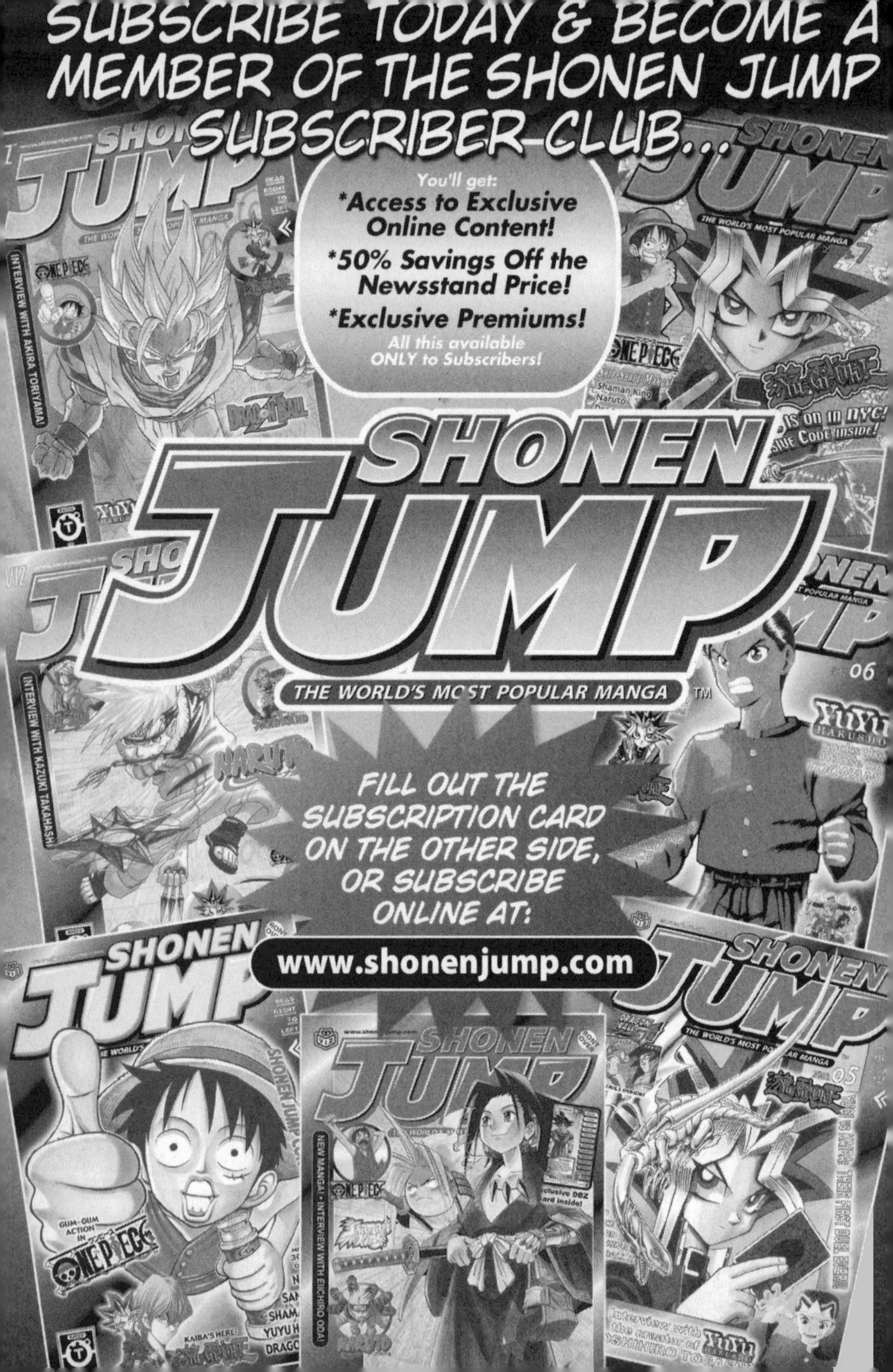
SUBSCRIBE TODAY & BECOME A MEMBER OF THE SHONEN JUMP SUBSCRIBER CLUB...
You'll get:
*Access to Exclusive Online Content!
*50% Savings Off the Newsstand Price!
*Exclusive Premiums!
All this available ONLY to Subscribers!
SHONEN JUMP
THE WORLD'S MOST POPULAR MANGA ™
FILL OUT THE SUBSCRIPTION CARD ON THE OTHER SIDE, OR SUBSCRIBE ONLINE AT:
www.shonenjump.com

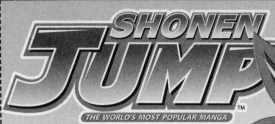

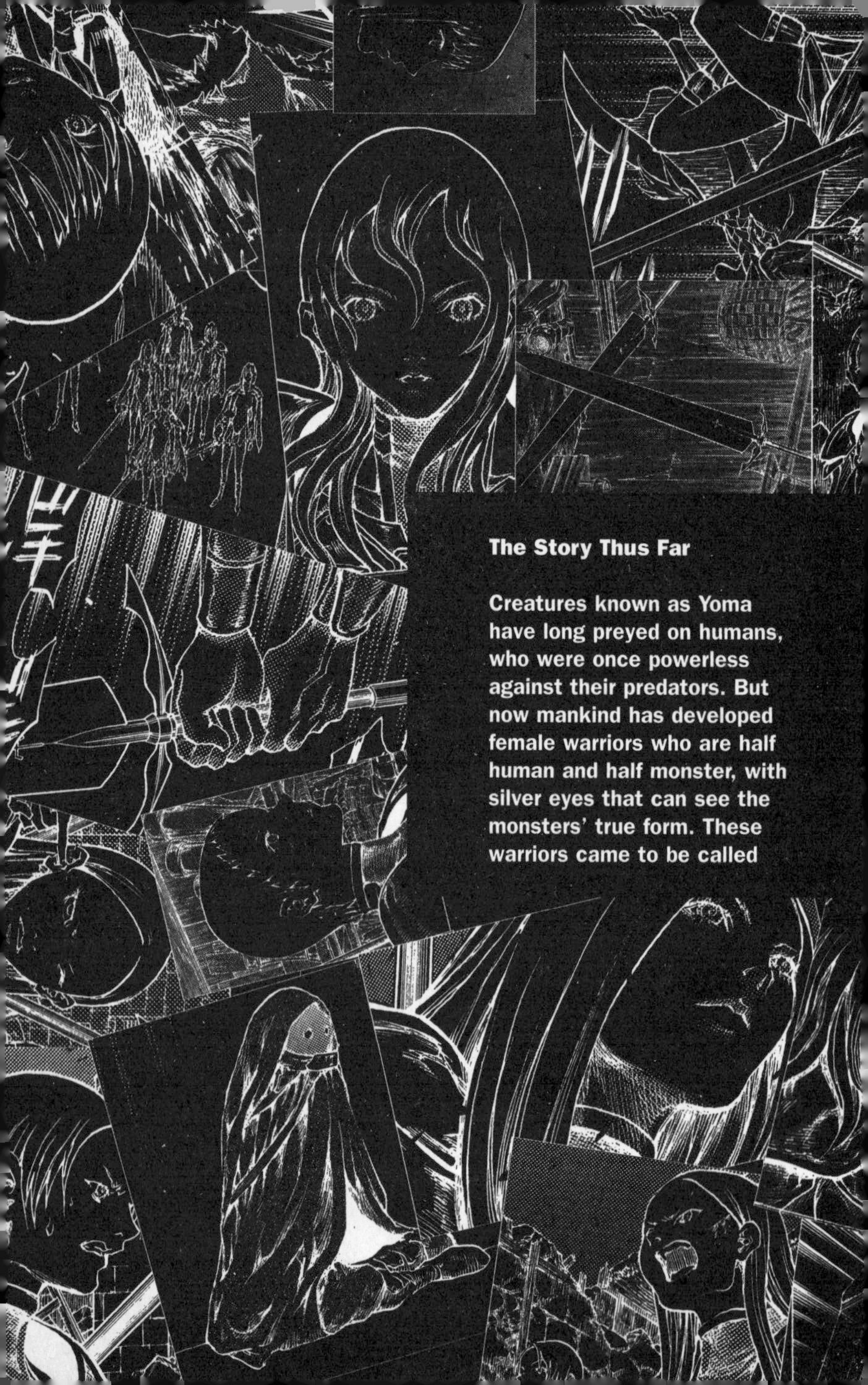

The Story Thus Far

Creatures known as Yoma have long preyed on humans, who were once powerless against their predators. But now mankind has developed female warriors who are half human and half monster, with silver eyes that can see the monsters' true form. These warriors came to be called

Claymore

Vol. 10

CONTENTS

Scene 52	The Battle of the North, Part 3	7
Scene 53	The Battle of the North, Part 4	39
Scene 54	The Battle of the North, Part 5	71
Scene 55	The Battle of the North, Part 6	103
Scene 56	The Battle of the North, Part 7	135
Scene 57	The Assault on Pieta, Part 1	159

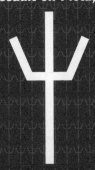

Scene 52: The Battle of the North, Part 3

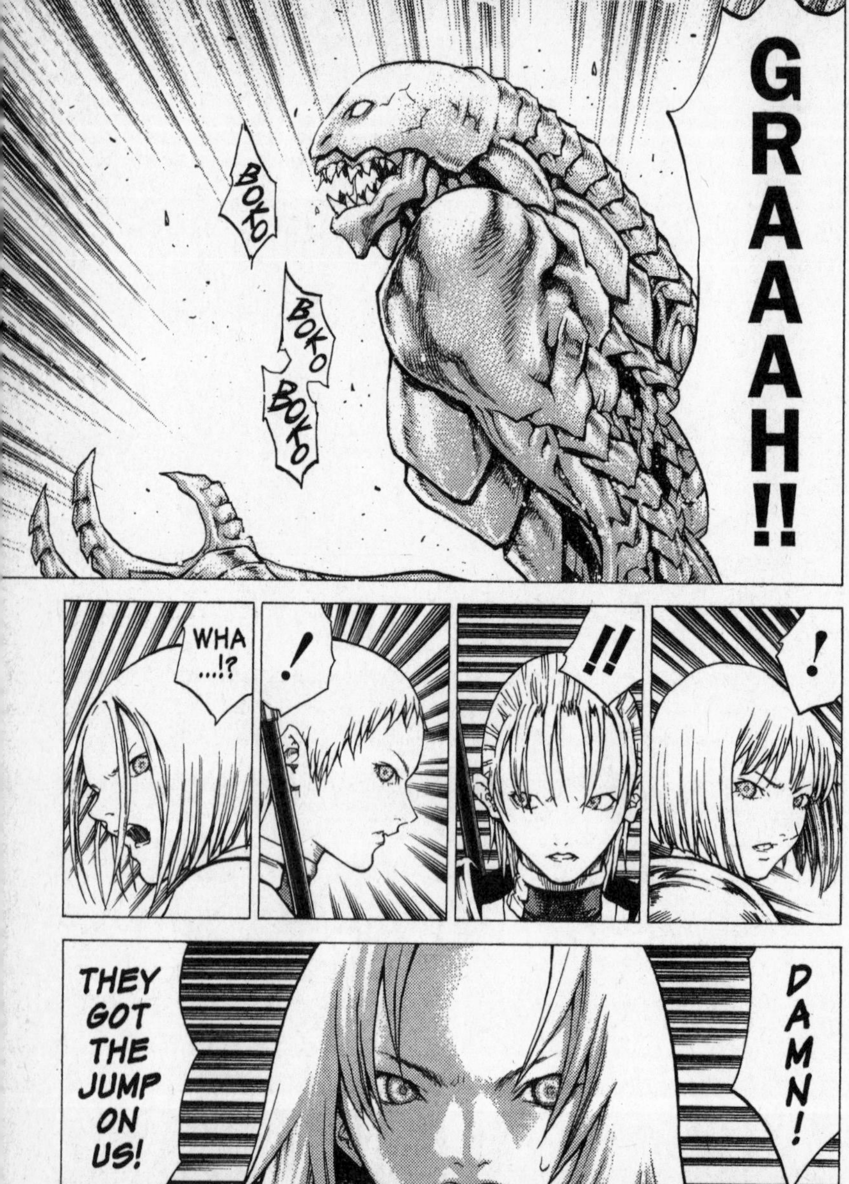
GRAAAH!!
BOKO
BOKO
BOKO
!
!!
!
WHA ...!?
DAMN!
THEY GOT THE JUMP ON US!

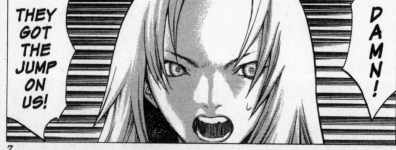

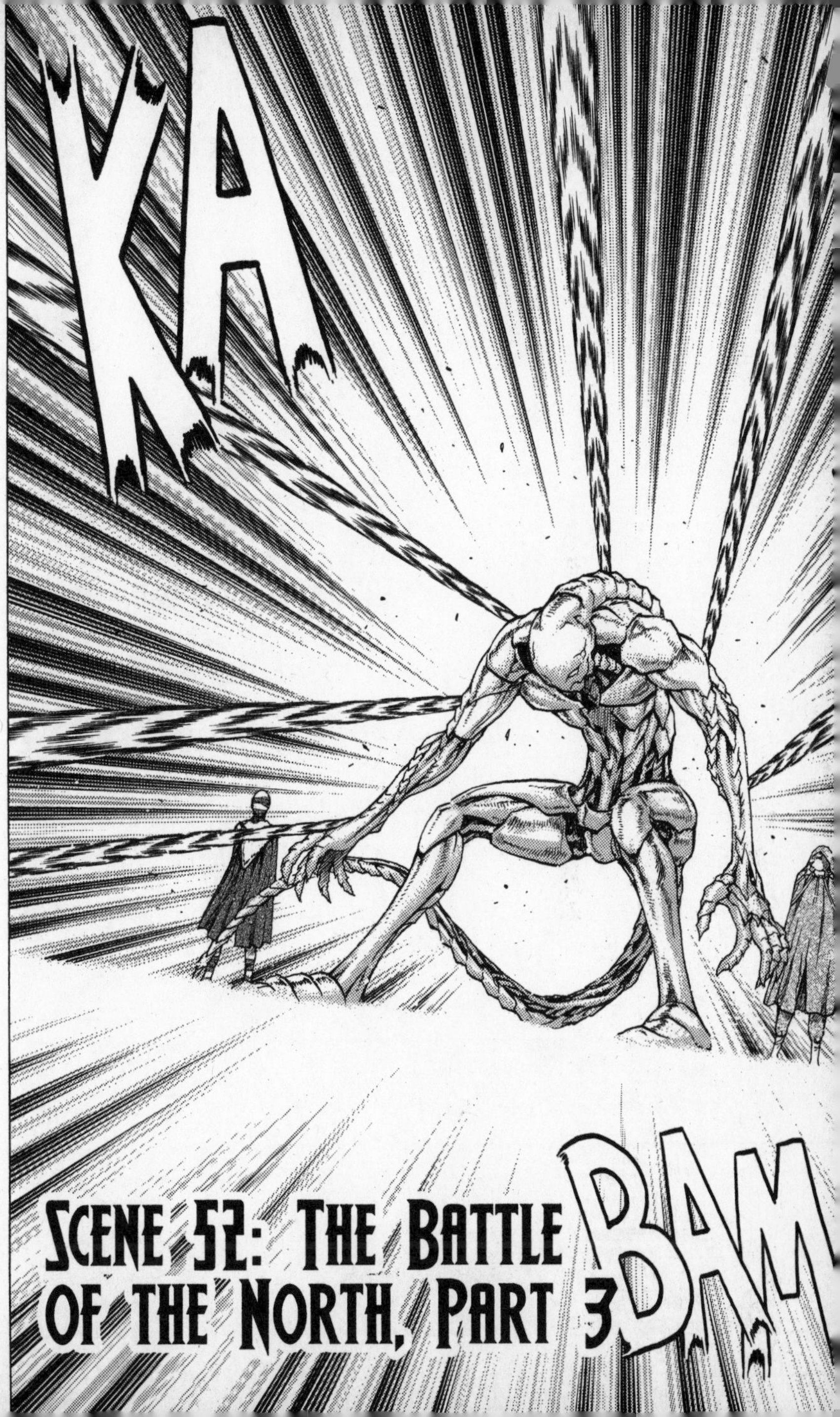
KA
SCENE 52: THE BATTLE OF THE NORTH, PART 3
BAM

READ THIS WAY

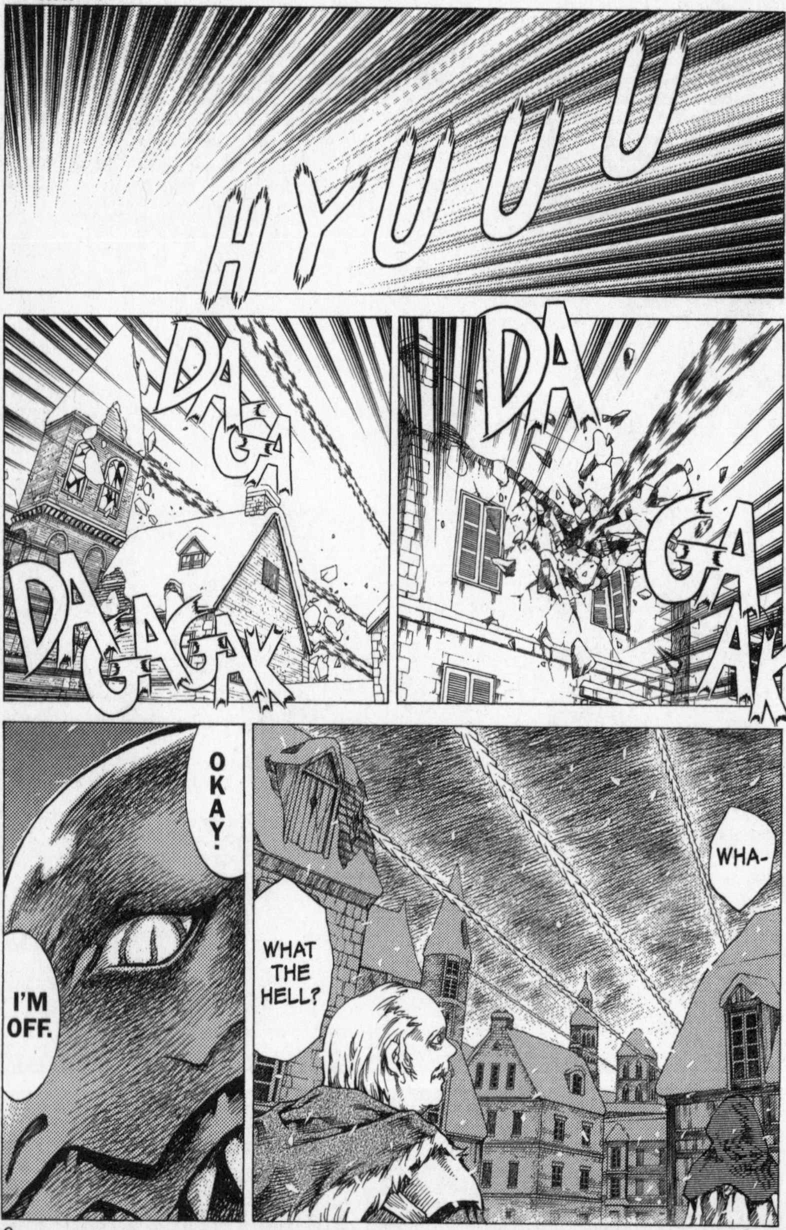
HYUUUU
DA GA GAK
DA GA
DA GA GAK
WHA-
WHAT THE HELL?
OKAY!
I'M OFF.

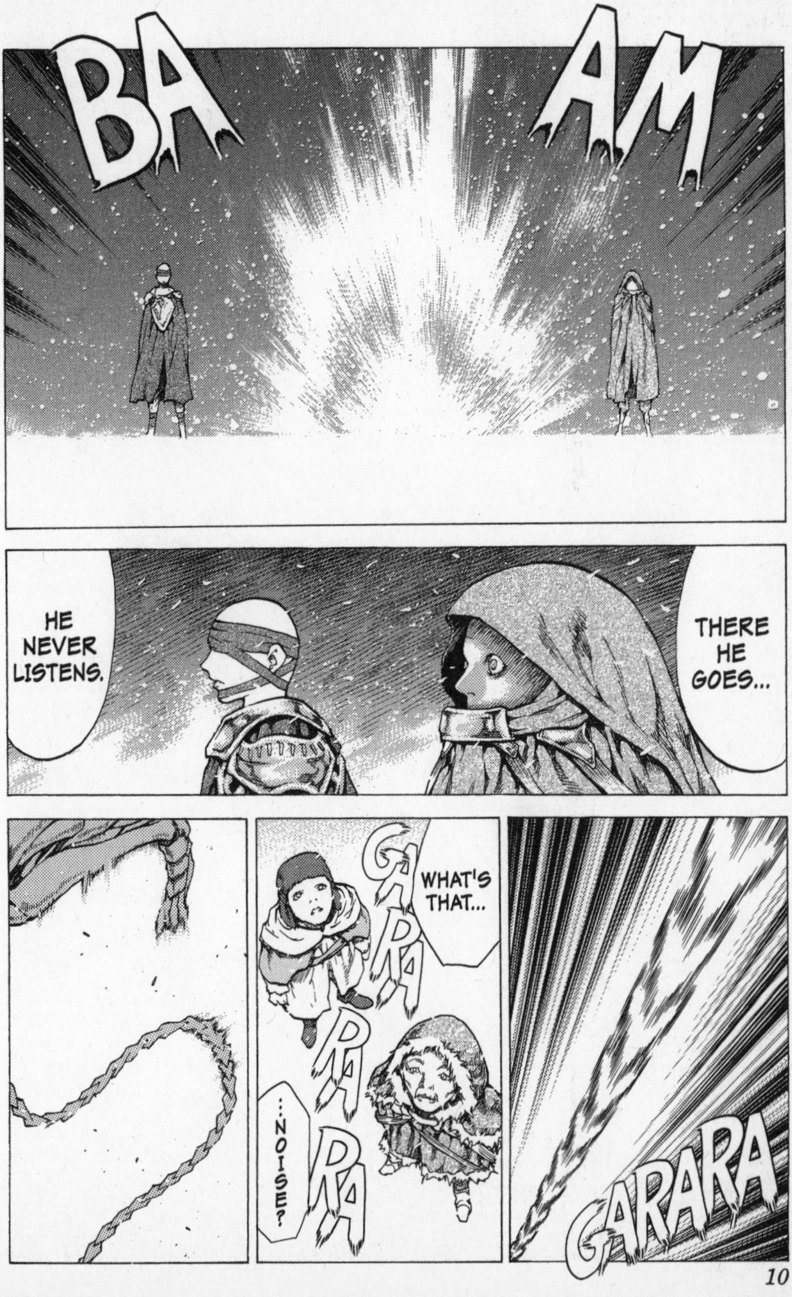
BA
AM
THERE HE GOES...
HE NEVER LISTENS.
GARARA
GARARARA
WHAT'S THAT...
...NOISE?

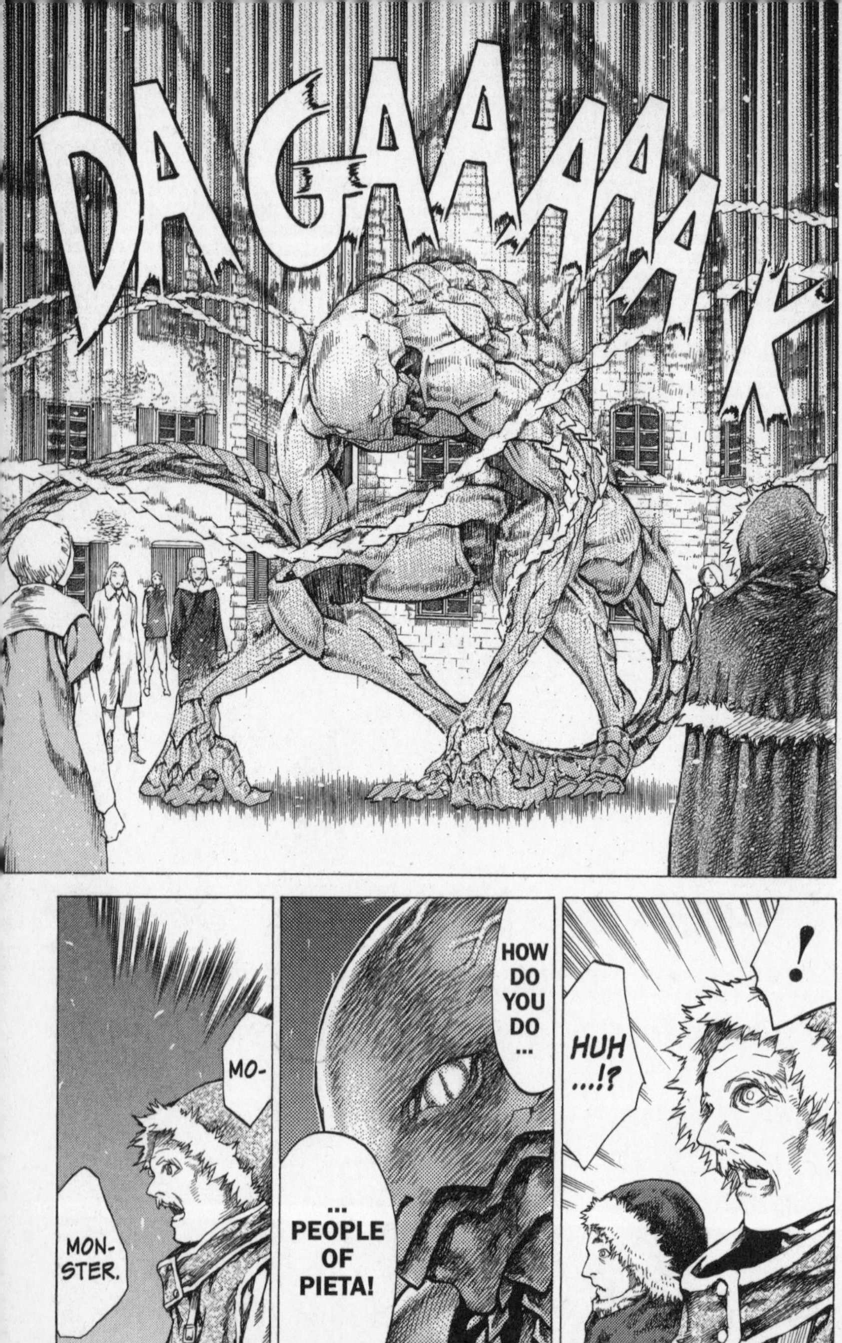
DAGAAAAAK
!
HUH ...!?
HOW DO YOU DO ...
... PEOPLE OF PIETA!
MO-
MON-STER.

DOBABABA
AND NOW ...
GOODBYE.

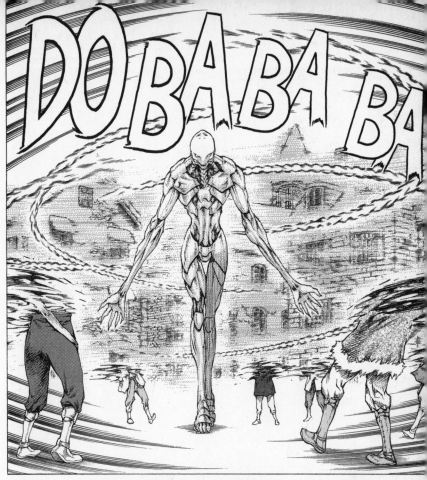

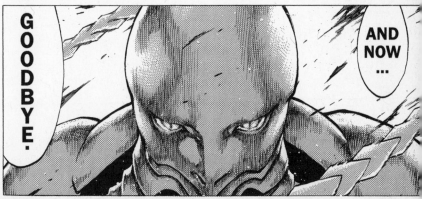

READ THIS WAY

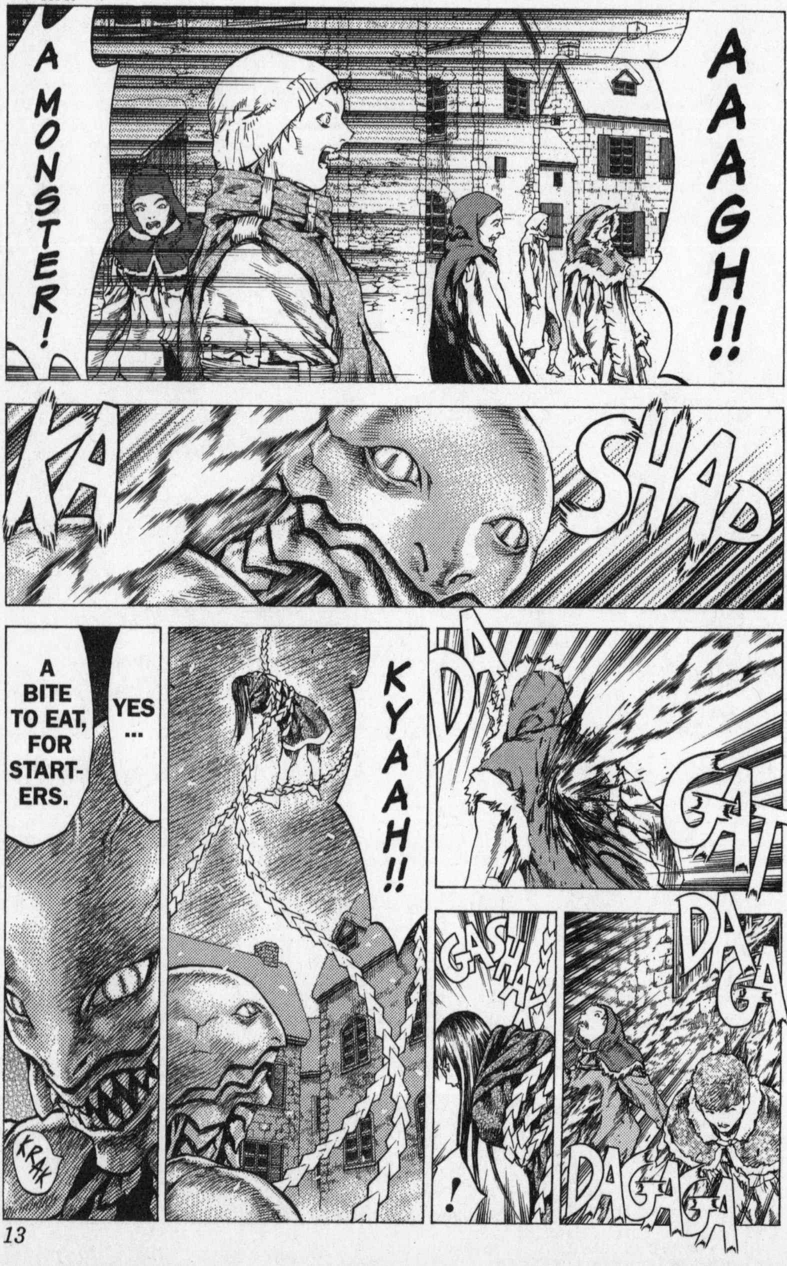

AAAGH!!
A MONSTER!
KA SHAD
DA
GAT
DAGA
DAGAGA
GASHAK
!
KYAAAH!!
YES...
A BITE TO EAT, FOR STARTERS.
KRAK

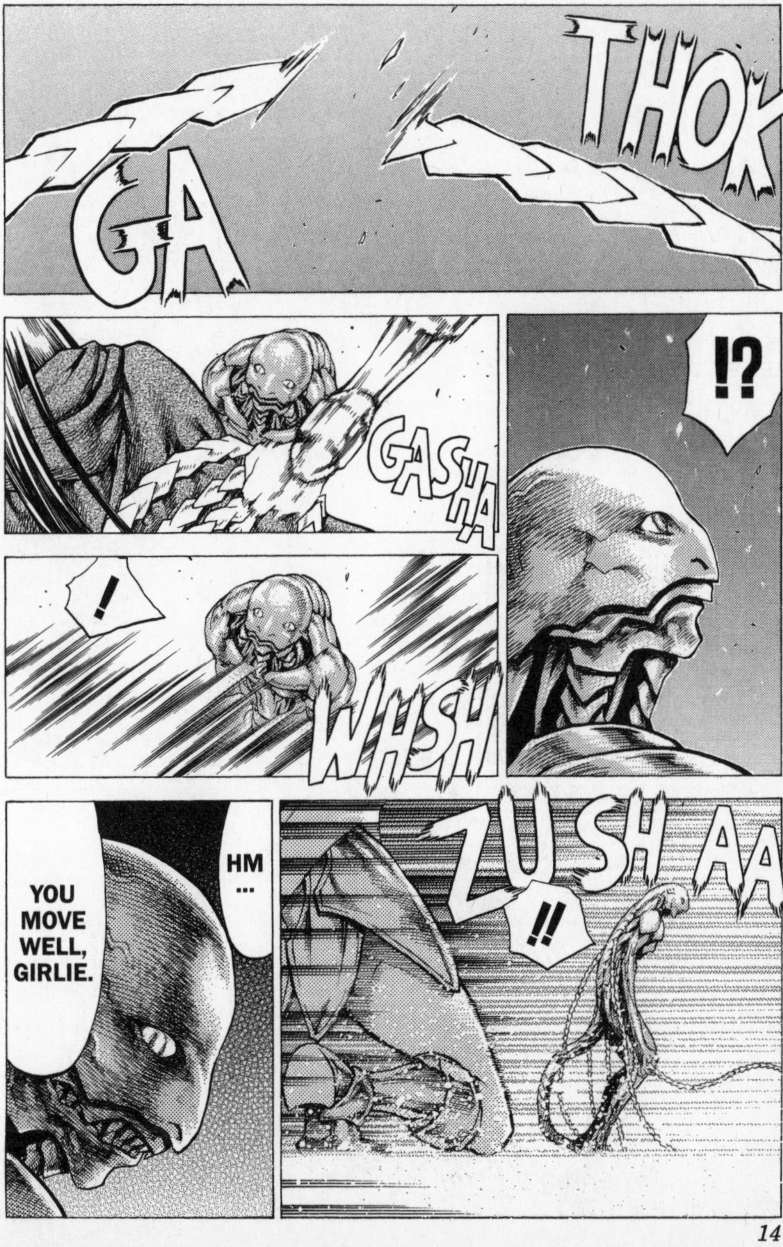
THOK
GA
!?
GASHA
!
WHSH
ZU SH AA
!!
HM...
YOU MOVE WELL, GIRLIE.

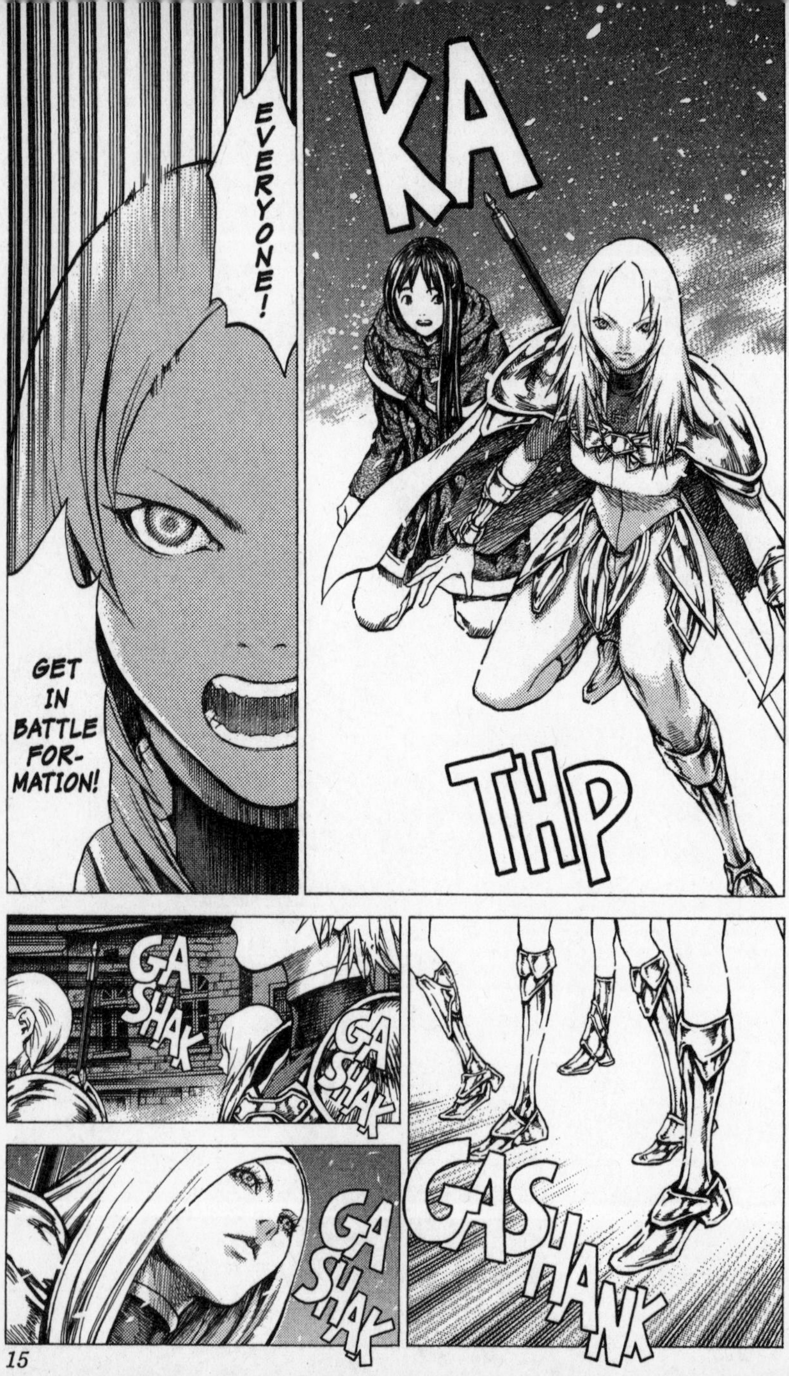
KA
THP
EVERYONE!
GET IN BATTLE FOR-MATION!
GASHANK
GA SHAK
GA SHAK
GA SHAK

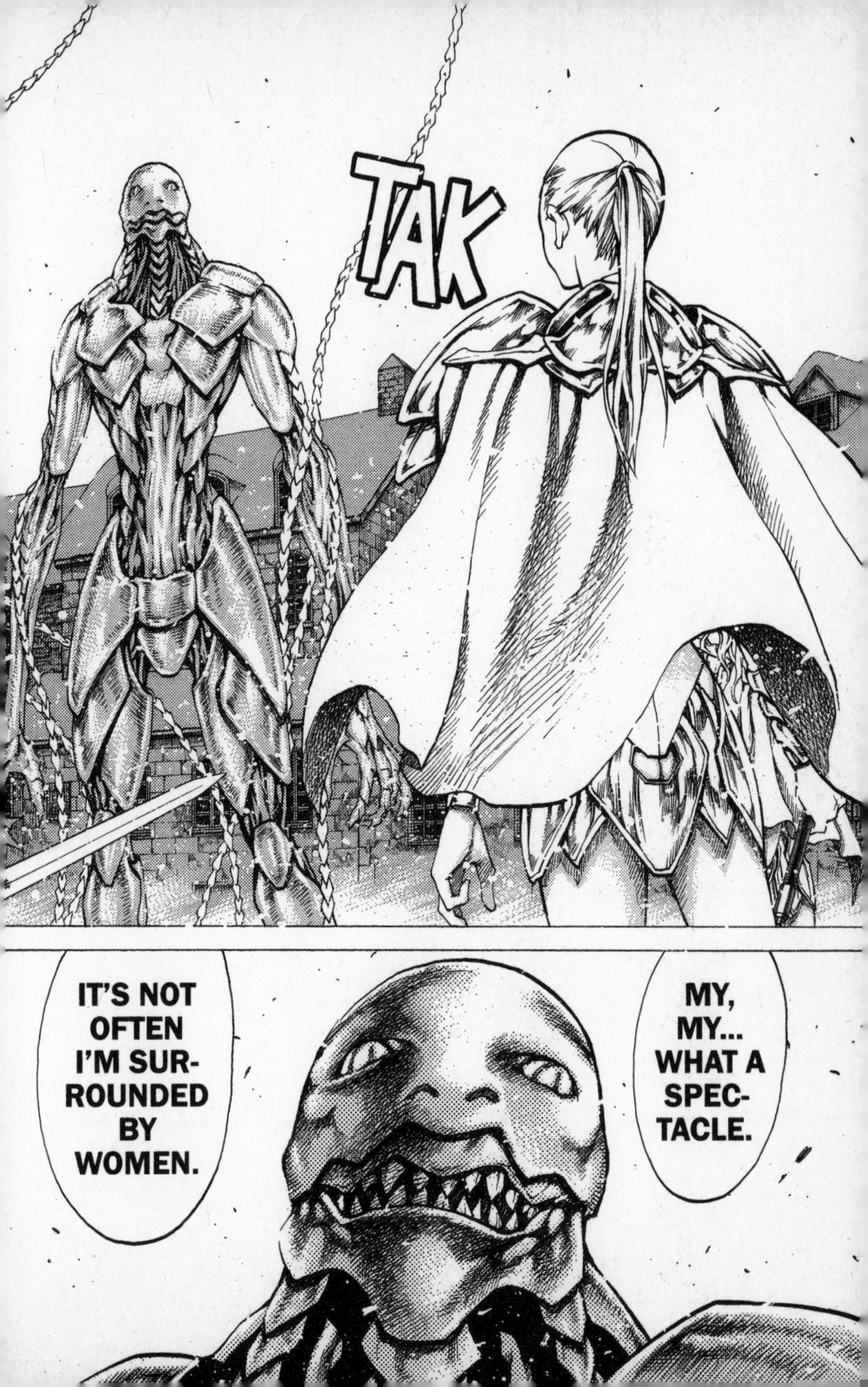
TAK
MY, MY... WHAT A SPECTACLE.
IT'S NOT OFTEN I'M SURROUNDED BY WOMEN.

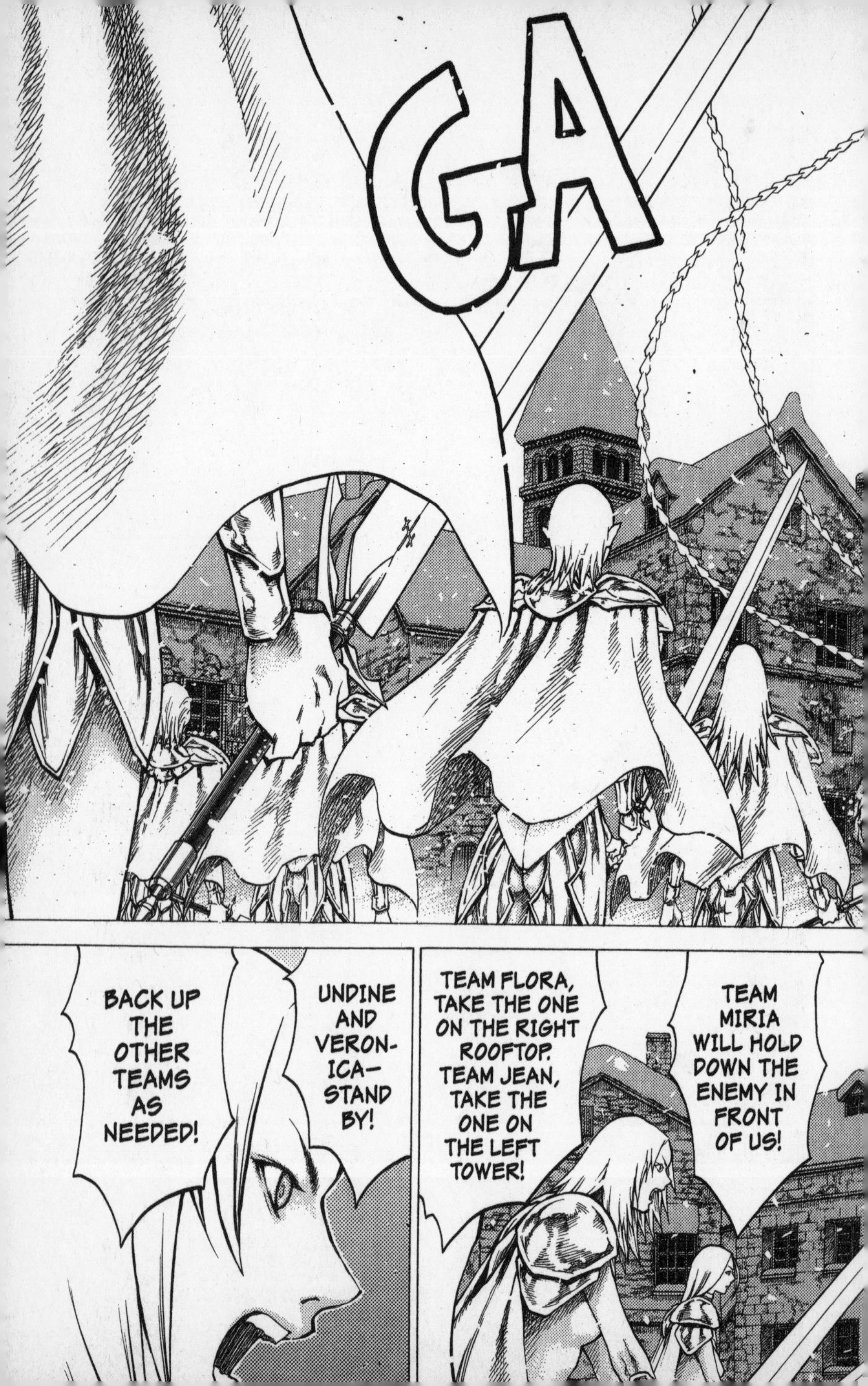
GA
TEAM MIRIA WILL HOLD DOWN THE ENEMY IN FRONT OF US!
TEAM FLORA, TAKE THE ONE ON THE RIGHT ROOFTOP. TEAM JEAN, TAKE THE ONE ON THE LEFT TOWER!
UNDINE AND VERON-ICA—STAND BY!
BACK UP THE OTHER TEAMS AS NEEDED!

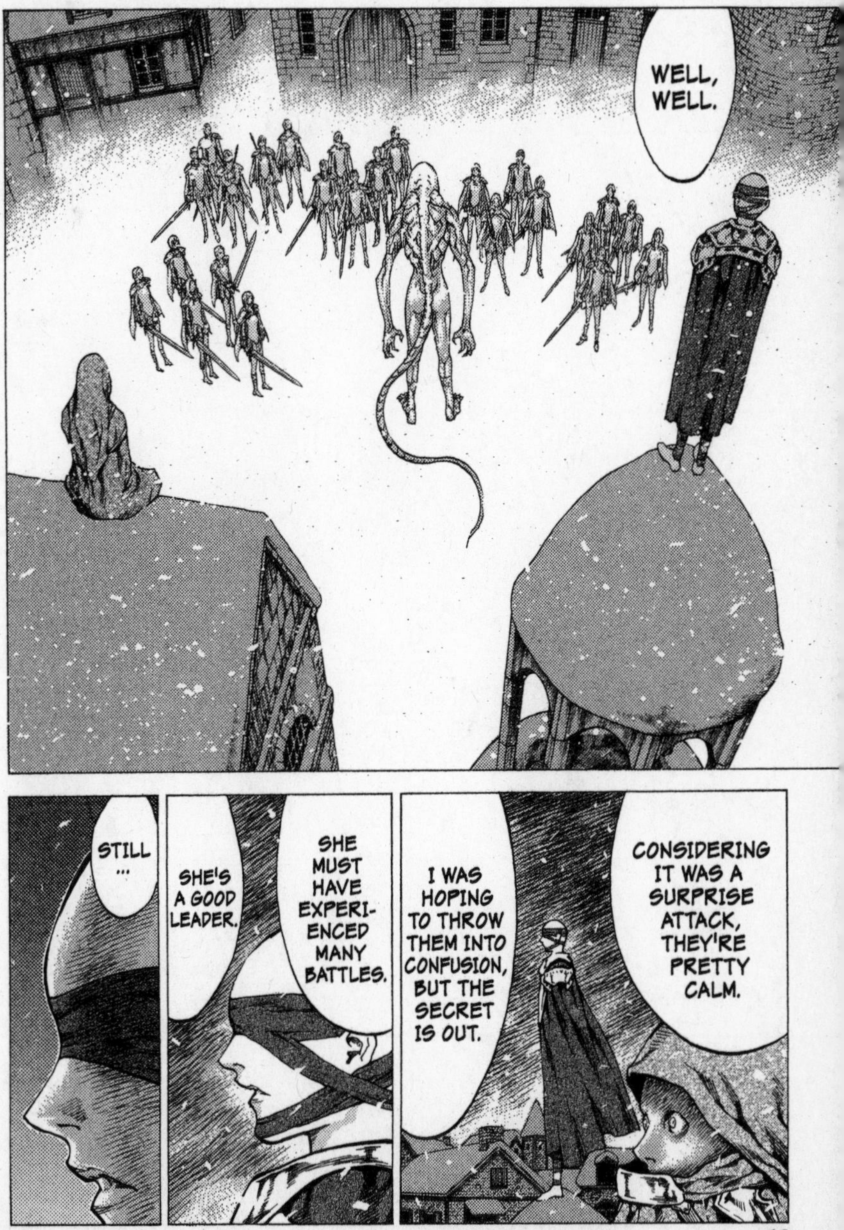
WELL, WELL.
CONSIDERING IT WAS A SURPRISE ATTACK, THEY'RE PRETTY CALM.
I WAS HOPING TO THROW THEM INTO CONFUSION, BUT THE SECRET IS OUT.
SHE MUST HAVE EXPERI-ENCED MANY BATTLES.
SHE'S A GOOD LEADER.
STILL ...

READ THIS WAY

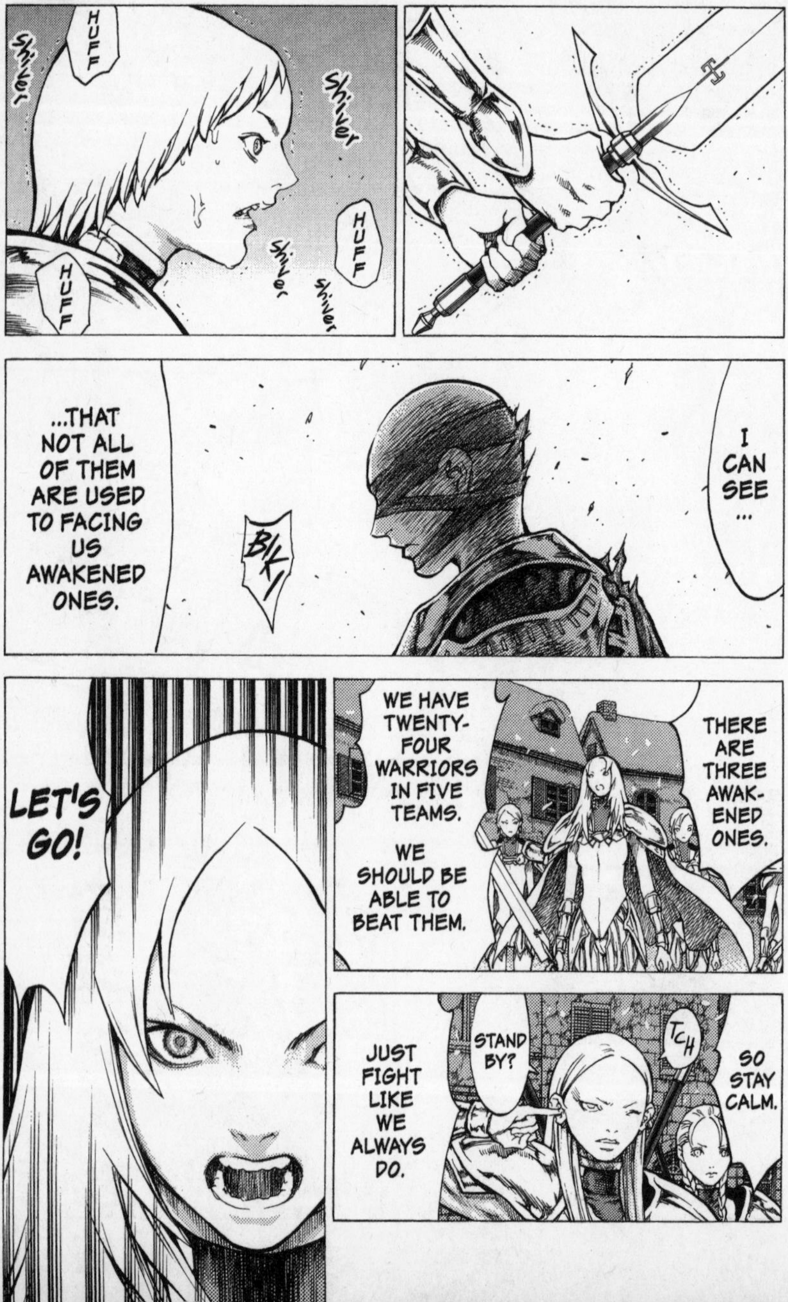
Shiver
HUFF
Shiver
Shiver
HUFF
Shiver
HUFF
I CAN SEE...
BIKI
...THAT NOT ALL OF THEM ARE USED TO FACING US AWAKENED ONES.
THERE ARE THREE AWAKENED ONES.
WE HAVE TWENTY-FOUR WARRIORS IN FIVE TEAMS.
WE SHOULD BE ABLE TO BEAT THEM.
SO STAY CALM.
TCH
STAND BY?
JUST FIGHT LIKE WE ALWAYS DO.
LET'S GO!

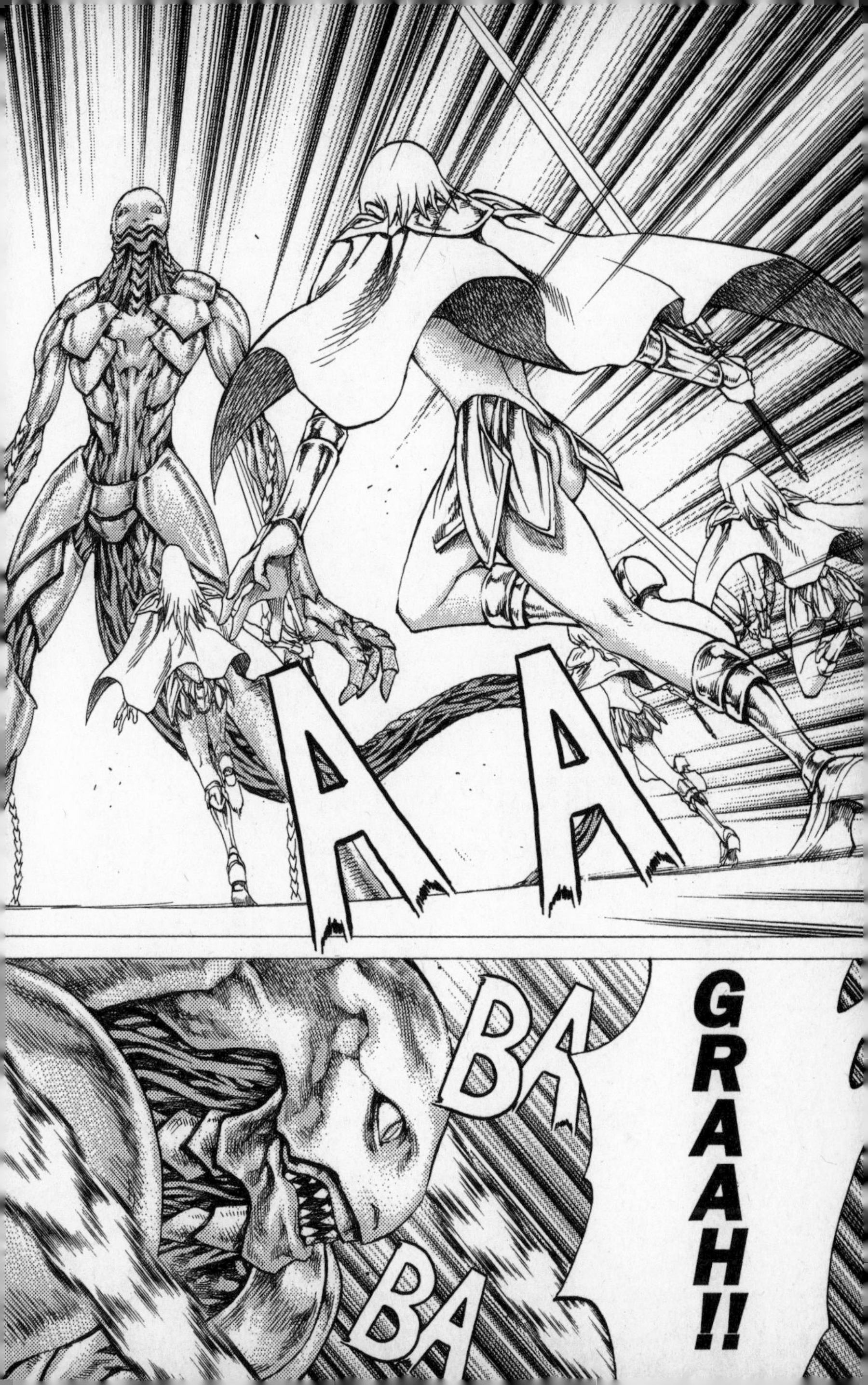
AA
GRAAAH!!
BA
BA

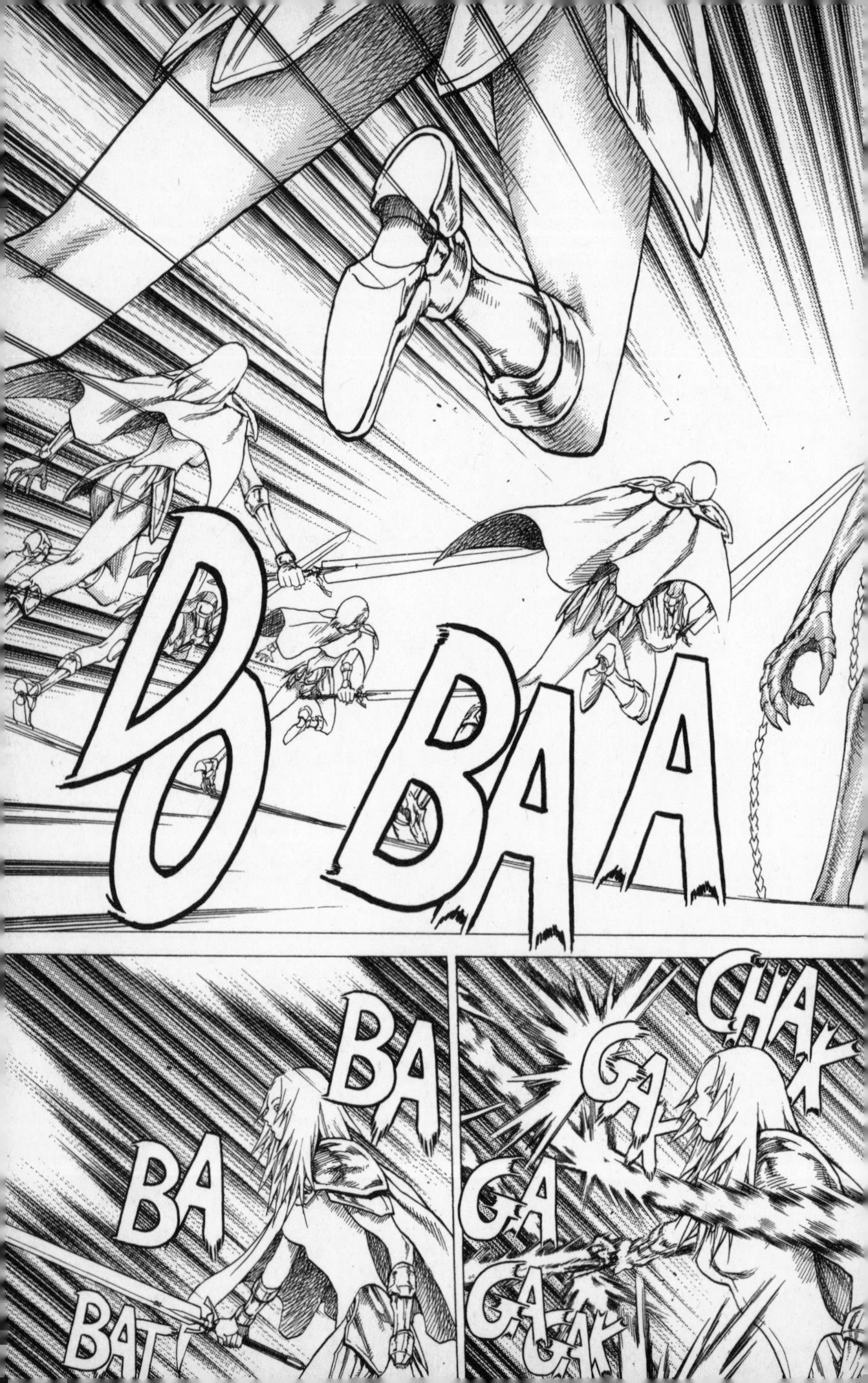
DO
BAAA
CHAK
GA
GAK
GA
GA
GAK
BA
BA
BATT

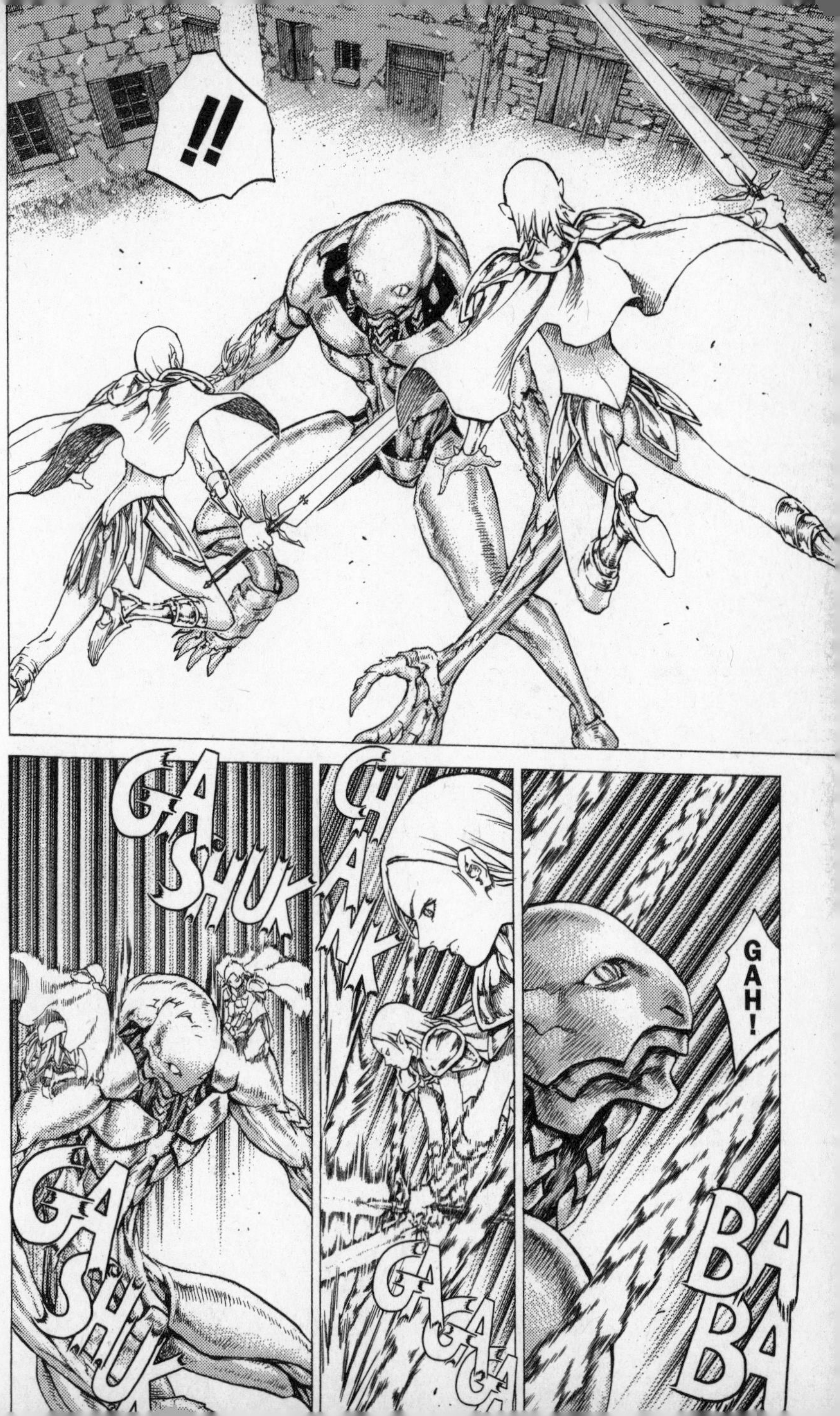
!!
GAH!
BABA
CHANK
GAGA
GASHUK
GASHU

READ THIS WAY

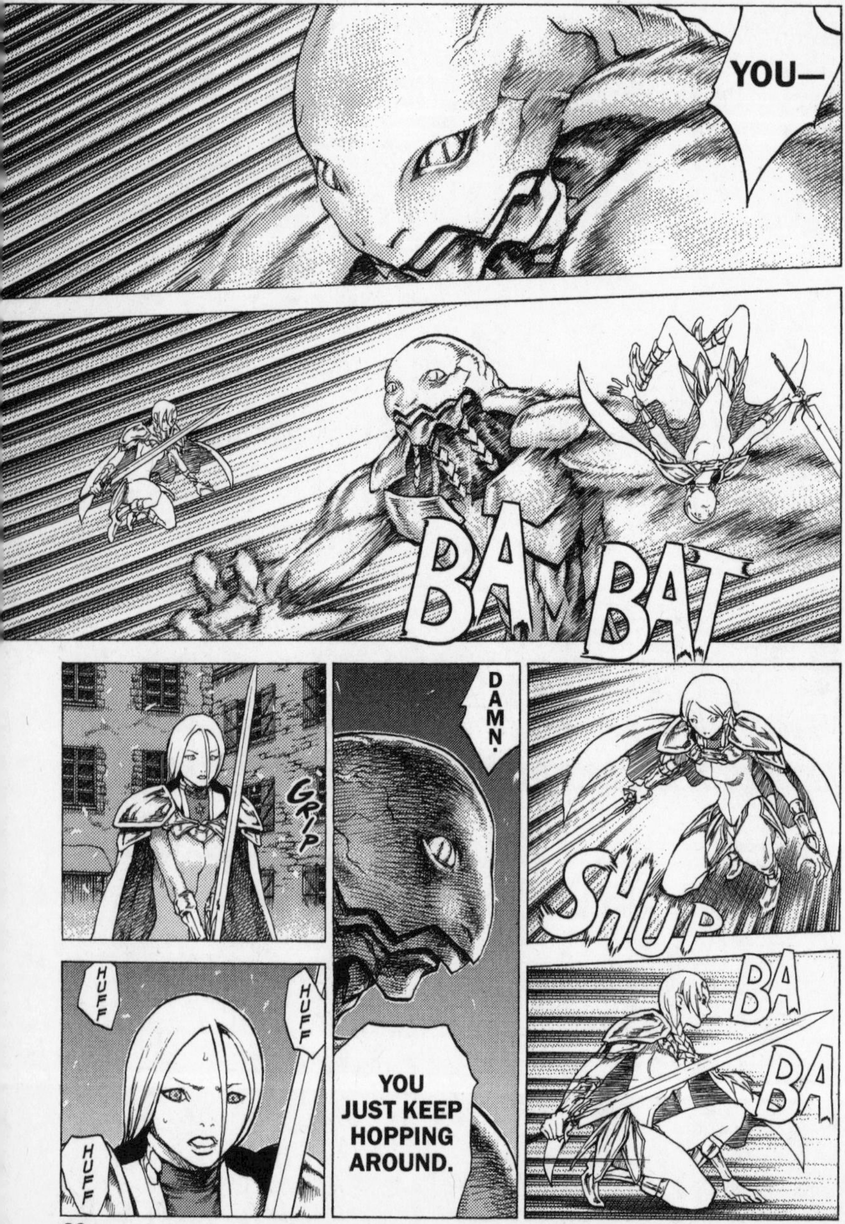
YOU—
BA BAT
SHUP
BA
BA
DAMN.
YOU JUST KEEP HOPPING AROUND.
GRIP
HUFF
HUFF
HUFF

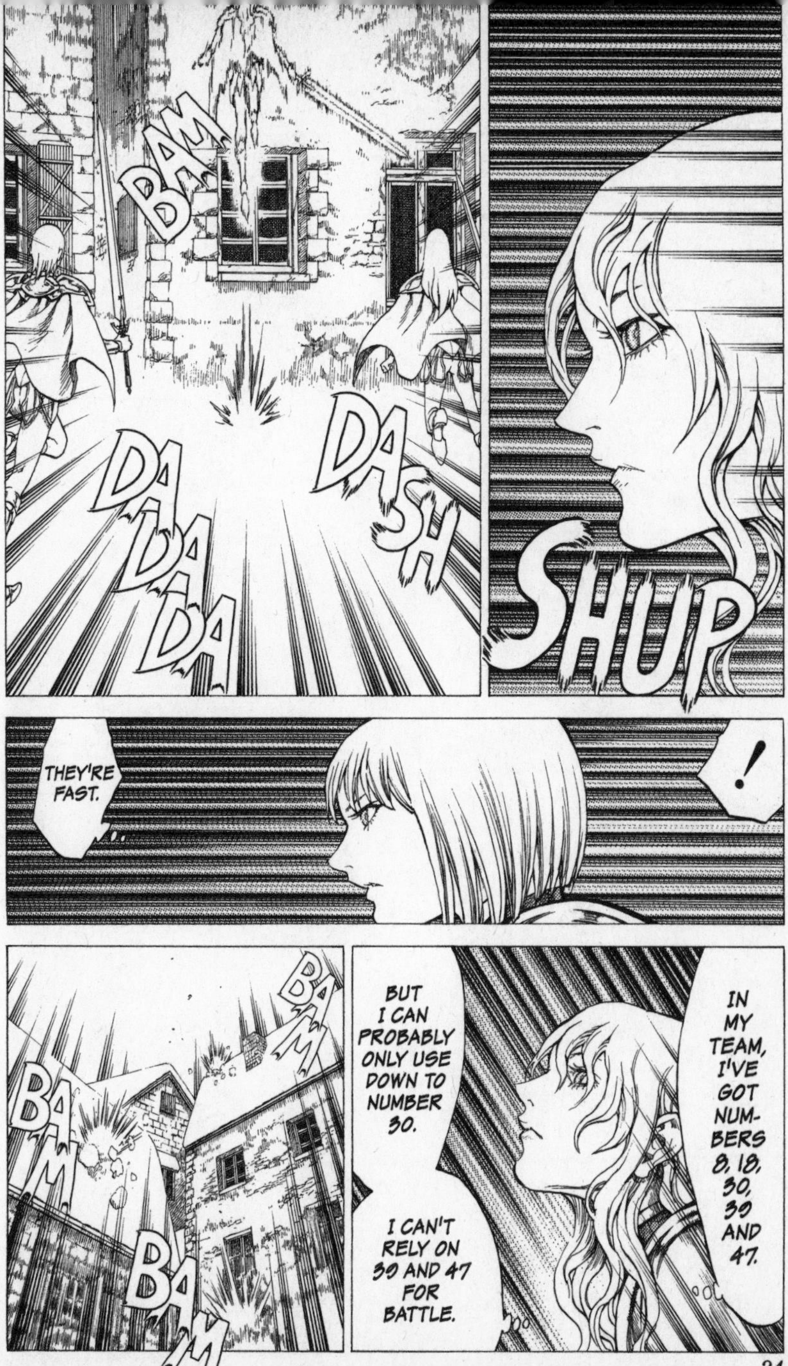
SHUP
BAM
DASH
DA DA DA
!
THEY'RE FAST...
IN MY TEAM, I'VE GOT NUMBERS 8, 18, 30, 39 AND 47.
BUT I CAN PROBABLY ONLY USE DOWN TO NUMBER 30.
I CAN'T RELY ON 39 AND 47 FOR BATTLE.
BAM
BAM
BAM
BAM

READ THIS WAY

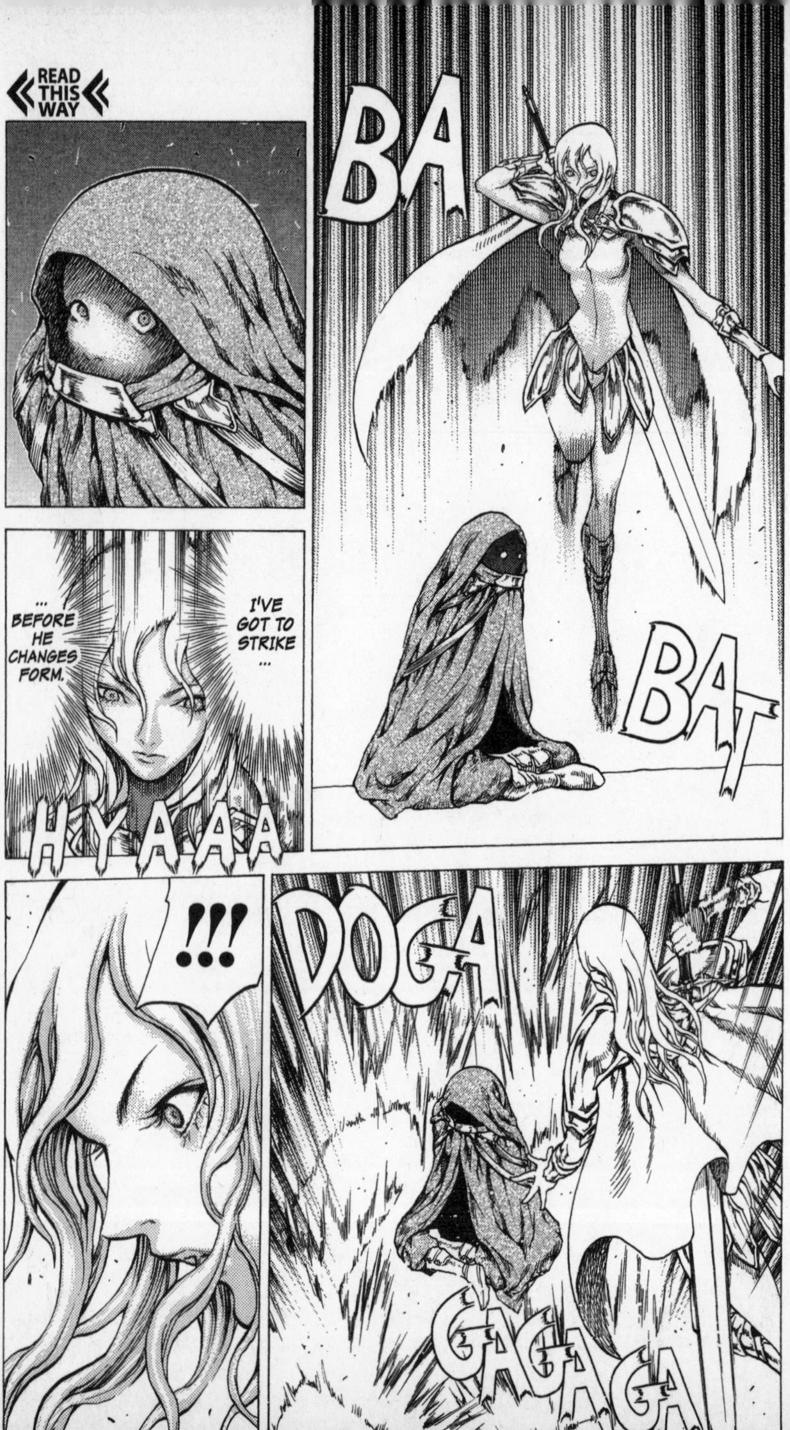
BA
BAT
I'VE GOT TO STRIKE ...
... BEFORE HE CHANGES FORM.
HYAAAA
DOGA
GAGAGA
!!!

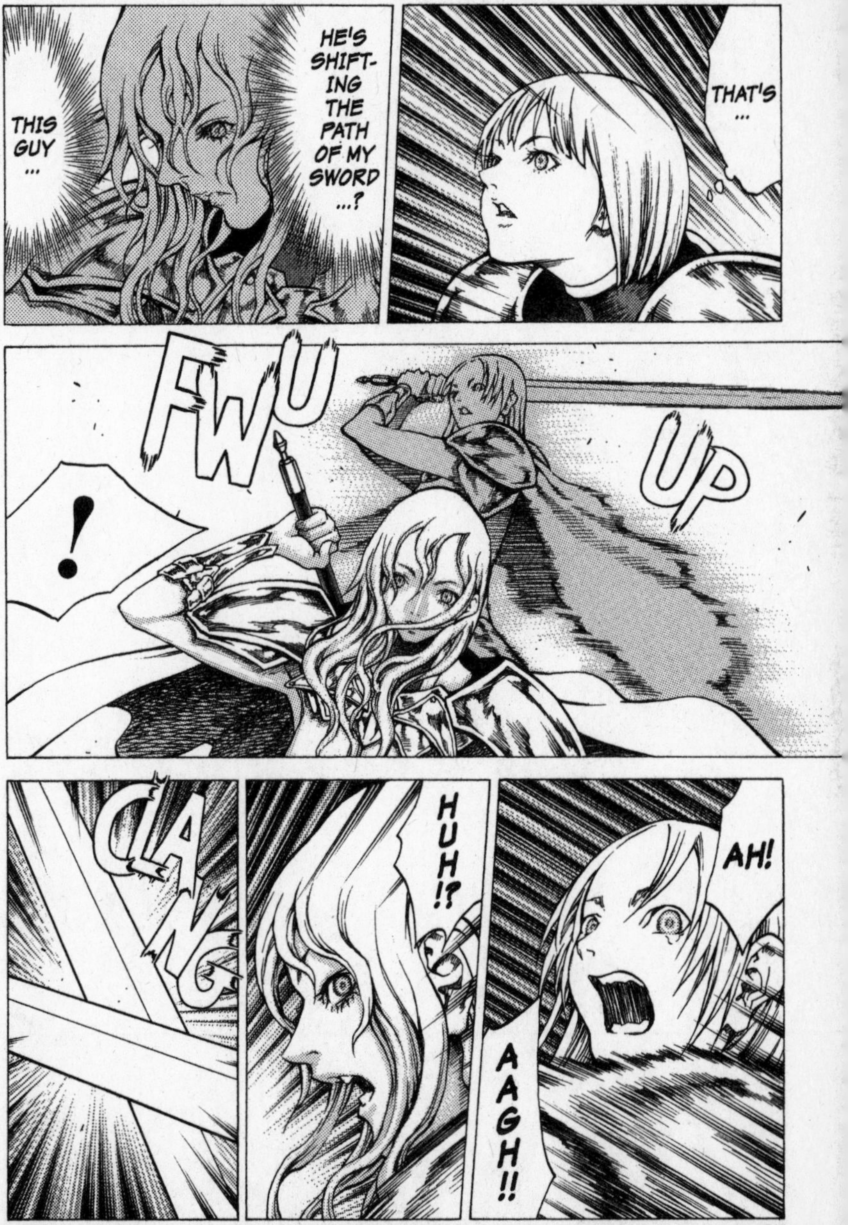
THAT'S ...
HE'S SHIFTING THE PATH OF MY SWORD ...?
THIS GUY ...
FWU
UP
!
AH!
AAGH!!
HUH!?
CLANG

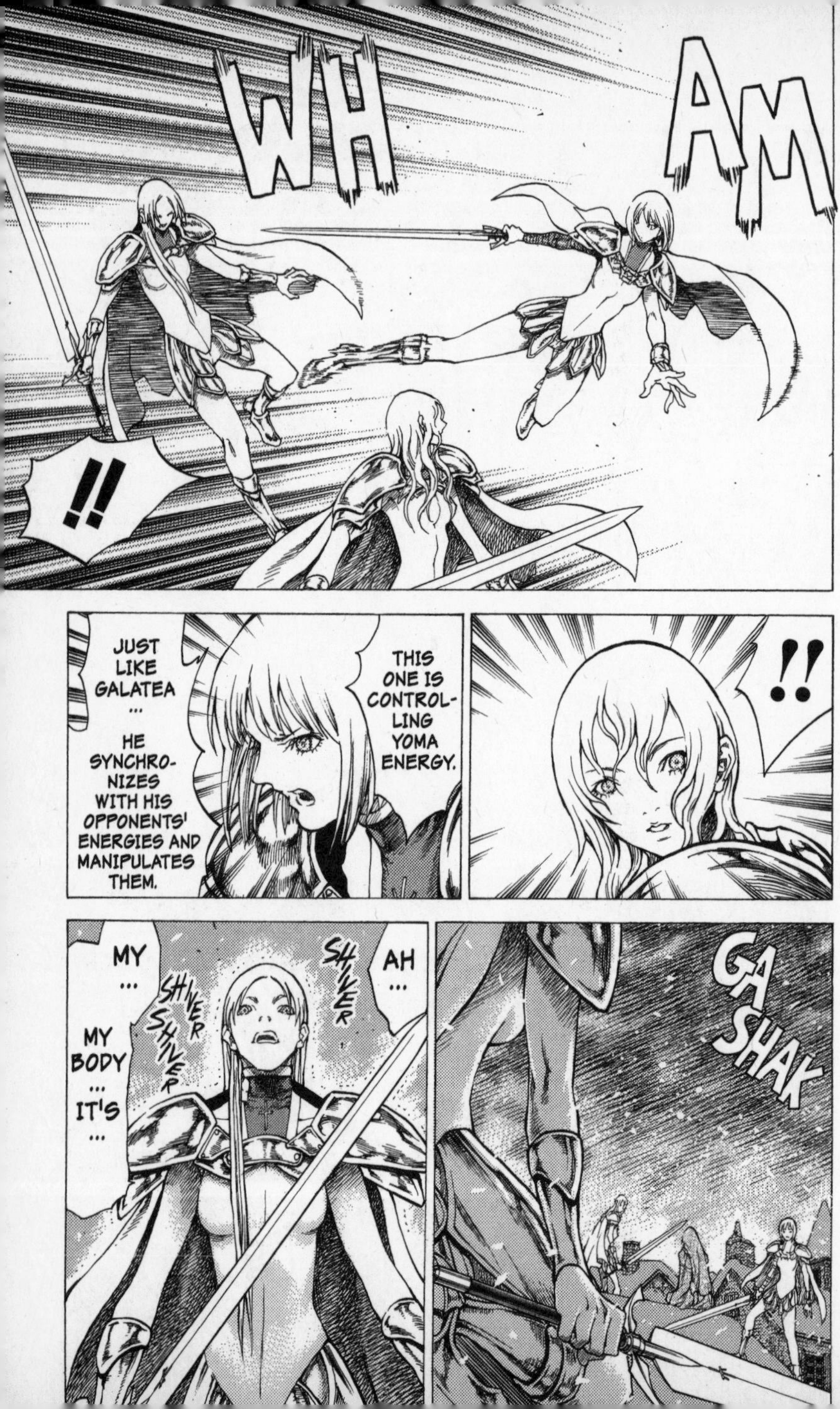
WHAM
!!
!!
THIS ONE IS CONTROLLING YOMA ENERGY.
JUST LIKE GALATEA ...
HE SYNCHRONIZES WITH HIS OPPONENTS' ENERGIES AND MANIPULATES THEM.
GASHAK
AH ...
SHIVER
SHIVER SHIVER
MY ...
MY BODY ... IT'S ...

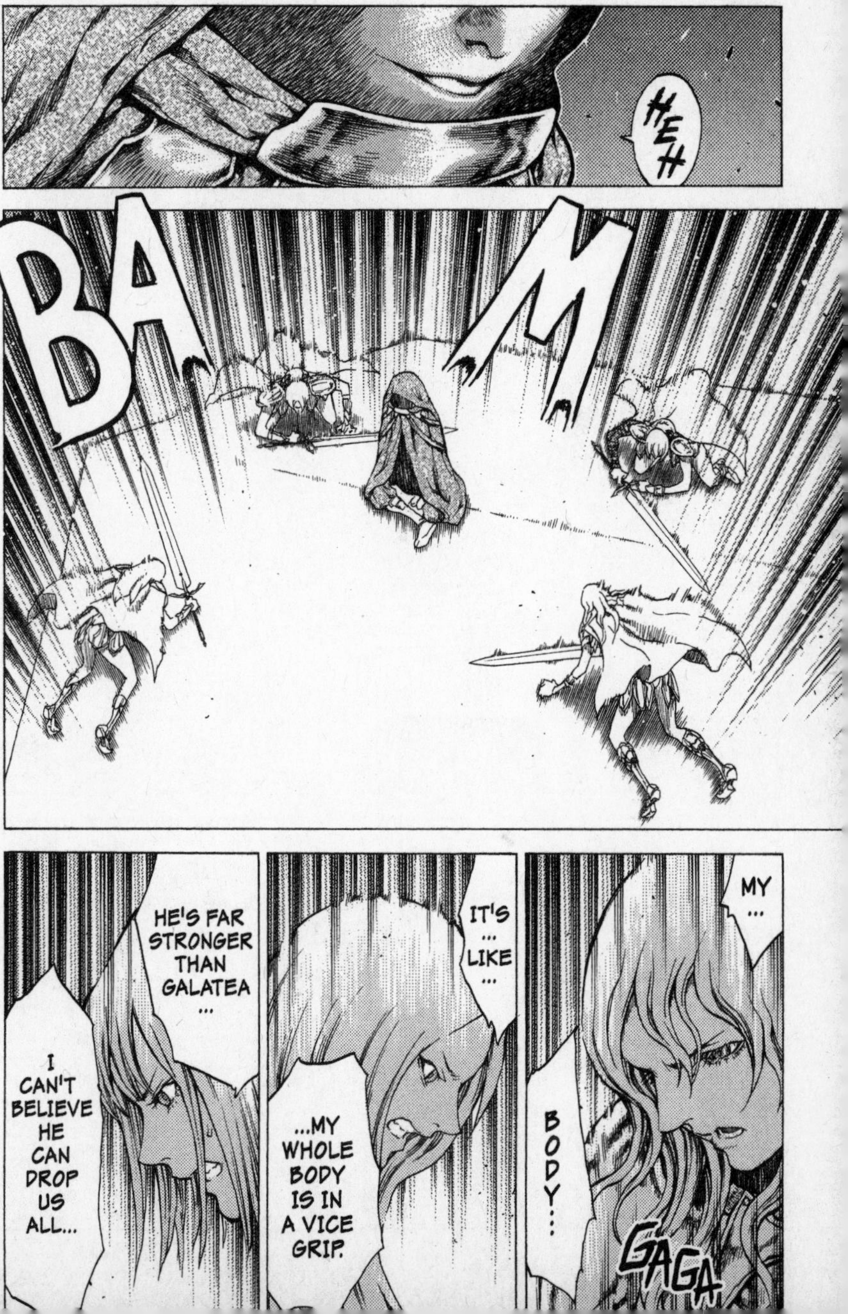
HEH
BAM
MY...
BODY...
GAGA
IT'S... LIKE...
...MY WHOLE BODY IS IN A VICE GRIP.
HE'S FAR STRONGER THAN GALATEA...
I CAN'T BELIEVE HE CAN DROP US ALL...

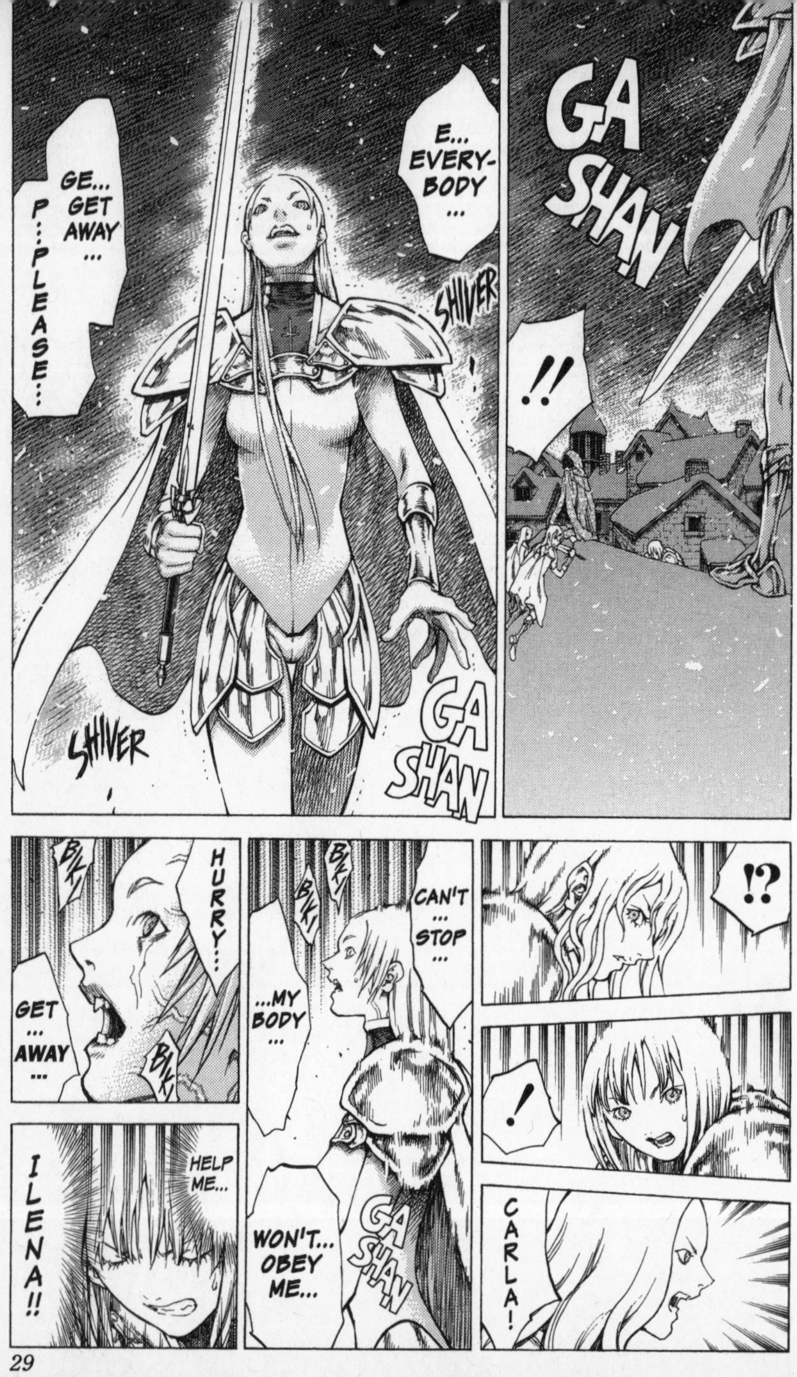

GA SHAN
!!
E... EVERYBODY...
SHIVER
GE... GET AWAY...
P...PLEASE...
SHIVER
GA SHAN
!?
!
CARLA!
BIKI
BIKI
CAN'T... STOP...
...MY BODY...
WON'T... OBEY ME...
GA SHAN
BIKI
HURRY...
GET... AWAY...
BIKI
HELP ME...
ILENA!!

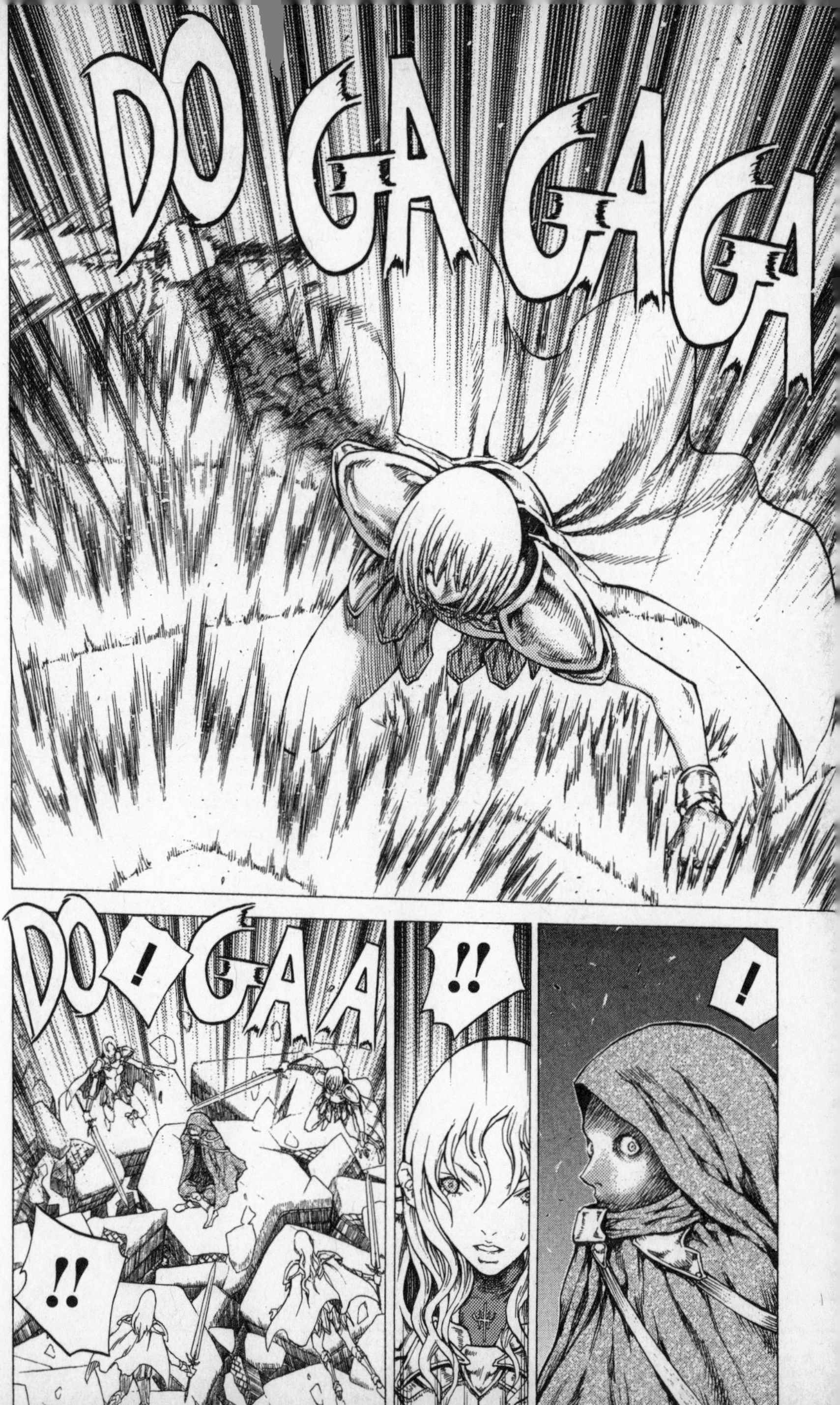
DOGAGAGA
!
!!
DOGAA
!
!!

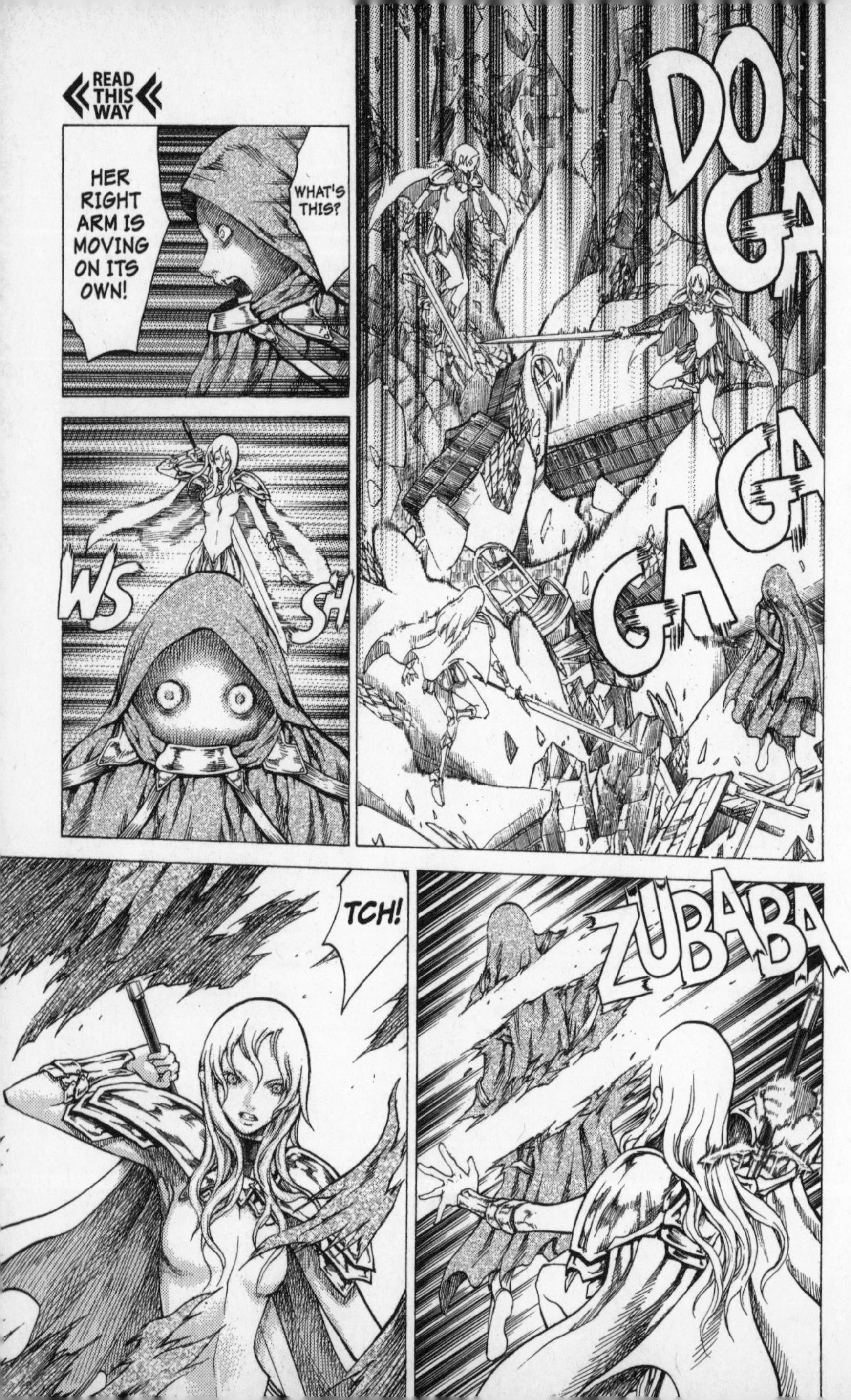
READ THIS WAY
DOGA
GAGA
GA
WHAT'S THIS?
HER RIGHT ARM IS MOVING ON ITS OWN!
WS
SH
ZUBABA
TCH!

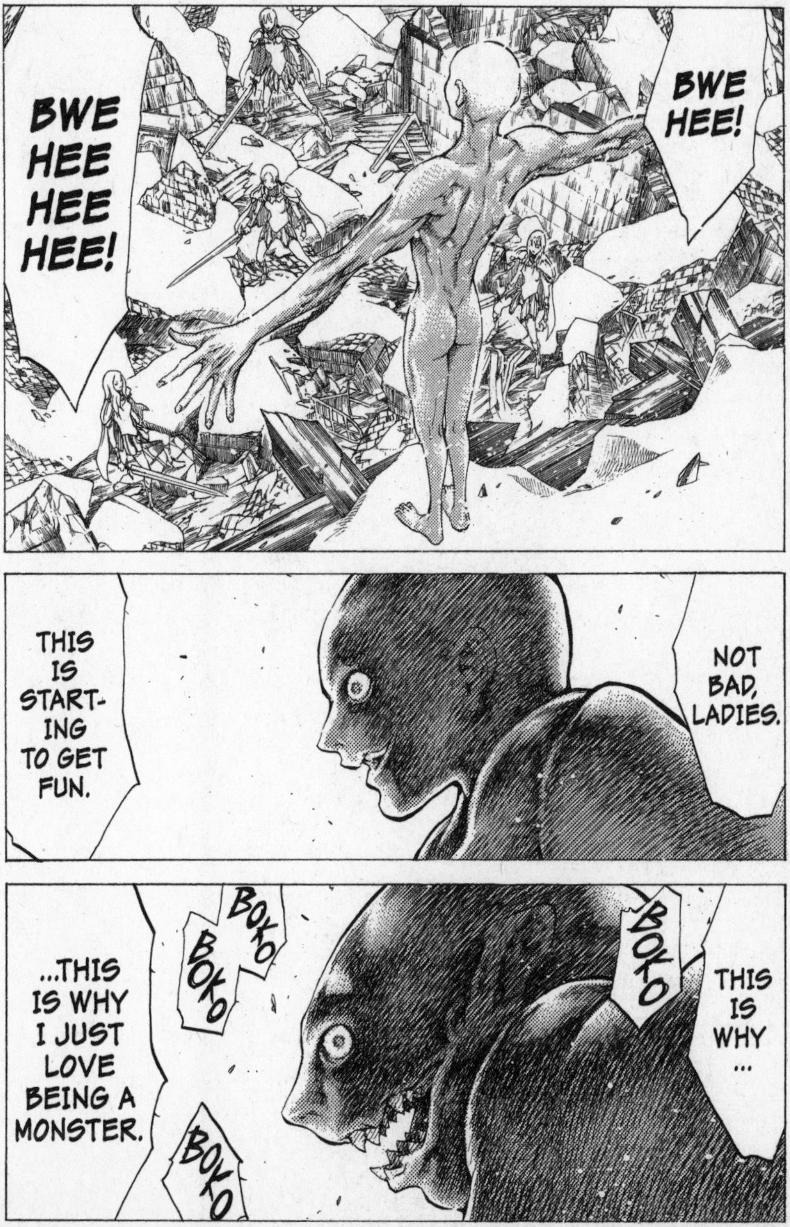
BWE HEE!
BWE HEE HEE HEE!
NOT BAD, LADIES.
THIS IS START-ING TO GET FUN.
THIS IS WHY ...
BOKO
BOKO
BOKO
...THIS IS WHY I JUST LOVE BEING A MONSTER.
BOKO

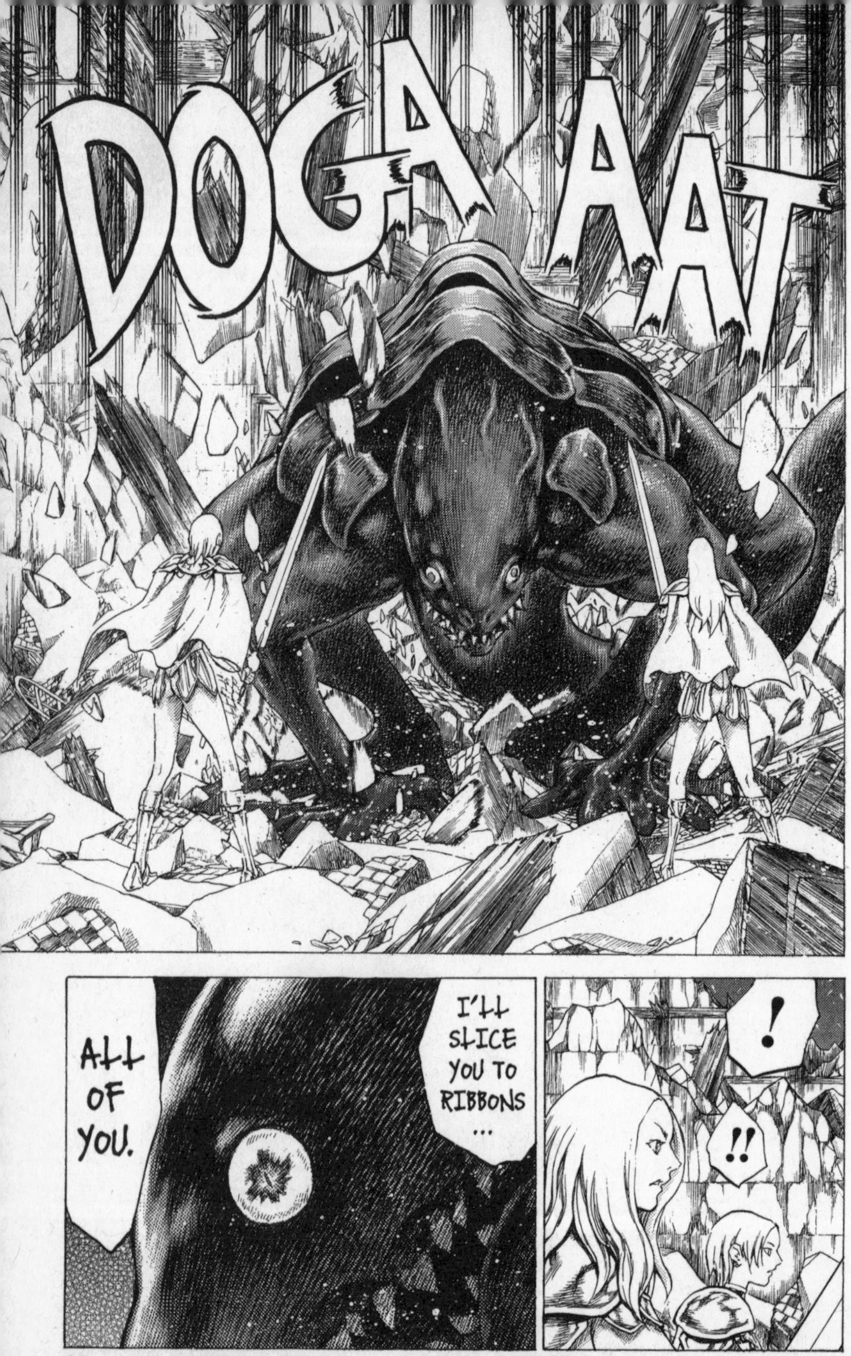
DOGAAAT
!
!!
I'LL SLICE YOU TO RIBBONS...
ALL OF YOU.

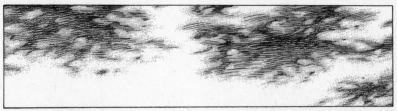

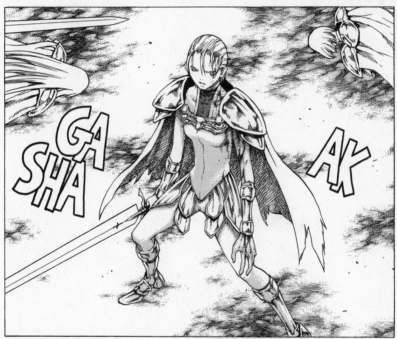

GA
SHA

AK

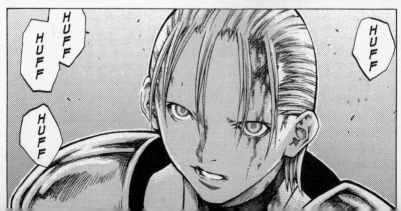

HUFF
HUFF
HUFF

HUFF

HUFF

READ THIS WAY

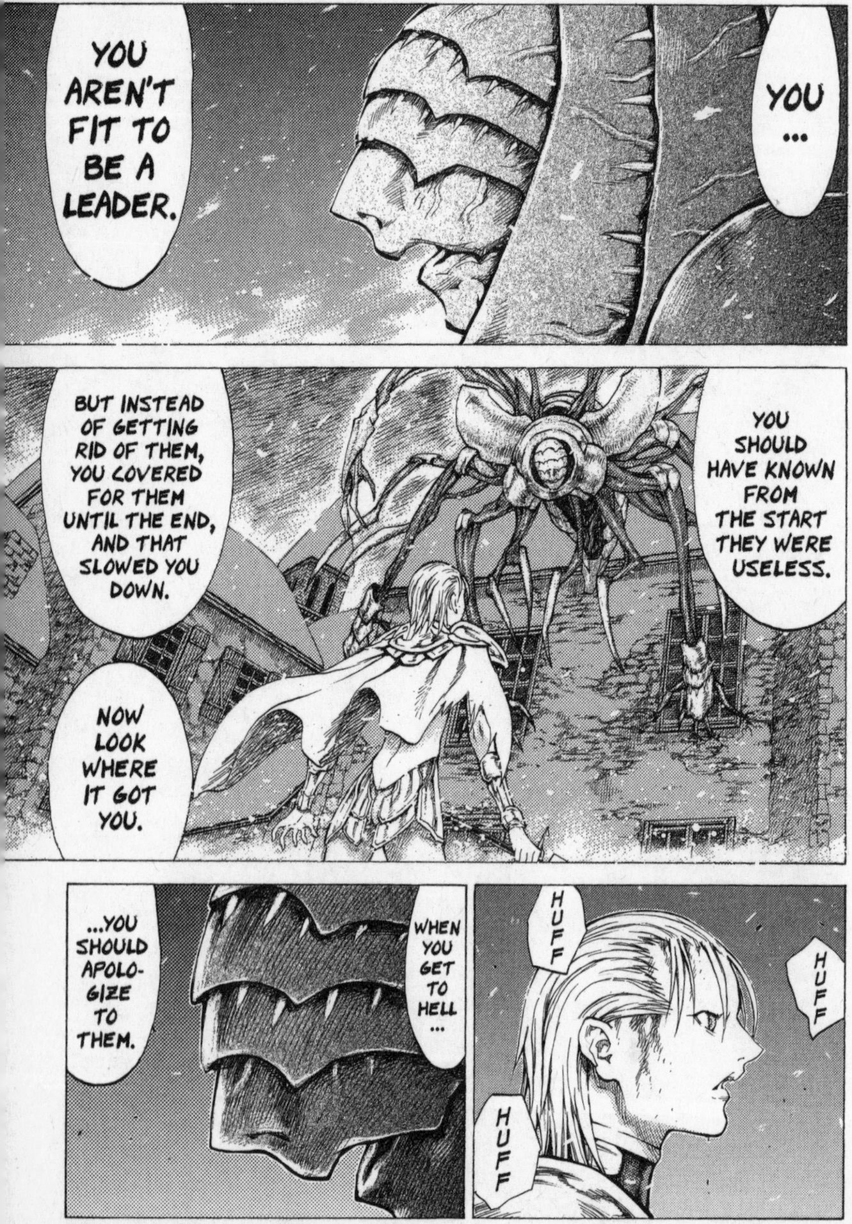
YOU ...
YOU AREN'T FIT TO BE A LEADER.
YOU SHOULD HAVE KNOWN FROM THE START THEY WERE USELESS.
BUT INSTEAD OF GETTING RID OF THEM, YOU COVERED FOR THEM UNTIL THE END, AND THAT SLOWED YOU DOWN.
NOW LOOK WHERE IT GOT YOU.
HUFF
HUFF
HUFF
WHEN YOU GET TO HELL ...
...YOU SHOULD APOLOGIZE TO THEM.

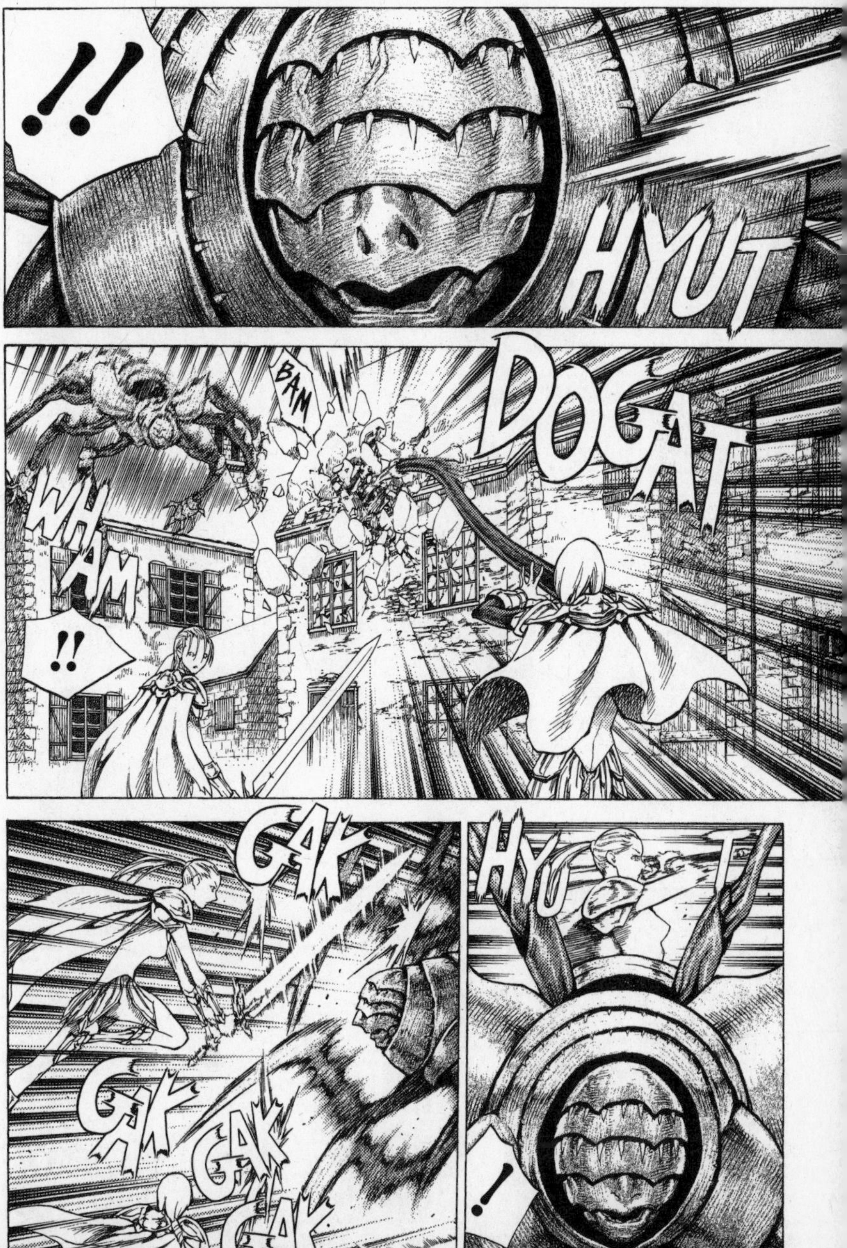
!!
HYUT
DOGAT
BAM
WHAM
!!
HYUT
!
GAK
GAK
GAK
GAK

READ THIS WAY

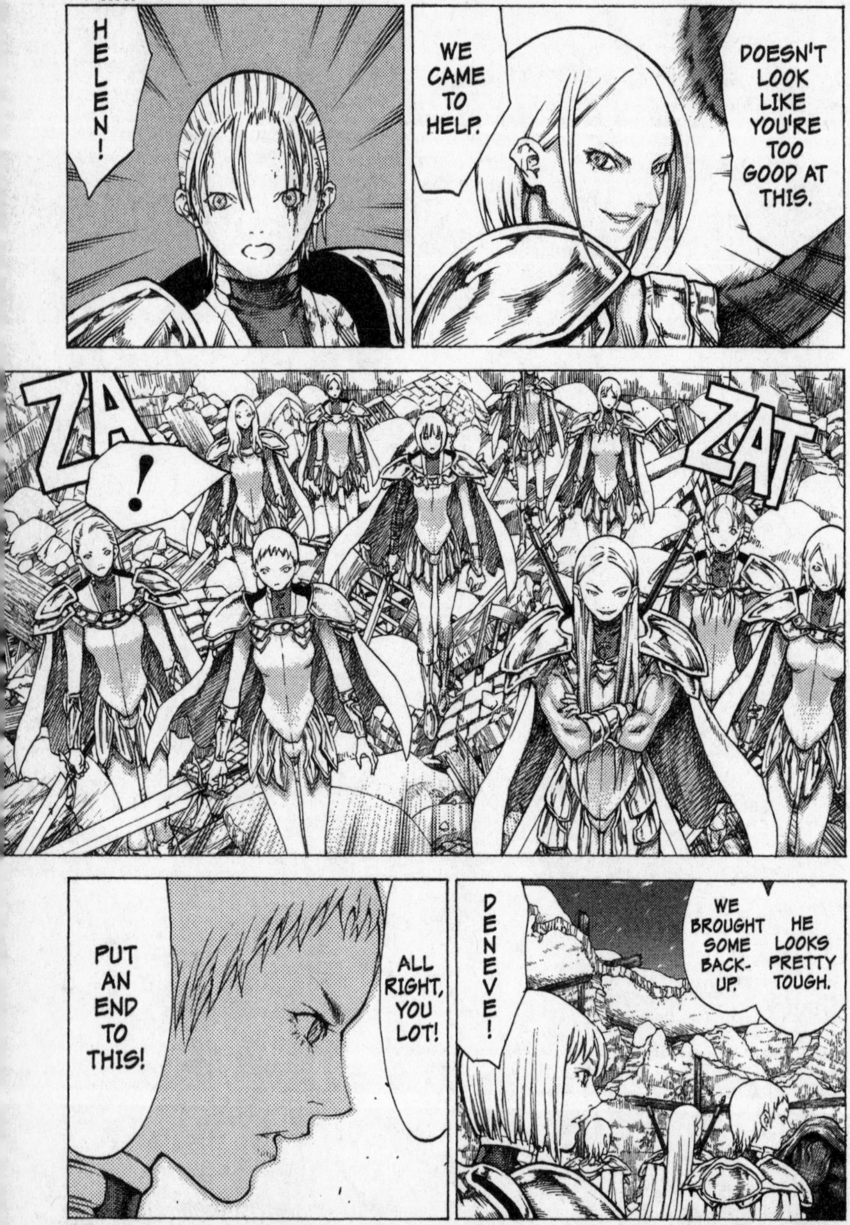

DOESN'T LOOK LIKE YOU'RE TOO GOOD AT THIS.
WE CAME TO HELP.
HELEN!
ZA ZAT
!
HE LOOKS PRETTY TOUGH.
WE BROUGHT SOME BACK-UP.
DENEVE!
ALL RIGHT, YOU LOT!
PUT AN END TO THIS!

クレイモア
Claymore™

Scene 53: The Battle of the North, Part 4

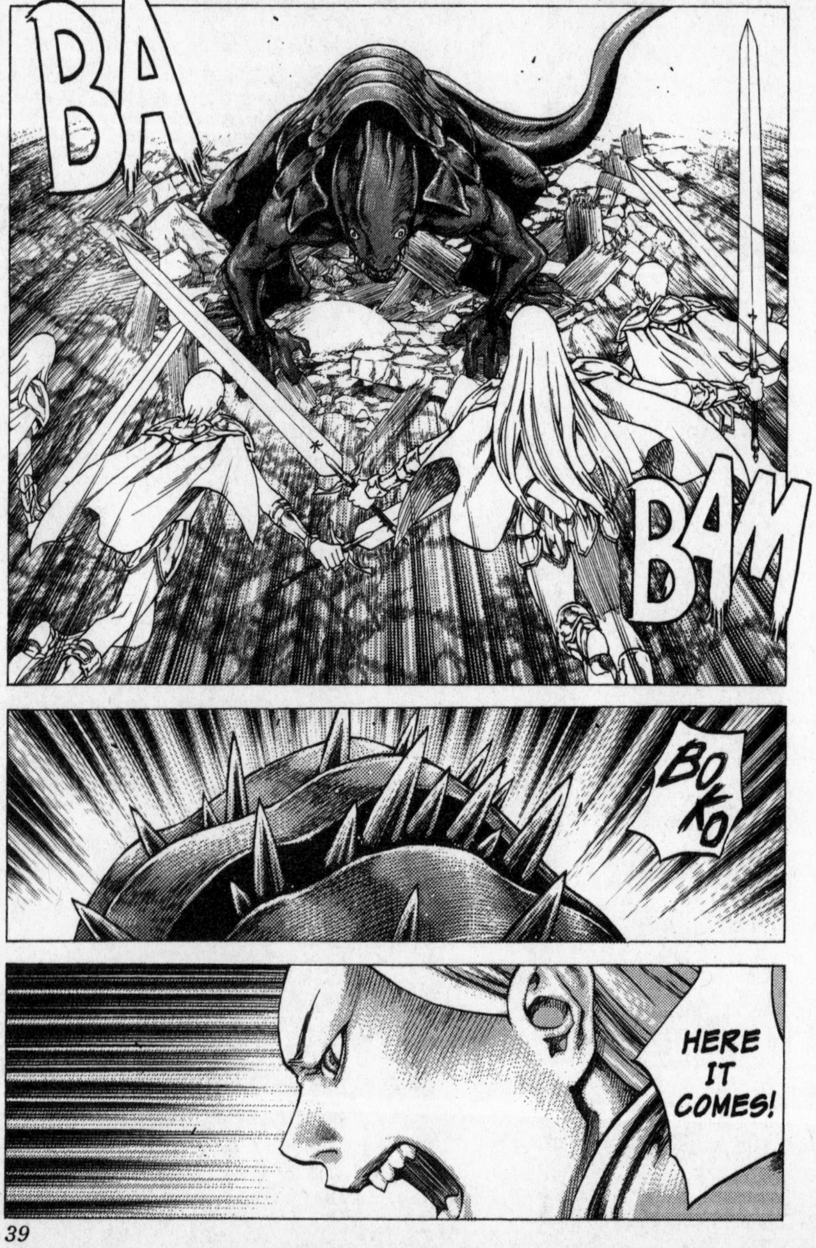
BA
BAM
BOKO
HERE IT COMES!

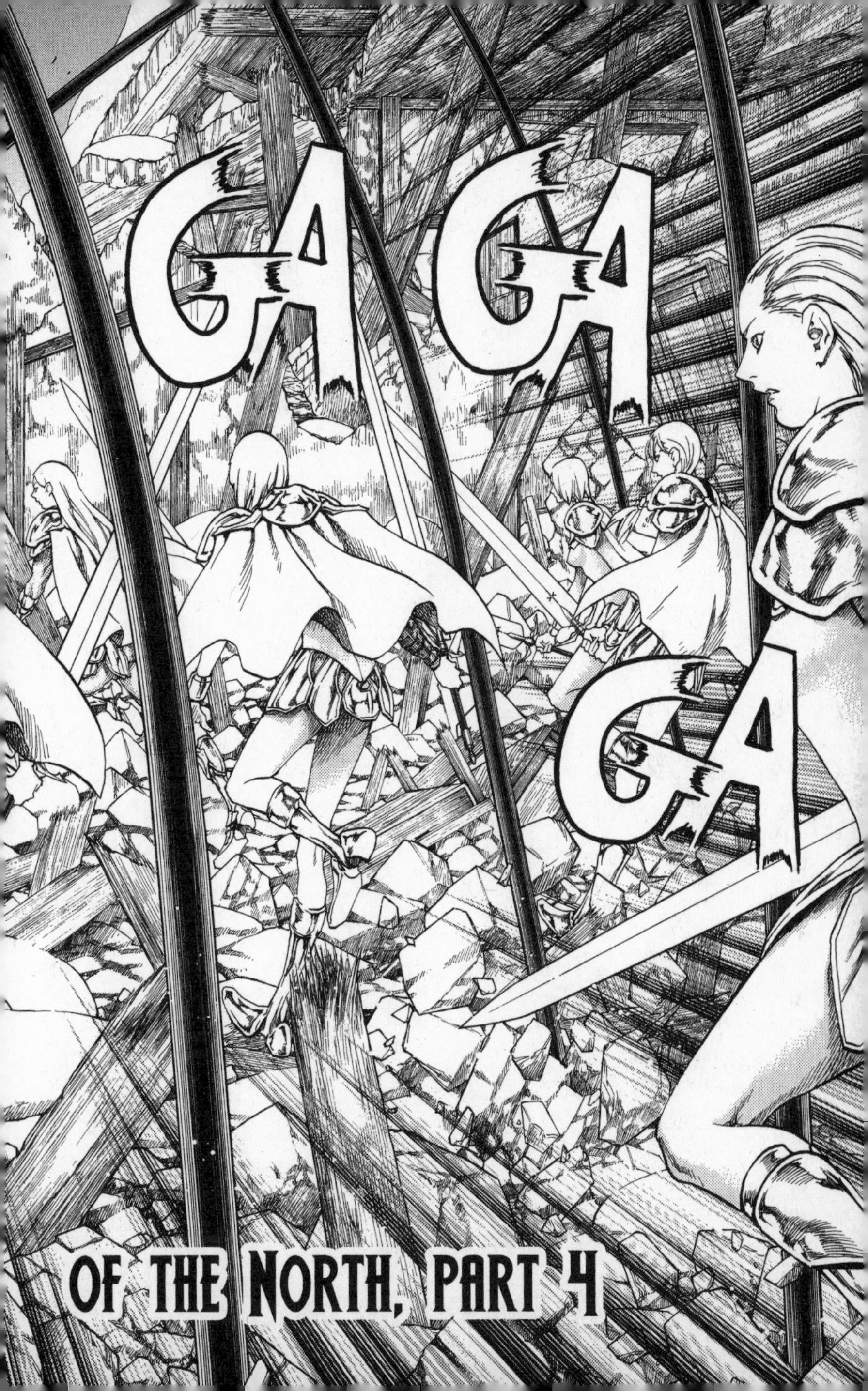
GA GA
GA
OF THE NORTH, PART 4

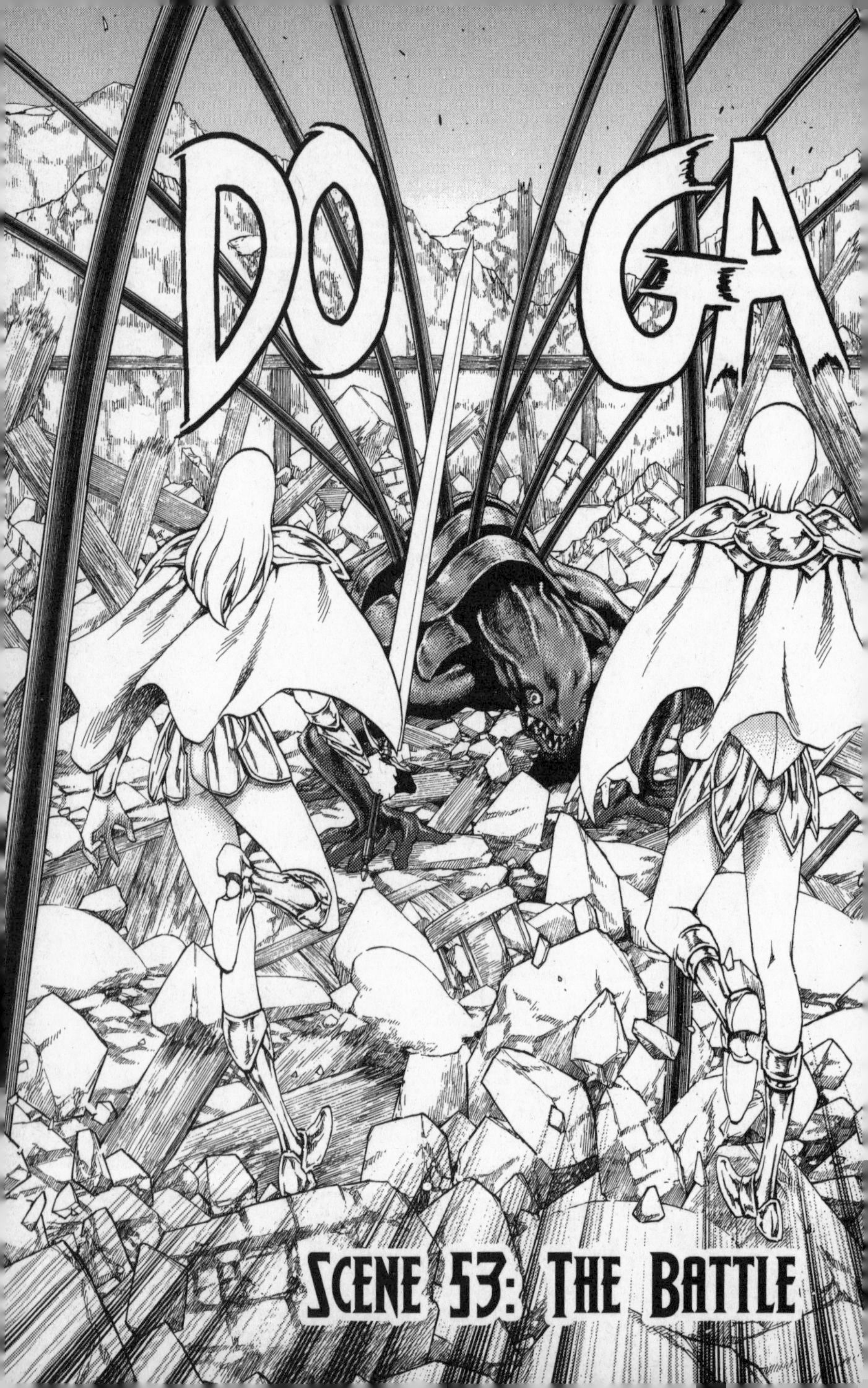
DO GA
SCENE 53: THE BATTLE

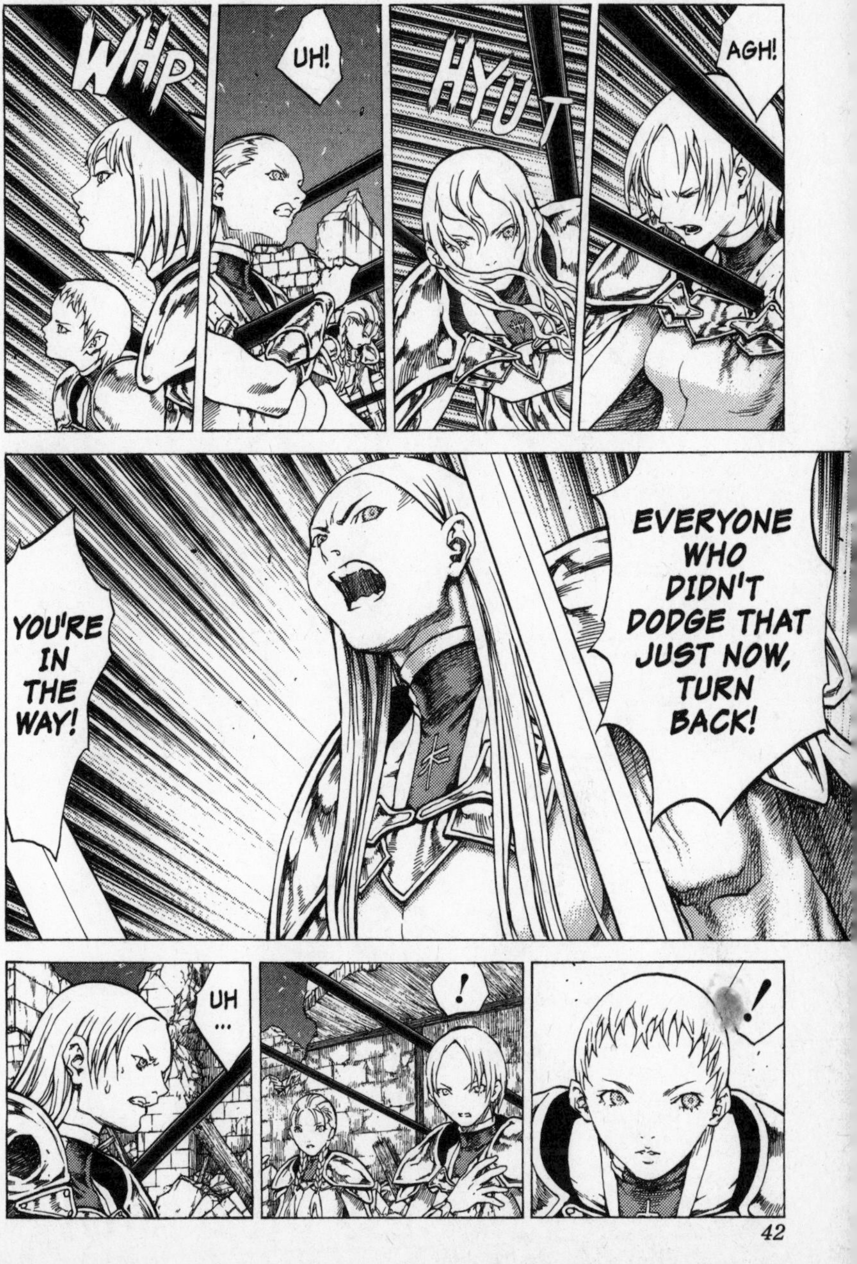
AGH!
HYUT
UH!
WHP
EVERYONE WHO DIDN'T DODGE THAT JUST NOW, TURN BACK!
YOU'RE IN THE WAY!
!
!
UH ...

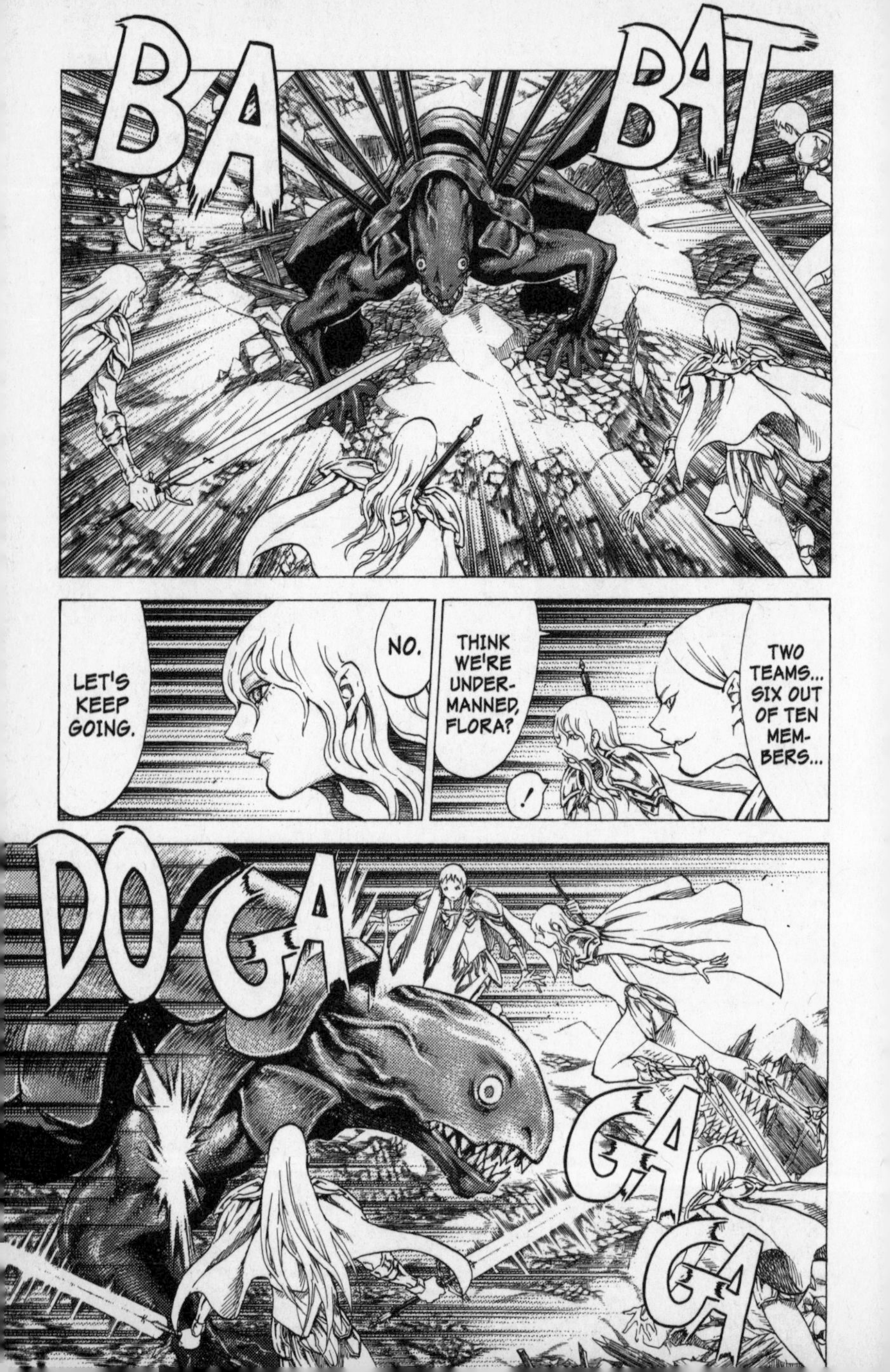
BA BAT
TWO TEAMS... SIX OUT OF TEN MEMBERS...
THINK WE'RE UNDER-MANNED, FLORA?
!
NO.
LET'S KEEP GOING.
DOGA
GA
GA

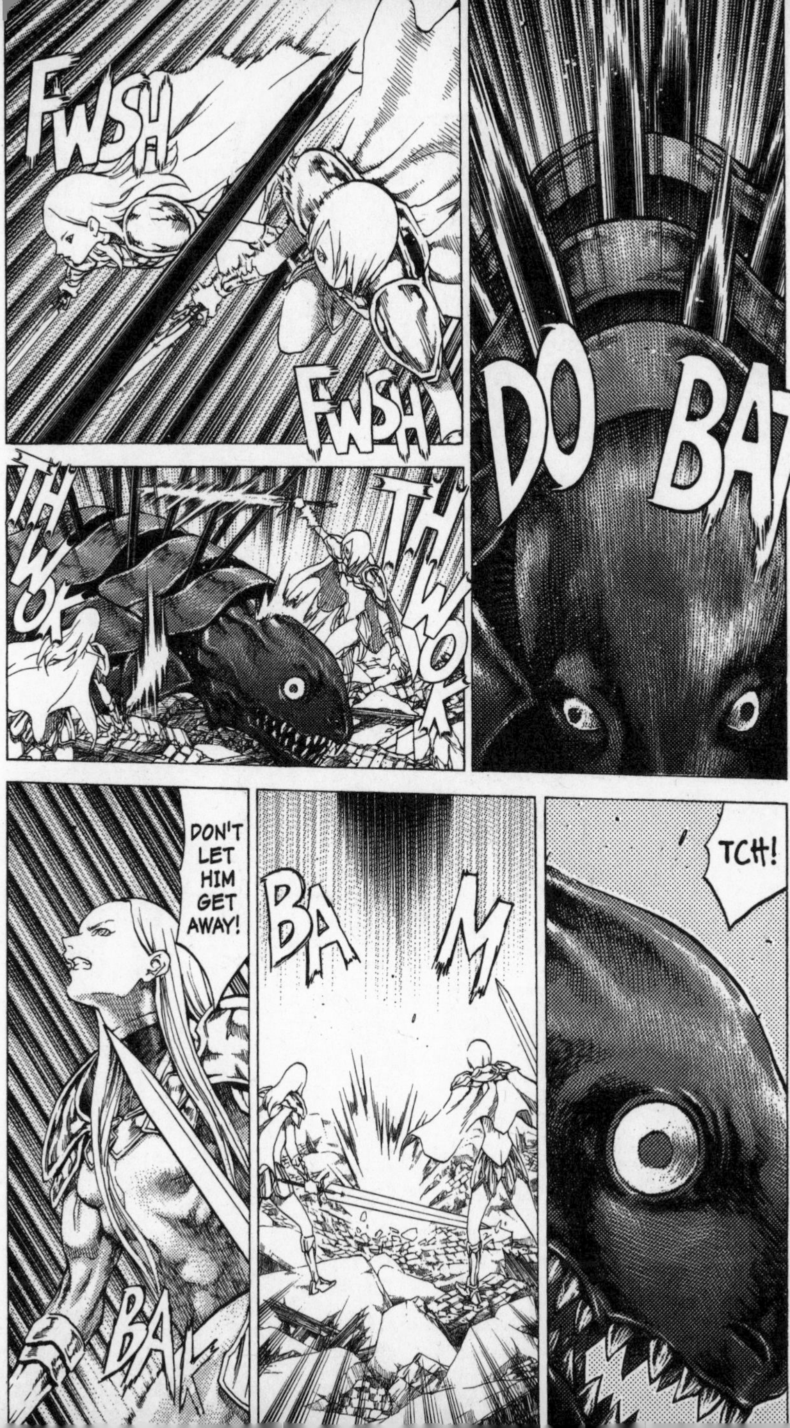
DO BAT
FWSH
FWSH
THWOK
THWOK
TCH!
BAM
DON'T LET HIM GET AWAY!
BAK

READ THIS WAY

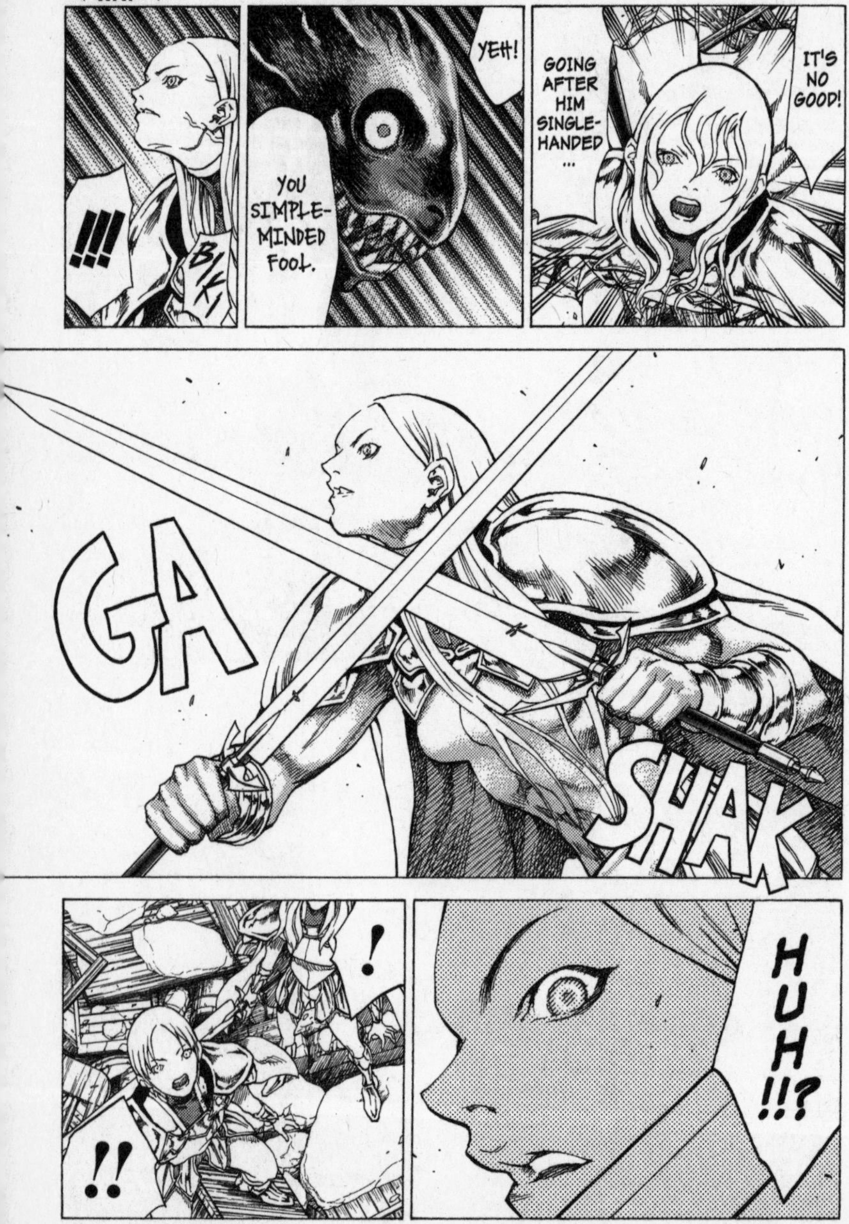
IT'S NO GOOD!
GOING AFTER HIM SINGLE-HANDED ...
YEH!
YOU SIMPLE-MINDED FOOL.
BIKI
!!!
GA
SHAK
HUH!!?
!
!!

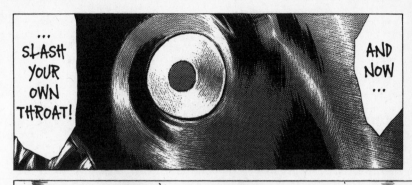

...SLASH YOUR OWN THROAT!

AND NOW ...

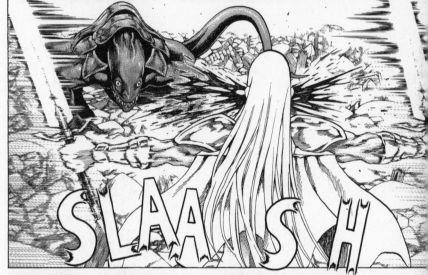

SLAASH

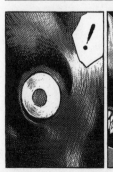

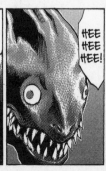

HEE HEE HEE!

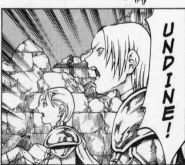

UNDINE!

46

READ THIS WAY

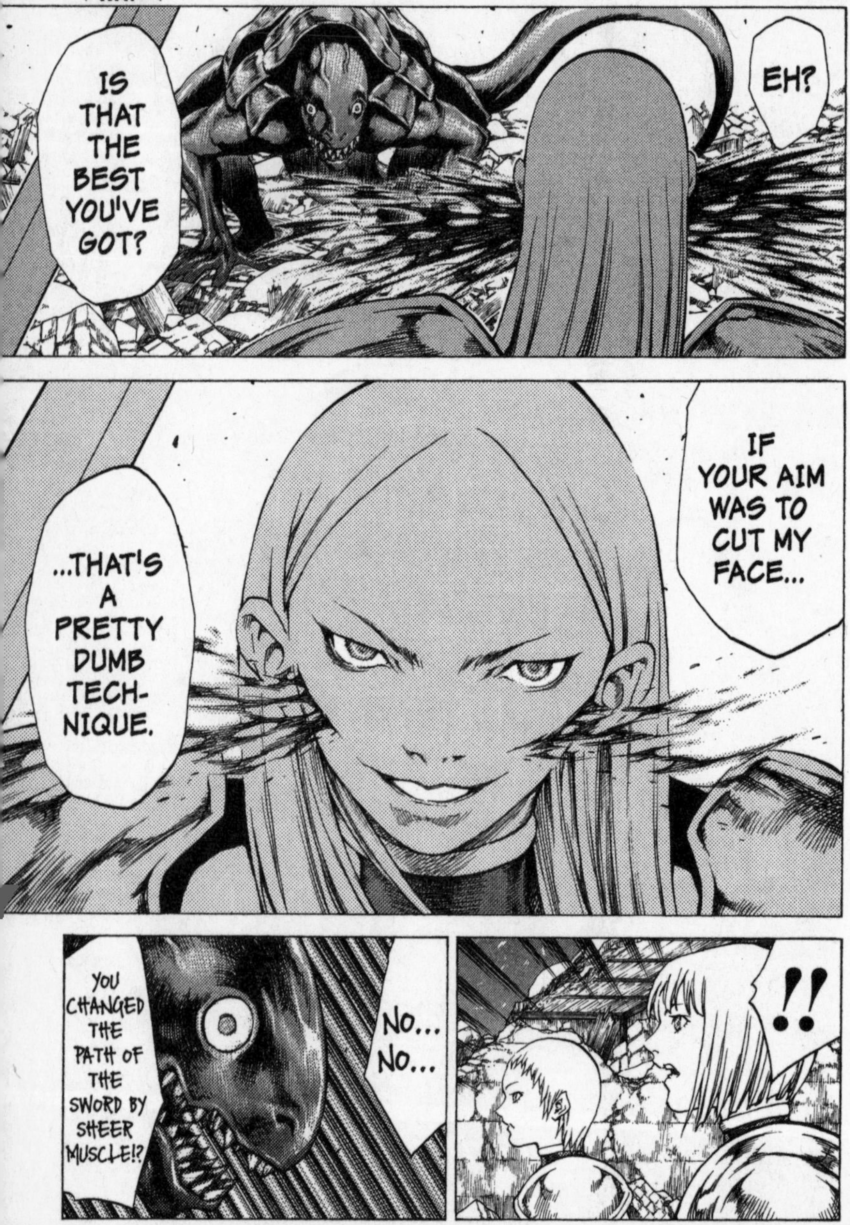

EH?
IS THAT THE BEST YOU'VE GOT?
IF YOUR AIM WAS TO CUT MY FACE...
...THAT'S A PRETTY DUMB TECH-NIQUE.
!!
NO... NO...
YOU CHANGED THE PATH OF THE SWORD BY SHEER MUSCLE!?

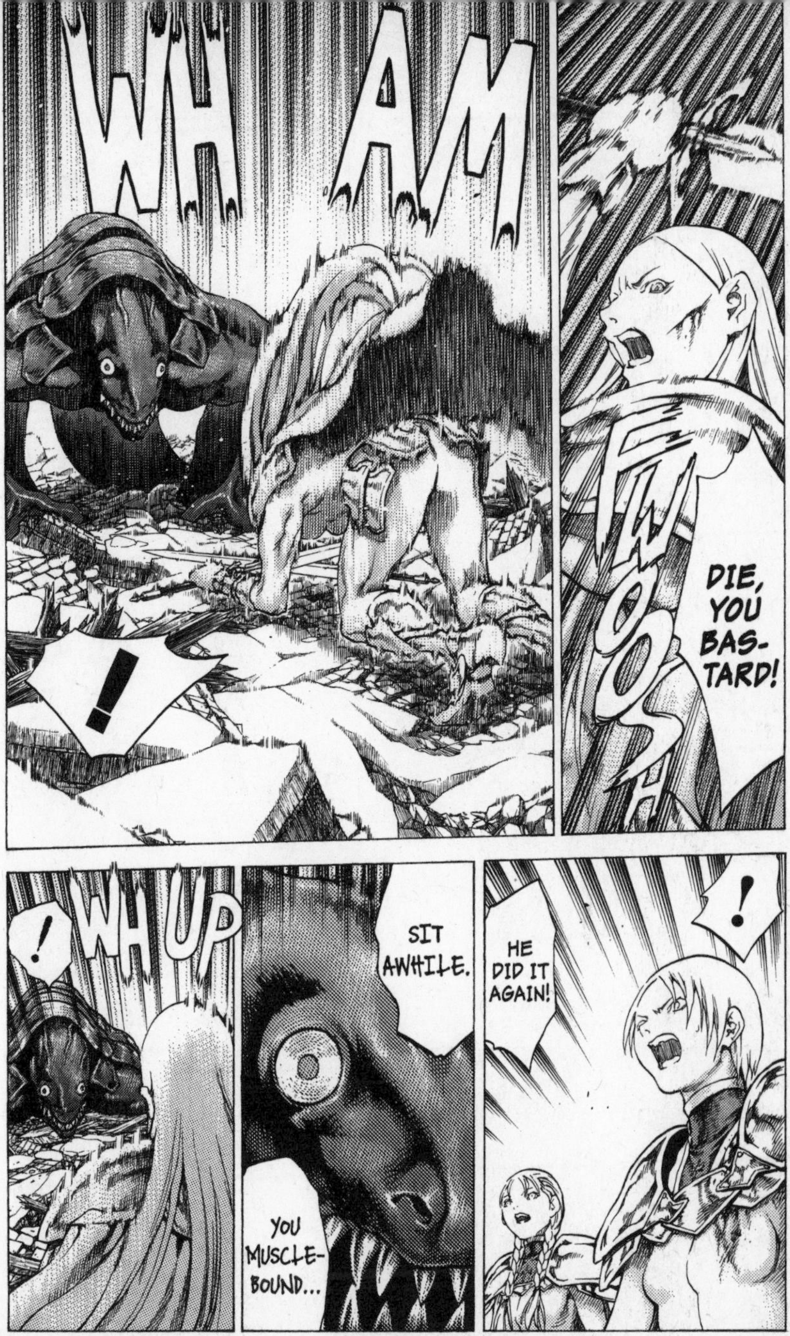
FWOOSH
DIE, YOU BASTARD!
WHAM
!
!
HE DID IT AGAIN!
SIT AWHILE.
YOU MUSCLE-BOUND...
WHUP
!

READ THIS WAY

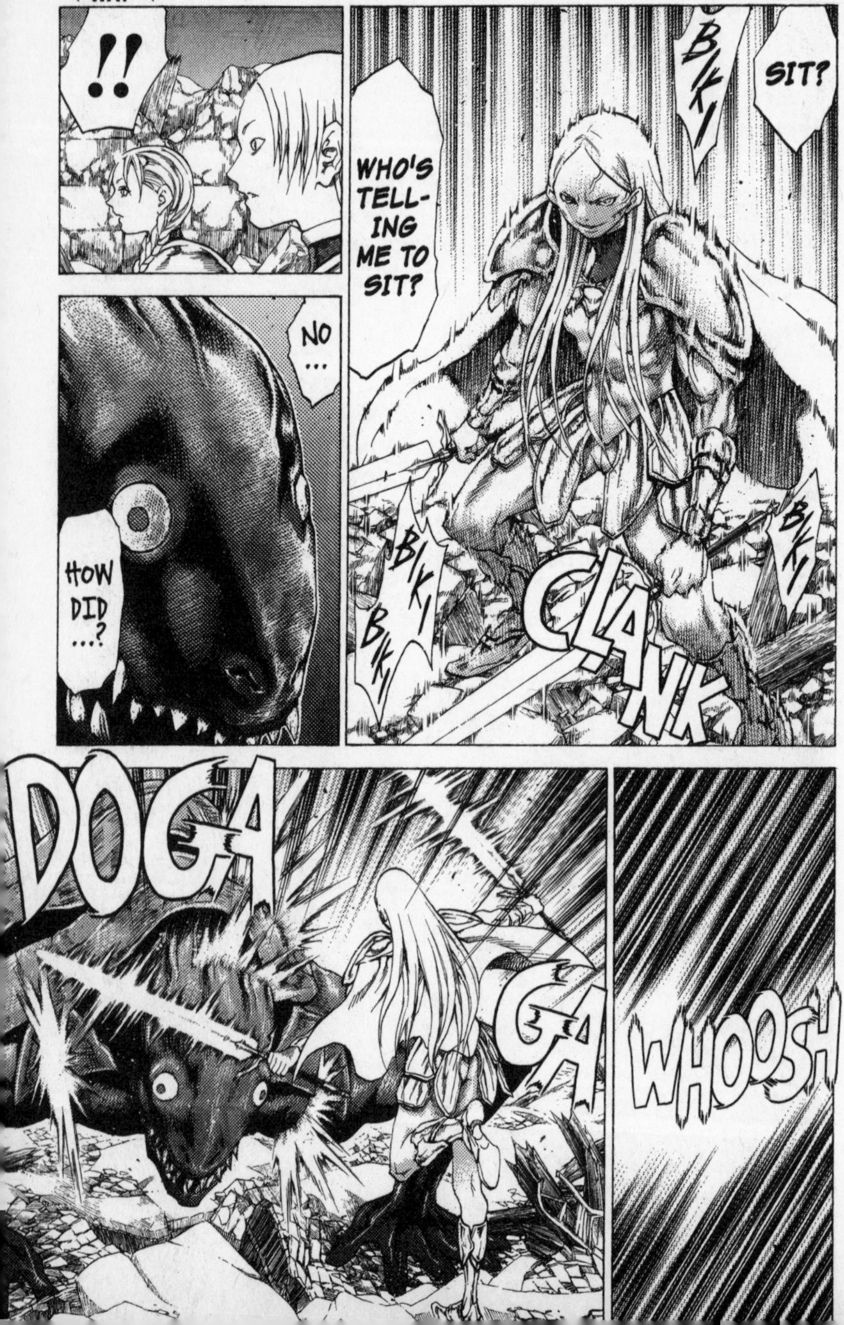
SIT?
BIKI
WHO'S TELLING ME TO SIT?
BIKI
CLANK
BIKI BIKI
!!
NO...
HOW DID...?
WHOOSH
DOGA
GA

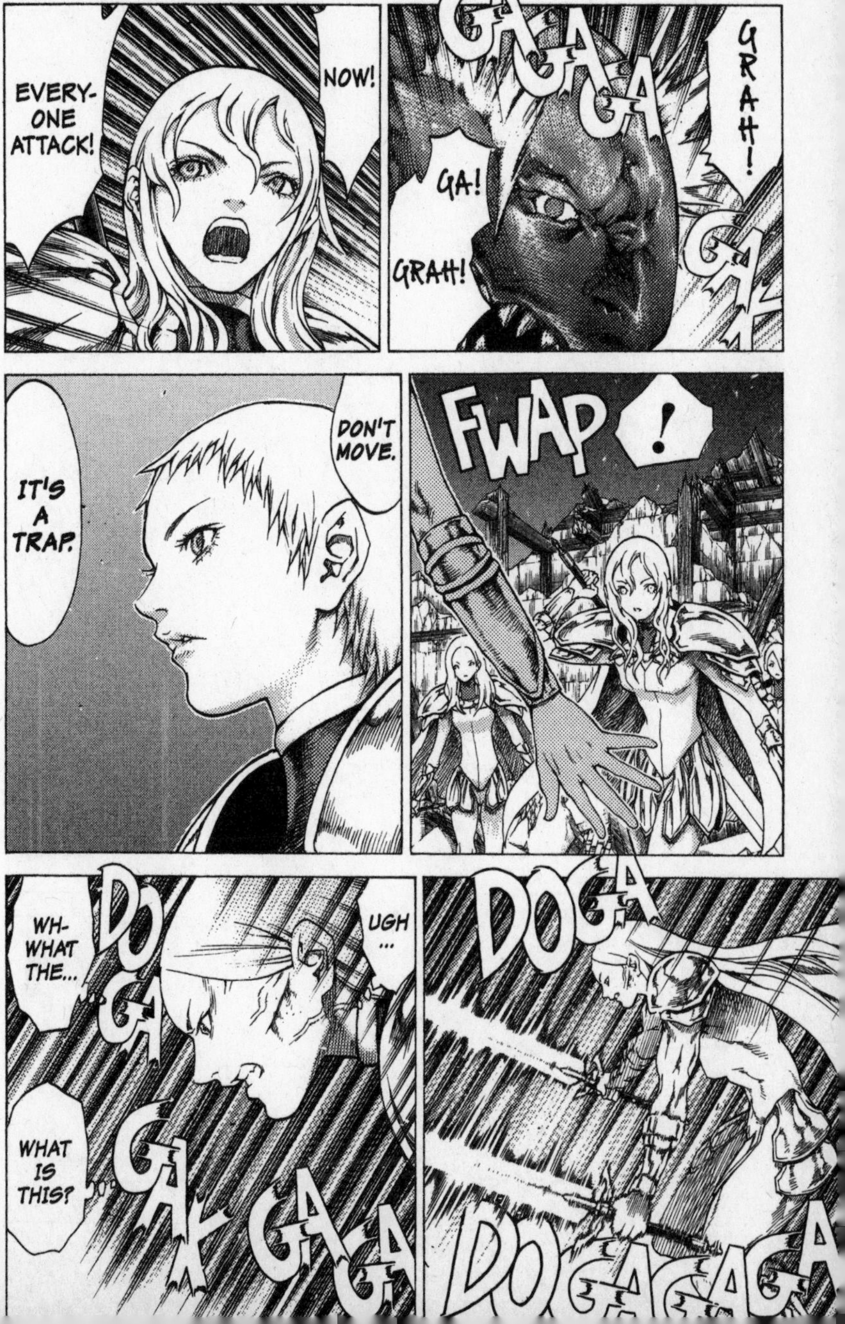
GAGAGA
GRAH!
GA!
GRAH!
GAGA
NOW!
EVERY-ONE ATTACK!
FWAP
!
DON'T MOVE.
IT'S A TRAP.
DOGA
DOGAGAGA
UGH...
WH-WHAT THE...
DOGA
WHAT IS THIS?
GAGAGAGA

READ THIS WAY

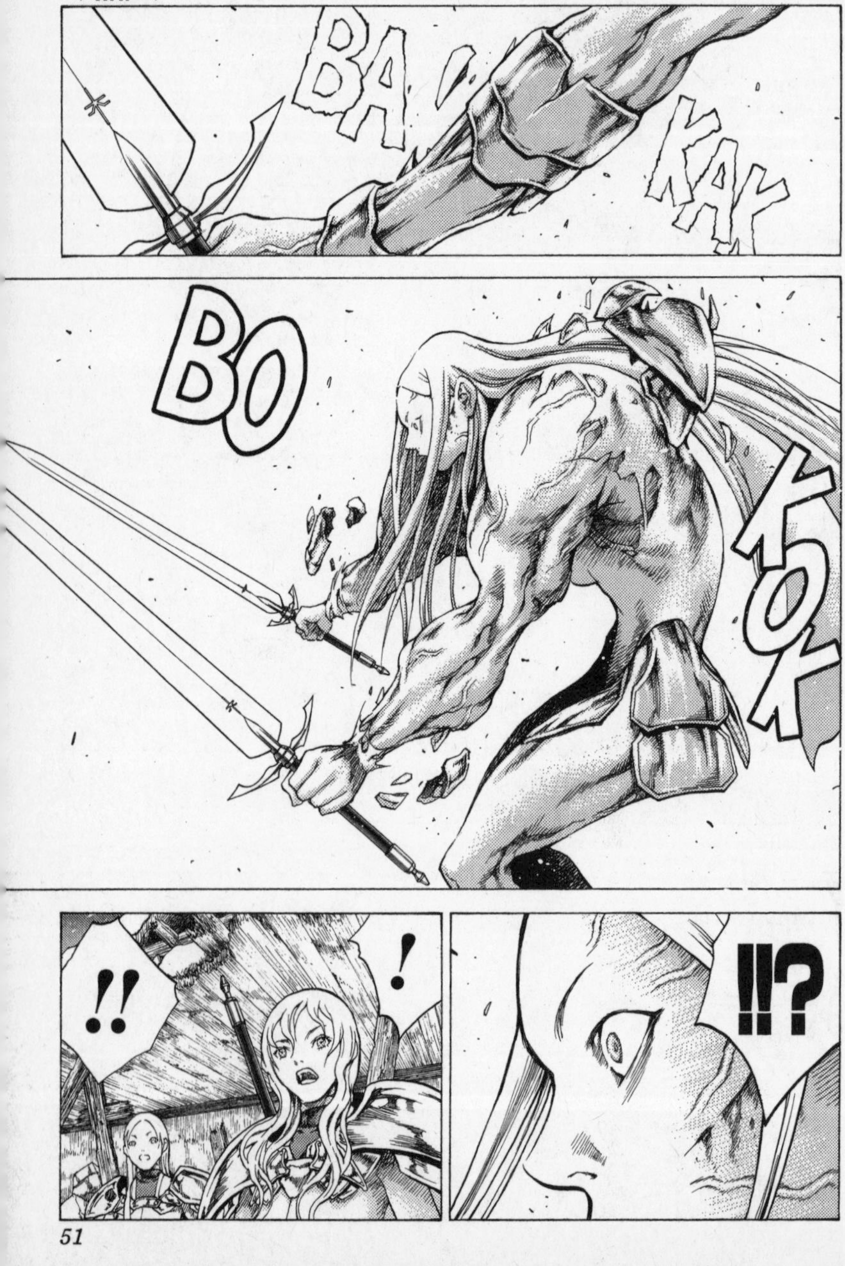
BA
KAY
BO
KOK
!!?
!
!!

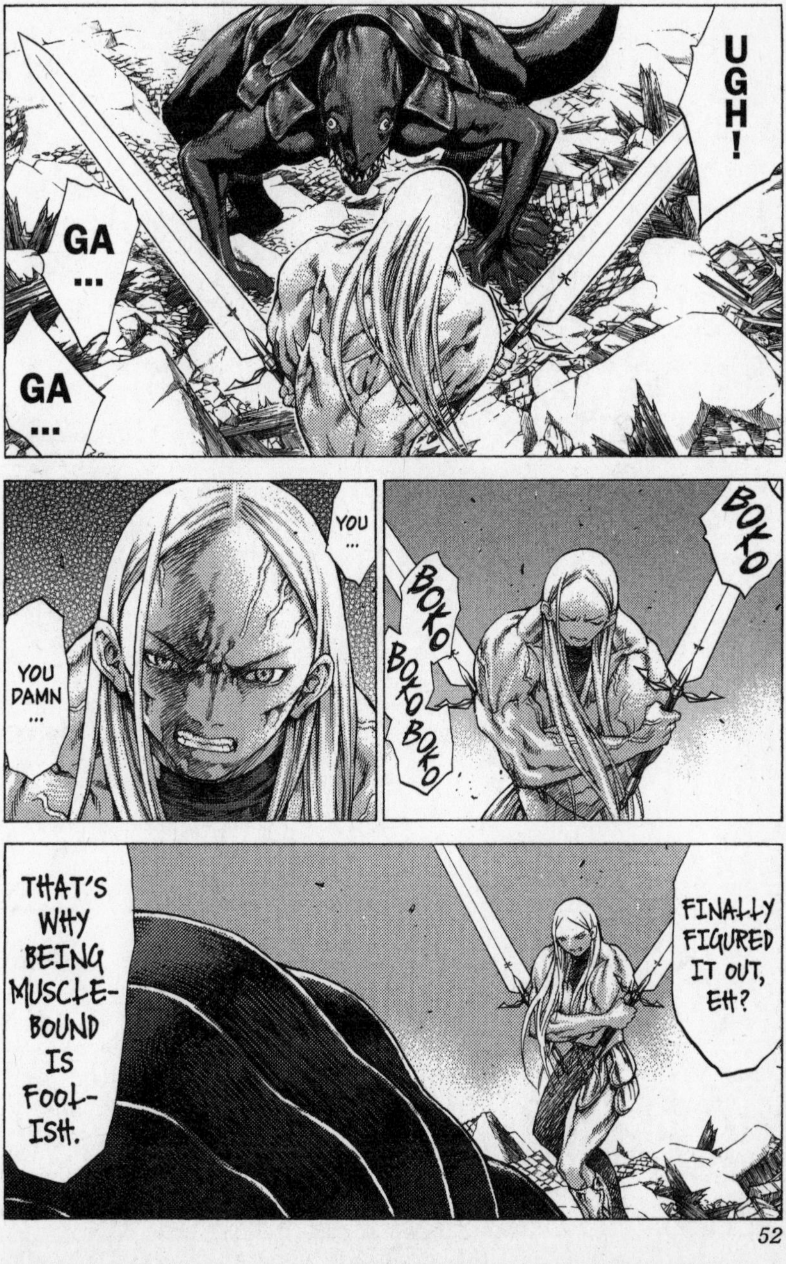
UGH!
GA ...
GA ...
BOKO
BOKO
BOKO
BOKO
BOKO
YOU ...
YOU DAMN ...
FINALLY FIGURED IT OUT, EH?
THAT'S WHY BEING MUSCLE-BOUND IS FOOLISH.

READ THIS WAY

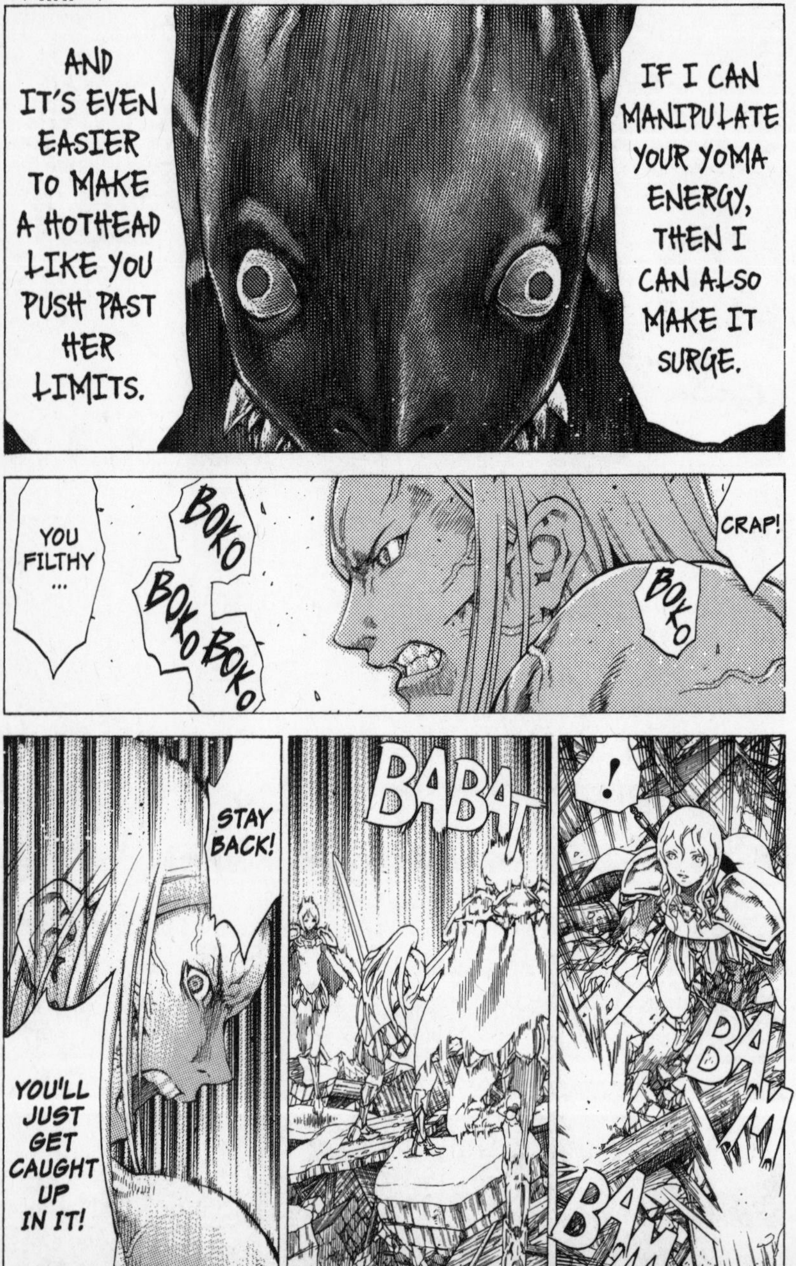
IF I CAN MANIPULATE YOUR YOMA ENERGY, THEN I CAN ALSO MAKE IT SURGE.
AND IT'S EVEN EASIER TO MAKE A HOTHEAD LIKE YOU PUSH PAST HER LIMITS.
CRAP!
BOKO
BOKO
BOKO BOKO
YOU FILTHY ...
!
BAM
BAM
BABAT
STAY BACK!
YOU'LL JUST GET CAUGHT UP IN IT!

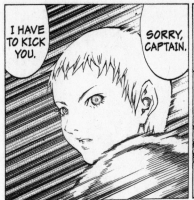

FWOOSH
!
SORRY, CAPTAIN.
I HAVE TO KICK YOU.
DOGAA
AGH!
CRASH
!
CLARE!

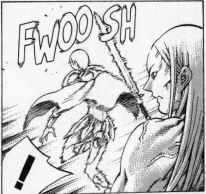

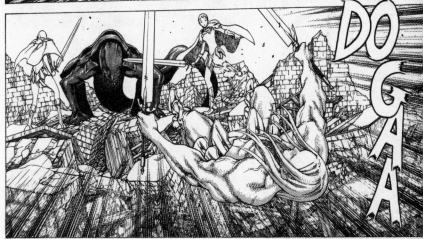

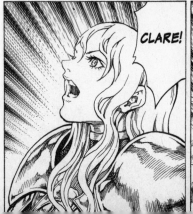

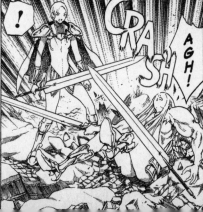

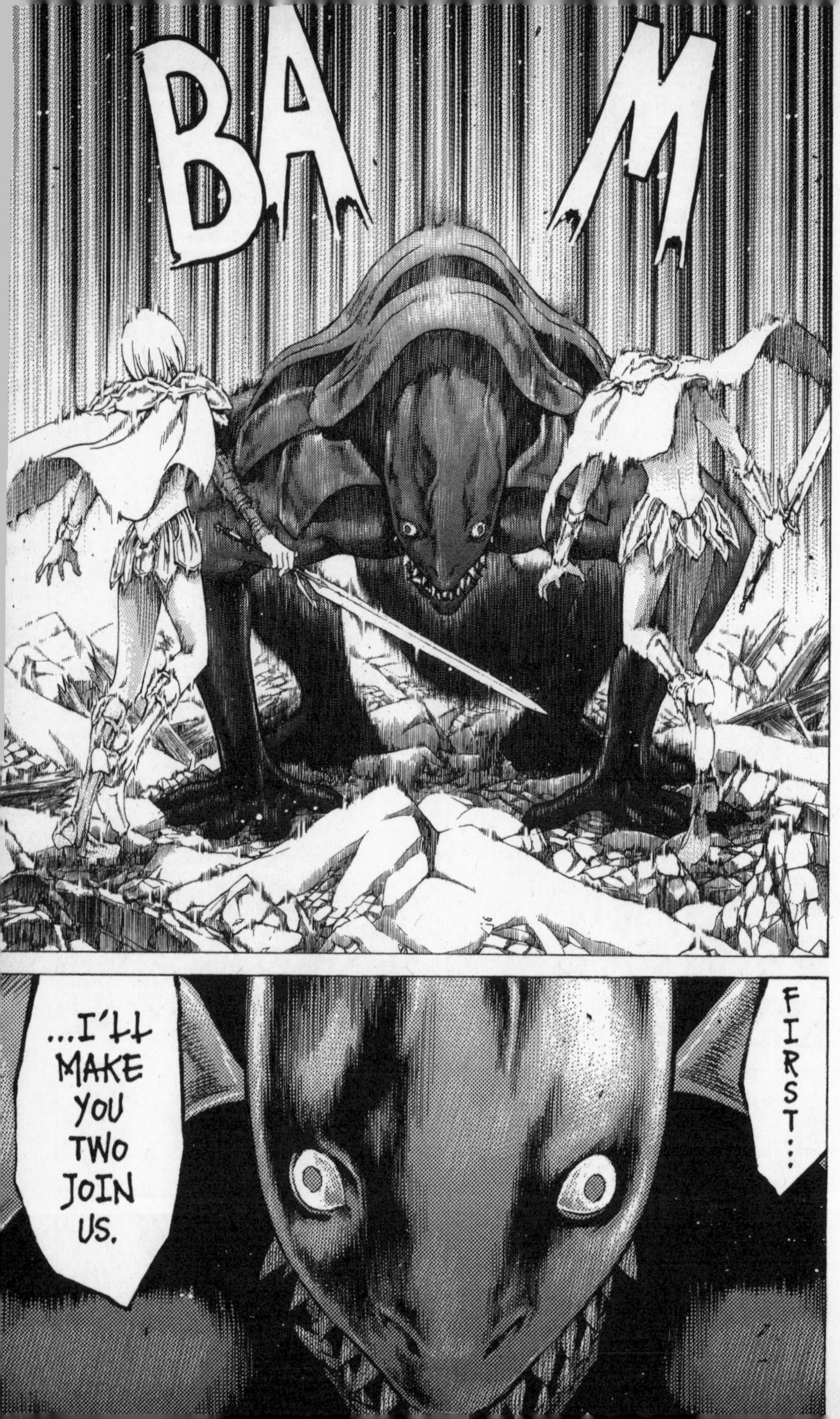
BAM
FIRST...
...I'll MAKE YOU TWO JOIN US.

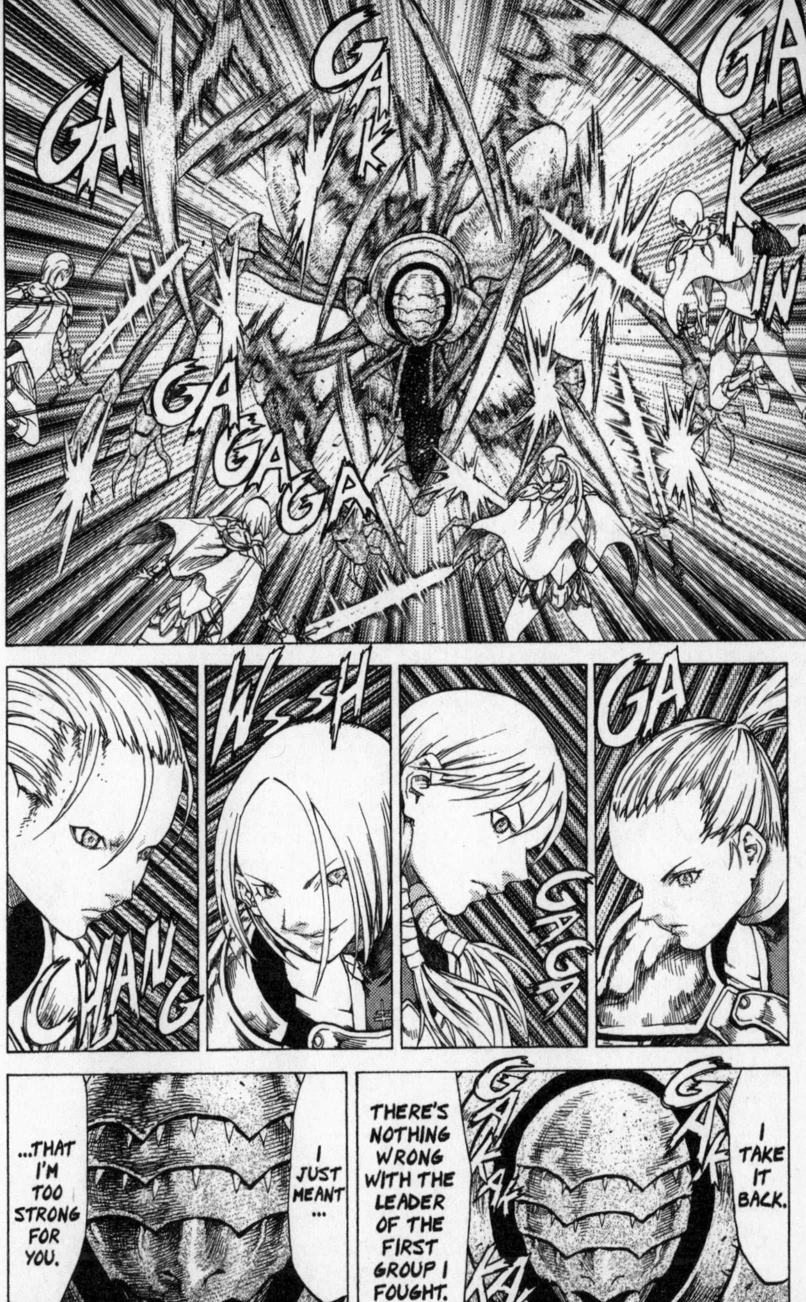
GA K IN
GAK
GA
GAGAGA
GA
GAGA
WSSH
CHANG
GAK
I TAKE IT BACK.
GAKAKAK
KAKAKAK
THERE'S NOTHING WRONG WITH THE LEADER OF THE FIRST GROUP I FOUGHT.
I JUST MEANT ...
...THAT I'M TOO STRONG FOR YOU.

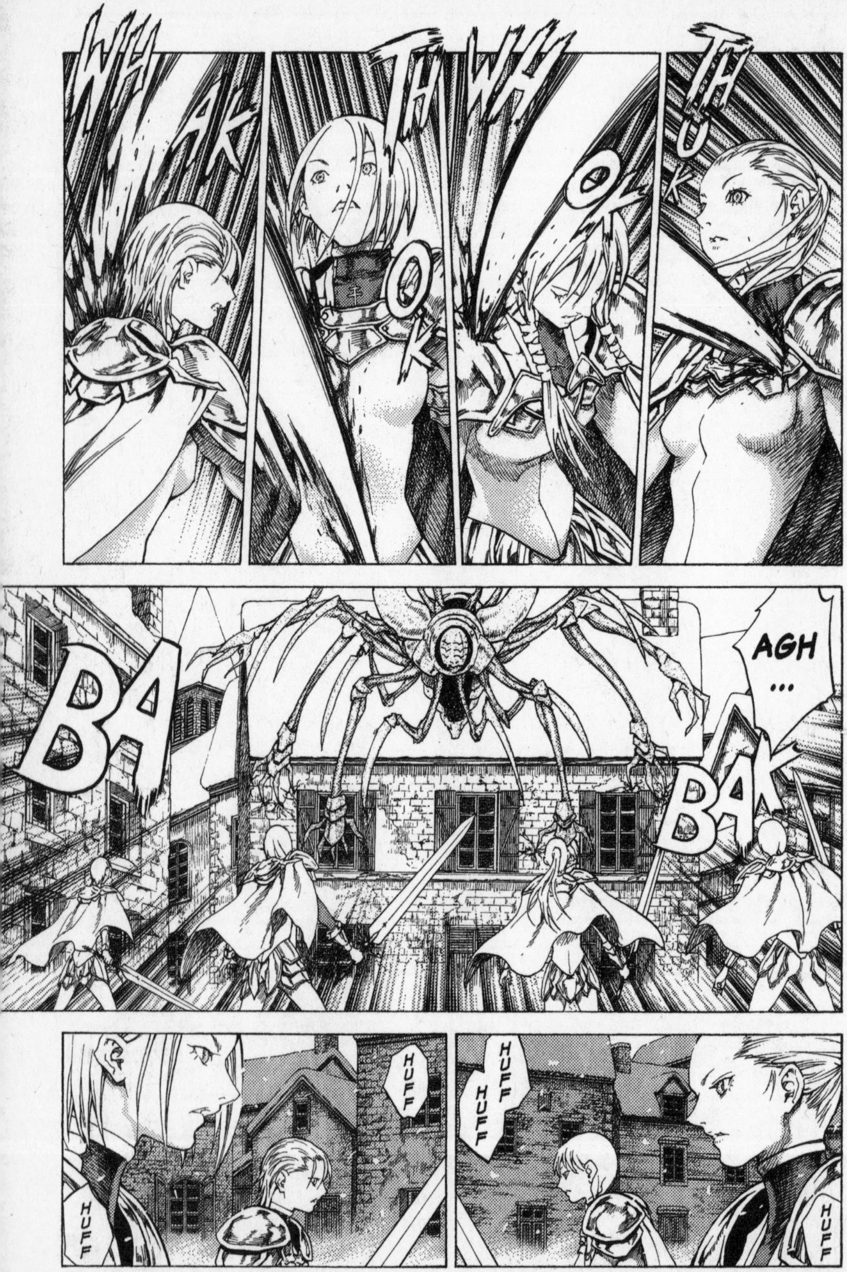
THUK
WHOK
THOK
WHAK
AGH ...
BAK
BA
HUFF HUFF
HUFF
HUFF
HUFF

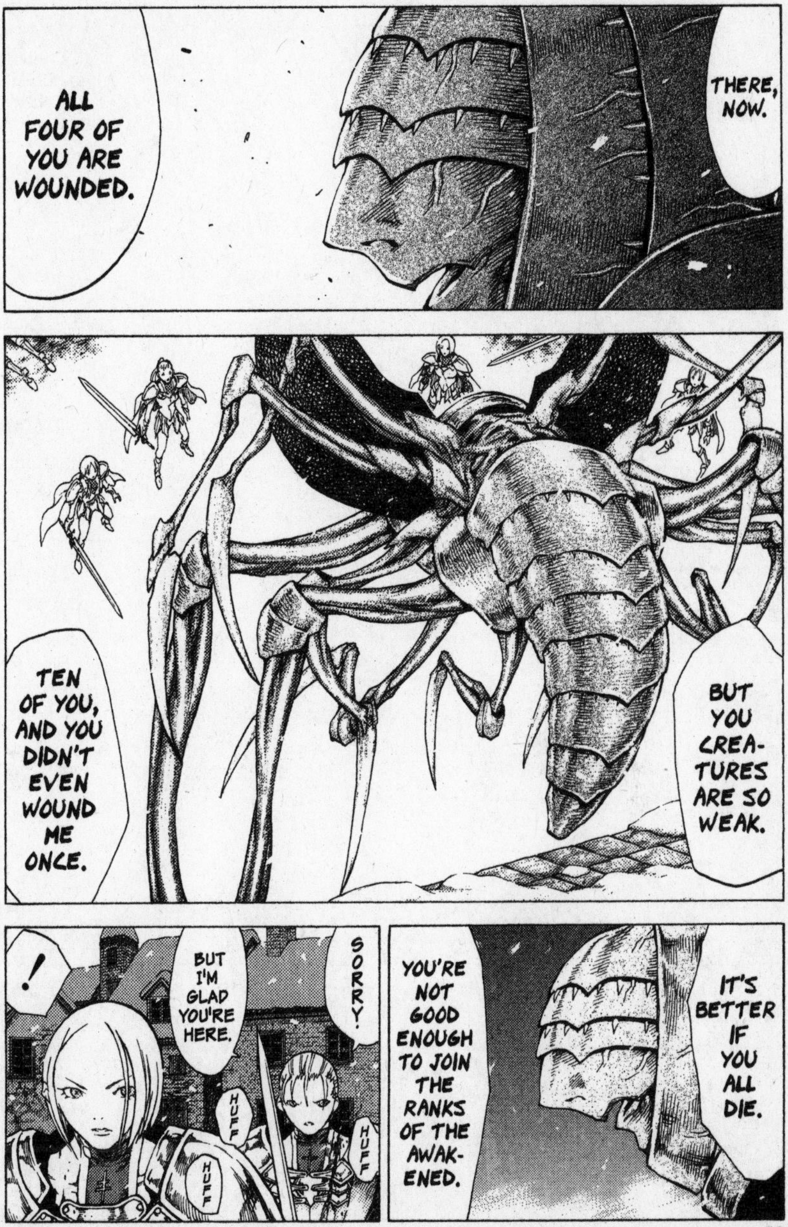
THERE, NOW.
ALL FOUR OF YOU ARE WOUNDED.
BUT YOU CREATURES ARE SO WEAK.
TEN OF YOU, AND YOU DIDN'T EVEN WOUND ME ONCE.
IT'S BETTER IF YOU ALL DIE.
YOU'RE NOT GOOD ENOUGH TO JOIN THE RANKS OF THE AWAKENED.
SORRY.
BUT I'M GLAD YOU'RE HERE.
!
HUFF
HUFF
HUFF

READ THIS WAY

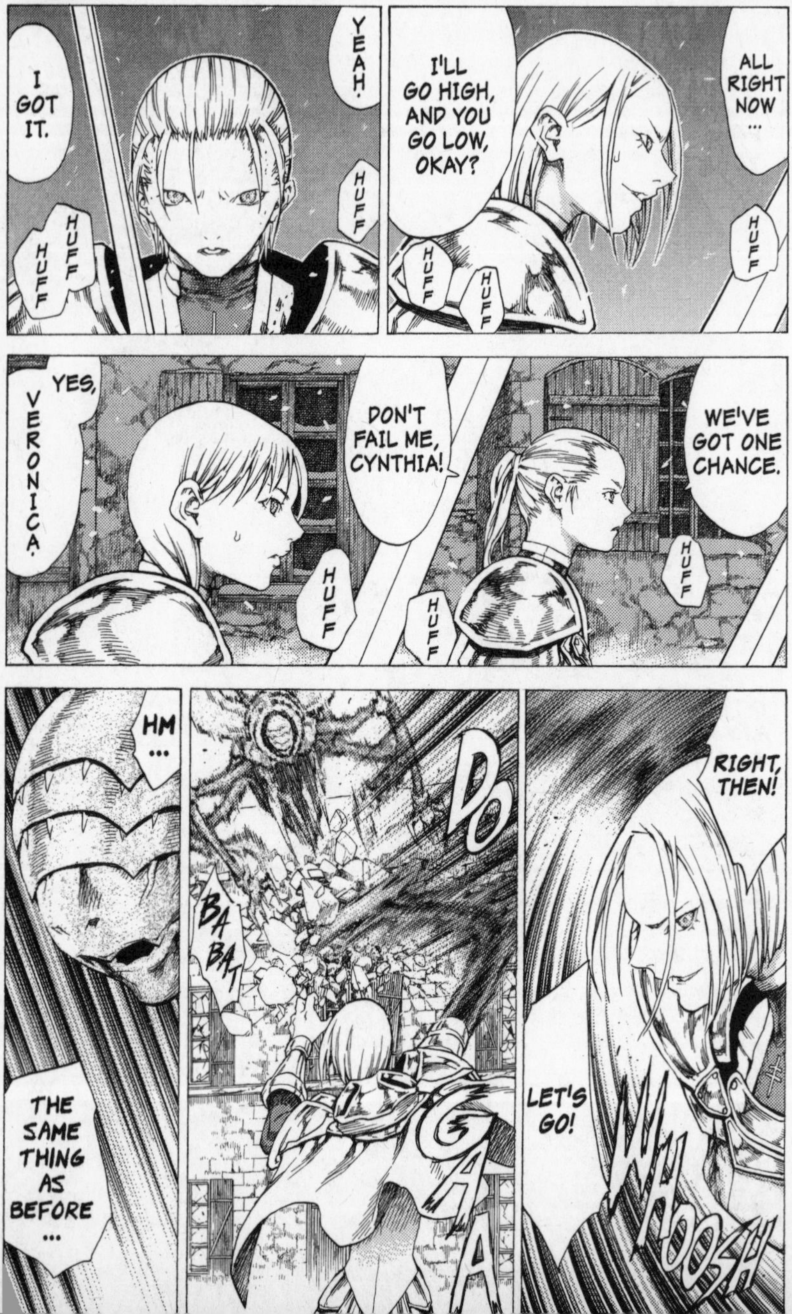
ALL RIGHT NOW ...
HUFF
I'LL GO HIGH, AND YOU GO LOW, OKAY?
HUFF
HUFF
YEAH.
I GOT IT.
HUFF
HUFF
HUFF
WE'VE GOT ONE CHANCE.
HUFF
DON'T FAIL ME, CYNTHIA!
HUFF
YES, VERONICA.
HUFF
RIGHT, THEN!
LET'S GO!
WHOOSH
DO
BA BAT
GA A
HM ...
THE SAME THING AS BEFORE ...

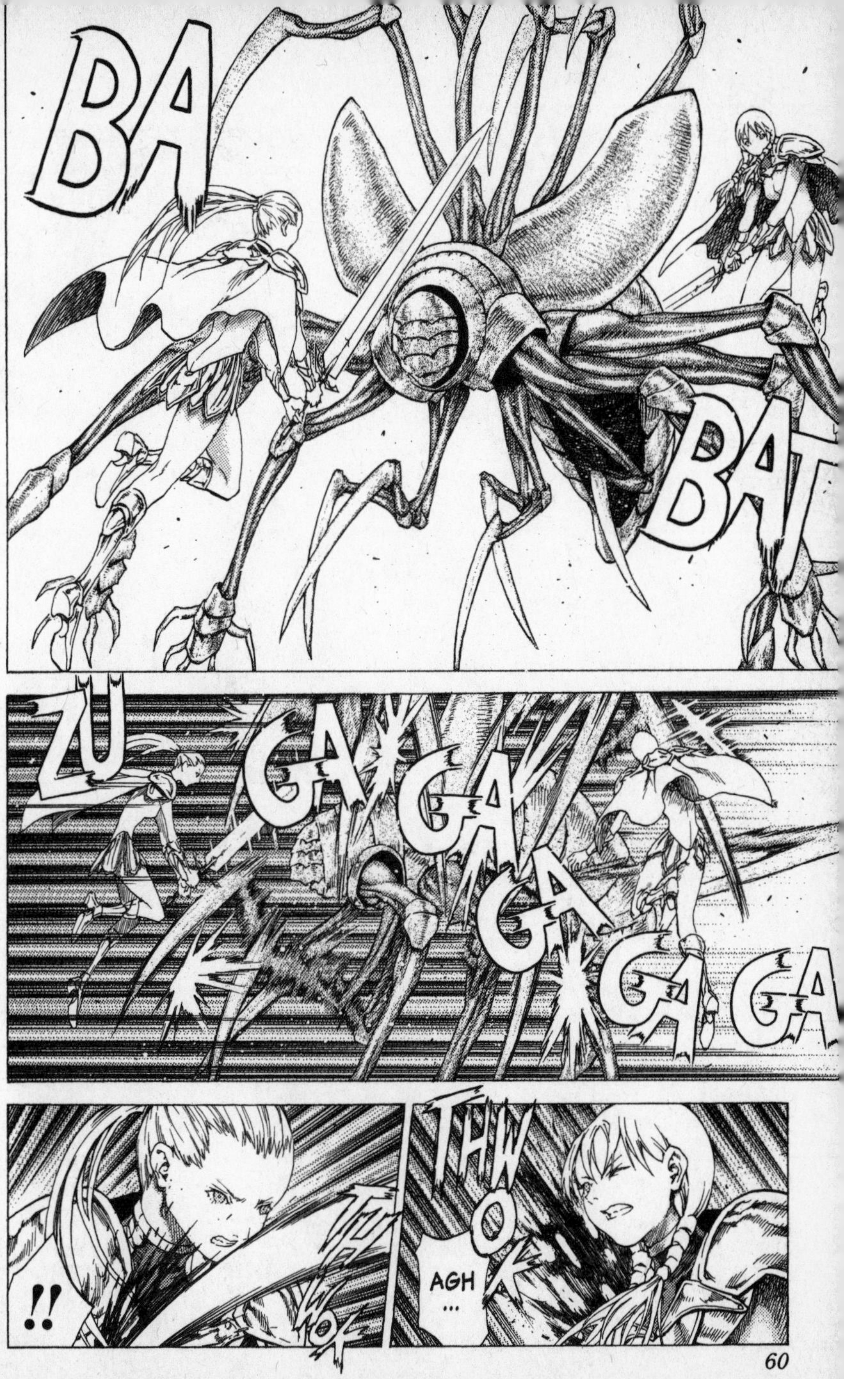
BA
BAT
ZU GA GA GA GA GA
THWOK
AGH ...
THWOK
!!

READ THIS WAY

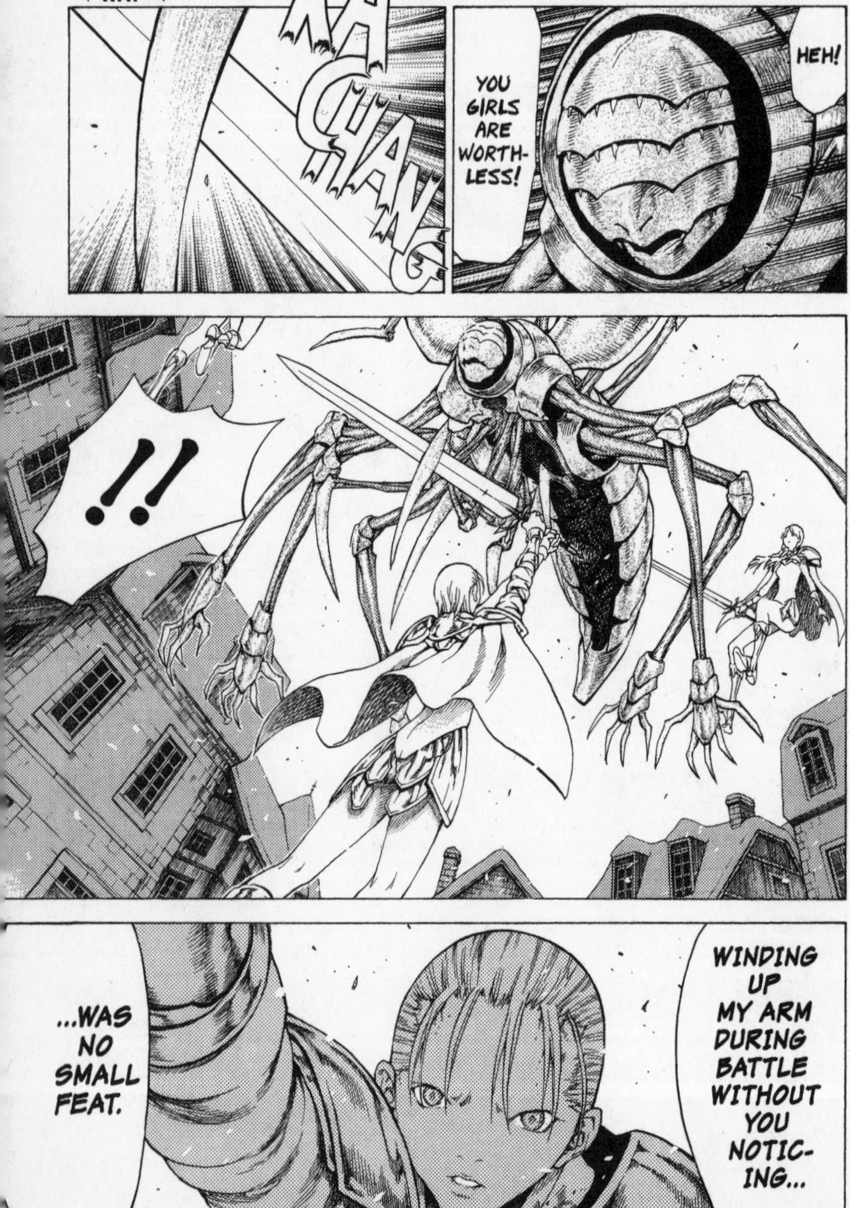
HEH!
YOU GIRLS ARE WORTHLESS!
KA CHANG
!!
WINDING UP MY ARM DURING BATTLE WITHOUT YOU NOTICING...
...WAS NO SMALL FEAT.

HUH !?
!!!
GA SHAP
AND THEN THE REST OF THE PLAN...
...IS FOR ME TO HIT YOU WITH THIS WHILE YOU'RE DISTRAC-TED.

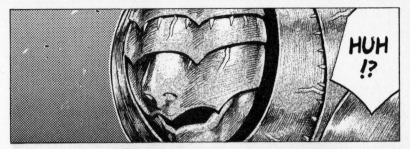

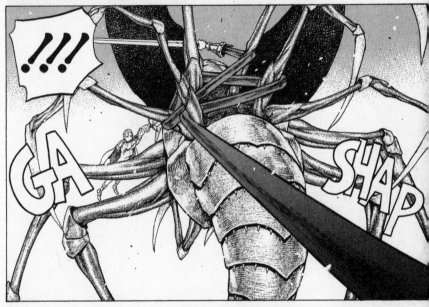

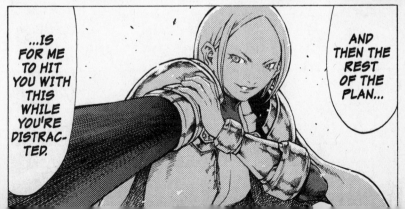

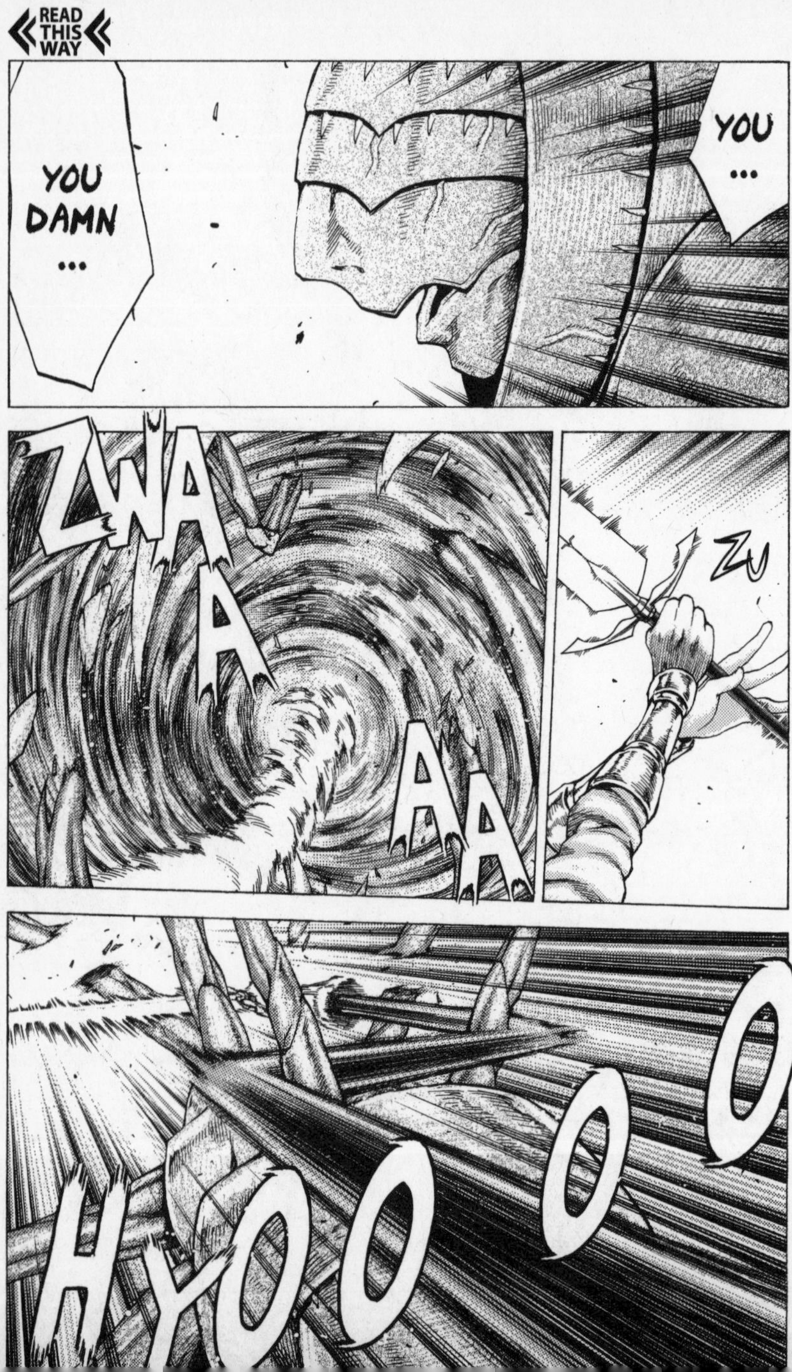
READ THIS WAY
YOU ...
YOU DAMN ...
ZU
ZWAAAA
HYOOOOO

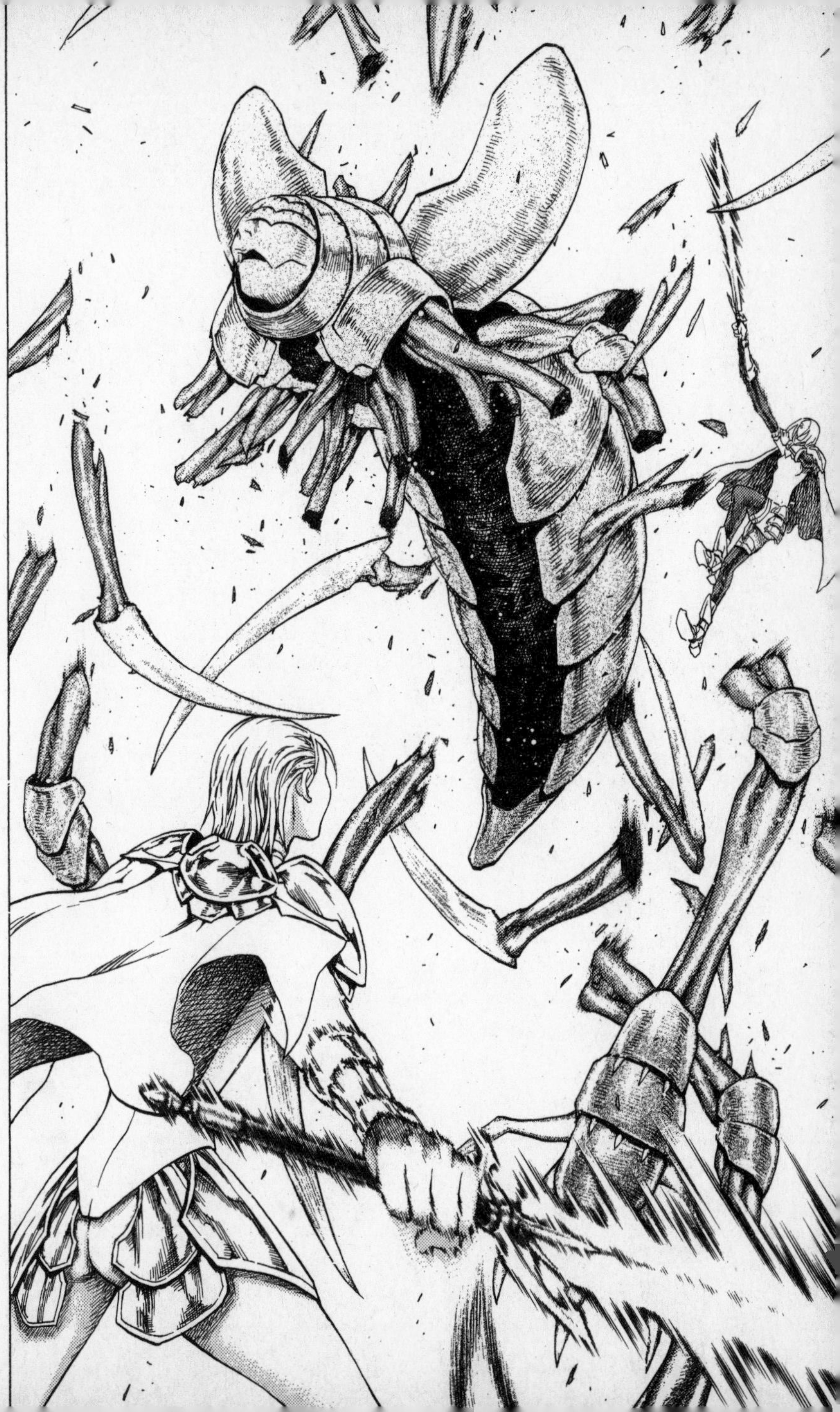

READ THIS WAY

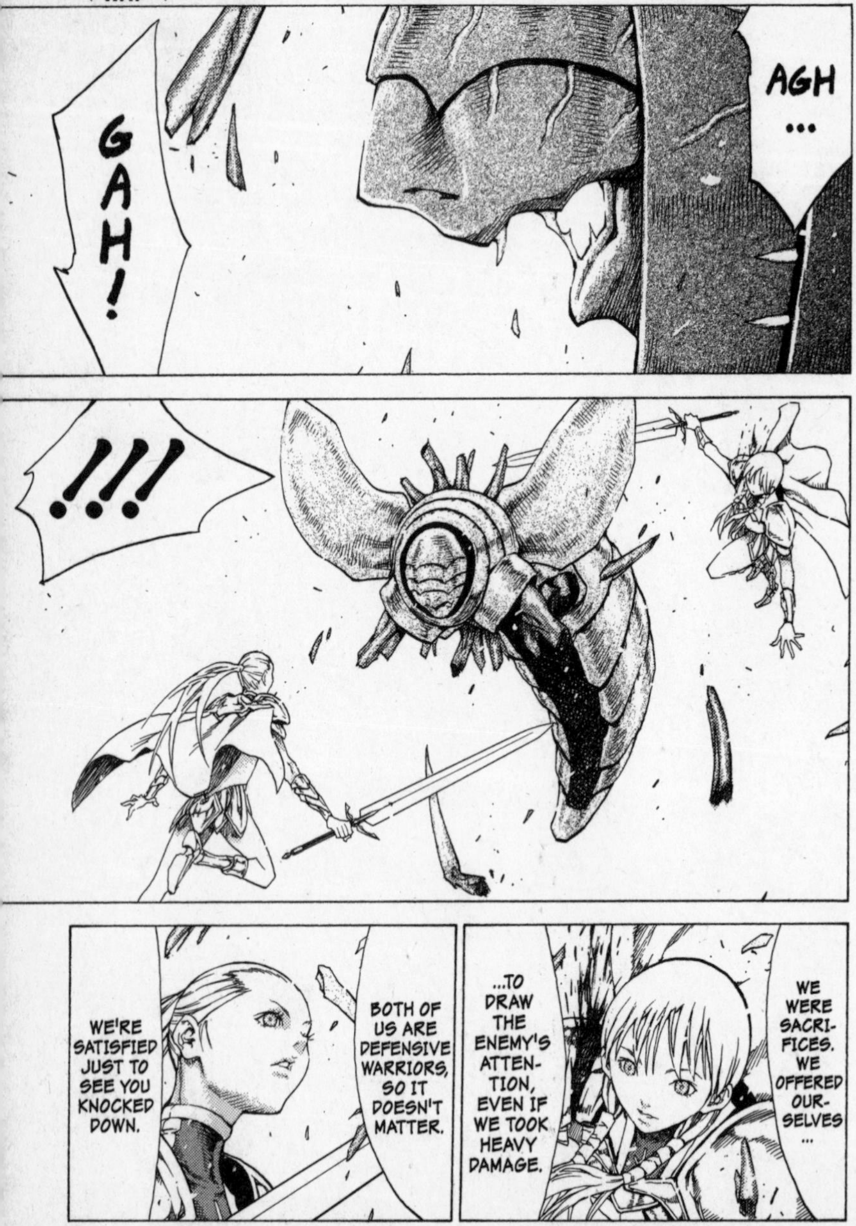
AGH ...
GAH!
!!!
WE WERE SACRIFICES. WE OFFERED OURSELVES ...
...TO DRAW THE ENEMY'S ATTENTION, EVEN IF WE TOOK HEAVY DAMAGE.
BOTH OF US ARE DEFENSIVE WARRIORS, SO IT DOESN'T MATTER.
WE'RE SATISFIED JUST TO SEE YOU KNOCKED DOWN.

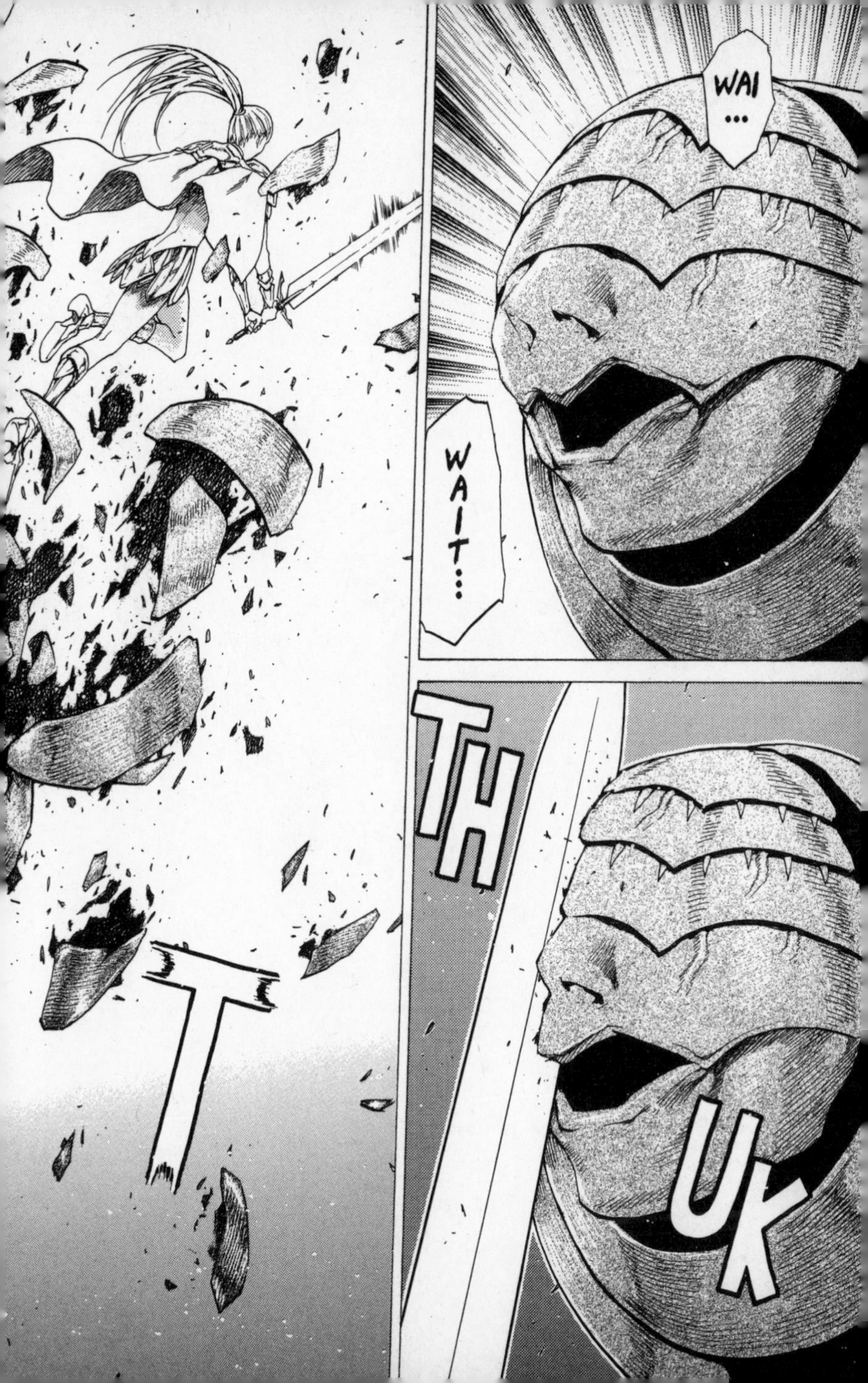
WAI ...
WAIT...
TH
UK
T

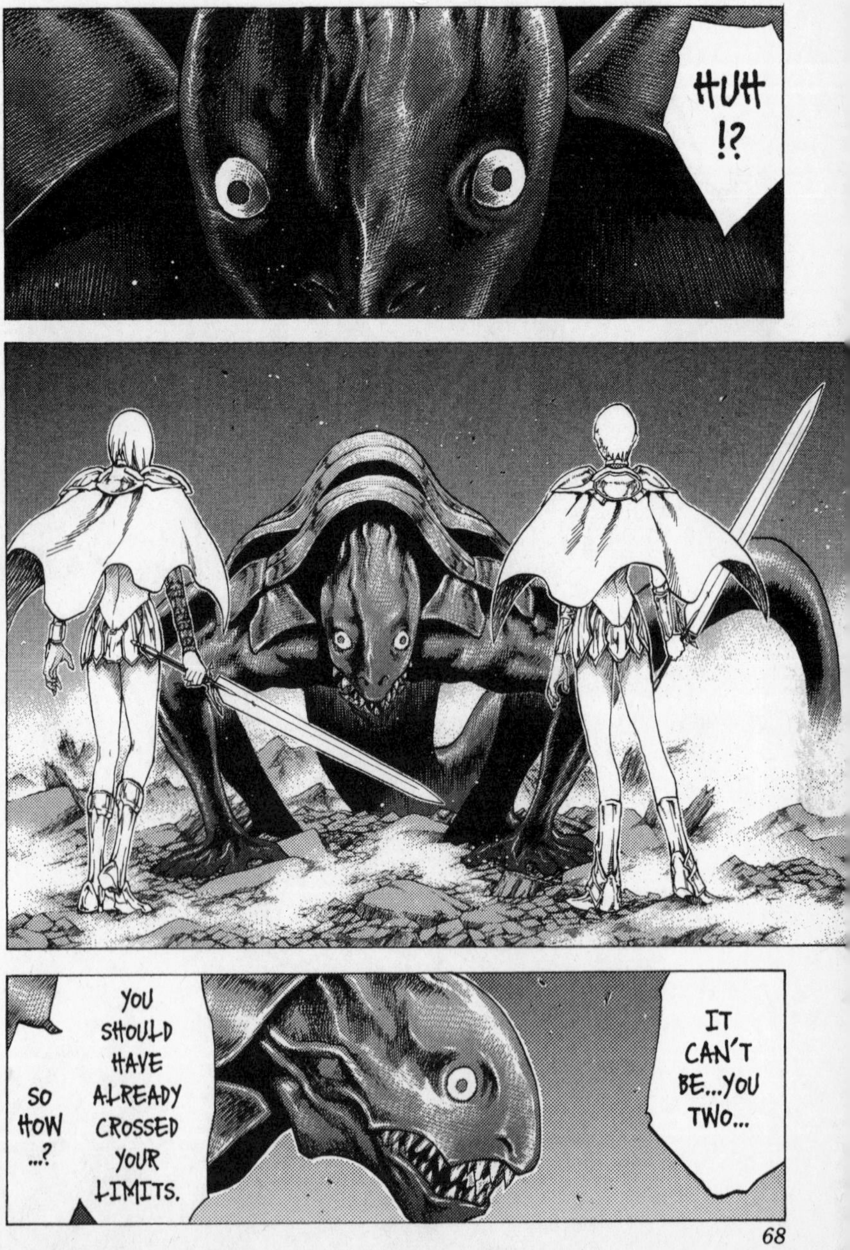
HUH!?
IT CAN'T BE...YOU TWO...
YOU SHOULD HAVE ALREADY CROSSED YOUR LIMITS.
SO HOW ...?

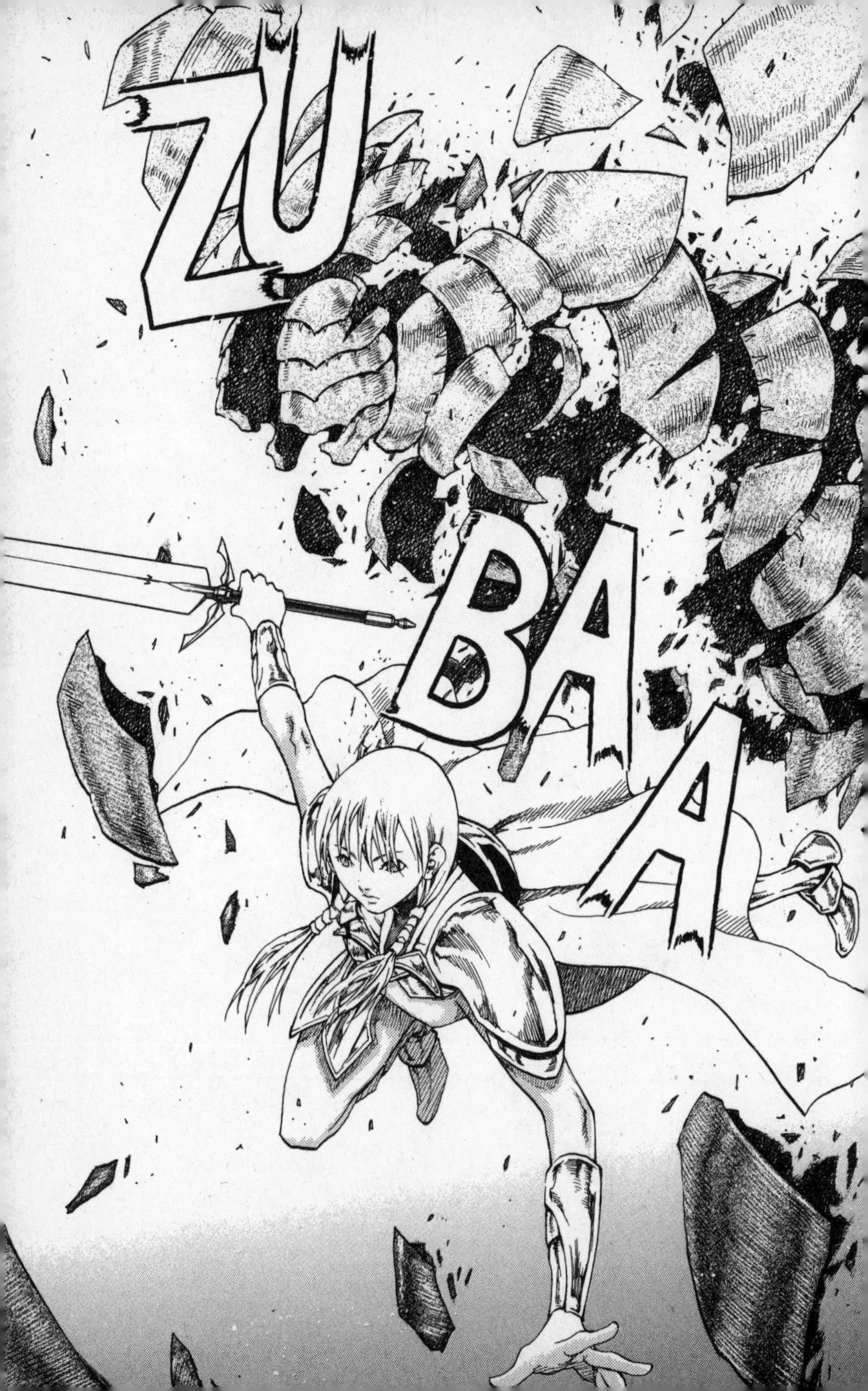
ZUBAAA

READ THIS WAY

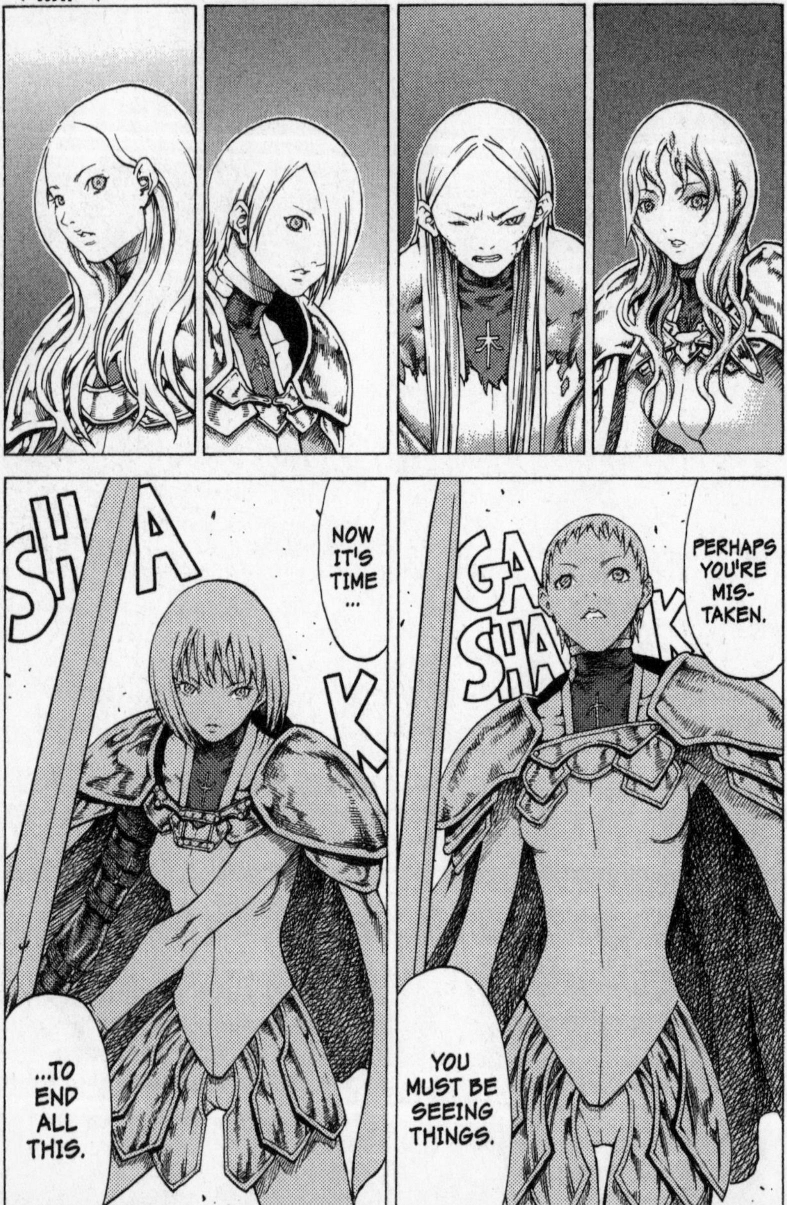

GASHAK
PERHAPS YOU'RE MIS-TAKEN.
YOU MUST BE SEEING THINGS.
SHAK
NOW IT'S TIME...
...TO END ALL THIS.

クレイモア
Claymore™

Scene 54: The Battle of the North, Part 5

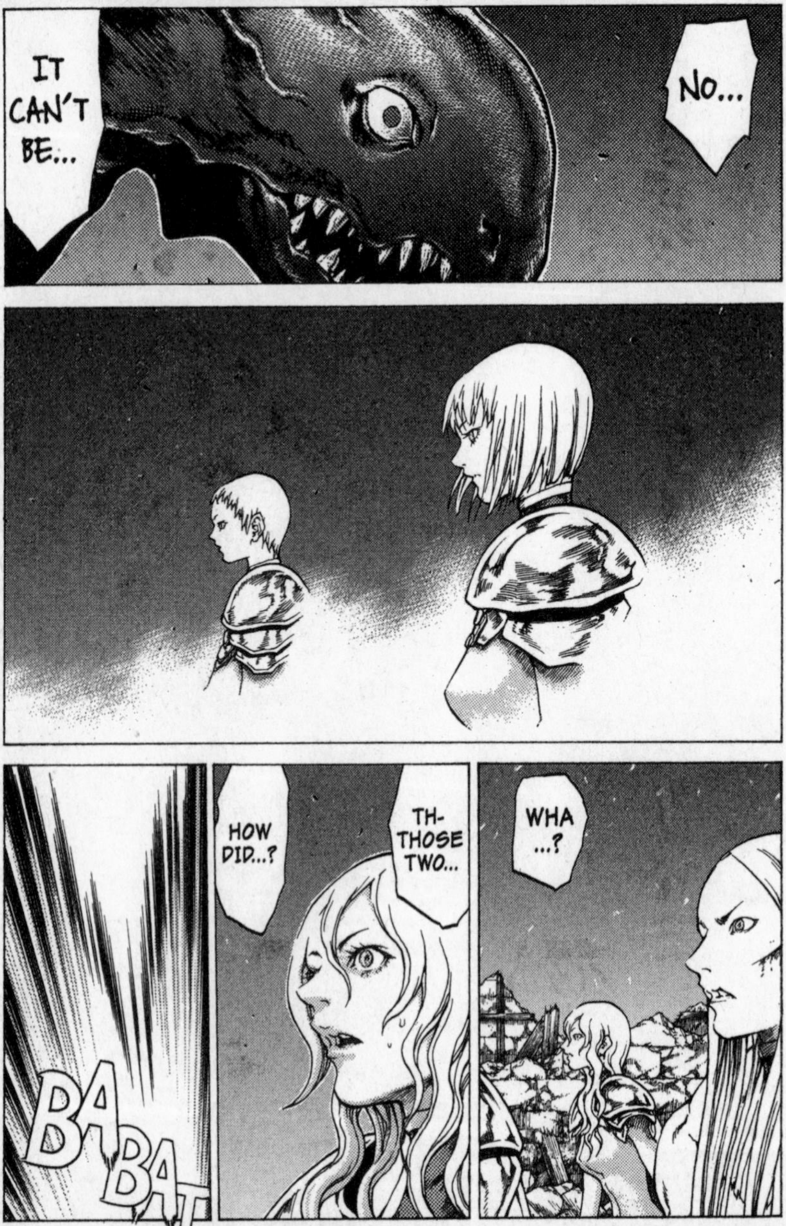

NO...
IT CAN'T BE...
WHA ...?
TH- THOSE TWO...
HOW DID...?
BABAT

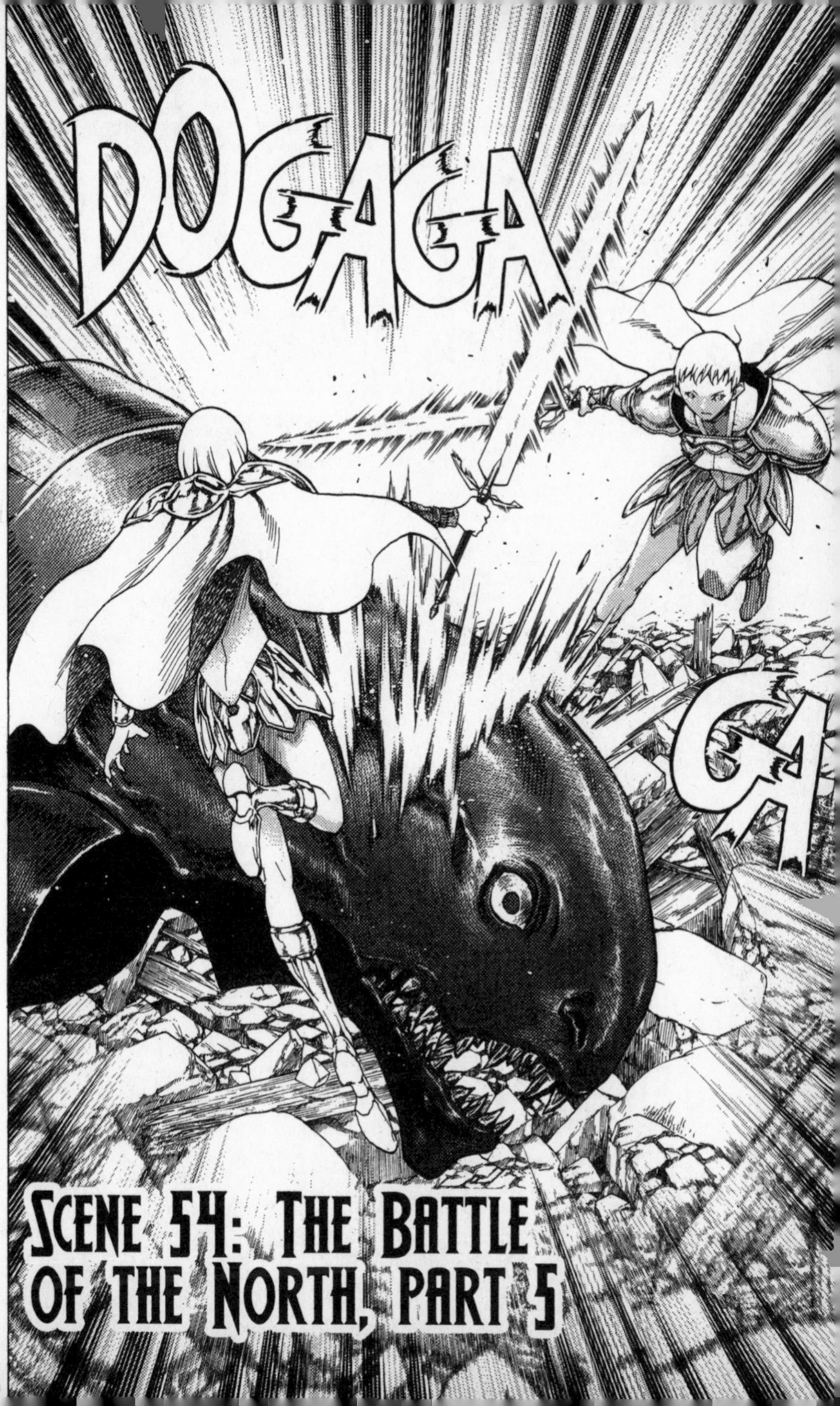
DOGAGA
GA

Scene 54: The Battle of the North, Part 5

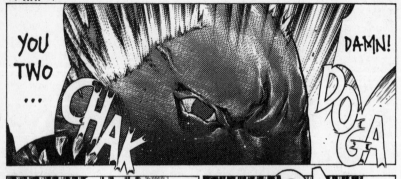

YOU TWO ...

DAMN!

CHAK

DOGA

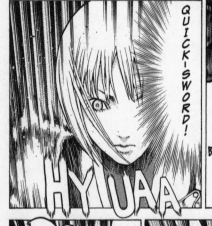

QUICKISWORD!

HYUAA

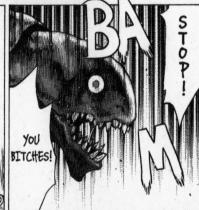

BAM

STOP!

YOU BITCHES!

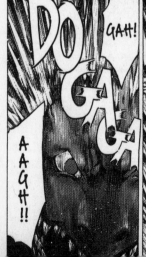

DOGA

GAH!

AAGH!!

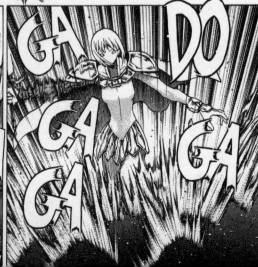

GA GA GA GA

DOGA GA

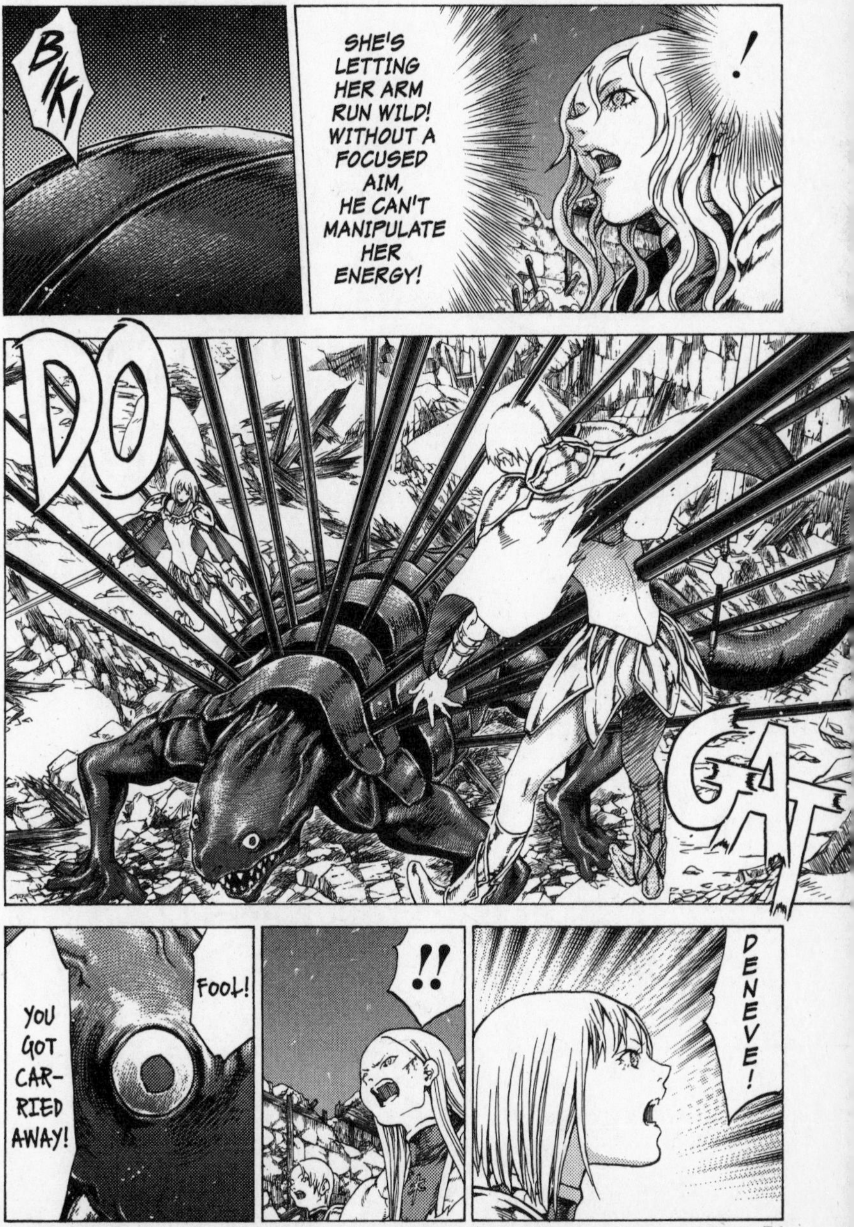
!
SHE'S LETTING HER ARM RUN WILD! WITHOUT A FOCUSED AIM, HE CAN'T MANIPULATE HER ENERGY!
BIKI
DO
GAT
DENEVE!
!!
FOOL!
YOU GOT CAR-RIED AWAY!

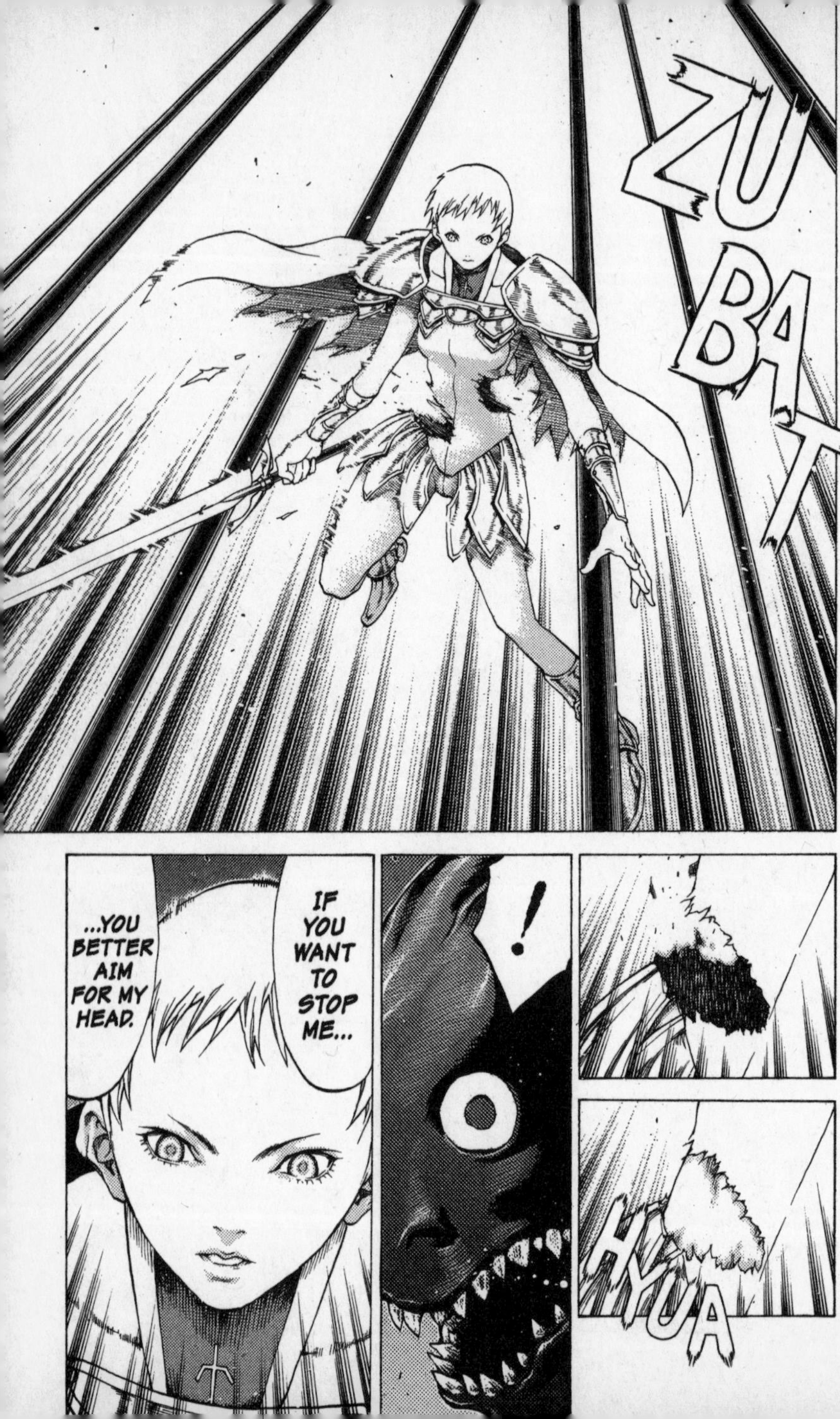
ZUBAT
HYUA
!
IF YOU WANT TO STOP ME...
...YOU BETTER AIM FOR MY HEAD.

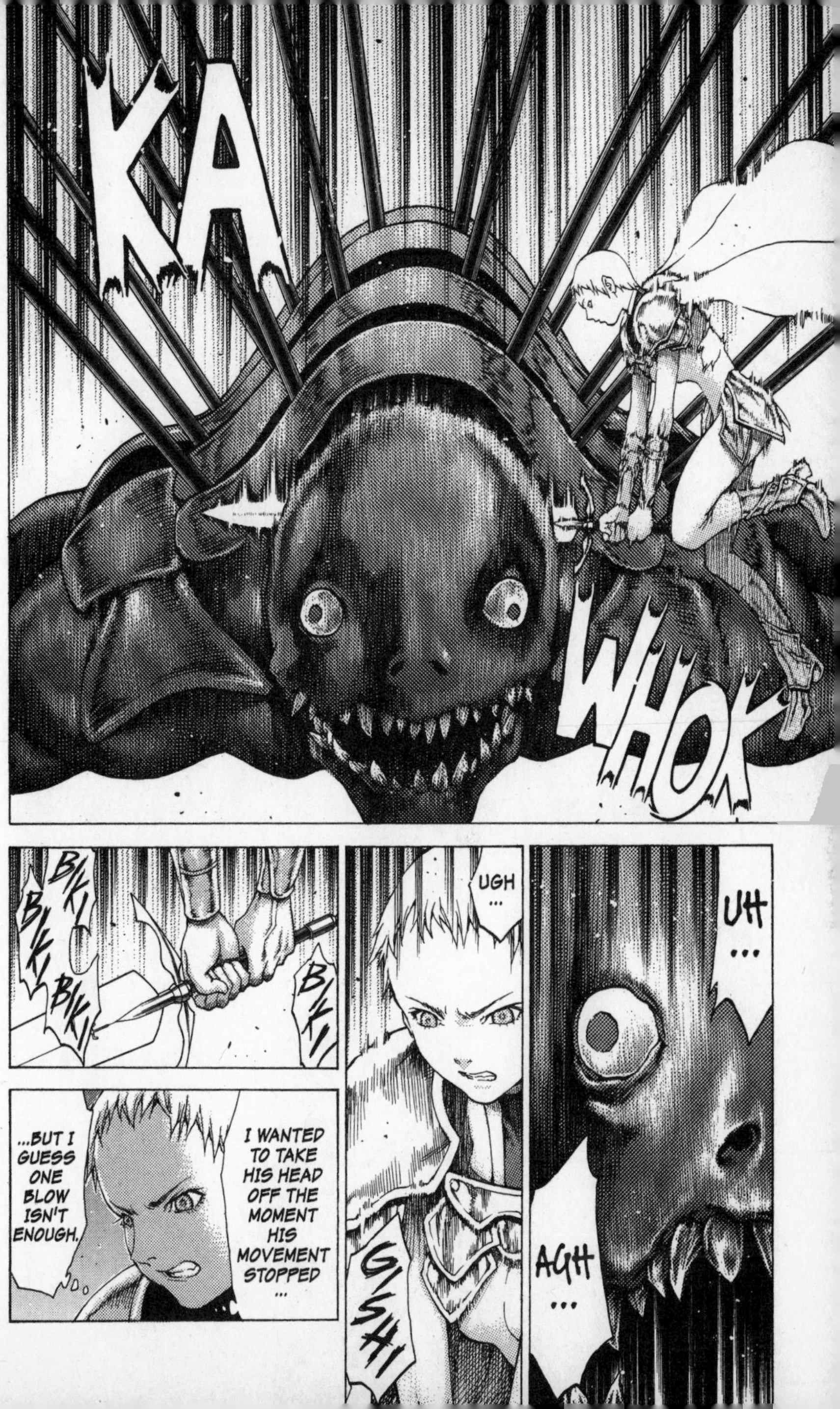
KA
WHOK
UH...
AGH...
UGH...
GISHI
BIKI BIKI BIKI
BIKI
I WANTED TO TAKE HIS HEAD OFF THE MOMENT HIS MOVEMENT STOPPED...
...BUT I GUESS ONE BLOW ISN'T ENOUGH.

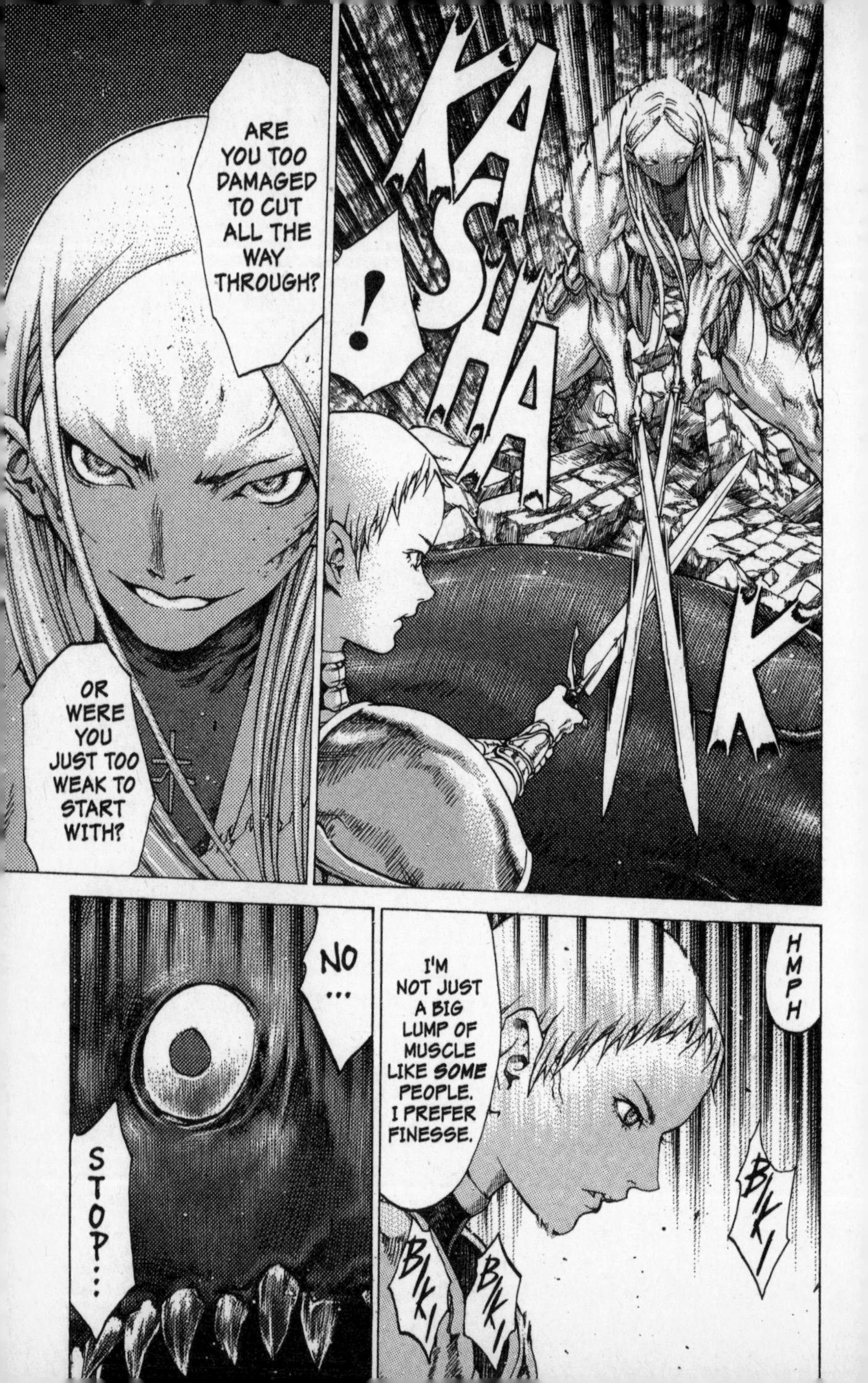
KASHAAK
!
ARE YOU TOO DAMAGED TO CUT ALL THE WAY THROUGH?
OR WERE YOU JUST TOO WEAK TO START WITH?
HMPH
I'M NOT JUST A BIG LUMP OF MUSCLE LIKE SOME PEOPLE. I PREFER FINESSE.
BIKI
BIKI
BIKI
NO...
STOP...

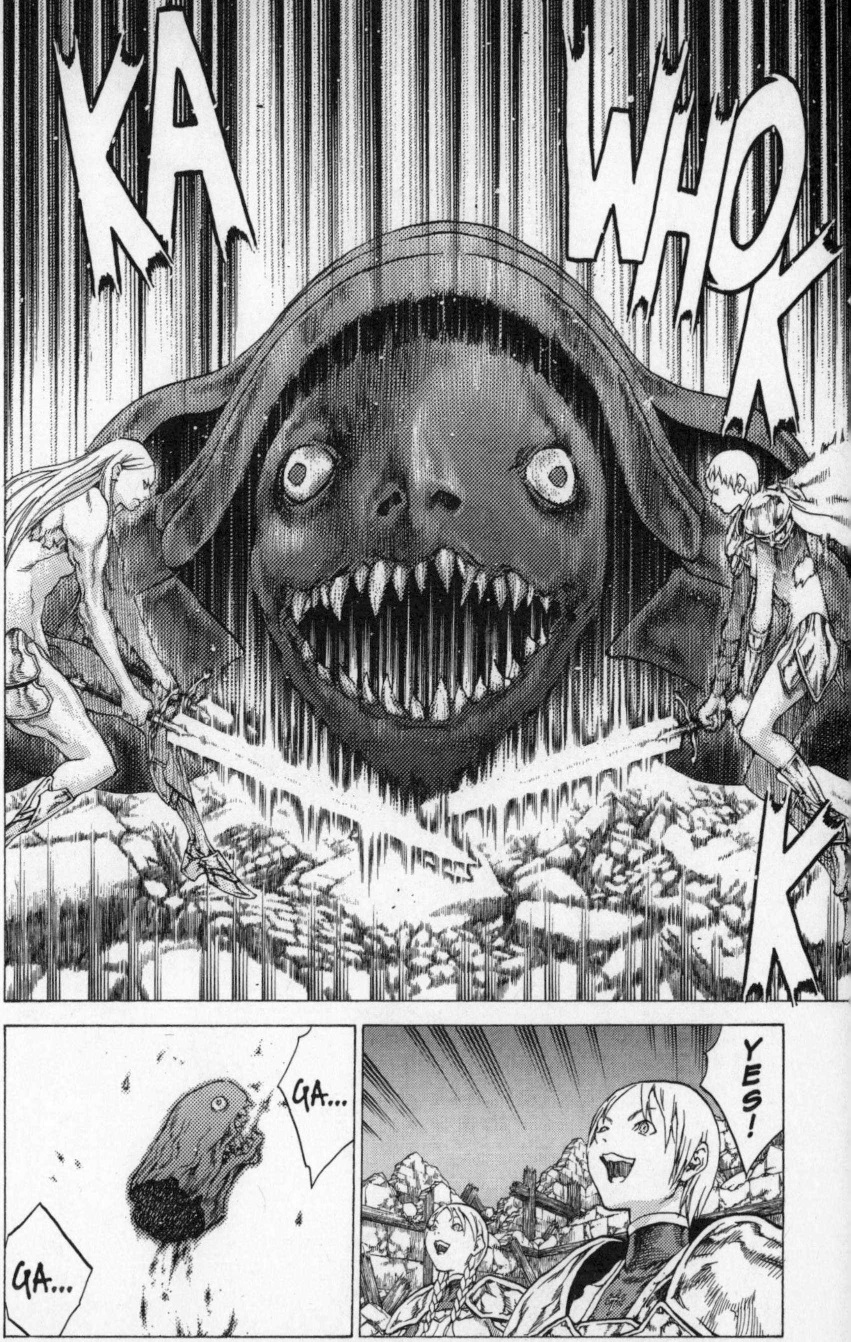
KA
WHOK
YES!
GA...
GA...

READ THIS WAY

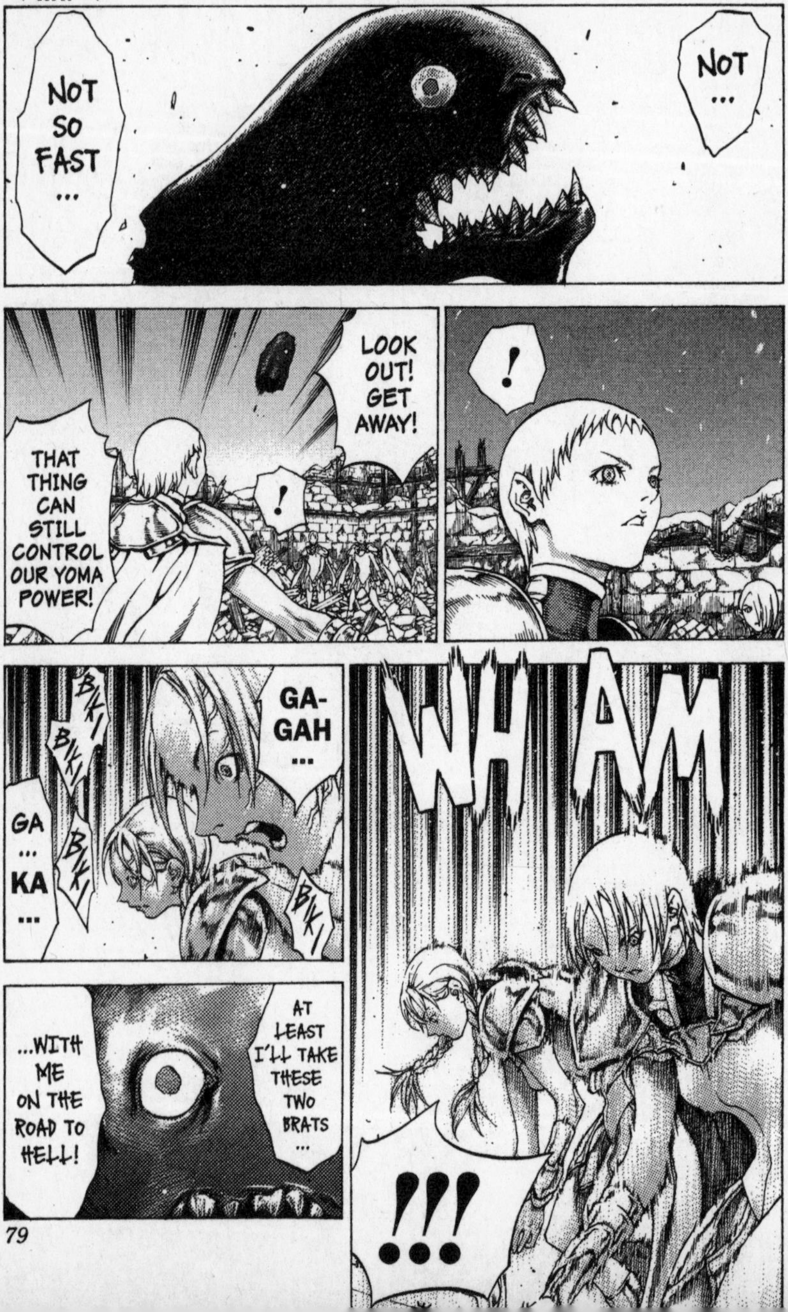
NOT ...
NOT SO FAST ...
!
LOOK OUT! GET AWAY!
THAT THING CAN STILL CONTROL OUR YOMA POWER!
!
WHAM
!!!
GA-GAH ...
BIKI BIKI
GA ... KA ...
BIKI BIKI
AT LEAST I'LL TAKE THESE TWO BRATS ...
...WITH ME ON THE ROAD TO HELL!

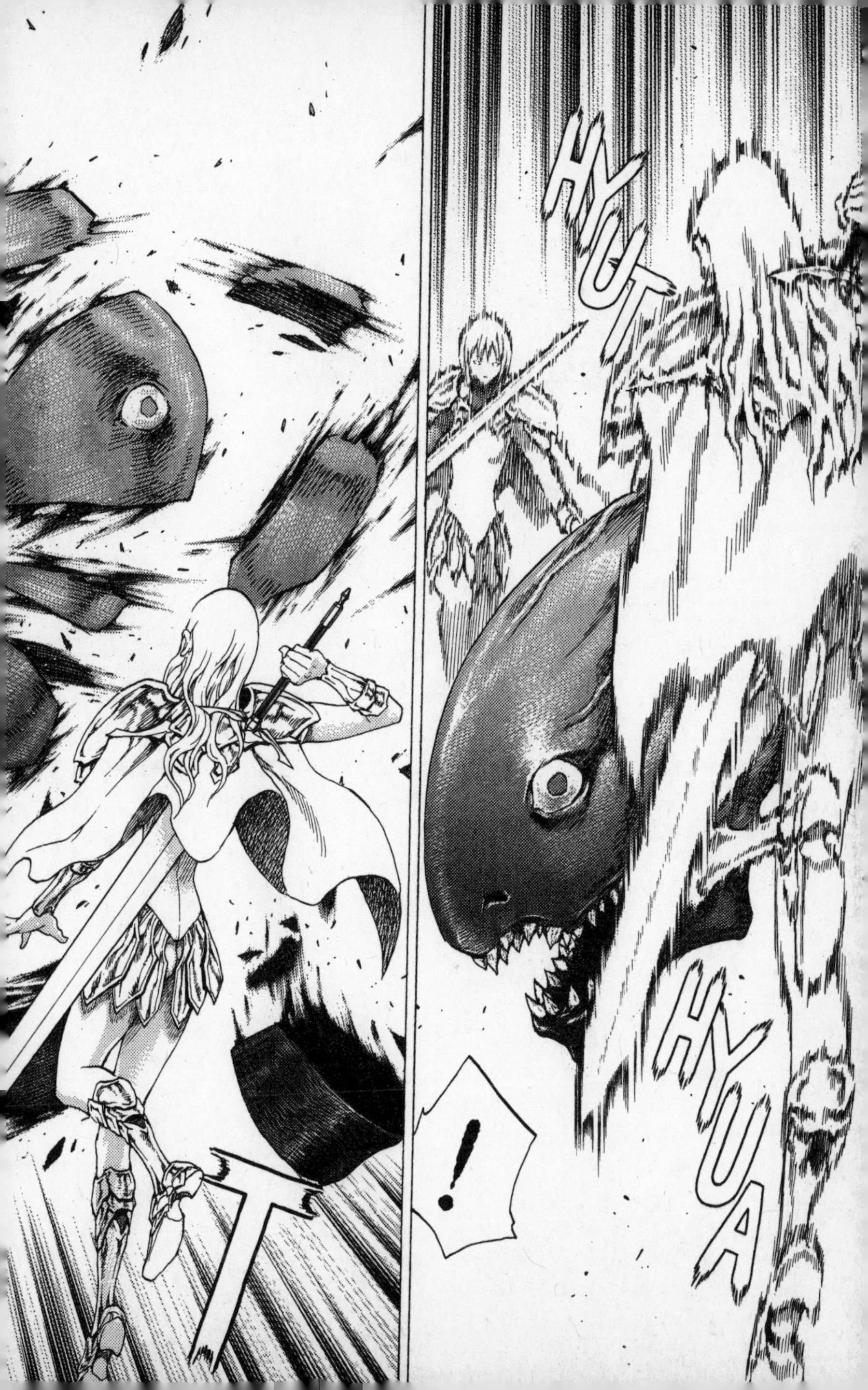
HYUT
HYUA
!
T

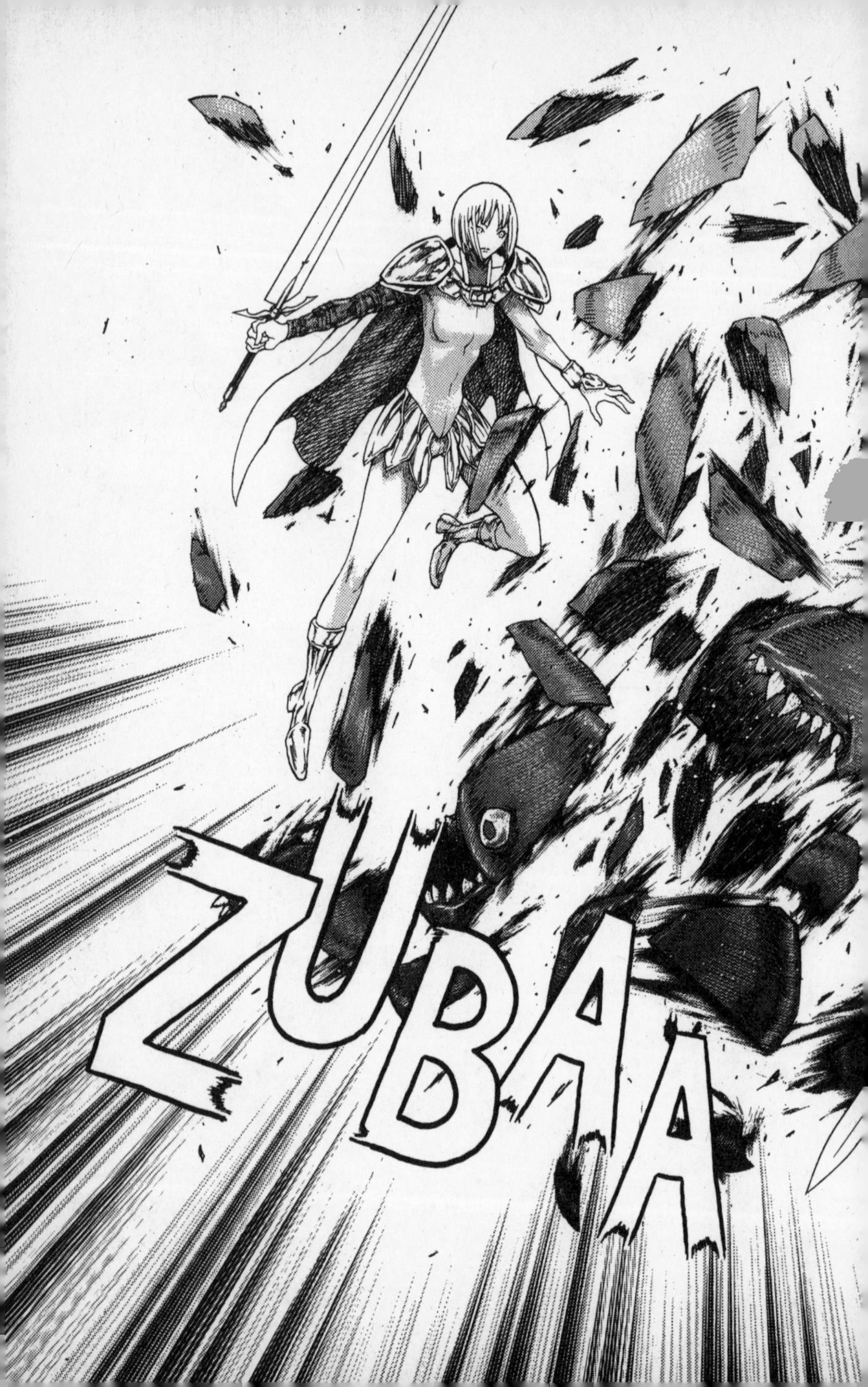
ZUBAA

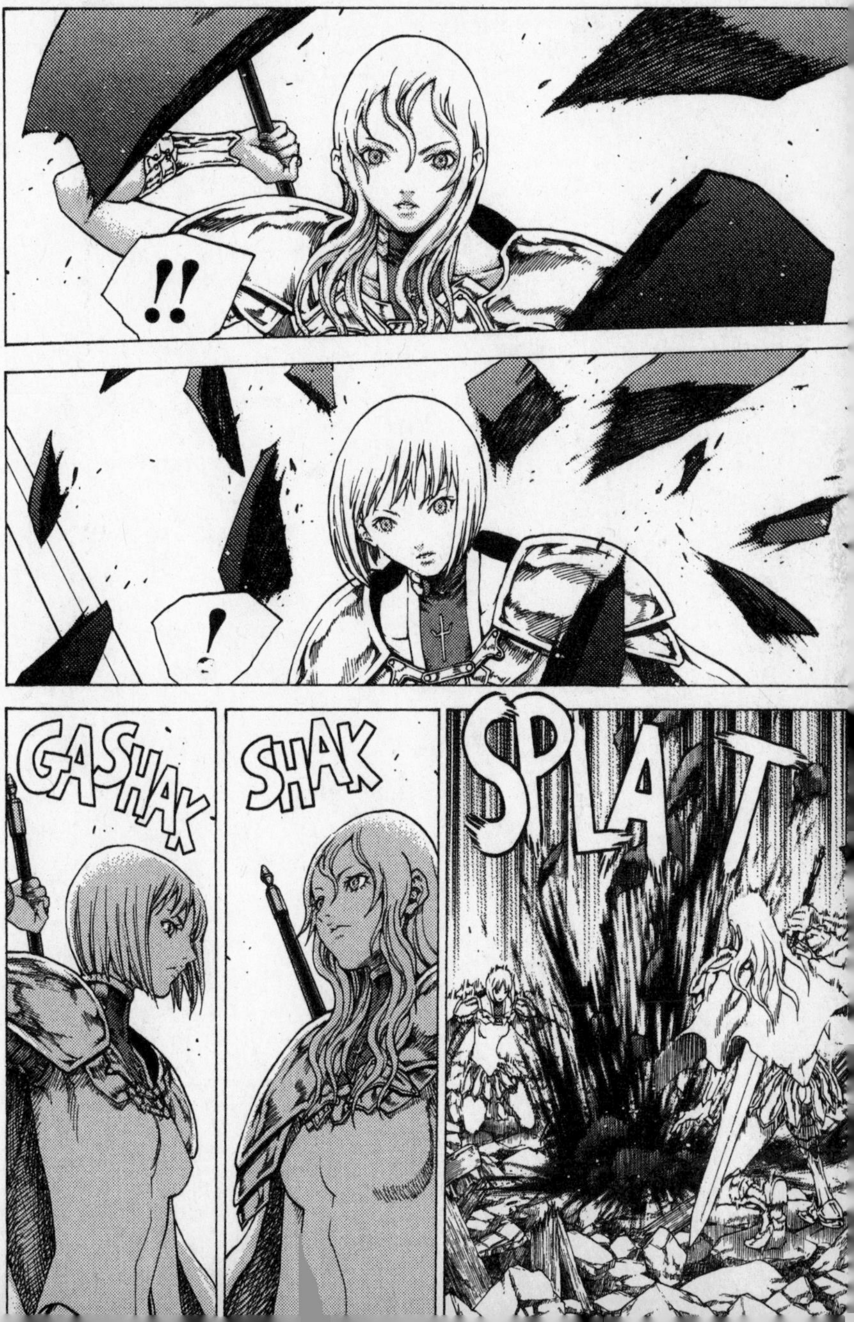
!!
!
SPLAT
SHAK
GASHAK

READ THIS WAY

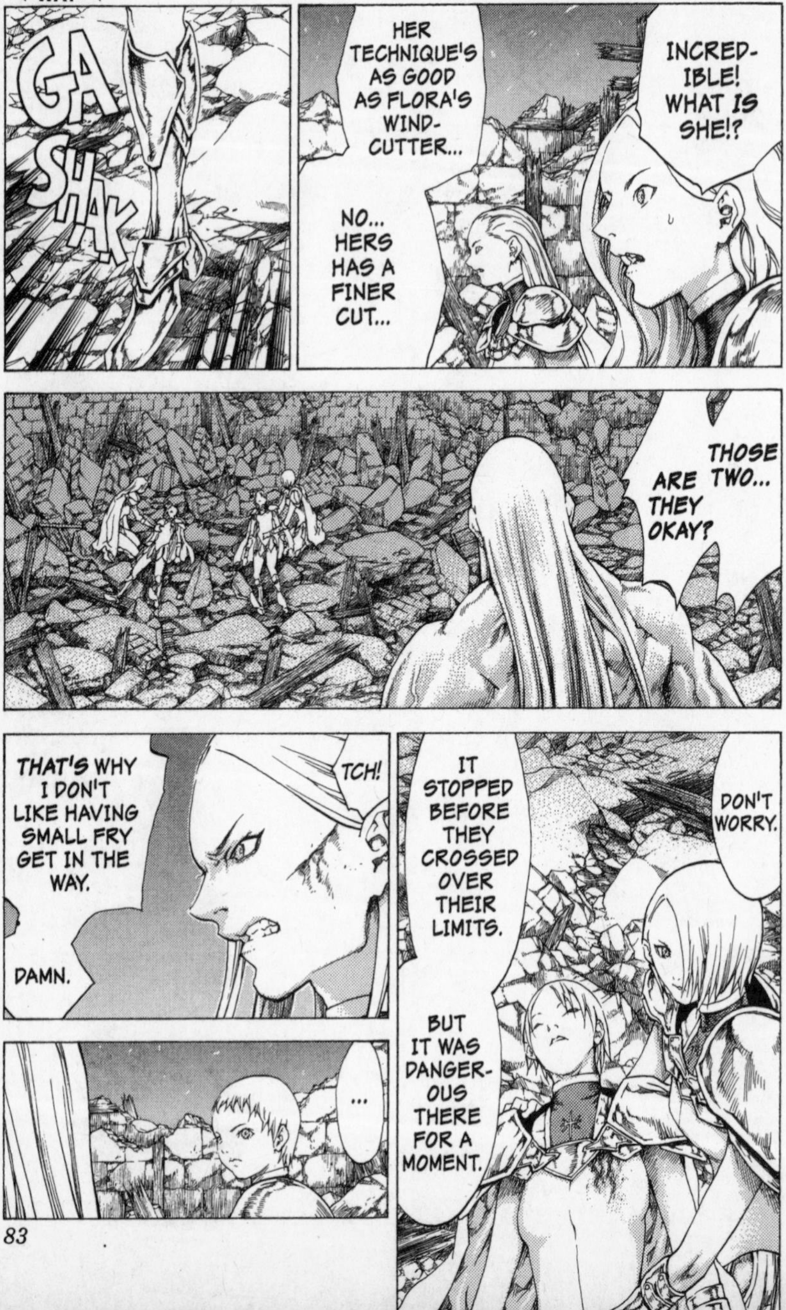

INCRED-IBLE! WHAT IS SHE!?
HER TECHNIQUE'S AS GOOD AS FLORA'S WIND-CUTTER...
NO... HERS HAS A FINER CUT...
GA SHAK
THOSE TWO... ARE THEY OKAY?
DON'T WORRY.
IT STOPPED BEFORE THEY CROSSED OVER THEIR LIMITS.
BUT IT WAS DANGER-OUS THERE FOR A MOMENT.
TCH!
THAT'S WHY I DON'T LIKE HAVING SMALL FRY GET IN THE WAY.
DAMN.
...

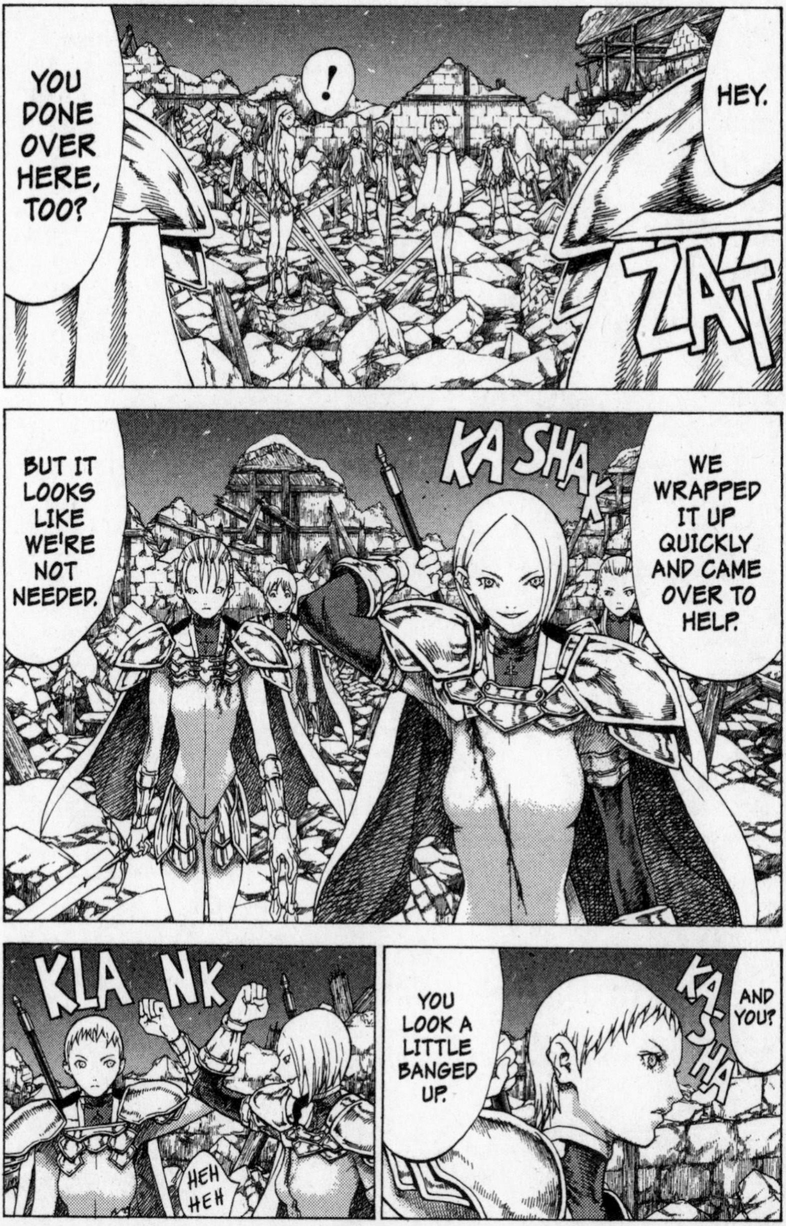
HEY.
ZA'T
!
YOU DONE OVER HERE, TOO?
WE WRAPPED IT UP QUICKLY AND CAME OVER TO HELP.
KA SHAK
BUT IT LOOKS LIKE WE'RE NOT NEEDED.
AND YOU?
KA-SHA
YOU LOOK A LITTLE BANGED UP.
KLA NK
HEH HEH

READ THIS WAY

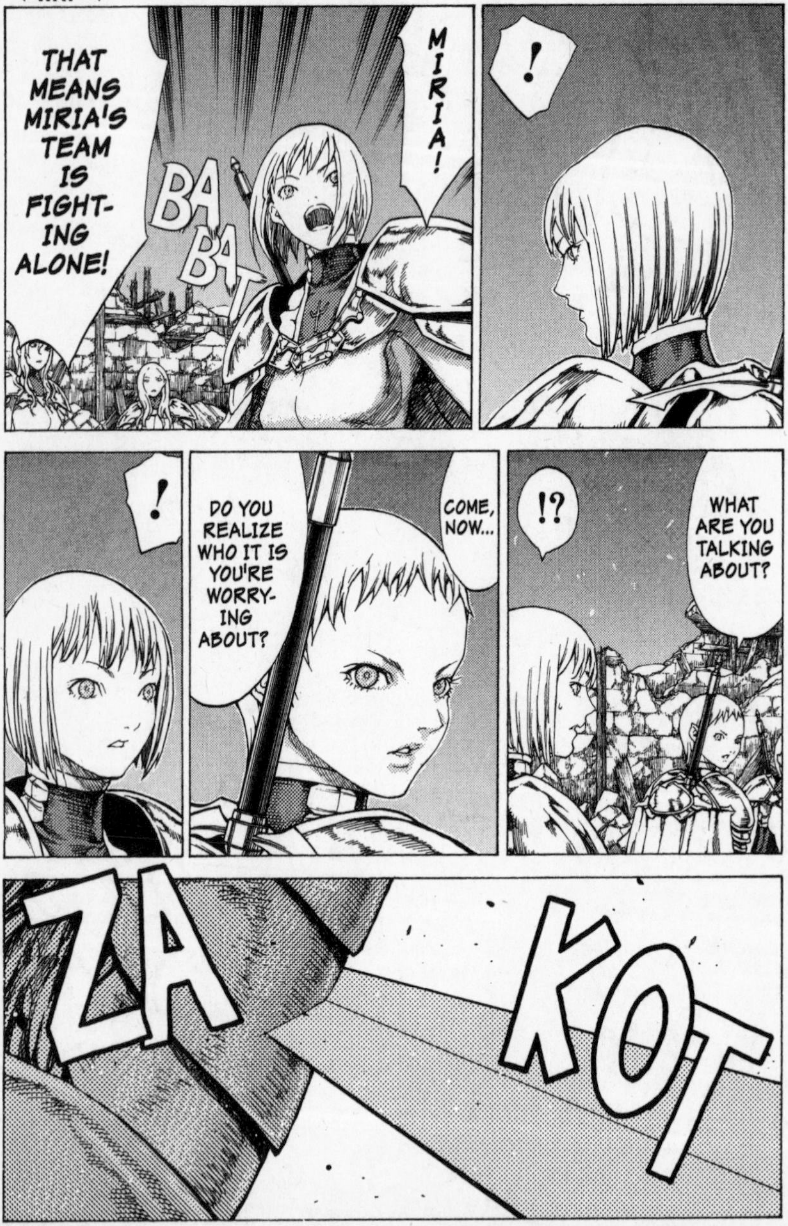
!
MIRIA!
THAT MEANS MIRIA'S TEAM IS FIGHTING ALONE!
BA BAT
WHAT ARE YOU TALKING ABOUT?
!?
COME, NOW...
DO YOU REALIZE WHO IT IS YOU'RE WORRYING ABOUT?
!
ZA KOT

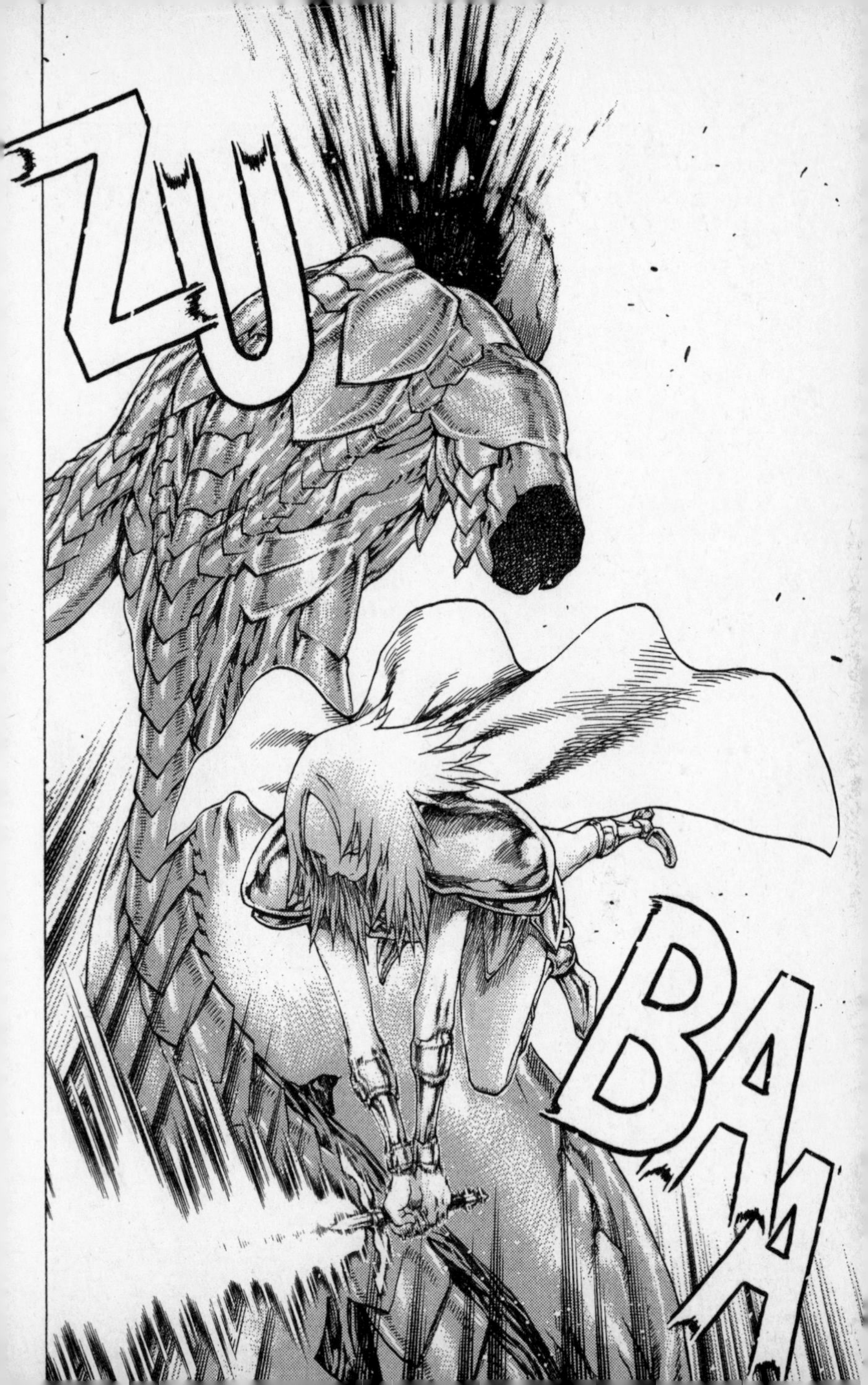
ZU
BAM

READ THIS WAY

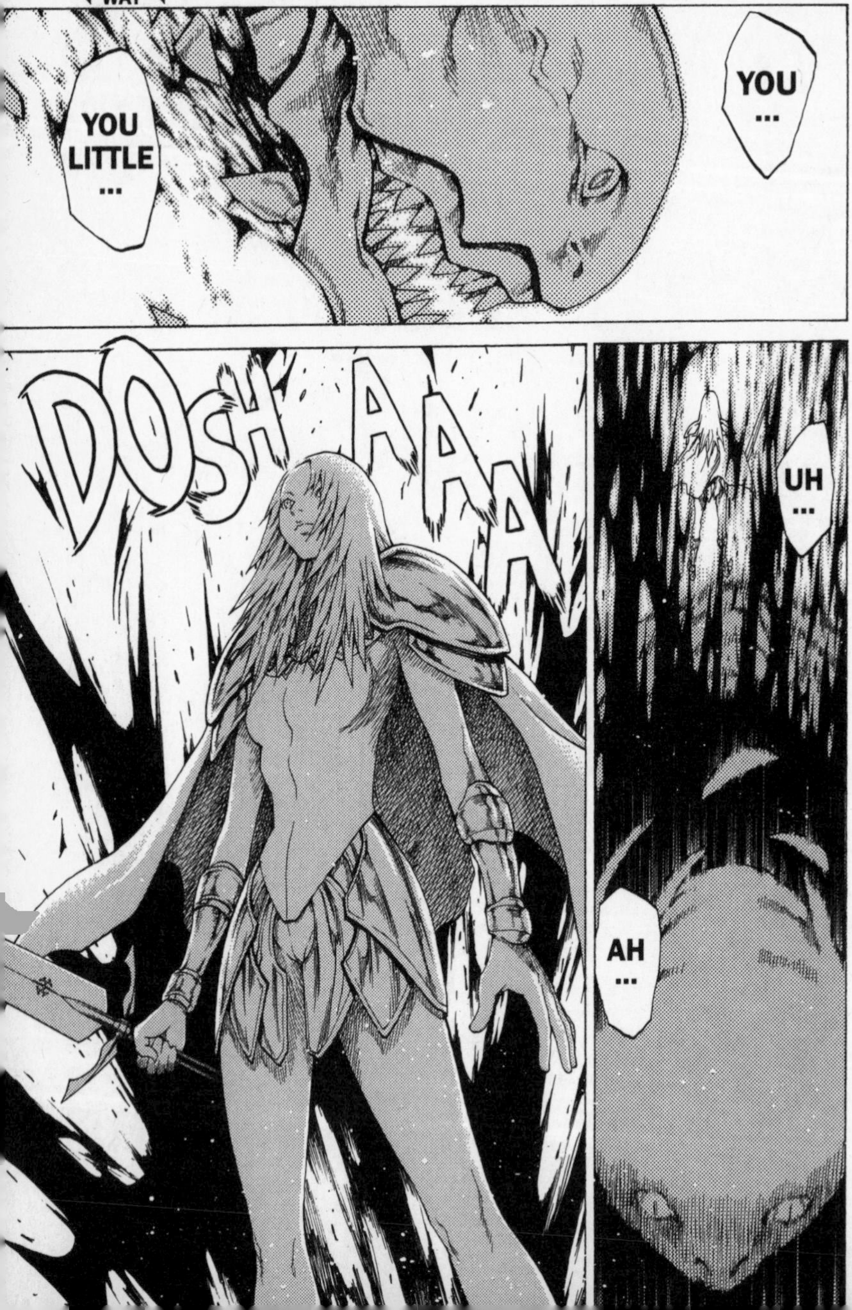
YOU ...
YOU LITTLE ...
UH ...
AH ...
DOSH
AAA

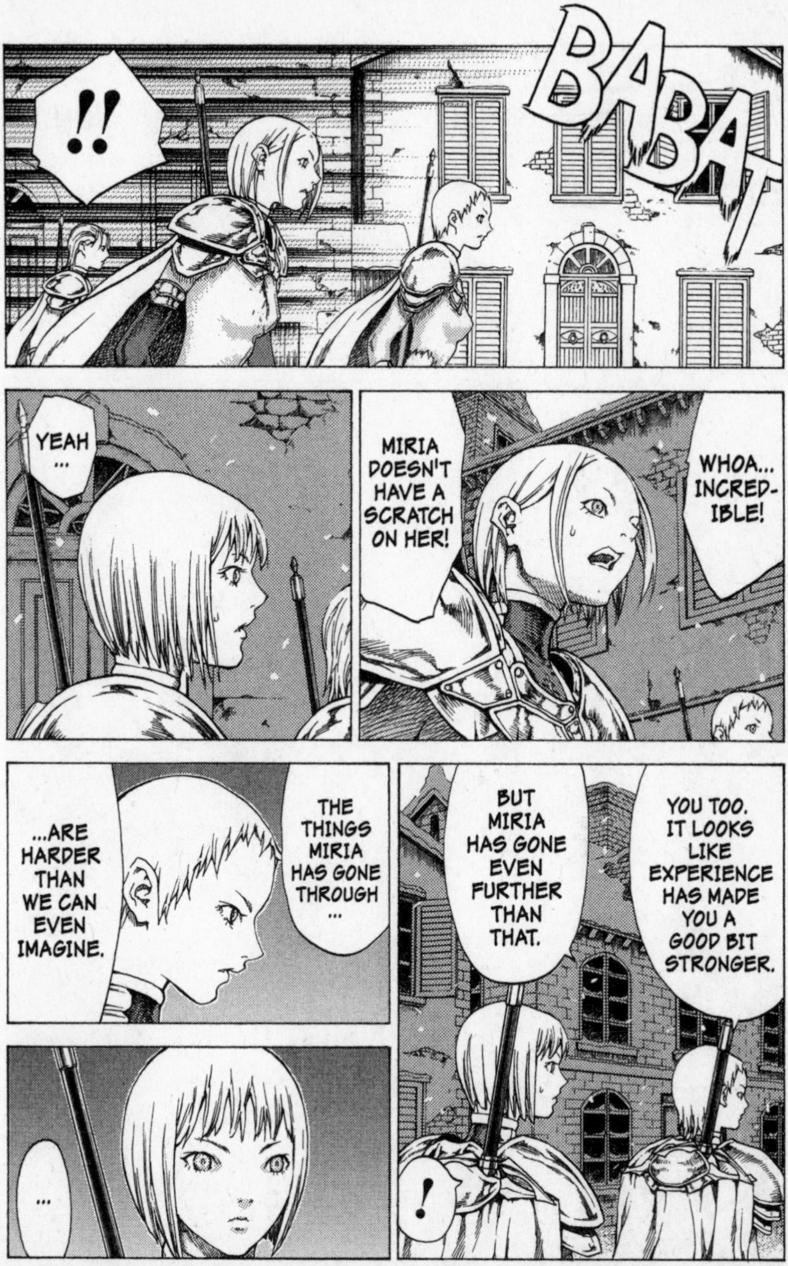
BABAT
!!
WHOA... INCRED-IBLE!
MIRIA DOESN'T HAVE A SCRATCH ON HER!
YEAH ...
YOU TOO. IT LOOKS LIKE EXPERIENCE HAS MADE YOU A GOOD BIT STRONGER.
BUT MIRIA HAS GONE EVEN FURTHER THAN THAT.
!
THE THINGS MIRIA HAS GONE THROUGH ...
...ARE HARDER THAN WE CAN EVEN IMAGINE.
...

READ THIS WAY

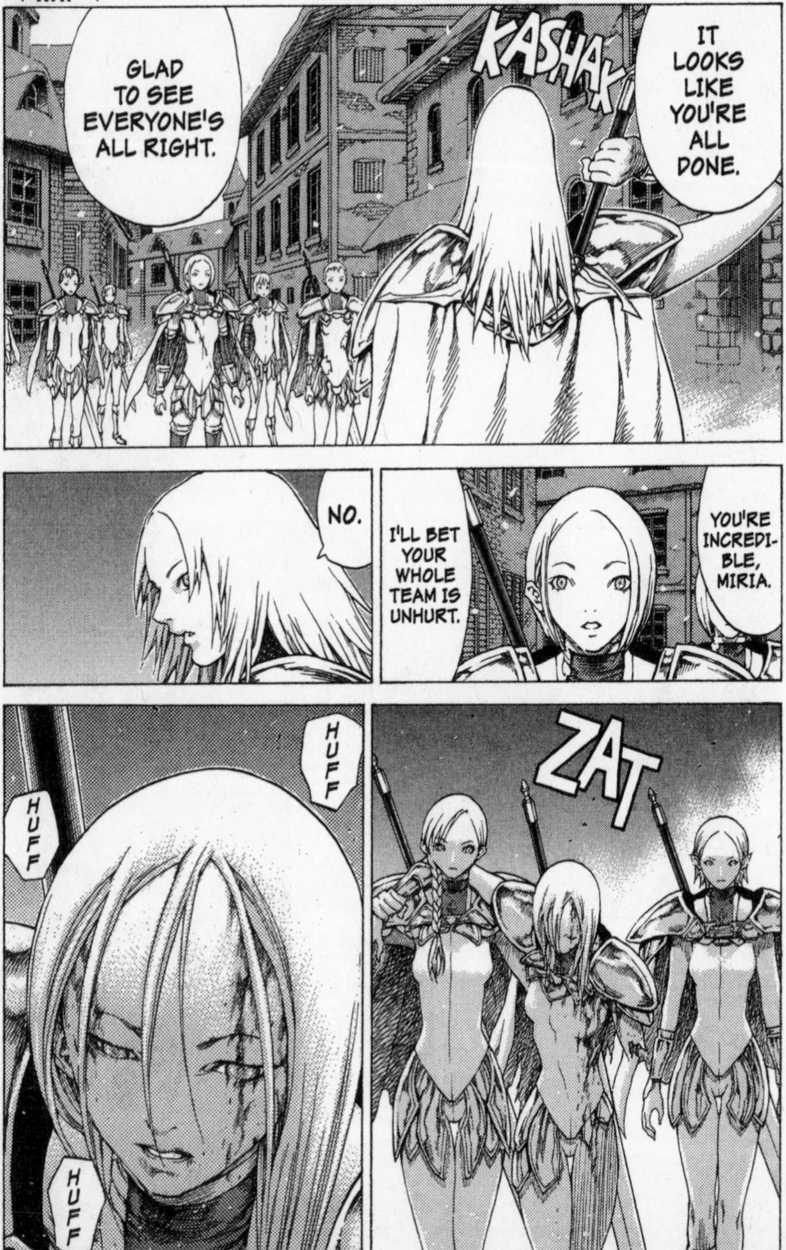
IT LOOKS LIKE YOU'RE ALL DONE.
KASHAK
GLAD TO SEE EVERYONE'S ALL RIGHT.
YOU'RE INCREDI-BLE, MIRIA.
I'LL BET YOUR WHOLE TEAM IS UNHURT.
NO.
ZAT
HUFF
HUFF
HUFF
HUFF
HUFF
HUFF

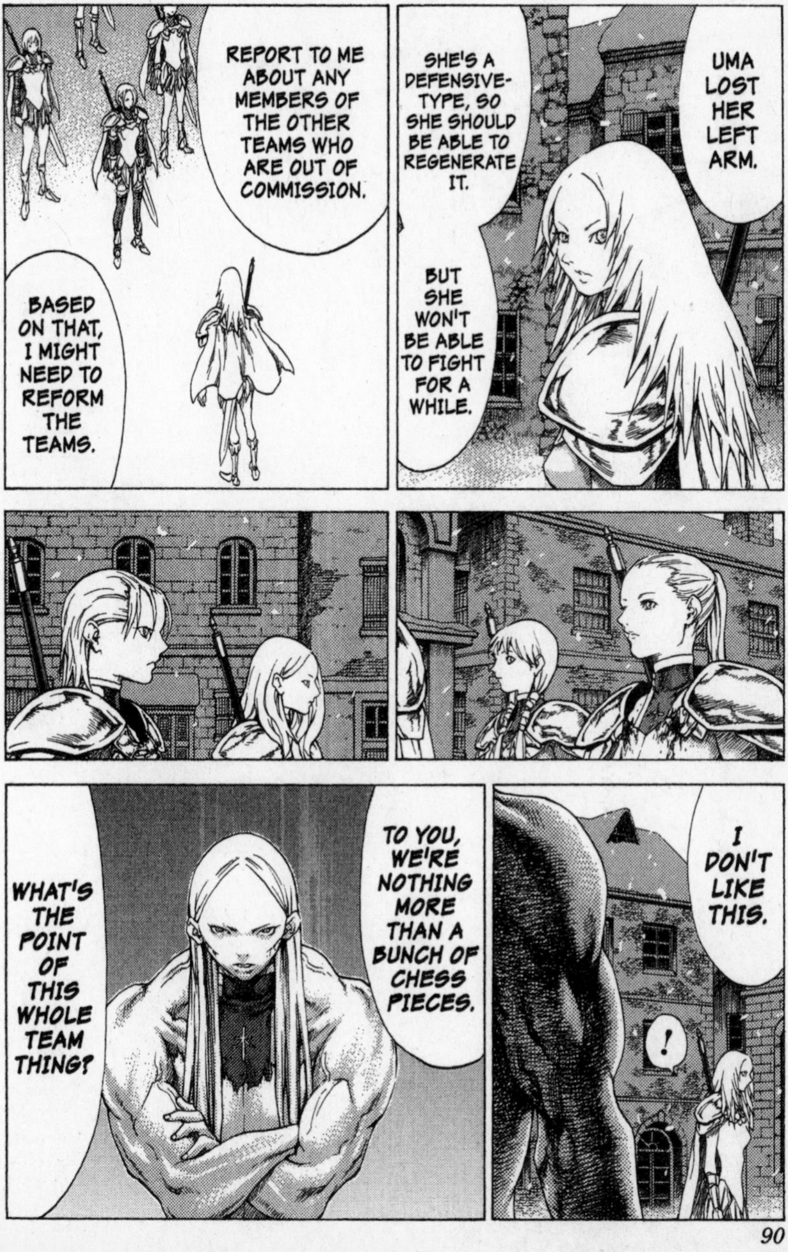

UMA LOST HER LEFT ARM.
SHE'S A DEFENSIVE-TYPE, SO SHE SHOULD BE ABLE TO REGENERATE IT.
BUT SHE WON'T BE ABLE TO FIGHT FOR A WHILE.
REPORT TO ME ABOUT ANY MEMBERS OF THE OTHER TEAMS WHO ARE OUT OF COMMISSION.
BASED ON THAT, I MIGHT NEED TO REFORM THE TEAMS.
I DON'T LIKE THIS.
!
TO YOU, WE'RE NOTHING MORE THAN A BUNCH OF CHESS PIECES.
WHAT'S THE POINT OF THIS WHOLE TEAM THING?

READ THIS WAY

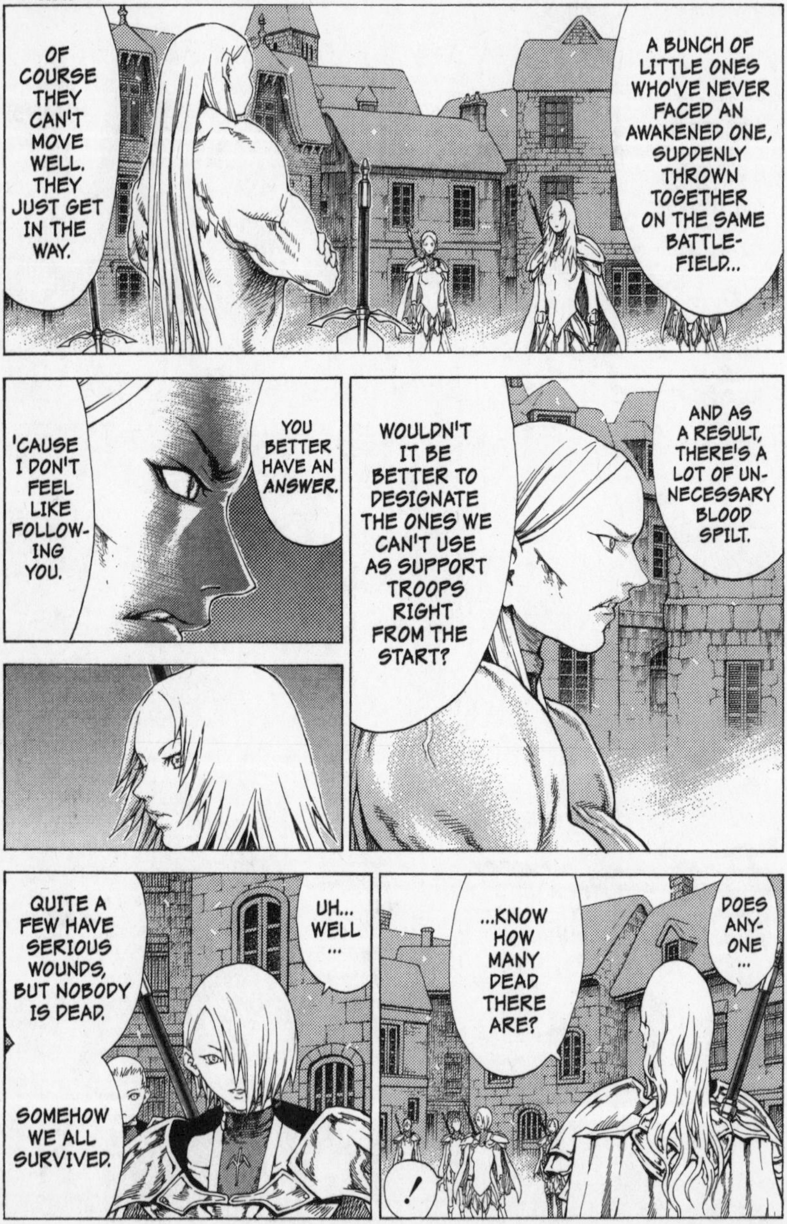
A BUNCH OF LITTLE ONES WHO'VE NEVER FACED AN AWAKENED ONE, SUDDENLY THROWN TOGETHER ON THE SAME BATTLE-FIELD...
OF COURSE THEY CAN'T MOVE WELL. THEY JUST GET IN THE WAY.
AND AS A RESULT, THERE'S A LOT OF UN-NECESSARY BLOOD SPILT.
WOULDN'T IT BE BETTER TO DESIGNATE THE ONES WE CAN'T USE AS SUPPORT TROOPS RIGHT FROM THE START?
YOU BETTER HAVE AN ANSWER.
'CAUSE I DON'T FEEL LIKE FOLLOW-ING YOU.
DOES ANY-ONE ...
...KNOW HOW MANY DEAD THERE ARE?
!
UH... WELL ...
QUITE A FEW HAVE SERIOUS WOUNDS, BUT NOBODY IS DEAD.
SOMEHOW WE ALL SURVIVED.

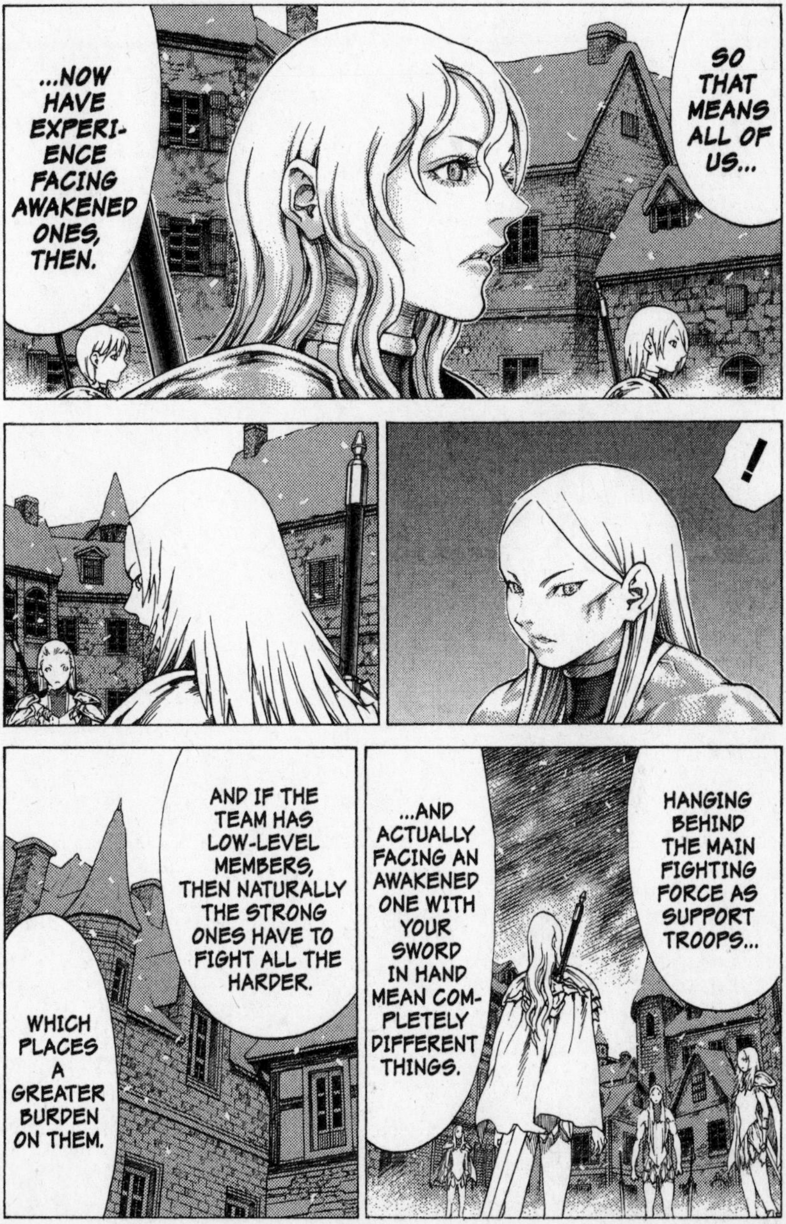
SO THAT MEANS ALL OF US...
...NOW HAVE EXPERI- ENCE FACING AWAKENED ONES, THEN.
!
HANGING BEHIND THE MAIN FIGHTING FORCE AS SUPPORT TROOPS...
...AND ACTUALLY FACING AN AWAKENED ONE WITH YOUR SWORD IN HAND MEAN COM- PLETELY DIFFERENT THINGS.
AND IF THE TEAM HAS LOW-LEVEL MEMBERS, THEN NATURALLY THE STRONG ONES HAVE TO FIGHT ALL THE HARDER.
WHICH PLACES A GREATER BURDEN ON THEM.

READ THIS WAY

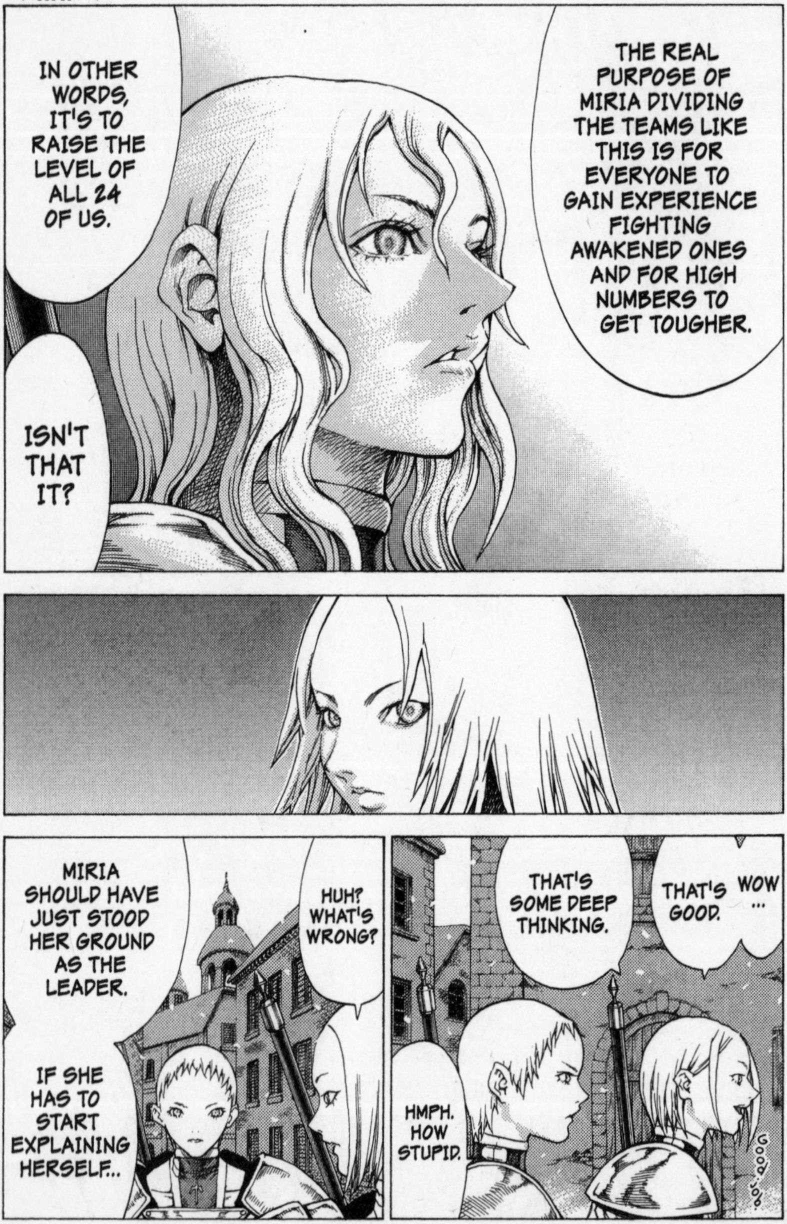
THE REAL PURPOSE OF MIRIA DIVIDING THE TEAMS LIKE THIS IS FOR EVERYONE TO GAIN EXPERIENCE FIGHTING AWAKENED ONES AND FOR HIGH NUMBERS TO GET TOUGHER.
IN OTHER WORDS, IT'S TO RAISE THE LEVEL OF ALL 24 OF US.
ISN'T THAT IT?
WOW...
THAT'S GOOD.
THAT'S SOME DEEP THINKING.
HMPH. HOW STUPID.
HUH? WHAT'S WRONG?
MIRIA SHOULD HAVE JUST STOOD HER GROUND AS THE LEADER.
IF SHE HAS TO START EXPLAINING HERSELF...

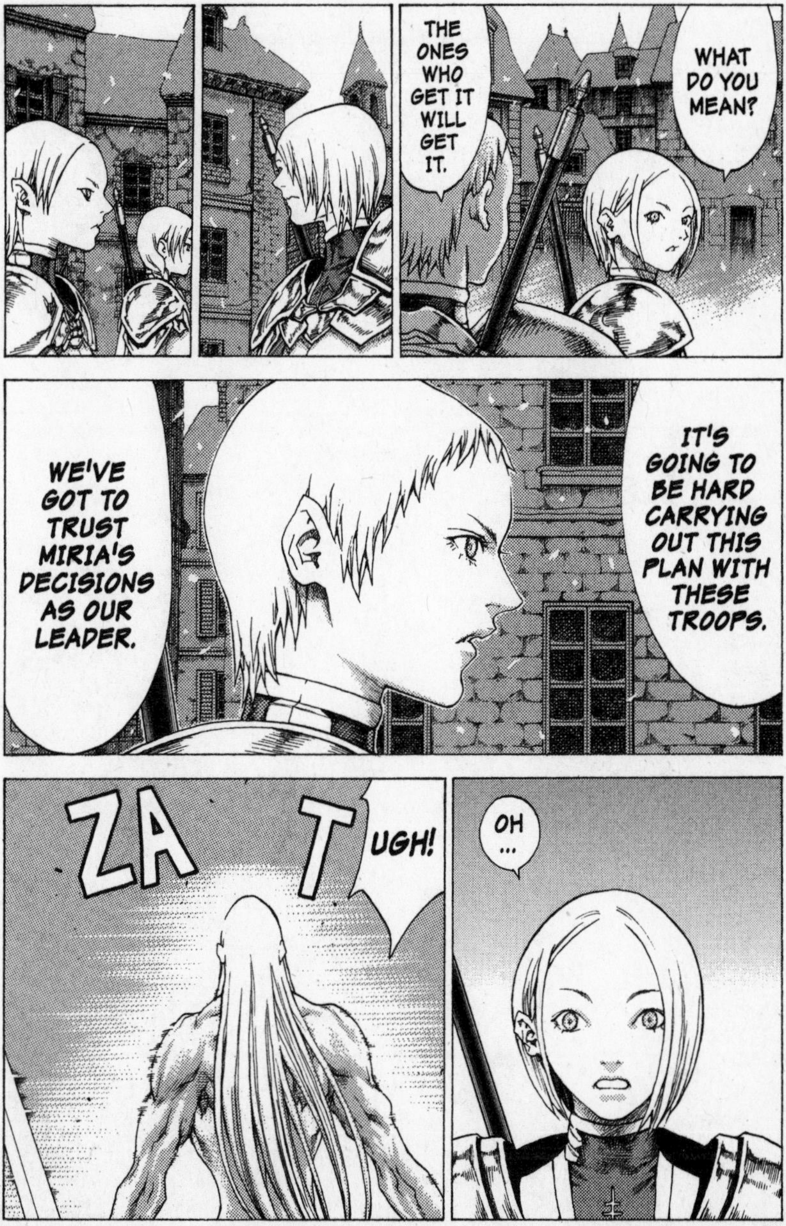
WHAT DO YOU MEAN?
THE ONES WHO GET IT WILL GET IT.
IT'S GOING TO BE HARD CARRYING OUT THIS PLAN WITH THESE TROOPS.
WE'VE GOT TO TRUST MIRIA'S DECISIONS AS OUR LEADER.
OH ...
ZA T
UGH!

READ THIS WAY

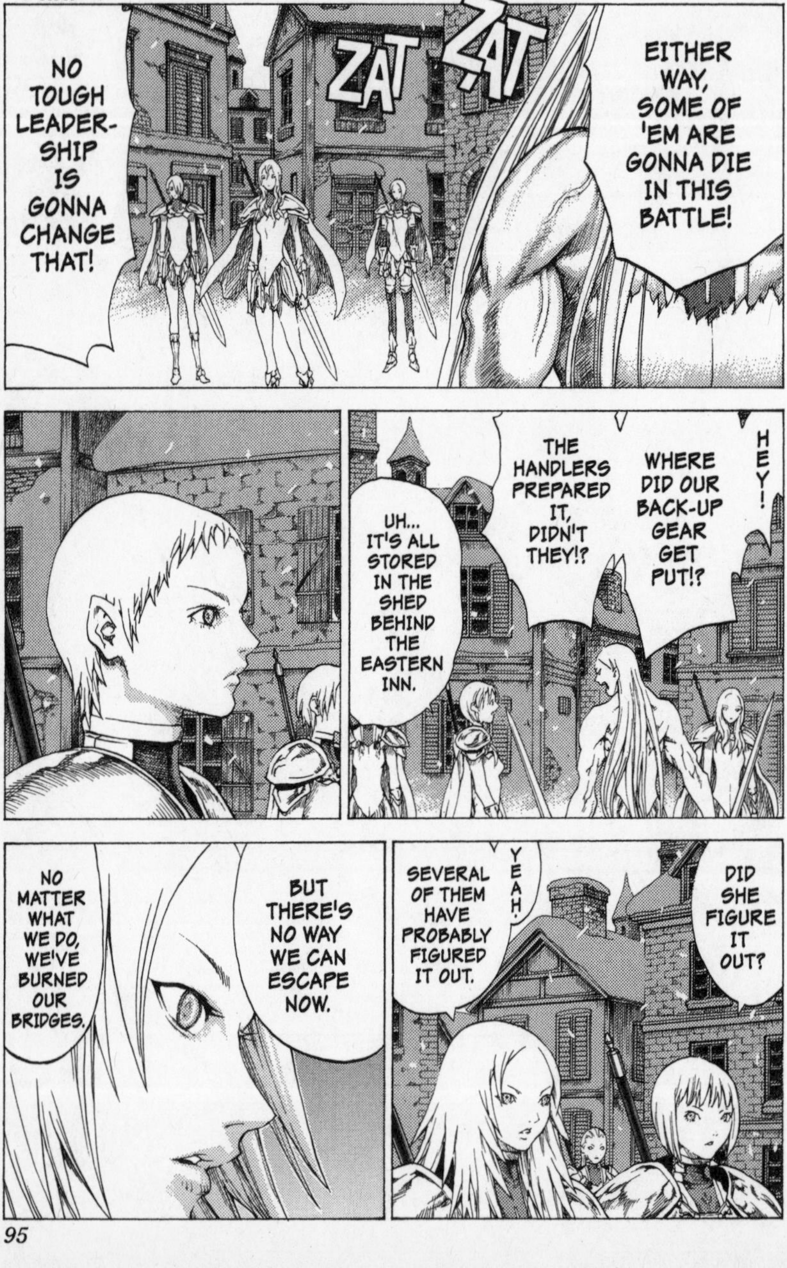
EITHER WAY, SOME OF 'EM ARE GONNA DIE IN THIS BATTLE!
ZAT ZAT
NO TOUGH LEADER-SHIP IS GONNA CHANGE THAT!
HEY!
WHERE DID OUR BACK-UP GEAR GET PUT!?
THE HANDLERS PREPARED IT, DIDN'T THEY!?
UH... IT'S ALL STORED IN THE SHED BEHIND THE EASTERN INN.
DID SHE FIGURE IT OUT?
YEAH!
SEVERAL OF THEM HAVE PROBABLY FIGURED IT OUT.
BUT THERE'S NO WAY WE CAN ESCAPE NOW.
NO MATTER WHAT WE DO, WE'VE BURNED OUR BRIDGES.

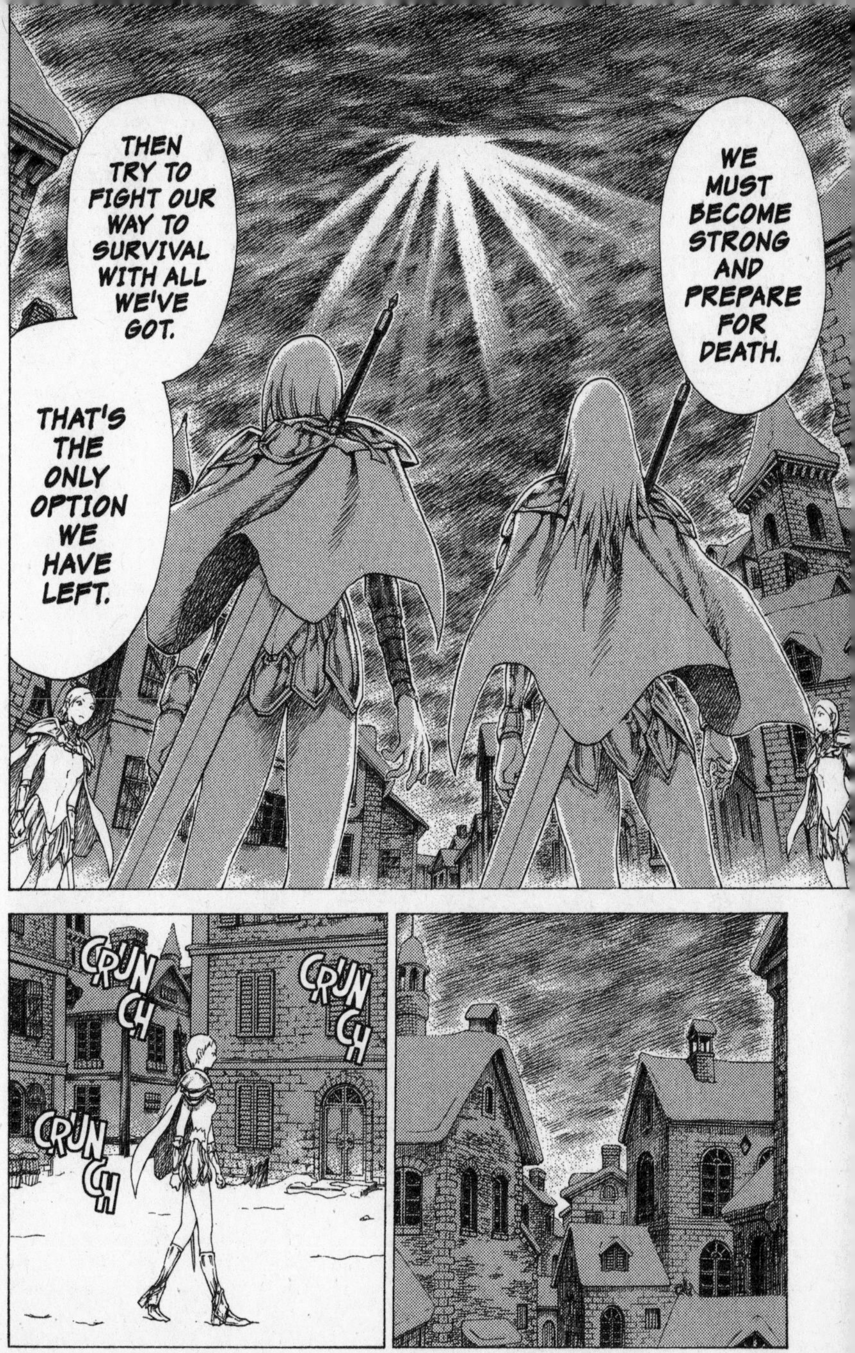
WE MUST BECOME STRONG AND PREPARE FOR DEATH.
THEN TRY TO FIGHT OUR WAY TO SURVIVAL WITH ALL WE'VE GOT.
THAT'S THE ONLY OPTION WE HAVE LEFT.
CRUNCH
CRUNCH
CRUNCH

READ THIS WAY

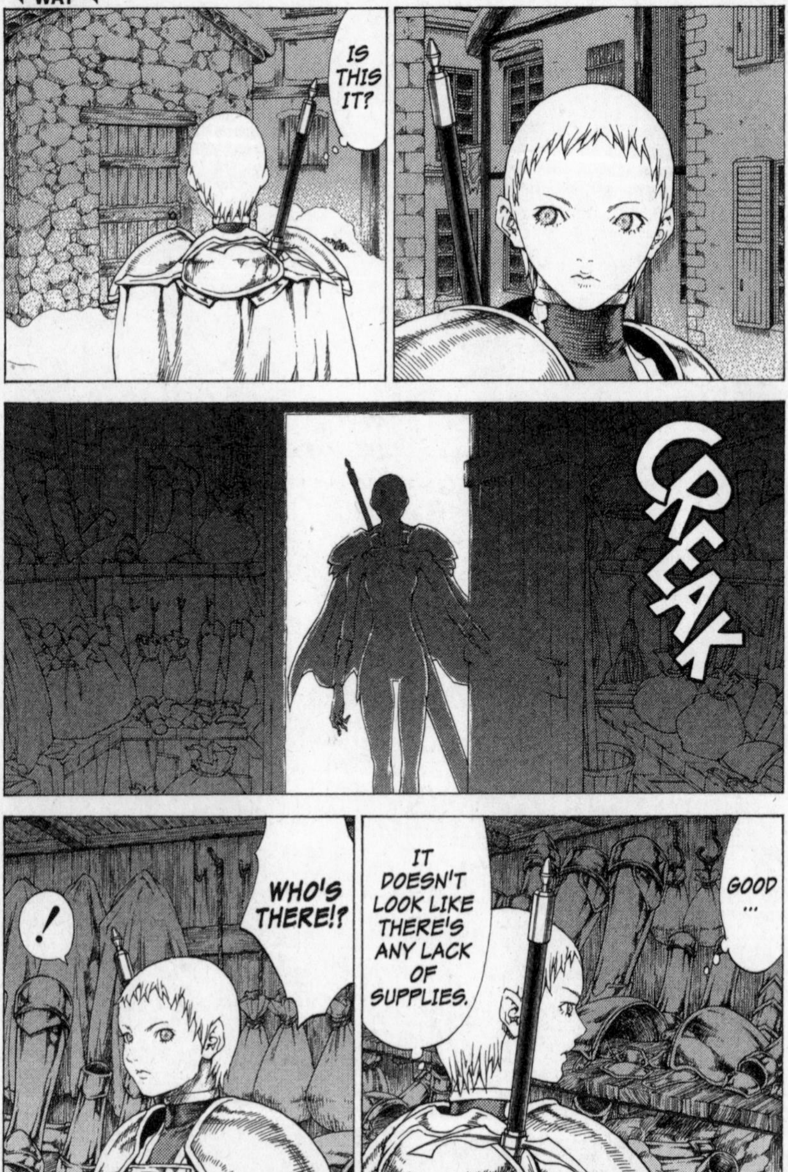
IS THIS IT?
CREAK
GOOD ...
IT DOESN'T LOOK LIKE THERE'S ANY LACK OF SUPPLIES.
WHO'S THERE!?
!

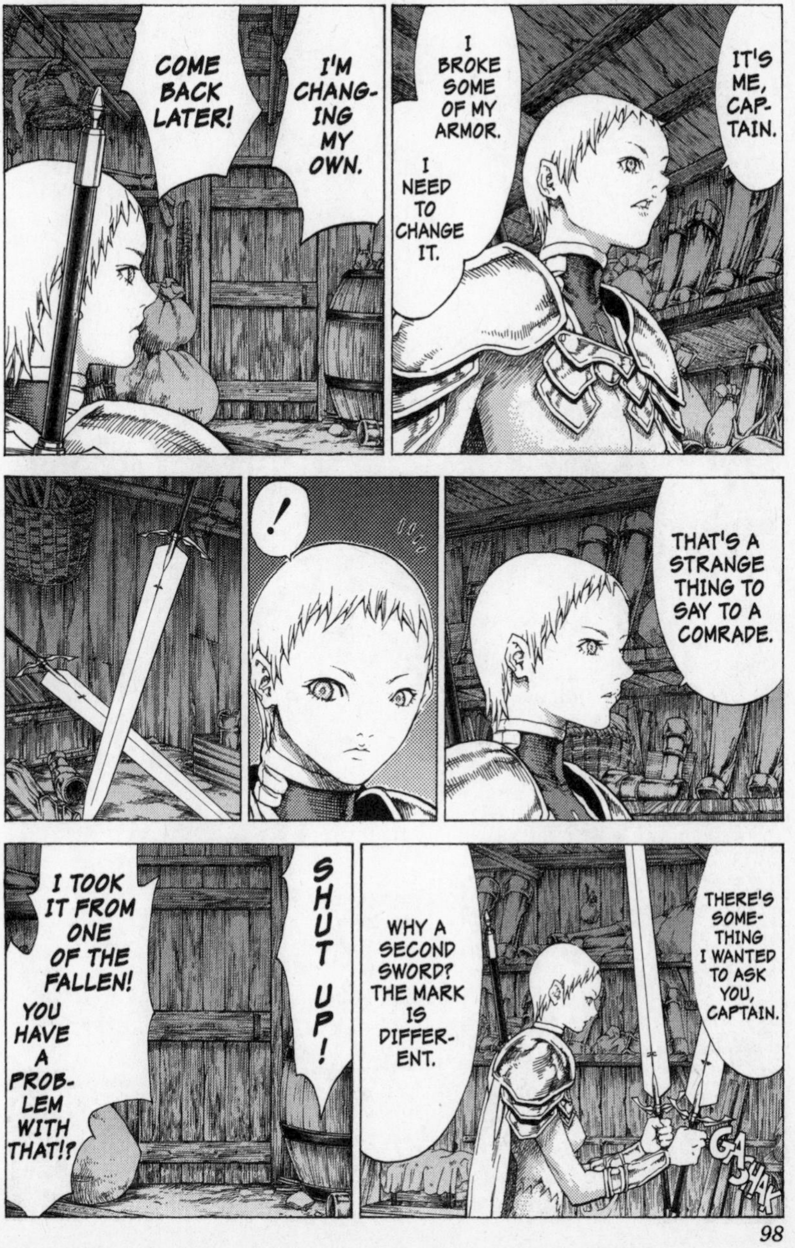
IT'S ME, CAPTAIN.
I BROKE SOME OF MY ARMOR.
I NEED TO CHANGE IT.
I'M CHANGING MY OWN.
COME BACK LATER!
THAT'S A STRANGE THING TO SAY TO A COMRADE.
!
THERE'S SOMETHING I WANTED TO ASK YOU, CAPTAIN.
GASHAK
WHY A SECOND SWORD? THE MARK IS DIFFERENT.
SHUT UP!
I TOOK IT FROM ONE OF THE FALLEN!
YOU HAVE A PROBLEM WITH THAT!?

READ THIS WAY

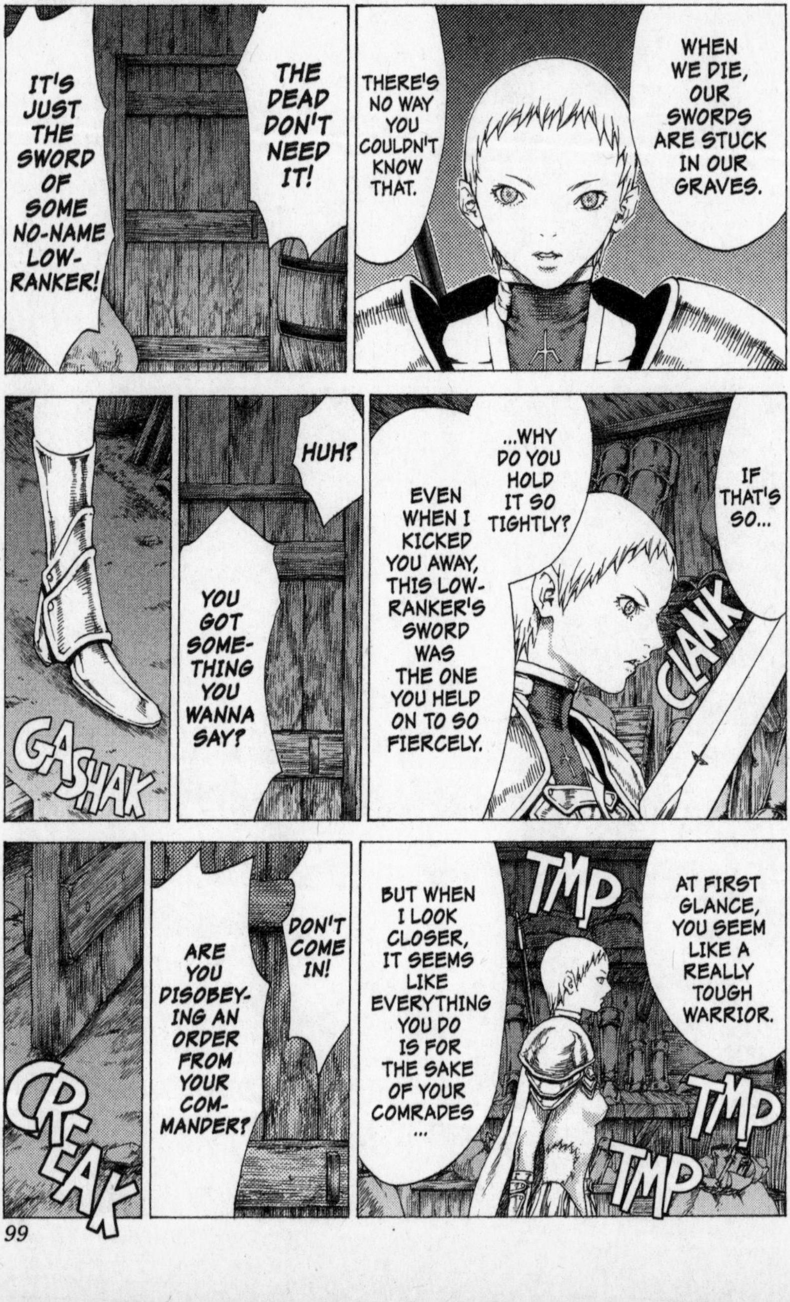
WHEN WE DIE, OUR SWORDS ARE STUCK IN OUR GRAVES.
THERE'S NO WAY YOU COULDN'T KNOW THAT.
THE DEAD DON'T NEED IT!
IT'S JUST THE SWORD OF SOME NO-NAME LOW-RANKER!
IF THAT'S SO...
CLANK
...WHY DO YOU HOLD IT SO TIGHTLY?
EVEN WHEN I KICKED YOU AWAY, THIS LOW-RANKER'S SWORD WAS THE ONE YOU HELD ON TO SO FIERCELY.
HUH?
YOU GOT SOMETHING YOU WANNA SAY?
GASHAK
TMP
AT FIRST GLANCE, YOU SEEM LIKE A REALLY TOUGH WARRIOR.
BUT WHEN I LOOK CLOSER, IT SEEMS LIKE EVERYTHING YOU DO IS FOR THE SAKE OF YOUR COMRADES...
TMP
TMP
DON'T COME IN!
ARE YOU DISOBEYING AN ORDER FROM YOUR COMMANDER?
CREAK

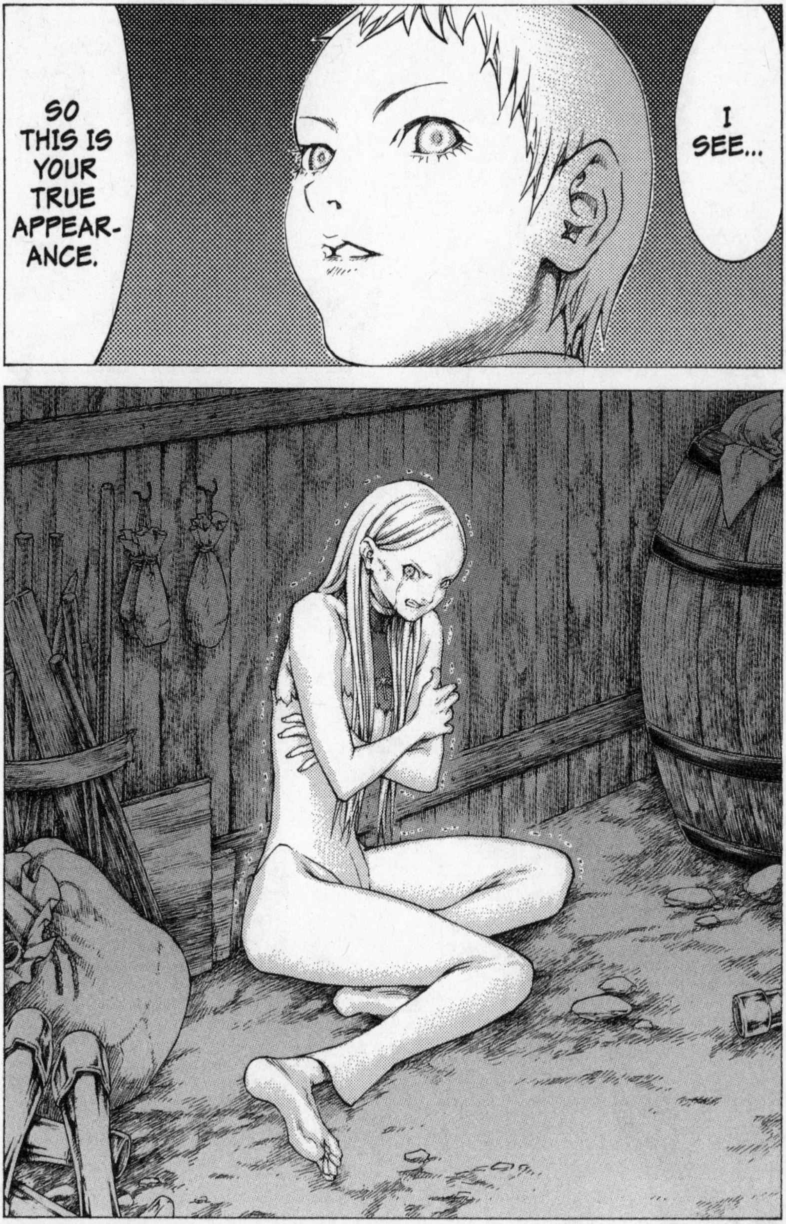
I SEE...
SO THIS IS YOUR TRUE APPEARANCE.

READ THIS WAY

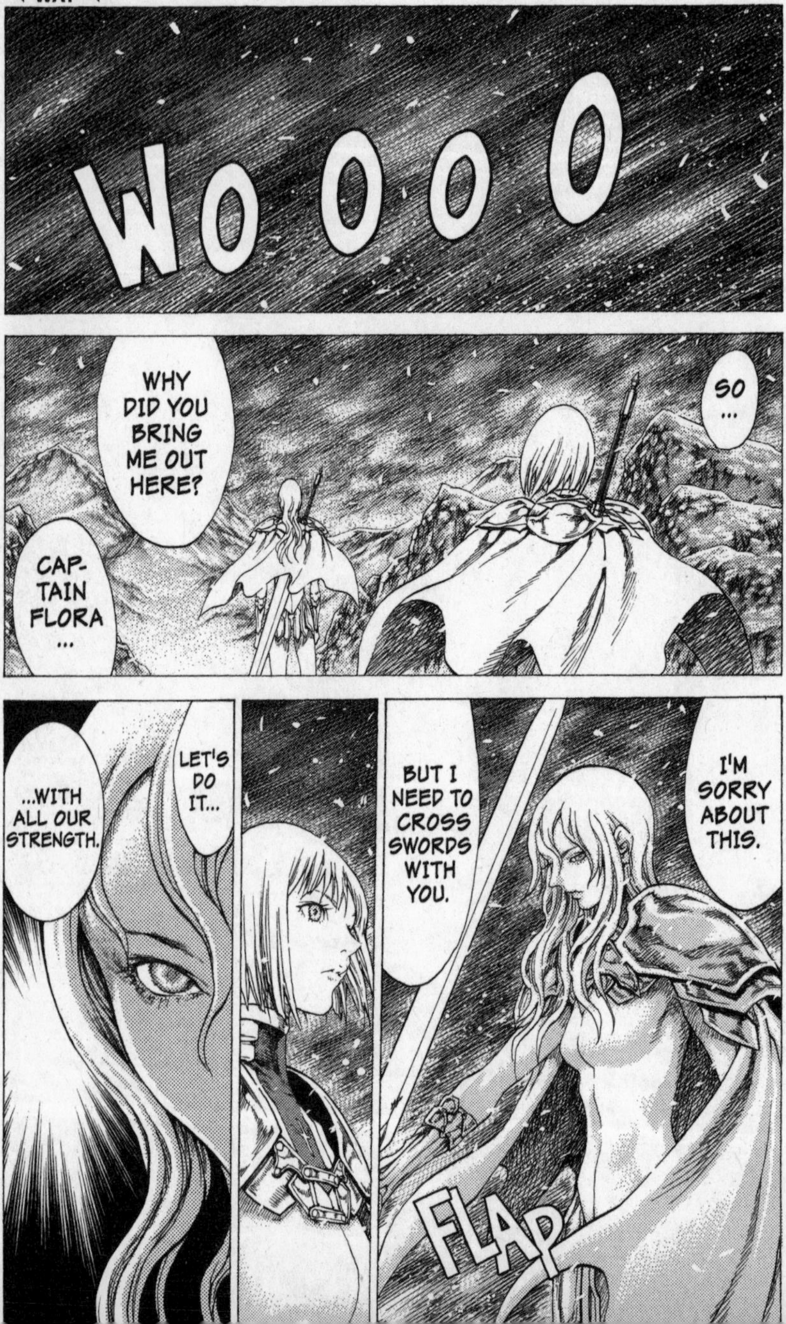
WOOOO
SO ...
WHY DID YOU BRING ME OUT HERE?
CAP-TAIN FLORA ...
I'M SORRY ABOUT THIS.
BUT I NEED TO CROSS SWORDS WITH YOU.
FLAP
LET'S DO IT...
...WITH ALL OUR STRENGTH.

クレイモア
Claymore™

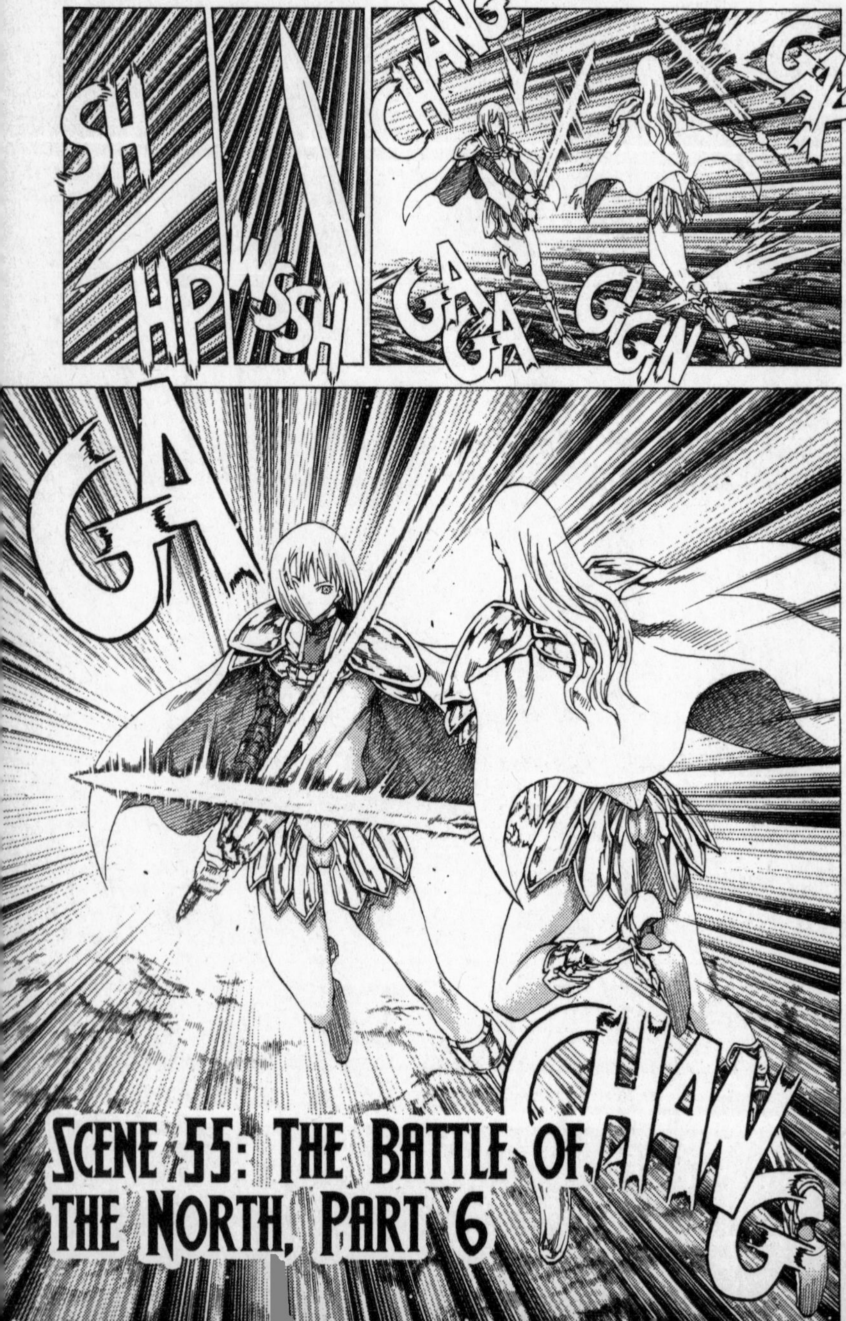
GA
CHANG
GIGN
GAGA
WSSH
SH
HP
GA
CHANG
SCENE 55: THE BATTLE OF THE NORTH, PART 6

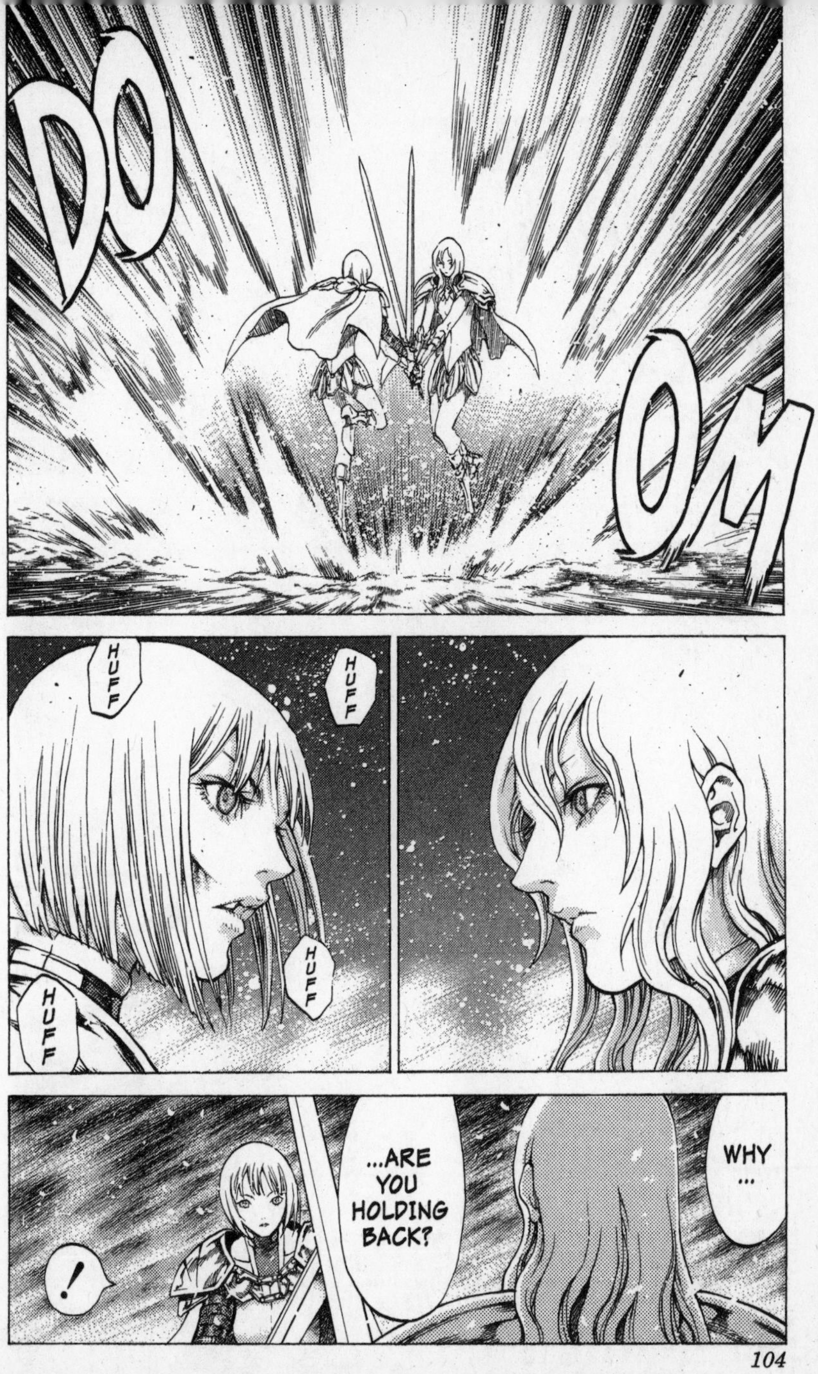
DO
OM
HUFF
HUFF
HUFF
HUFF
WHY ...
...ARE YOU HOLDING BACK?
!

READ THIS WAY

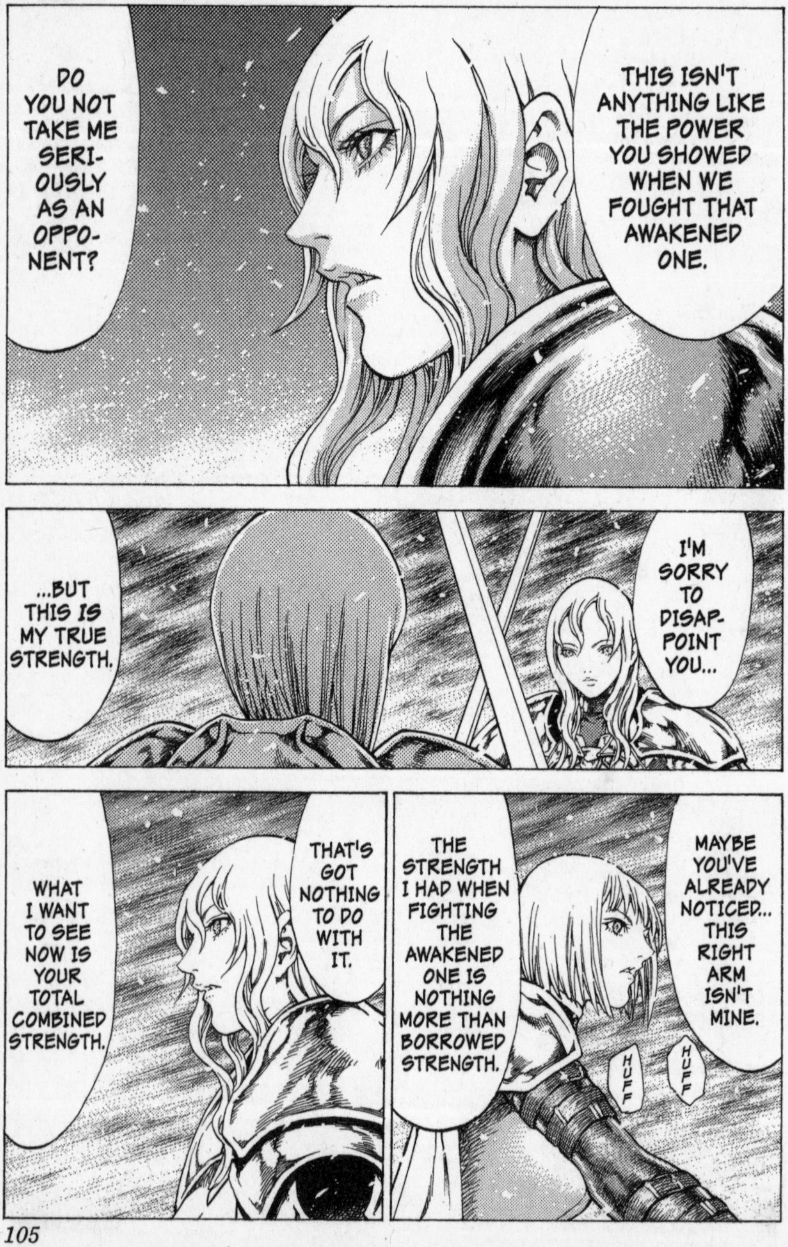
THIS ISN'T ANYTHING LIKE THE POWER YOU SHOWED WHEN WE FOUGHT THAT AWAKENED ONE.
DO YOU NOT TAKE ME SERIOUSLY AS AN OPPONENT?
I'M SORRY TO DISAPPOINT YOU...
...BUT THIS *IS* MY TRUE STRENGTH.
MAYBE YOU'VE ALREADY NOTICED... THIS RIGHT ARM ISN'T MINE.
HUFF
HUFF
THE STRENGTH I HAD WHEN FIGHTING THE AWAKENED ONE IS NOTHING MORE THAN BORROWED STRENGTH.
THAT'S GOT NOTHING TO DO WITH IT.
WHAT I WANT TO SEE NOW IS YOUR TOTAL COMBINED STRENGTH.

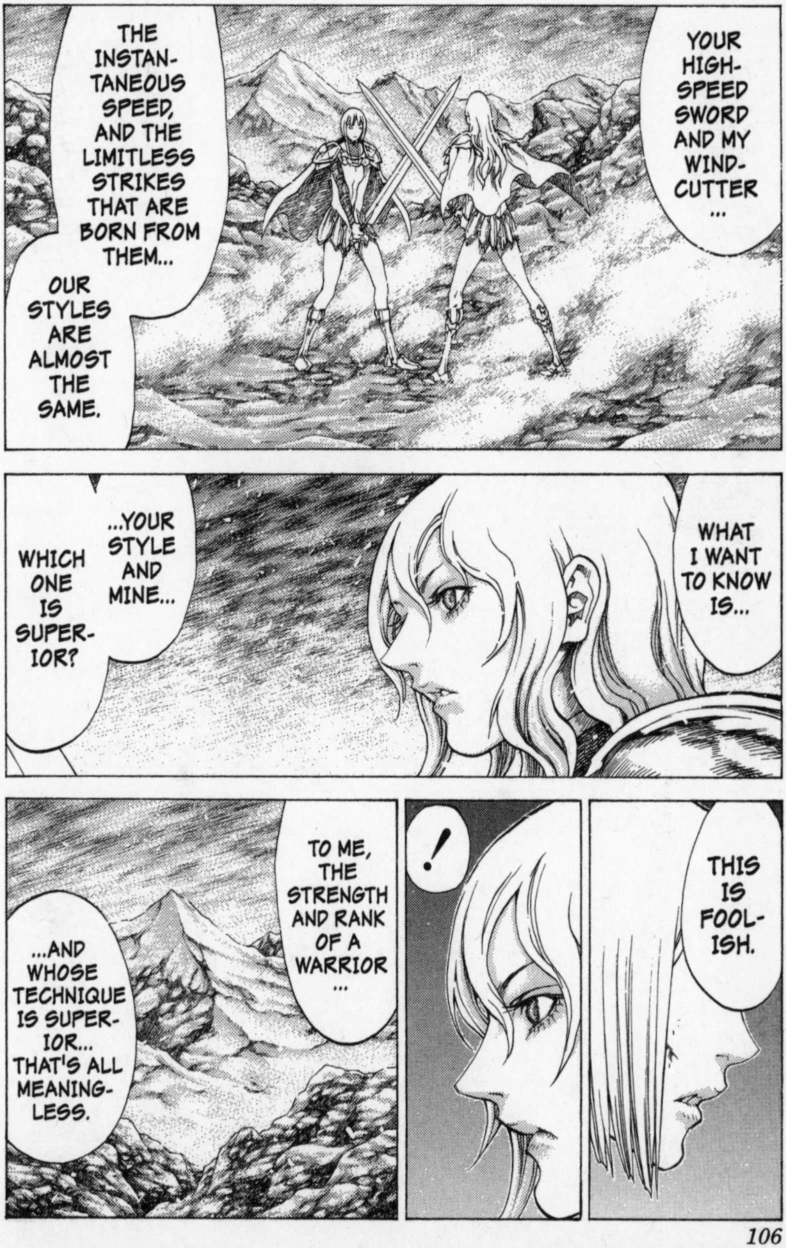
YOUR HIGH-SPEED SWORD AND MY WIND-CUTTER ...
THE INSTANTANEOUS SPEED, AND THE LIMITLESS STRIKES THAT ARE BORN FROM THEM...
OUR STYLES ARE ALMOST THE SAME.
WHAT I WANT TO KNOW IS...
...YOUR STYLE AND MINE...
WHICH ONE IS SUPERIOR?
THIS IS FOOLISH.
!
TO ME, THE STRENGTH AND RANK OF A WARRIOR ...
...AND WHOSE TECHNIQUE IS SUPERIOR... THAT'S ALL MEANINGLESS.

READ THIS WAY

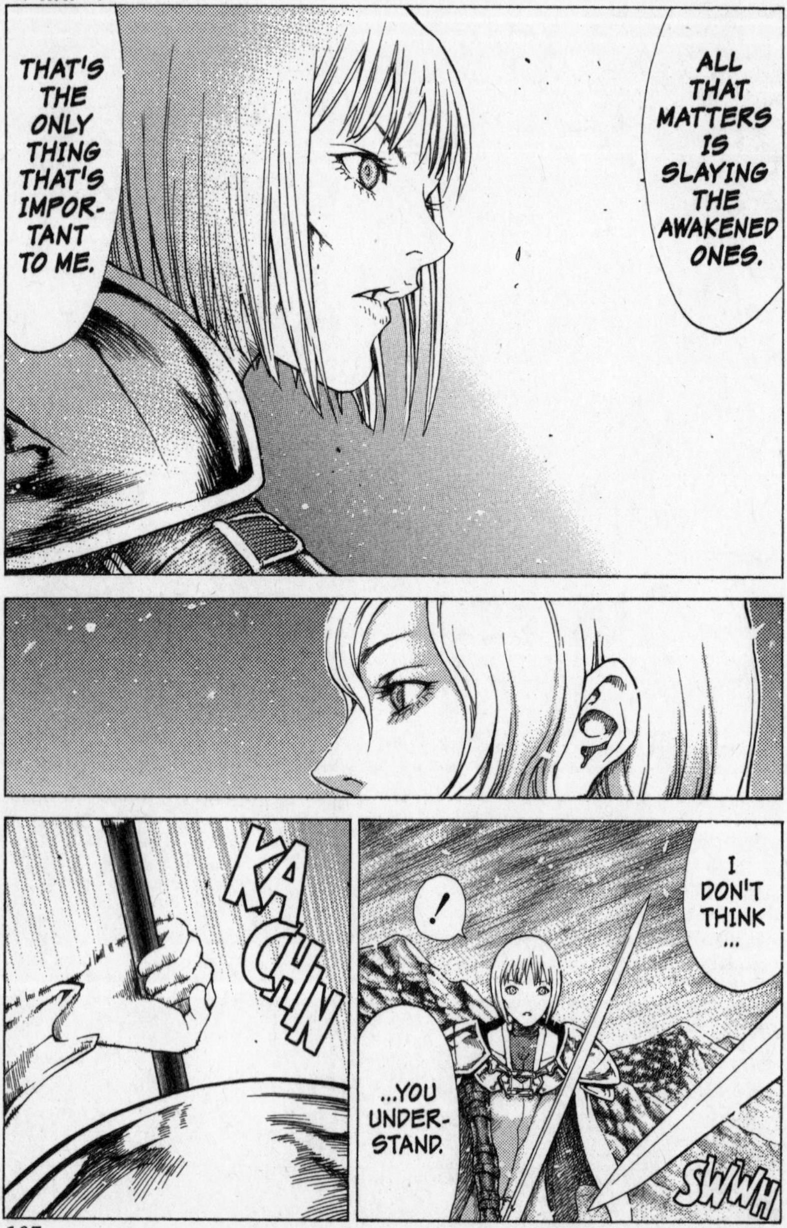
ALL THAT MATTERS IS SLAYING THE AWAKENED ONES.
THAT'S THE ONLY THING THAT'S IMPORTANT TO ME.
!
I DON'T THINK ...
...YOU UNDERSTAND.
SWWH
KACHIN

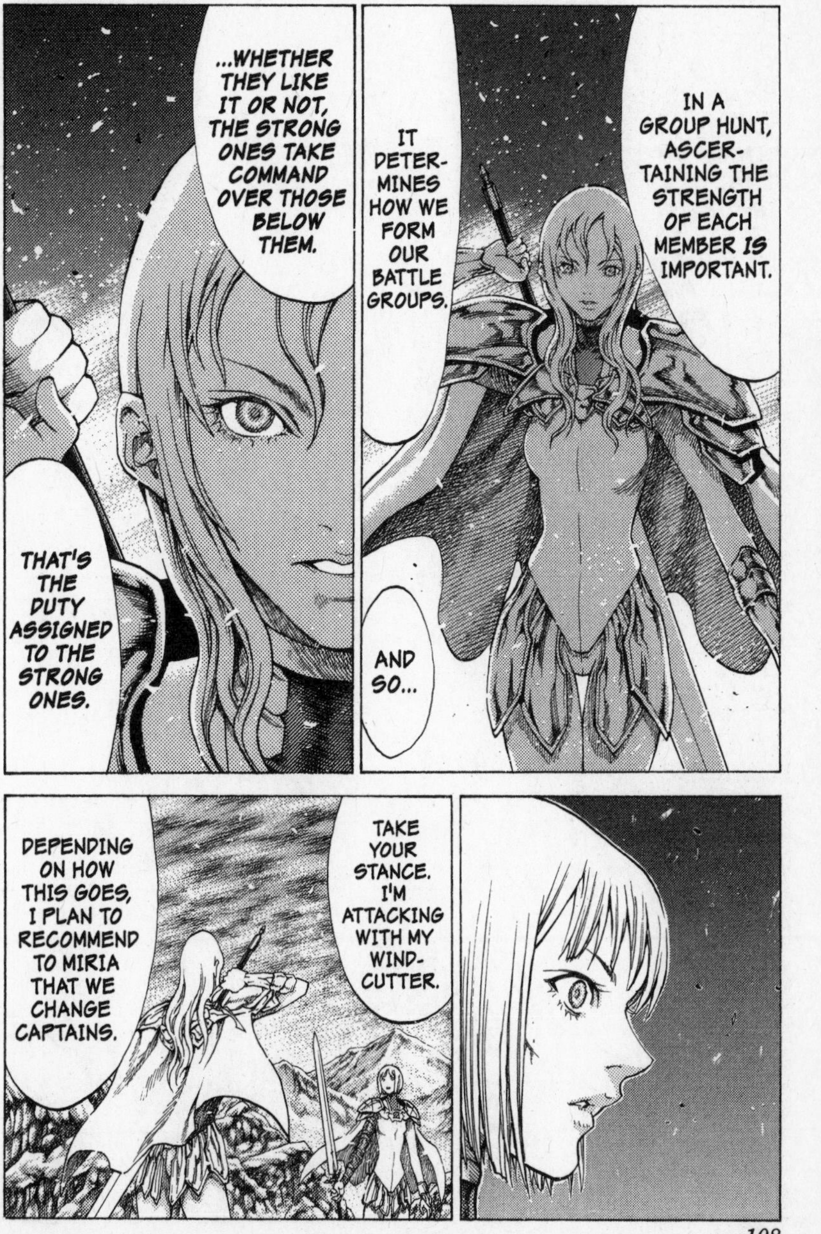
IN A GROUP HUNT, ASCER-TAINING THE STRENGTH OF EACH MEMBER IS IMPORTANT.
IT DETER-MINES HOW WE FORM OUR BATTLE GROUPS.
AND SO...
...WHETHER THEY LIKE IT OR NOT, THE STRONG ONES TAKE COMMAND OVER THOSE BELOW THEM.
THAT'S THE DUTY ASSIGNED TO THE STRONG ONES.
TAKE YOUR STANCE. I'M ATTACKING WITH MY WIND-CUTTER.
DEPENDING ON HOW THIS GOES, I PLAN TO RECOMMEND TO MIRIA THAT WE CHANGE CAPTAINS.

READ THIS WAY

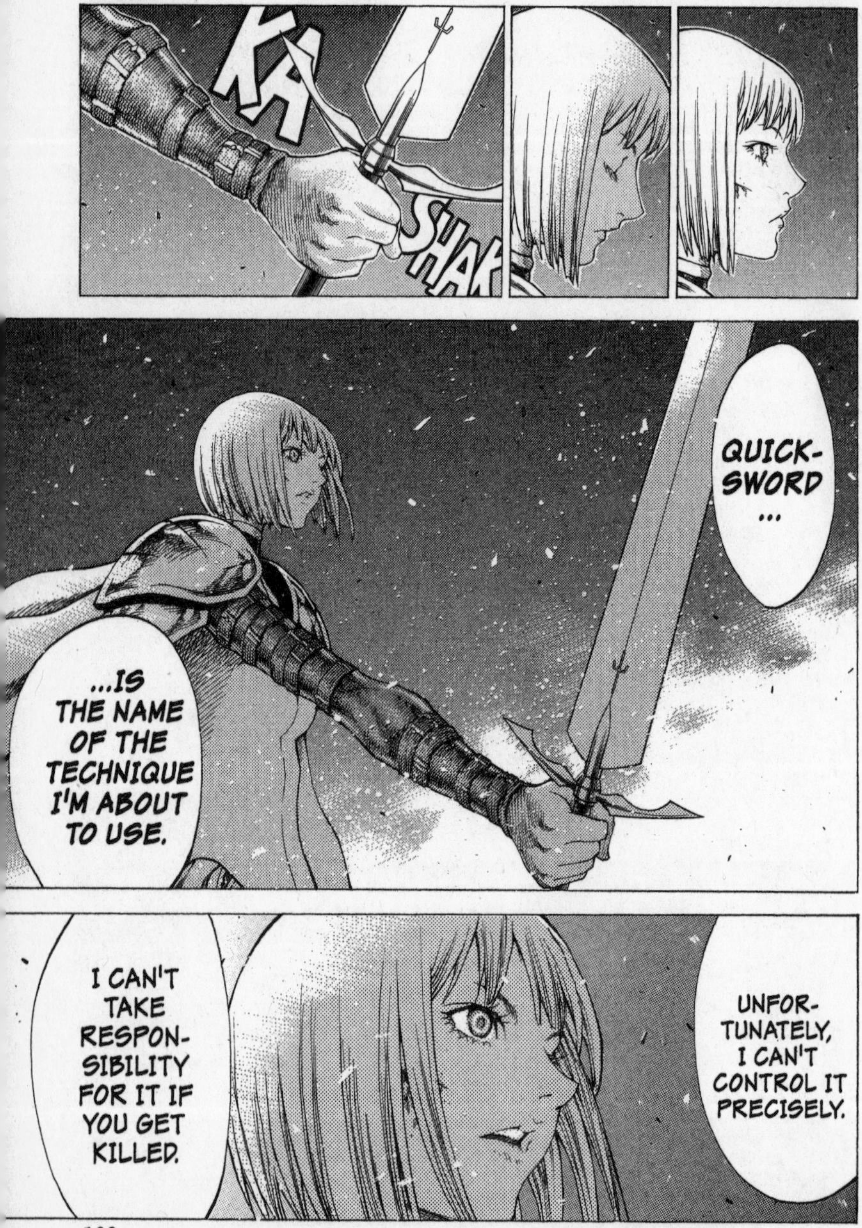
KA
SHAK
QUICK-SWORD...
...IS THE NAME OF THE TECHNIQUE I'M ABOUT TO USE.
UNFOR-TUNATELY, I CAN'T CONTROL IT PRECISELY.
I CAN'T TAKE RESPON-SIBILITY FOR IT IF YOU GET KILLED.

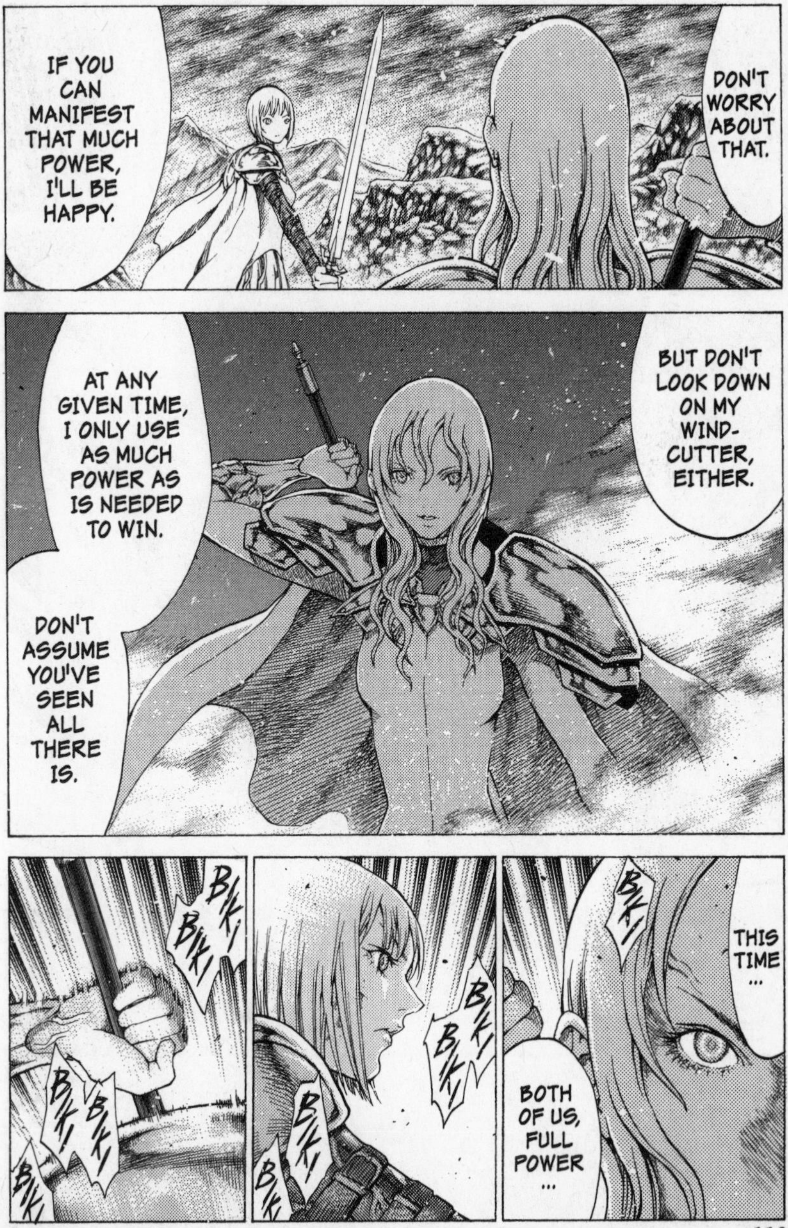
DON'T WORRY ABOUT THAT.
IF YOU CAN MANIFEST THAT MUCH POWER, I'LL BE HAPPY.
BUT DON'T LOOK DOWN ON MY WIND-CUTTER, EITHER.
AT ANY GIVEN TIME, I ONLY USE AS MUCH POWER AS IS NEEDED TO WIN.
DON'T ASSUME YOU'VE SEEN ALL THERE IS.
BIKI
THIS TIME...
BOTH OF US, FULL POWER...
BIKI
BIKI
BIKI
BIKI
BIKI
BIKI
BIKI
BIKI

READ THIS WAY

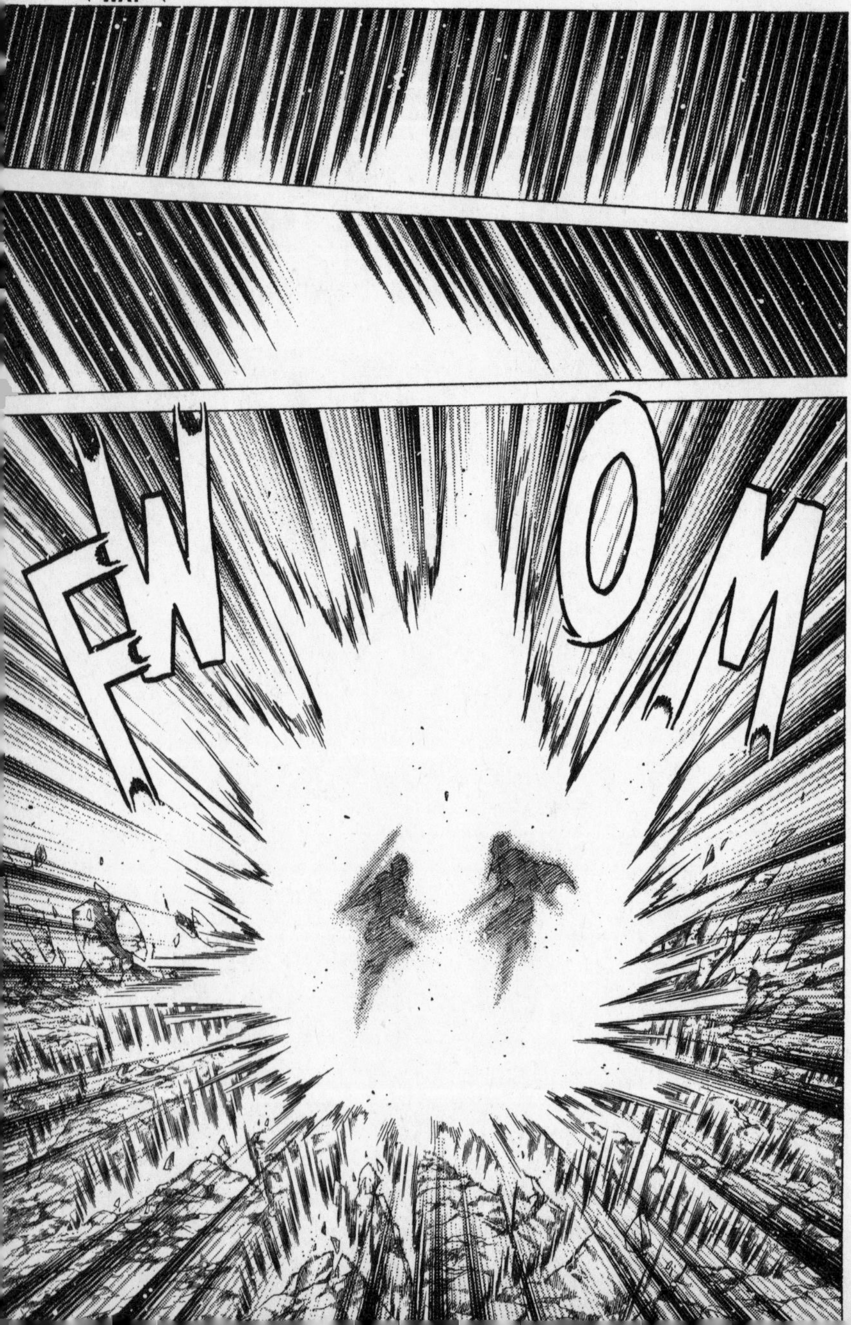
FWOM

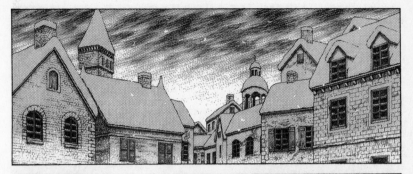

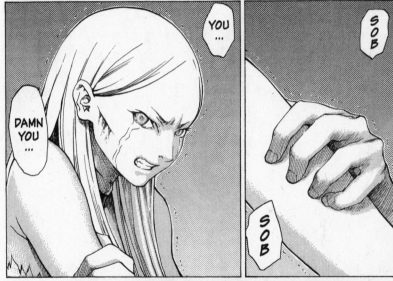

YOU
...

DAMN
YOU
...

SOB

SOB

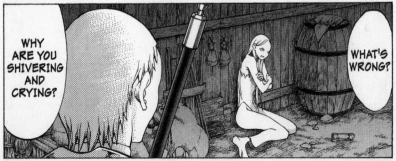

WHY
ARE YOU
SHIVERING
AND
CRYING?

WHAT'S
WRONG?

READ THIS WAY

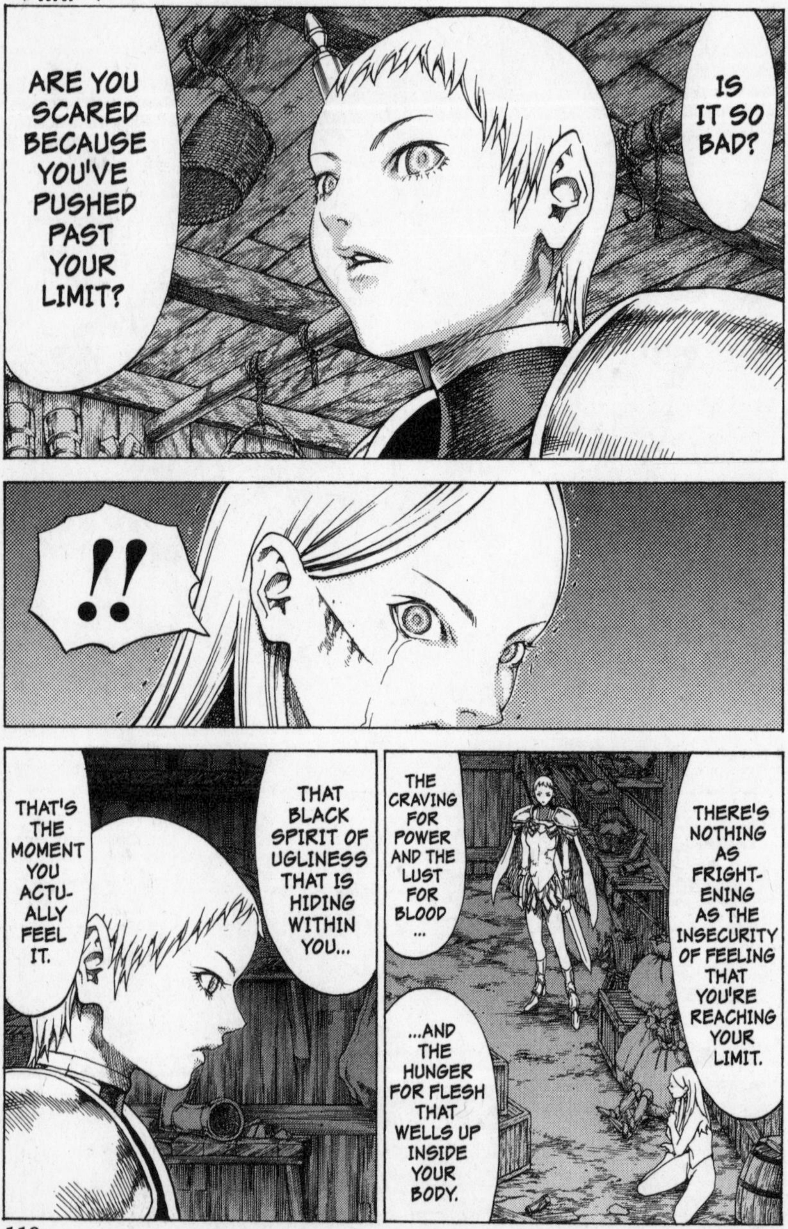

IS IT SO BAD?
ARE YOU SCARED BECAUSE YOU'VE PUSHED PAST YOUR LIMIT?
!!
THERE'S NOTHING AS FRIGHT-ENING AS THE INSECURITY OF FEELING THAT YOU'RE REACHING YOUR LIMIT.
THE CRAVING FOR POWER AND THE LUST FOR BLOOD ...
...AND THE HUNGER FOR FLESH THAT WELLS UP INSIDE YOUR BODY.
THAT BLACK SPIRIT OF UGLINESS THAT IS HIDING WITHIN YOU...
THAT'S THE MOMENT YOU ACTU-ALLY FEEL IT.

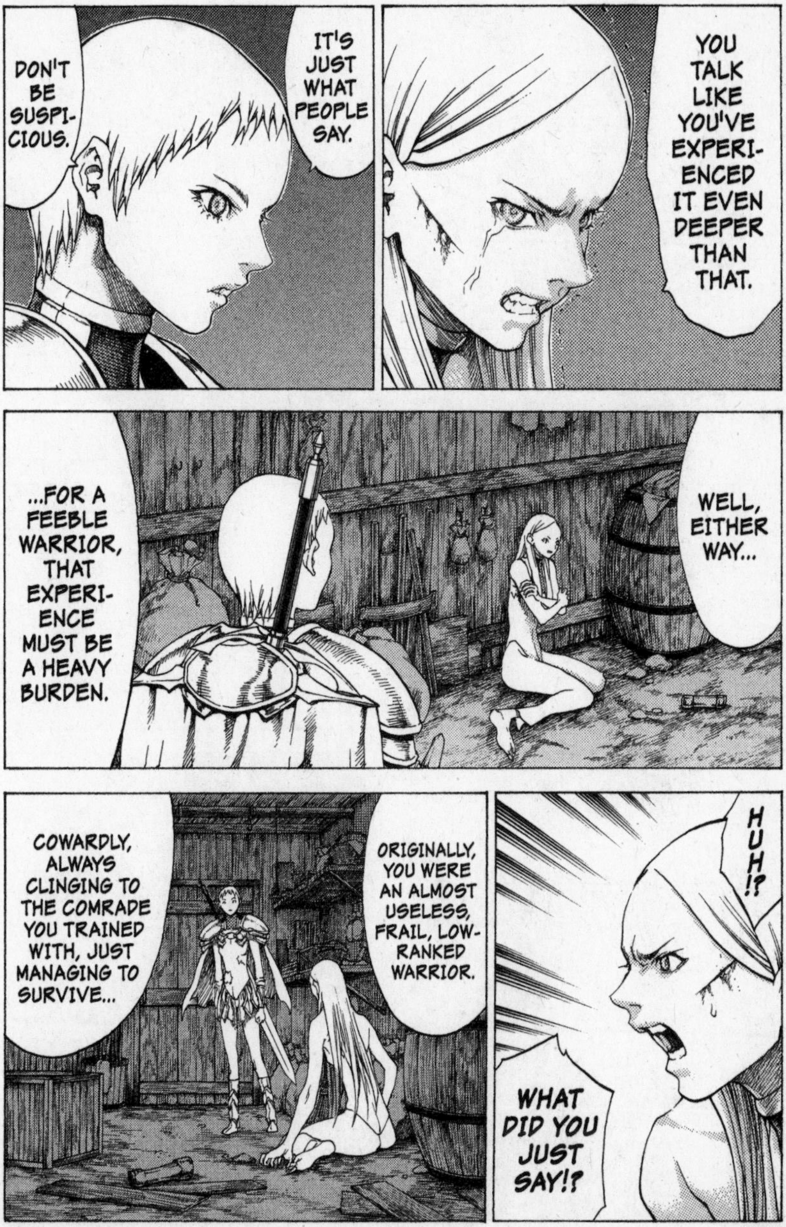
YOU TALK LIKE YOU'VE EXPERIENCED IT EVEN DEEPER THAN THAT.
IT'S JUST WHAT PEOPLE SAY.
DON'T BE SUSPICIOUS.
WELL, EITHER WAY...
...FOR A FEEBLE WARRIOR, THAT EXPERIENCE MUST BE A HEAVY BURDEN.
HUH!?
WHAT DID YOU JUST SAY!?
ORIGINALLY, YOU WERE AN ALMOST USELESS, FRAIL, LOW-RANKED WARRIOR.
COWARDLY, ALWAYS CLINGING TO THE COMRADE YOU TRAINED WITH, JUST MANAGING TO SURVIVE...

READ THIS WAY

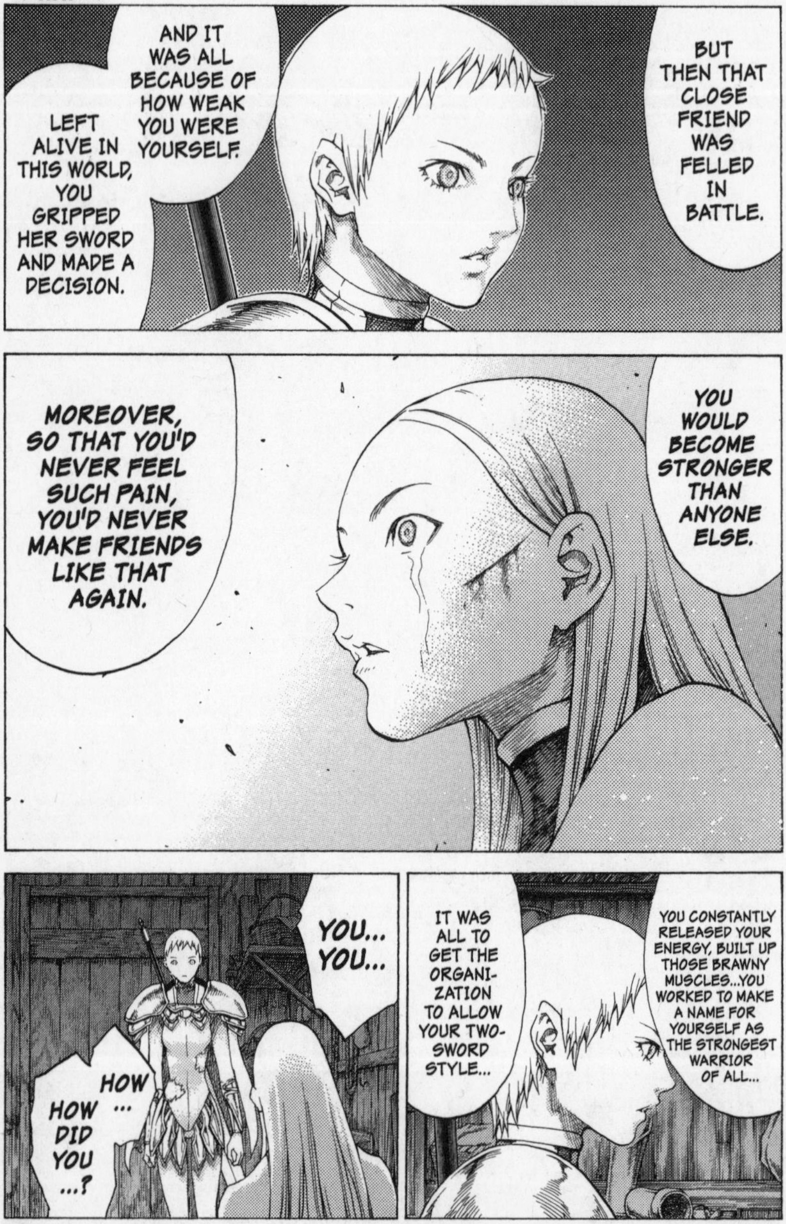
BUT THEN THAT CLOSE FRIEND WAS FELLED IN BATTLE.
AND IT WAS ALL BECAUSE OF HOW WEAK YOU WERE YOURSELF.
LEFT ALIVE IN THIS WORLD, YOU GRIPPED HER SWORD AND MADE A DECISION.
YOU WOULD BECOME STRONGER THAN ANYONE ELSE.
MOREOVER, SO THAT YOU'D NEVER FEEL SUCH PAIN, YOU'D NEVER MAKE FRIENDS LIKE THAT AGAIN.
YOU CONSTANTLY RELEASED YOUR ENERGY, BUILT UP THOSE BRAWNY MUSCLES...YOU WORKED TO MAKE A NAME FOR YOURSELF AS THE STRONGEST WARRIOR OF ALL...
IT WAS ALL TO GET THE ORGANIZATION TO ALLOW YOUR TWO-SWORD STYLE...
YOU... YOU...
HOW... HOW DID YOU ...?

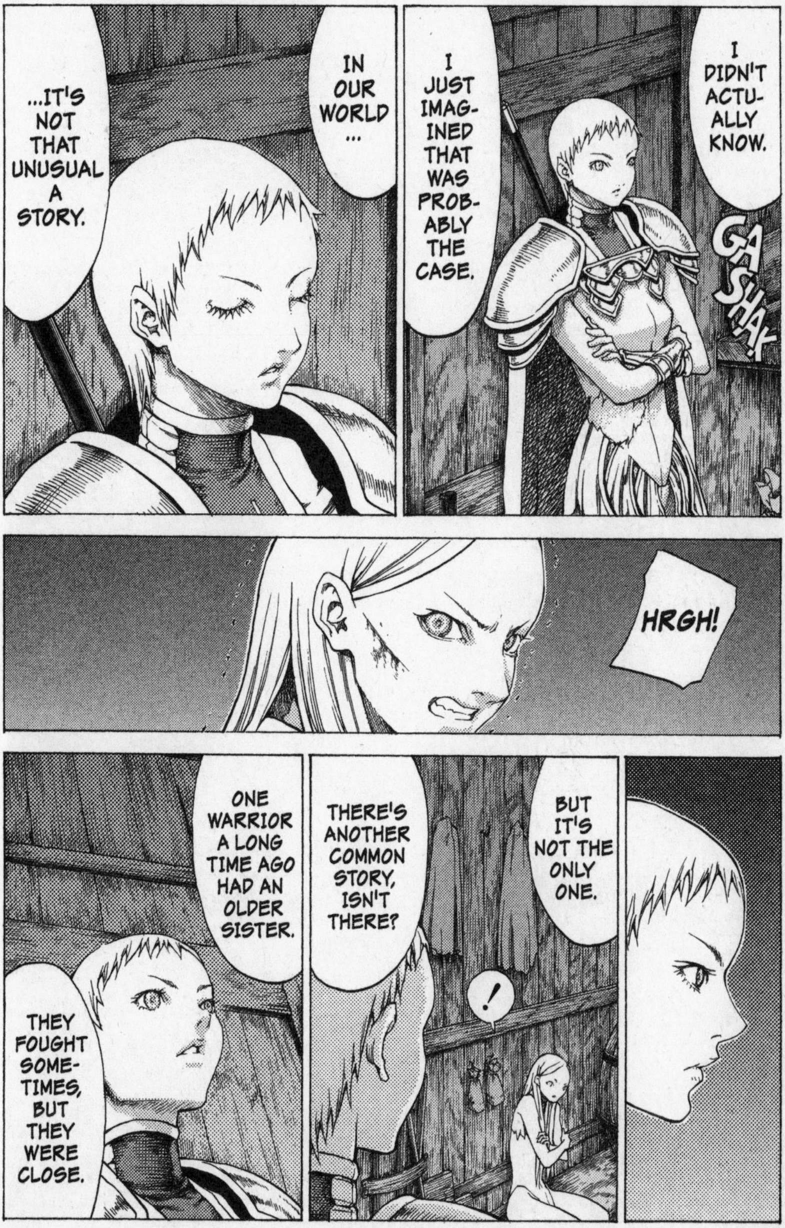
I DIDN'T ACTUALLY KNOW.
GASHAK
I JUST IMAGINED THAT WAS PROBABLY THE CASE.
IN OUR WORLD...
...IT'S NOT THAT UNUSUAL A STORY.
HRGH!
BUT IT'S NOT THE ONLY ONE.
THERE'S ANOTHER COMMON STORY, ISN'T THERE?
!
ONE WARRIOR A LONG TIME AGO HAD AN OLDER SISTER.
THEY FOUGHT SOMETIMES, BUT THEY WERE CLOSE.

READ THIS WAY

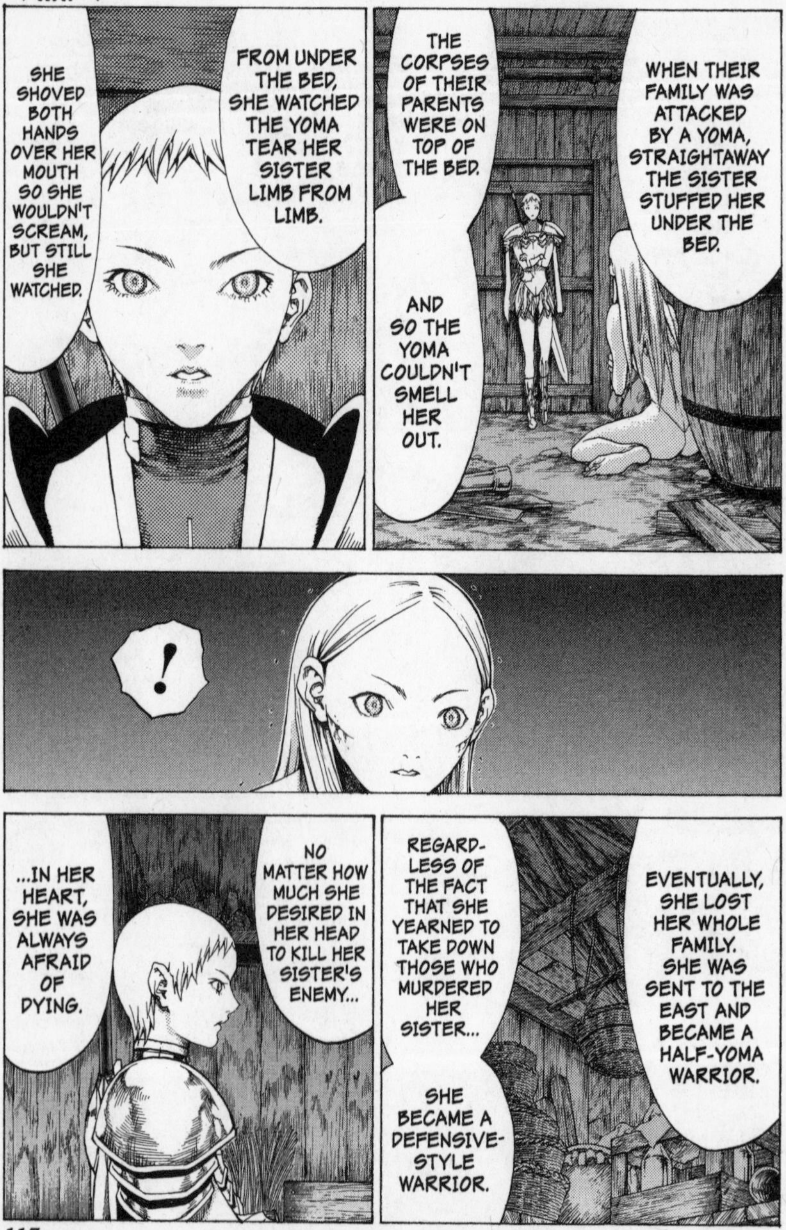
WHEN THEIR FAMILY WAS ATTACKED BY A YOMA, STRAIGHTAWAY THE SISTER STUFFED HER UNDER THE BED.
THE CORPSES OF THEIR PARENTS WERE ON TOP OF THE BED.
AND SO THE YOMA COULDN'T SMELL HER OUT.
FROM UNDER THE BED, SHE WATCHED THE YOMA TEAR HER SISTER LIMB FROM LIMB.
SHE SHOVED BOTH HANDS OVER HER MOUTH SO SHE WOULDN'T SCREAM, BUT STILL SHE WATCHED.
!
EVENTUALLY, SHE LOST HER WHOLE FAMILY. SHE WAS SENT TO THE EAST AND BECAME A HALF-YOMA WARRIOR.
REGARDLESS OF THE FACT THAT SHE YEARNED TO TAKE DOWN THOSE WHO MURDERED HER SISTER...
SHE BECAME A DEFENSIVE-STYLE WARRIOR.
NO MATTER HOW MUCH SHE DESIRED IN HER HEAD TO KILL HER SISTER'S ENEMY...
...IN HER HEART, SHE WAS ALWAYS AFRAID OF DYING.

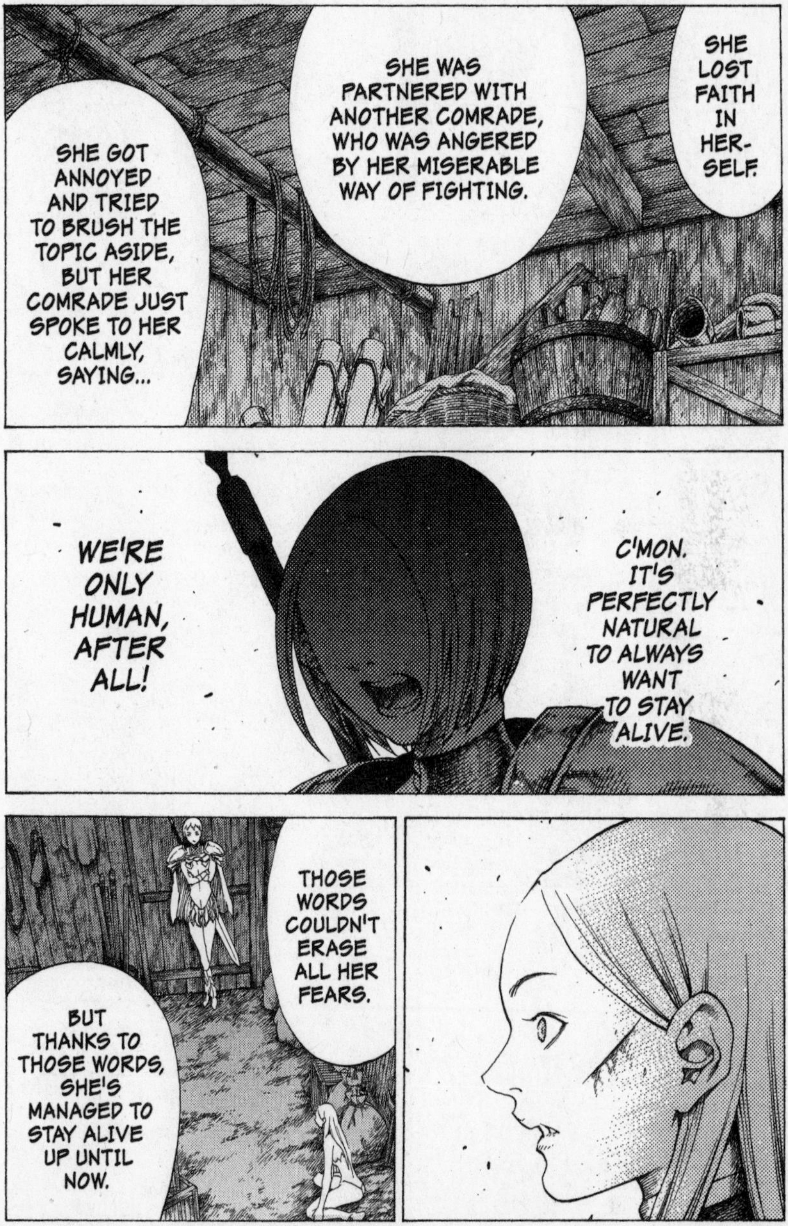
SHE LOST FAITH IN HER-SELF.
SHE WAS PARTNERED WITH ANOTHER COMRADE, WHO WAS ANGERED BY HER MISERABLE WAY OF FIGHTING.
SHE GOT ANNOYED AND TRIED TO BRUSH THE TOPIC ASIDE, BUT HER COMRADE JUST SPOKE TO HER CALMLY, SAYING...
C'MON. IT'S PERFECTLY NATURAL TO ALWAYS WANT TO STAY ALIVE.
WE'RE ONLY HUMAN, AFTER ALL!
THOSE WORDS COULDN'T ERASE ALL HER FEARS.
BUT THANKS TO THOSE WORDS, SHE'S MANAGED TO STAY ALIVE UP UNTIL NOW.

READ THIS WAY

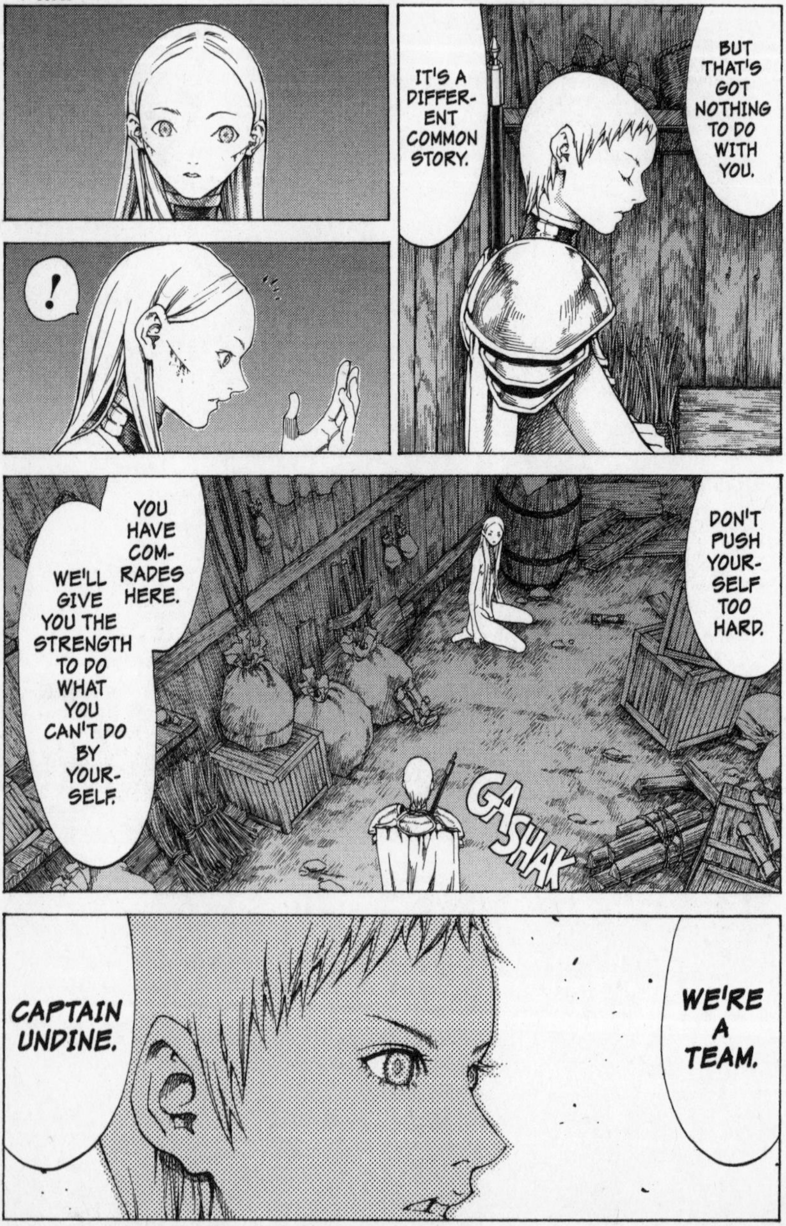
BUT THAT'S GOT NOTHING TO DO WITH YOU.
IT'S A DIFFER-ENT COMMON STORY.
!
DON'T PUSH YOUR-SELF TOO HARD.
GASHAK
YOU HAVE COM-RADES HERE.
WE'LL GIVE YOU THE STRENGTH TO DO WHAT YOU CAN'T DO BY YOUR-SELF.
WE'RE A TEAM.
CAPTAIN UNDINE.

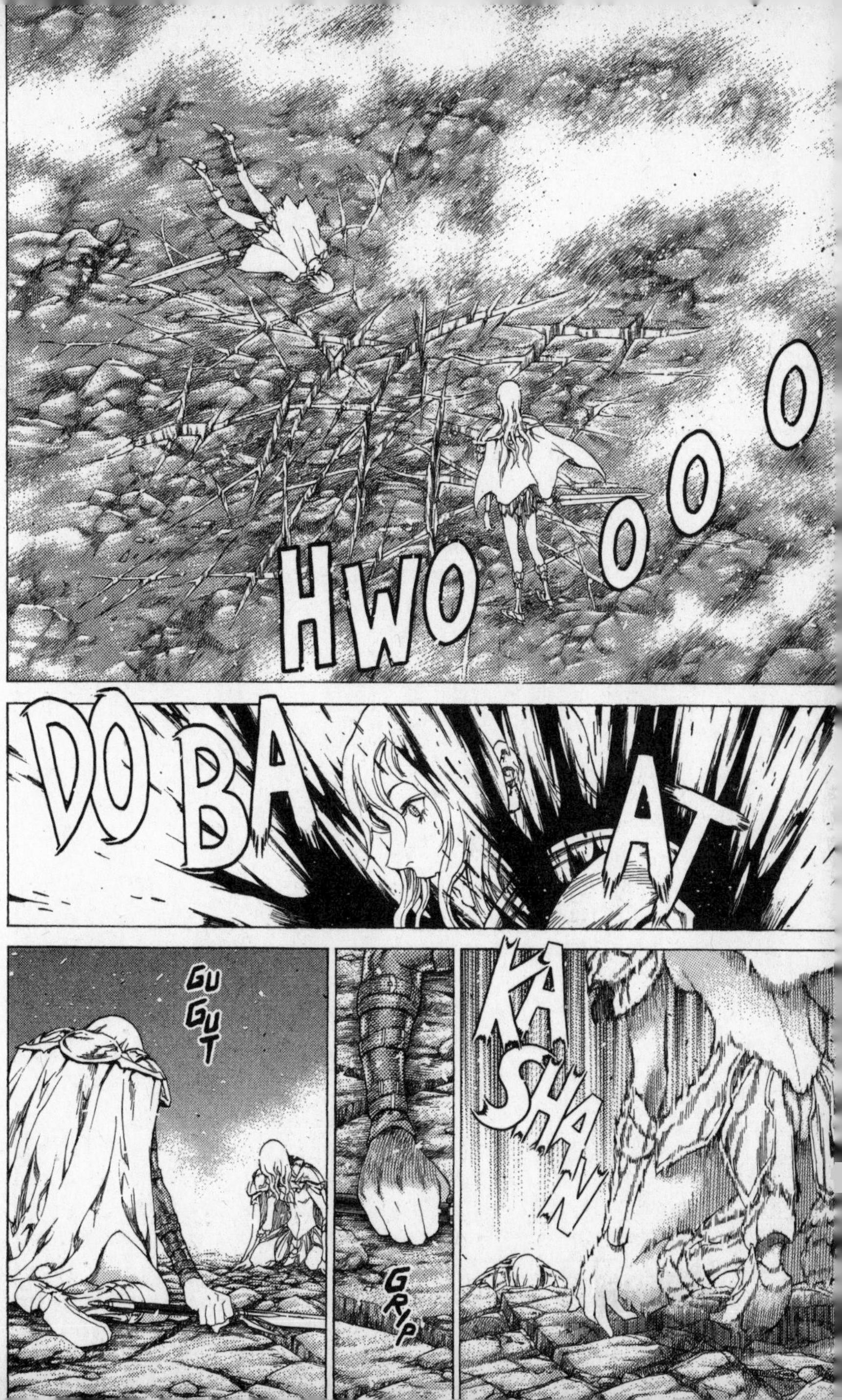
HWOOOOO
DOBAAT
KASHAN
GRIP
GUGUT

READ THIS WAY

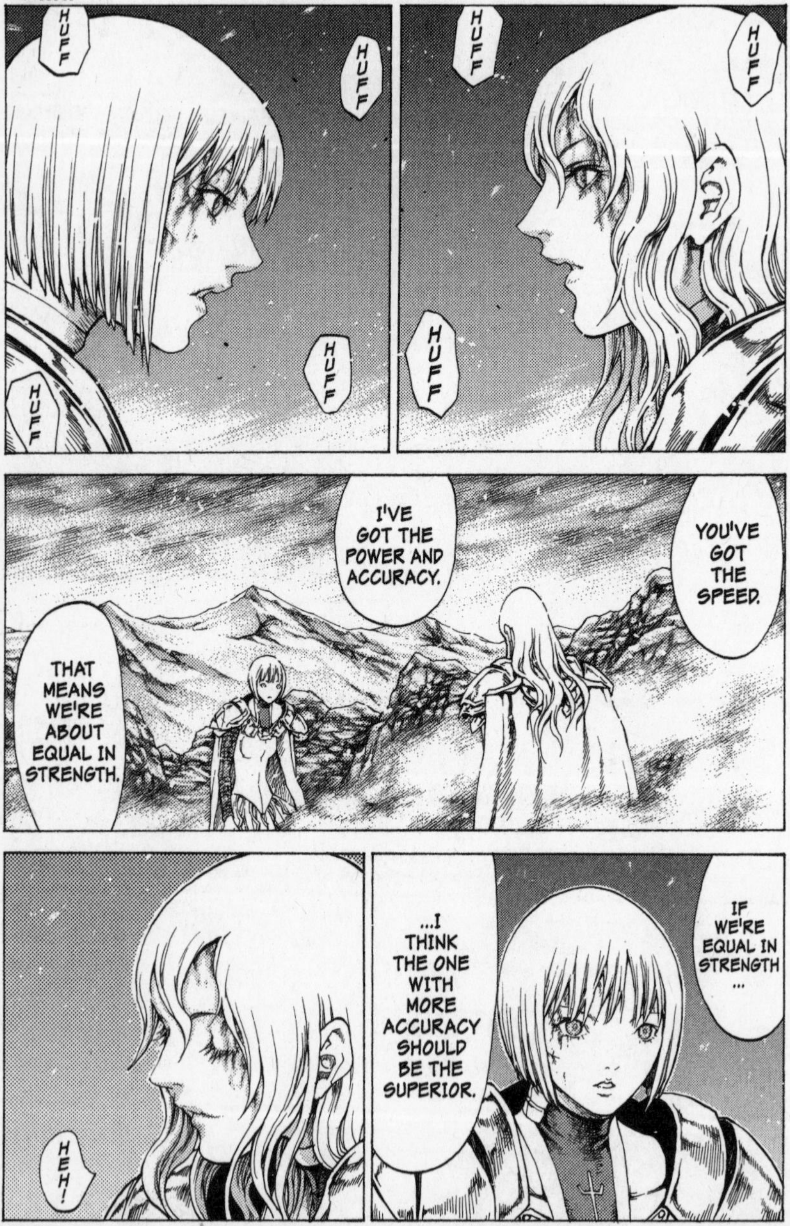
HUFF
HUFF
HUFF
HUFF
HUFF
HUFF
YOU'VE GOT THE SPEED.
I'VE GOT THE POWER AND ACCURACY.
THAT MEANS WE'RE ABOUT EQUAL IN STRENGTH.
IF WE'RE EQUAL IN STRENGTH...
...I THINK THE ONE WITH MORE ACCURACY SHOULD BE THE SUPERIOR.
HEH!

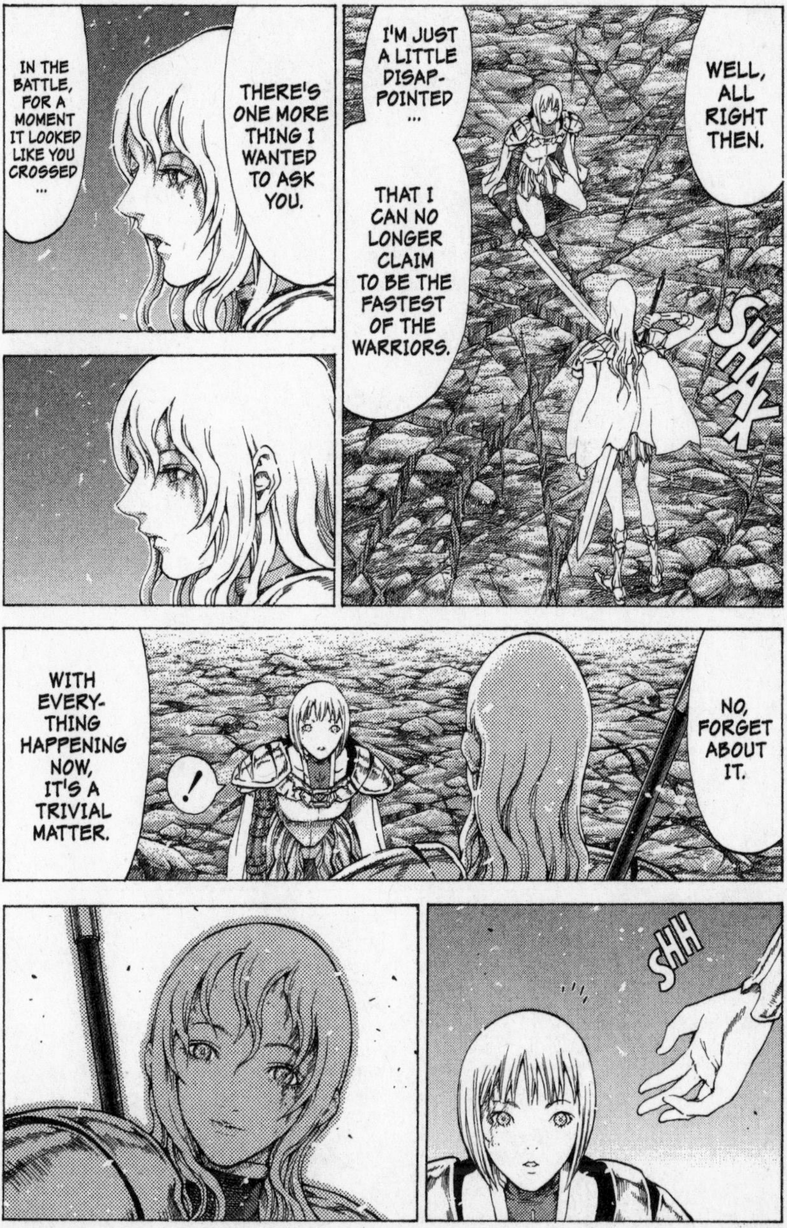
WELL, ALL RIGHT THEN.
I'M JUST A LITTLE DISAP-POINTED ...
THAT I CAN NO LONGER CLAIM TO BE THE FASTEST OF THE WARRIORS.
SHAK
THERE'S ONE MORE THING I WANTED TO ASK YOU.
IN THE BATTLE, FOR A MOMENT IT LOOKED LIKE YOU CROSSED ...
NO, FORGET ABOUT IT.
!
WITH EVERY-THING HAPPENING NOW, IT'S A TRIVIAL MATTER.
SHH

READ THIS WAY

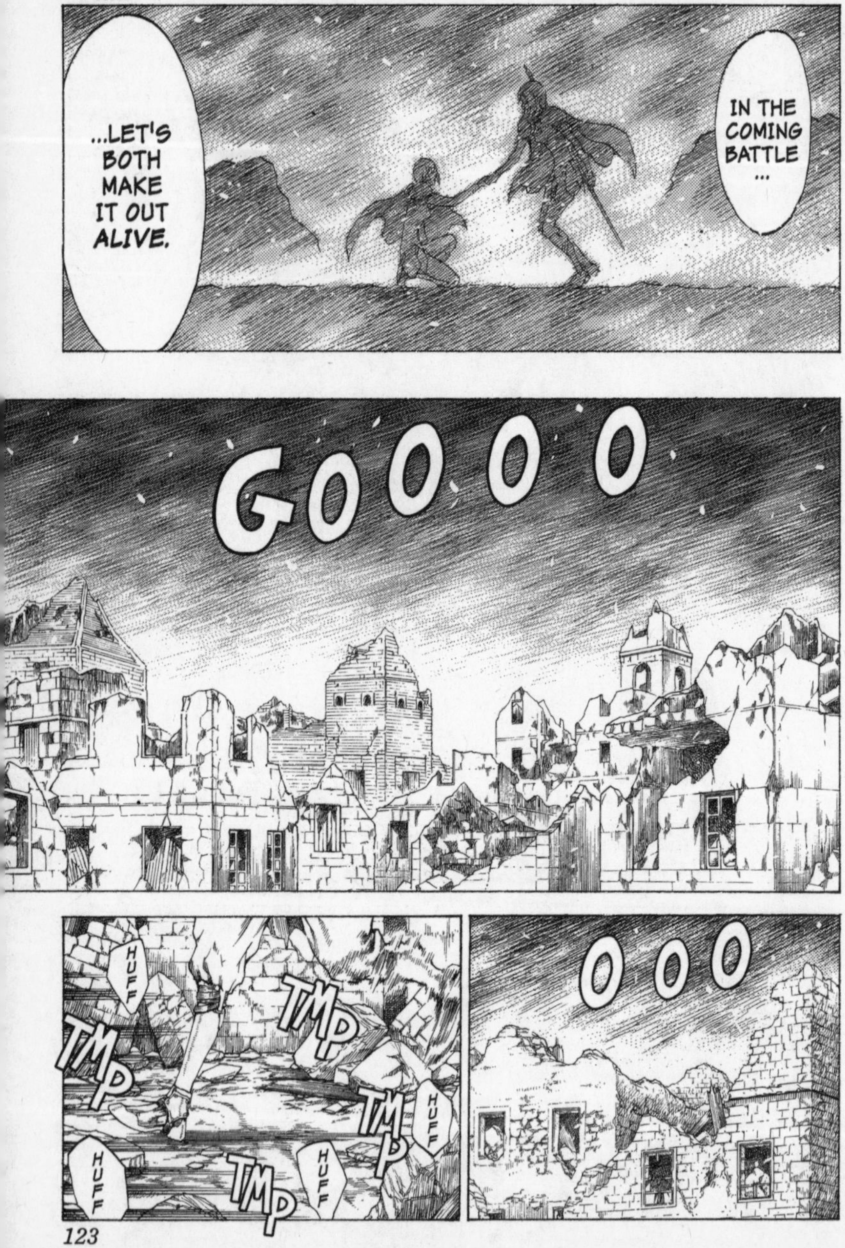
IN THE COMING BATTLE ...
...LET'S BOTH MAKE IT OUT ALIVE.
GOOOO
OOO
TMP
HUFF
TMP
HUFF
TMP
HUFF
TMP
HUFF

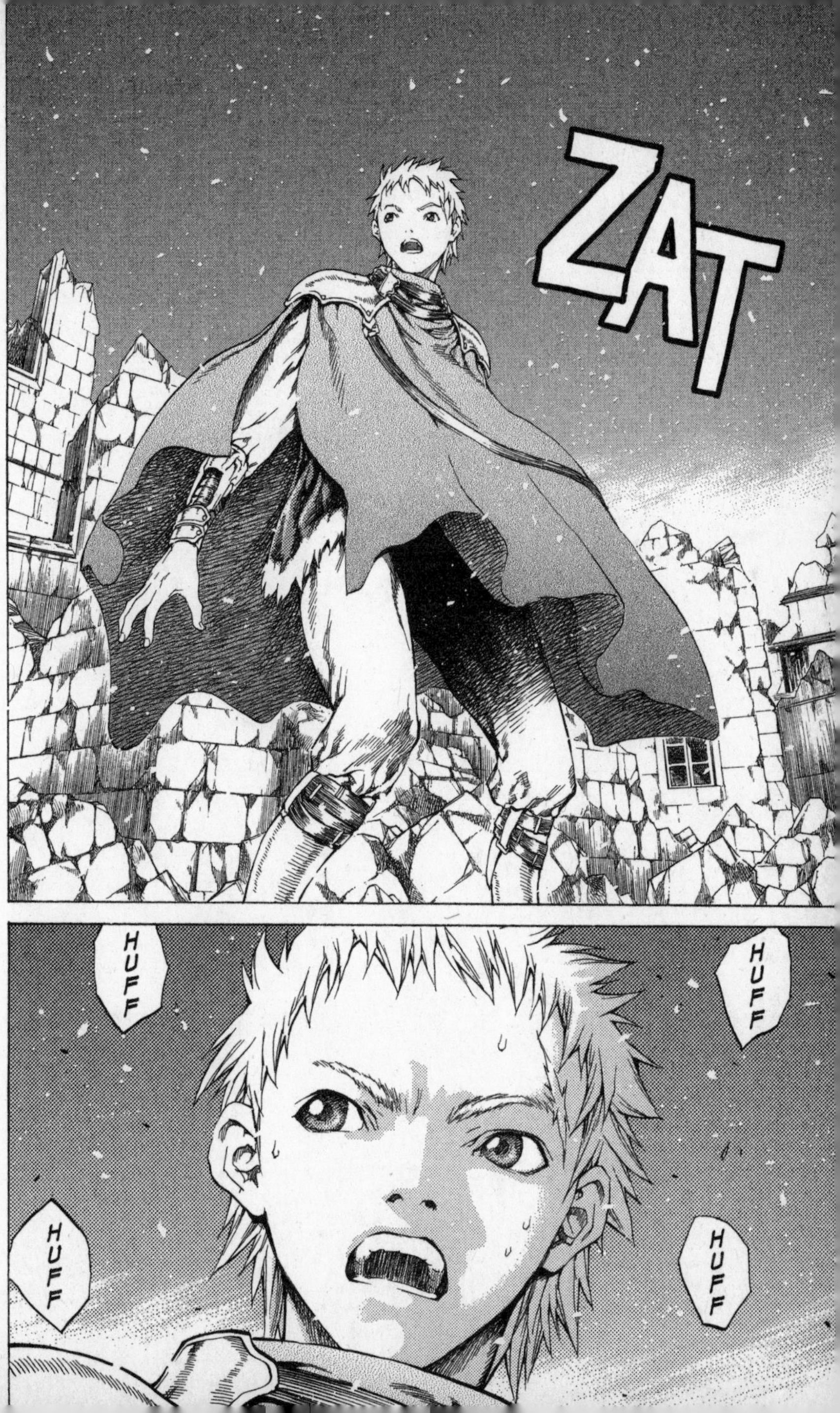
ZAT
HUFF
HUFF
HUFF
HUFF

READ THIS WAY

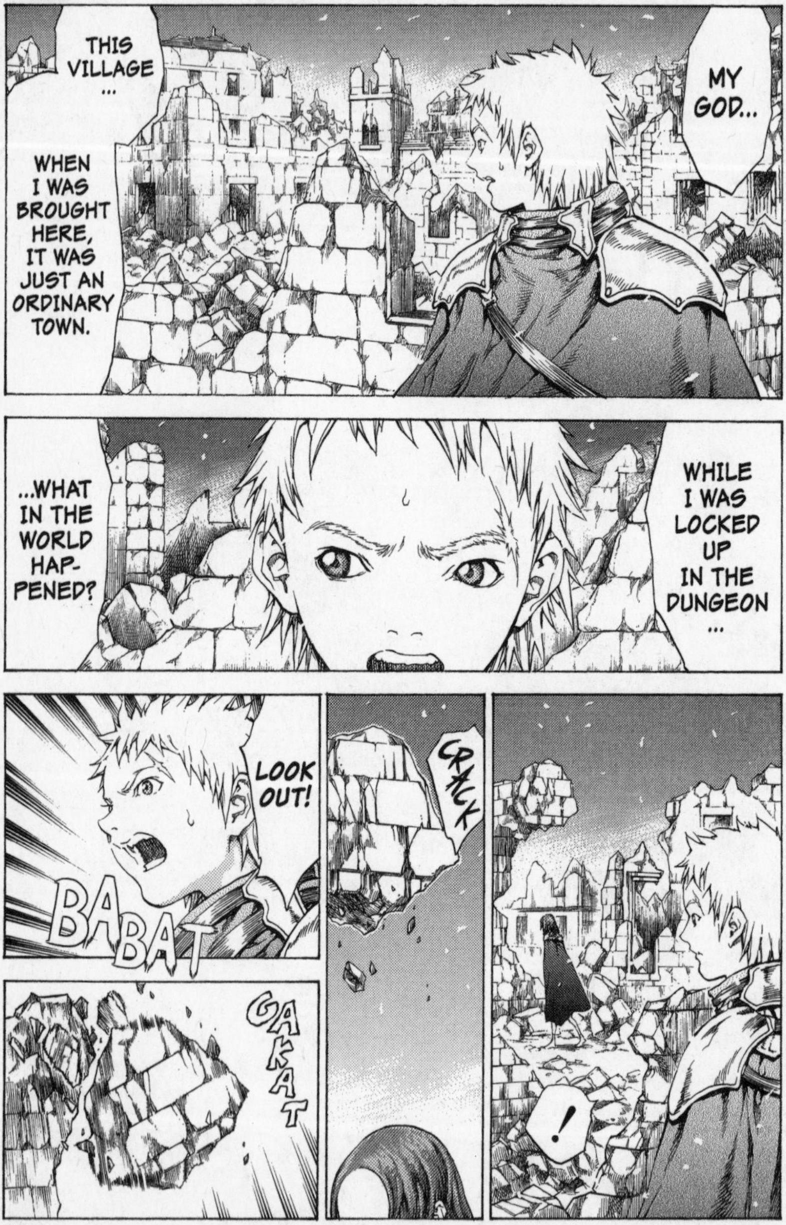
MY GOD...
THIS VILLAGE ...
WHEN I WAS BROUGHT HERE, IT WAS JUST AN ORDINARY TOWN.
WHILE I WAS LOCKED UP IN THE DUNGEON ...
...WHAT IN THE WORLD HAP-PENED?
!
CRACK
LOOK OUT!
BABAT
GAKAT

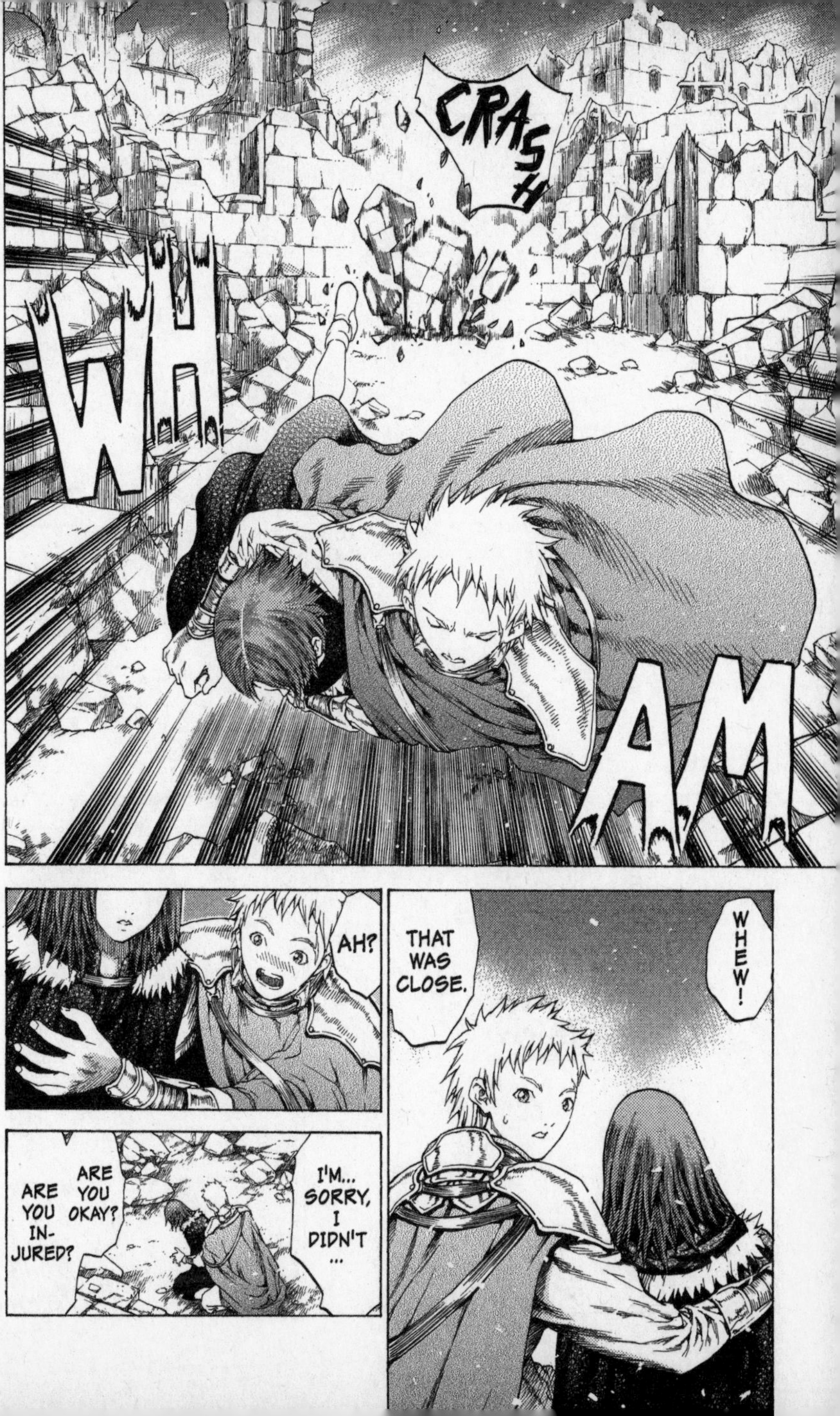
CRASH
WHAM
WHEW!
THAT WAS CLOSE.
AH?
I'M... SORRY, I DIDN'T ...
ARE YOU OKAY?
ARE YOU INJURED?

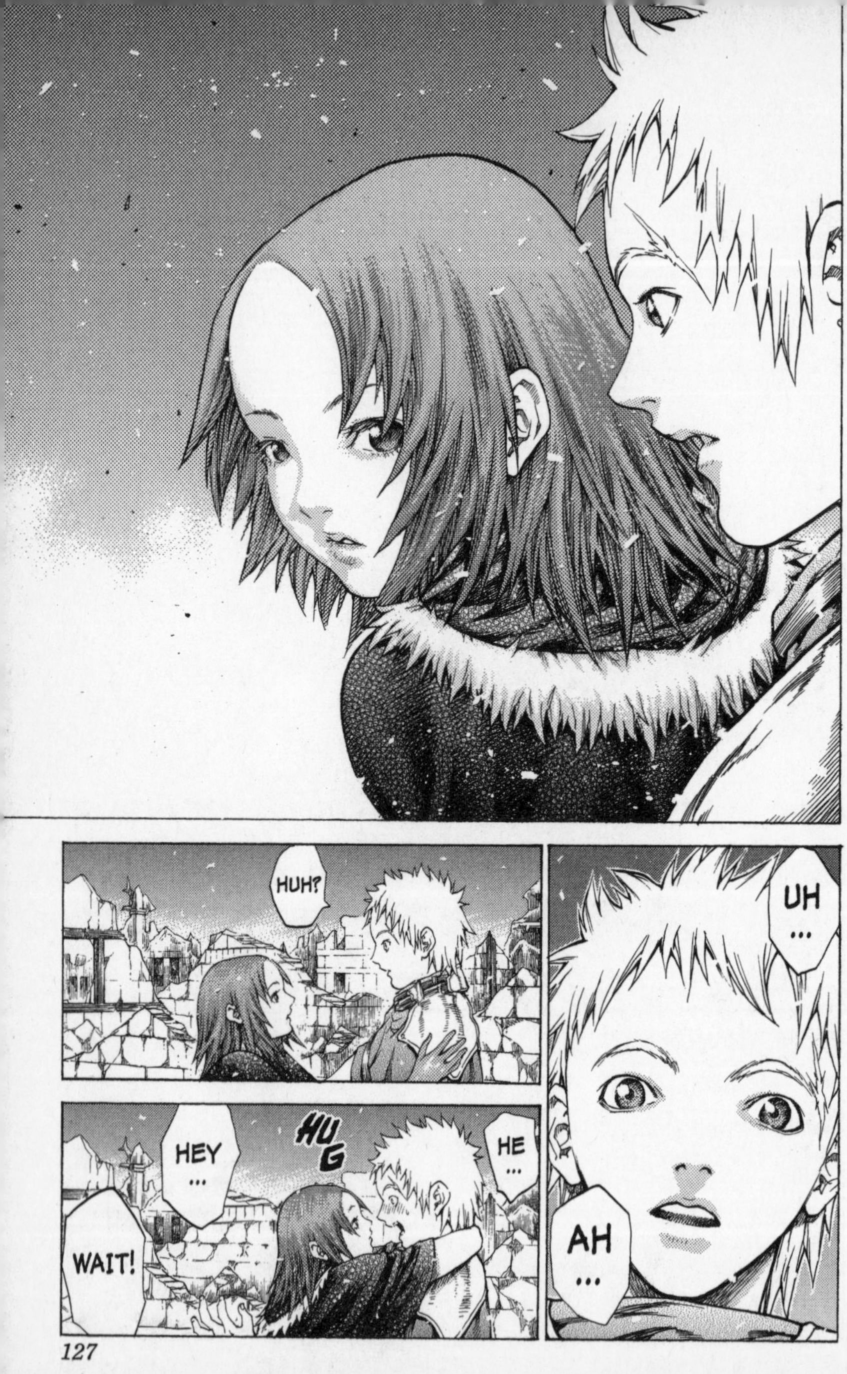
UH ...
AH ...
HUH?
HE ...
HUG
HEY ...
WAIT!

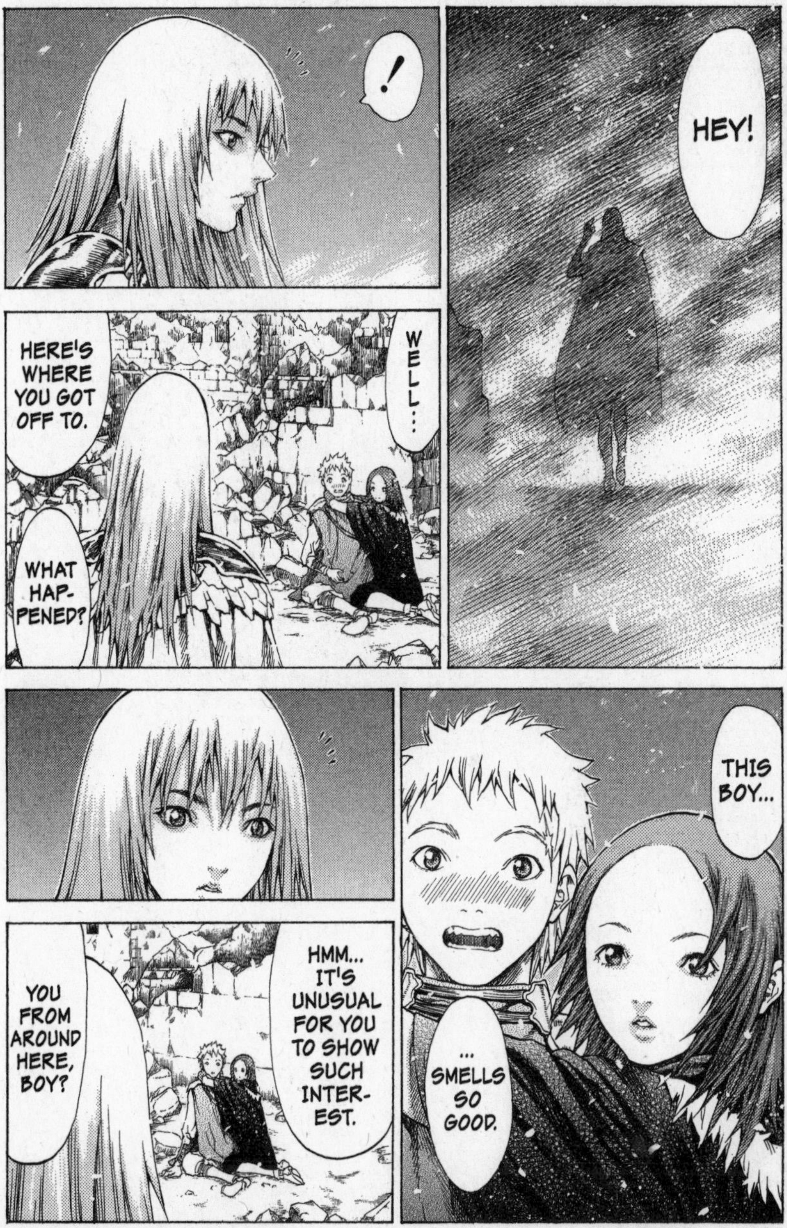
HEY!
!
WELL...
HERE'S WHERE YOU GOT OFF TO.
WHAT HAPPENED?
THIS BOY...
...SMELLS SO GOOD.
HMM... IT'S UNUSUAL FOR YOU TO SHOW SUCH INTEREST.
YOU FROM AROUND HERE, BOY?

READ THIS WAY

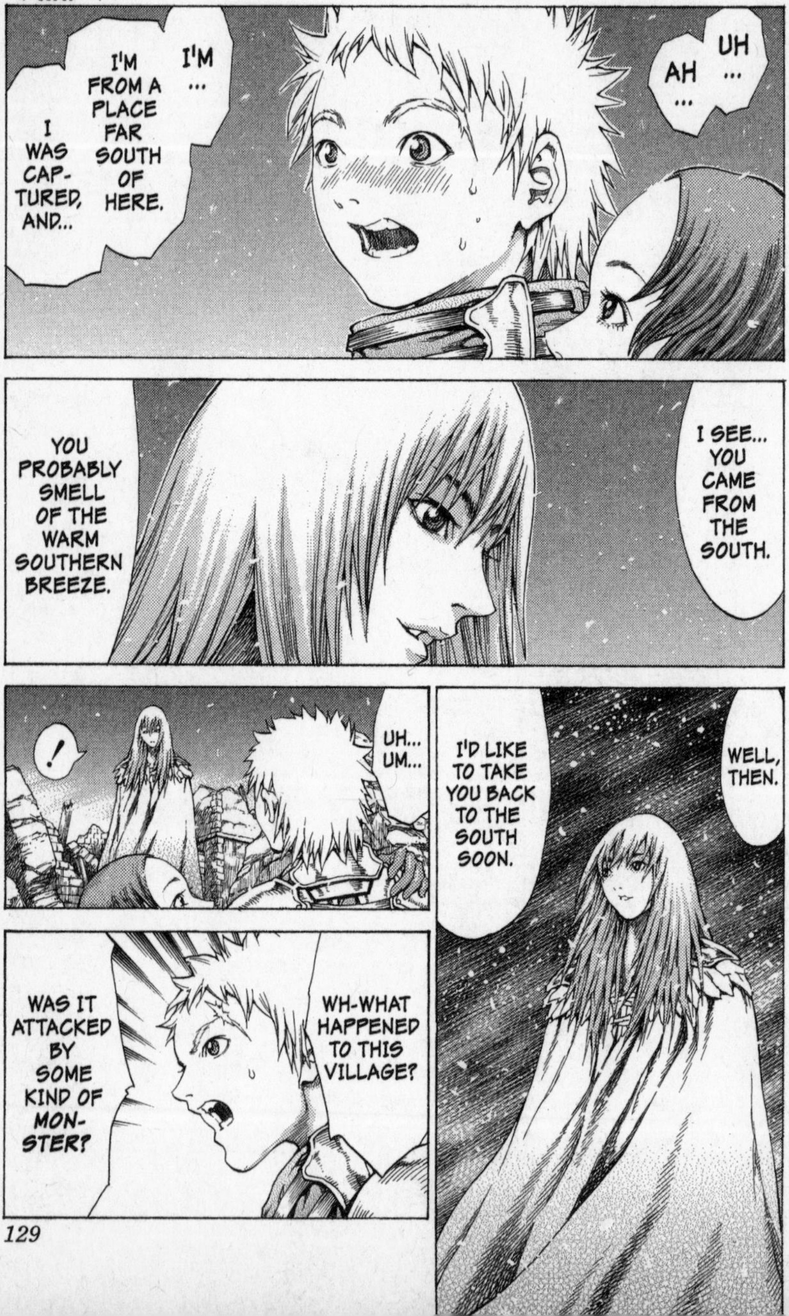
UH ...
AH ...
I'M ...
I'M FROM A PLACE FAR SOUTH OF HERE.
I WAS CAPTURED, AND...
I SEE... YOU CAME FROM THE SOUTH.
YOU PROBABLY SMELL OF THE WARM SOUTHERN BREEZE.
WELL, THEN.
I'D LIKE TO TAKE YOU BACK TO THE SOUTH SOON.
UH... UM...
!
WH-WHAT HAPPENED TO THIS VILLAGE?
WAS IT ATTACKED BY SOME KIND OF MONSTER?

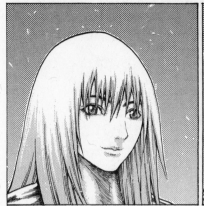

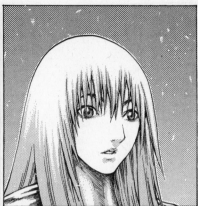

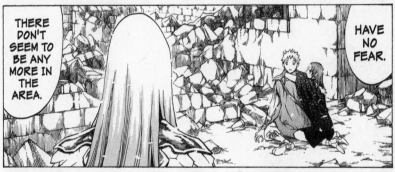

HAVE NO FEAR.
THERE DON'T SEEM TO BE ANY MORE IN THE AREA.
WSSH
AGH!
IT'S COLD OUT HERE.
LET'S HURRY HOME.
YOU CAN COME WITH US.
HUH?
THAT GIRL NEVER GETS CLOSE TO PEOPLE LIKE THIS.
WOULD YOU MIND STAYING WITH HER AWHILE?

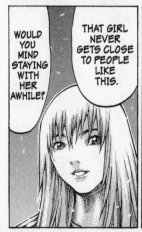

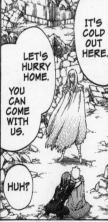

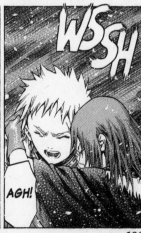

READ THIS WAY

UH ...
AH ... OKAY ...
ZUU
LET'S GO...
...PRISCILLA.

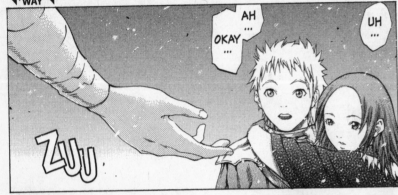

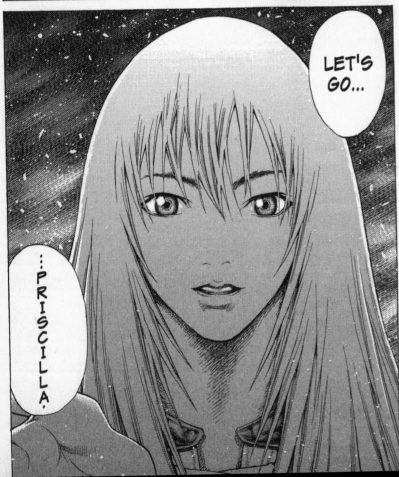

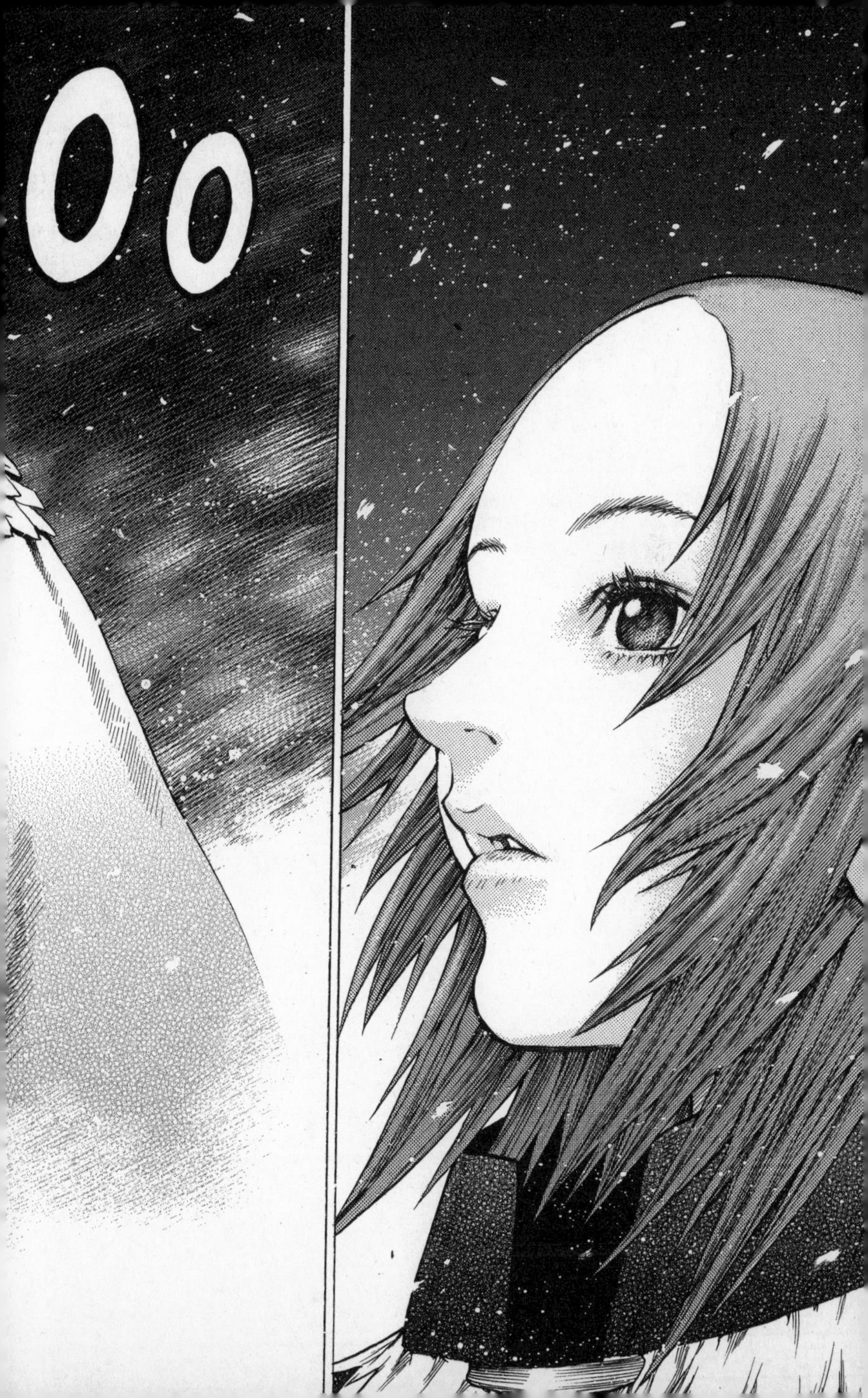
Oo

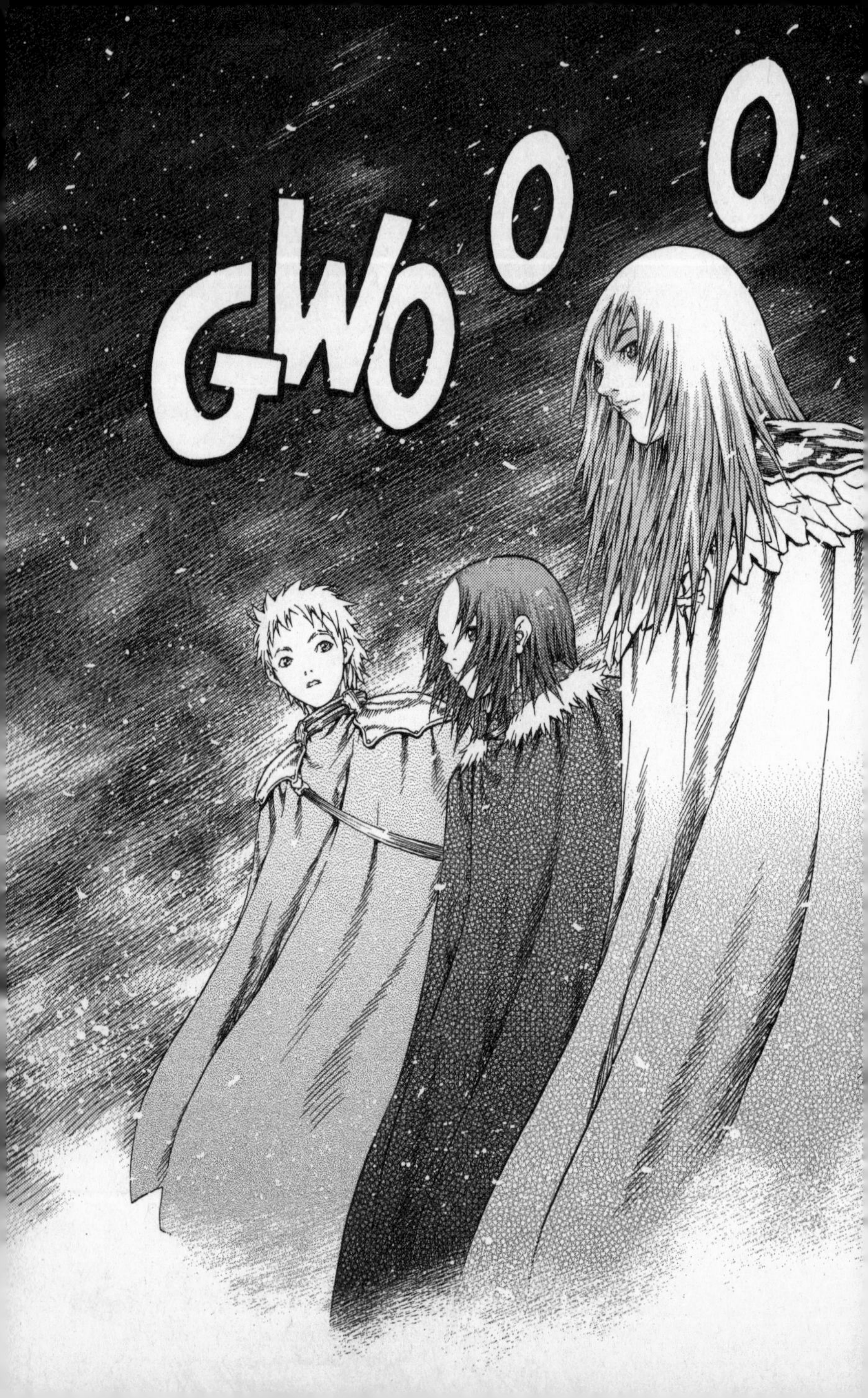
GWO O O

クレイモア

Claymore™

Scene 56: The Battle of the North, Part 7

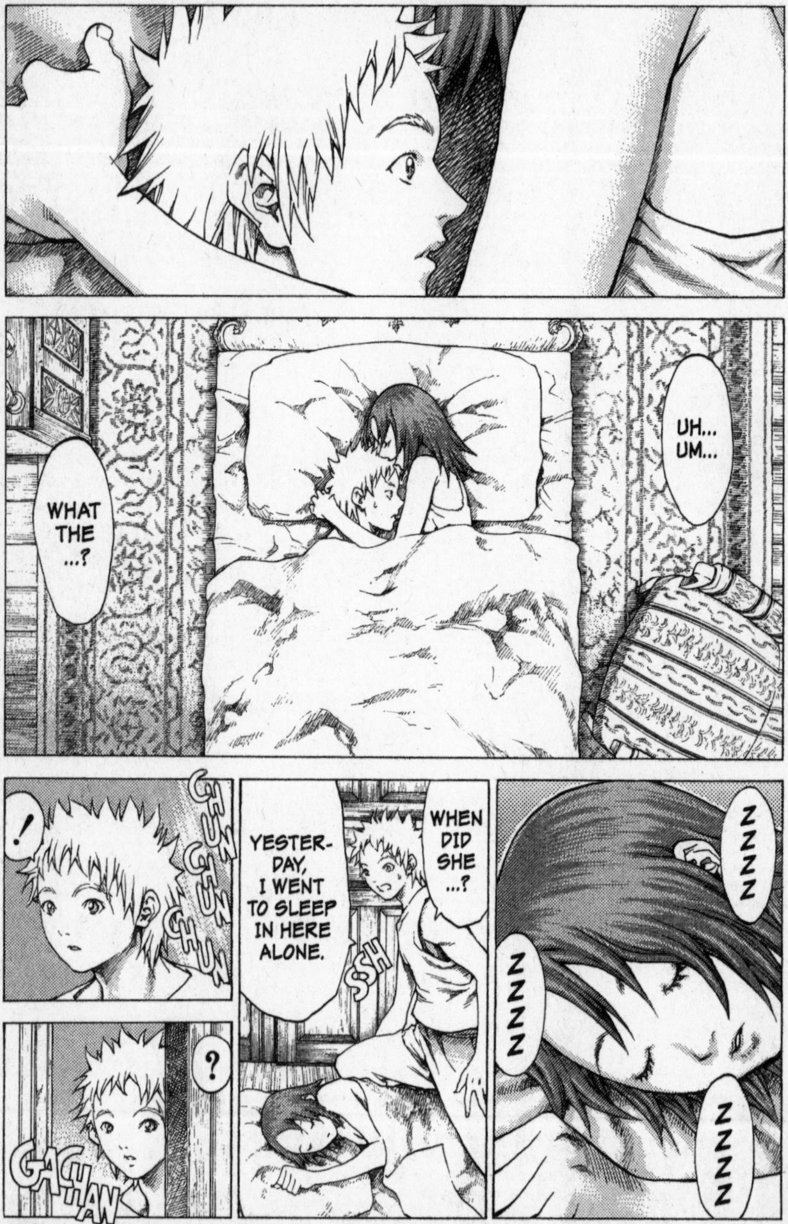
UH... UM...
WHAT THE ...?
ZZZZ
ZZZZ
ZZZZ
WHEN DID SHE ...?
YESTER-DAY, I WENT TO SLEEP IN HERE ALONE.
SSH
!
CHUN CHUN CHUN
?
GACHAN

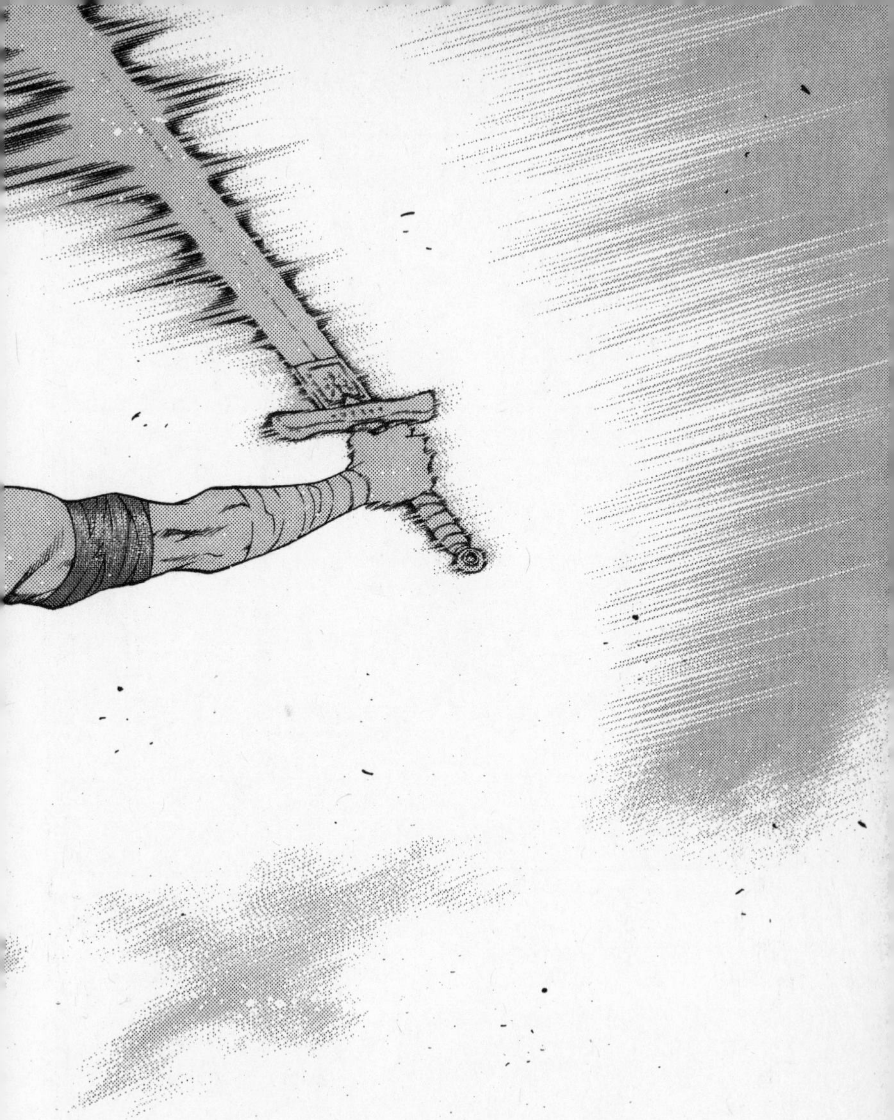

Scene 56: The Battle of the North, Part 7

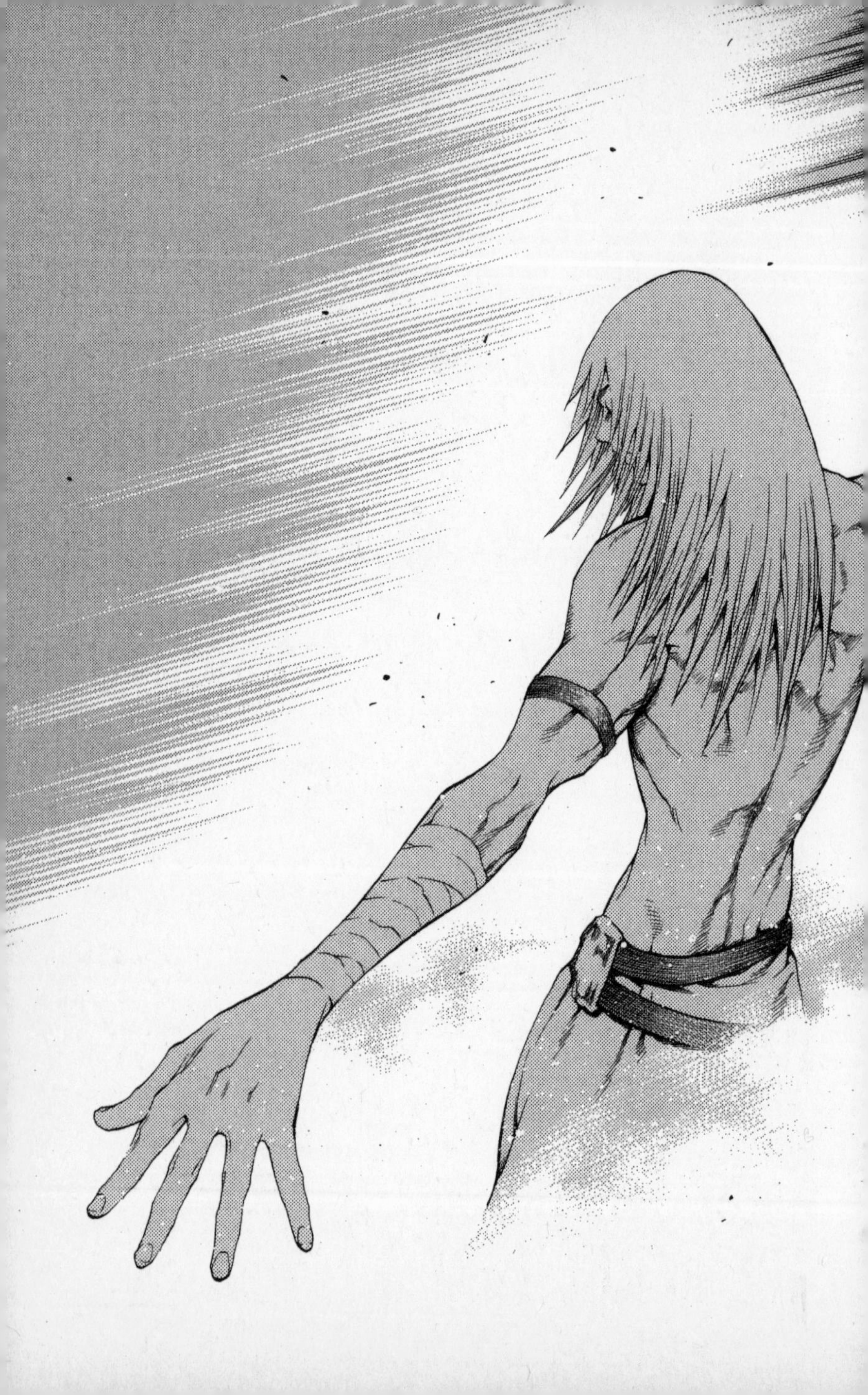

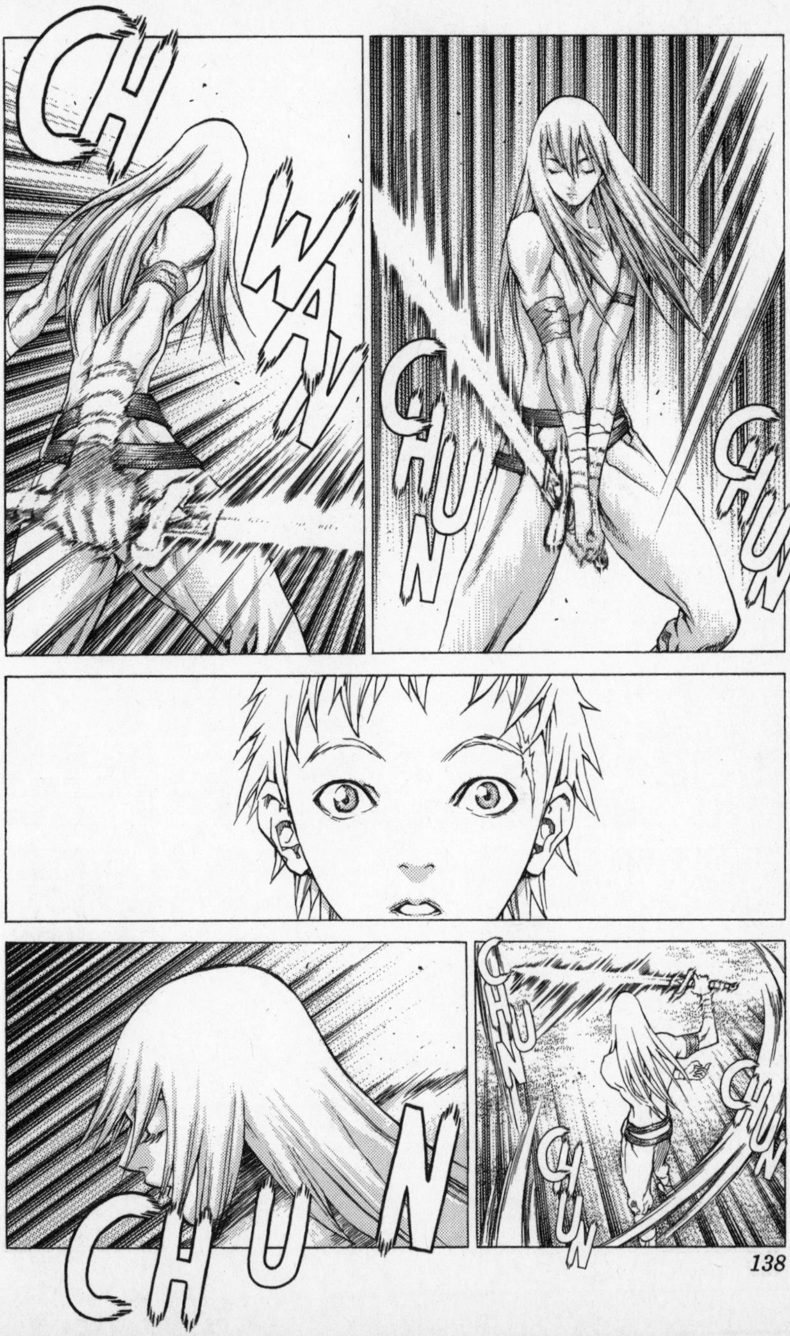
CHUN
CHUN
CHWAN
CHUN
CHUN
CHUN
CHUN

READ THIS WAY

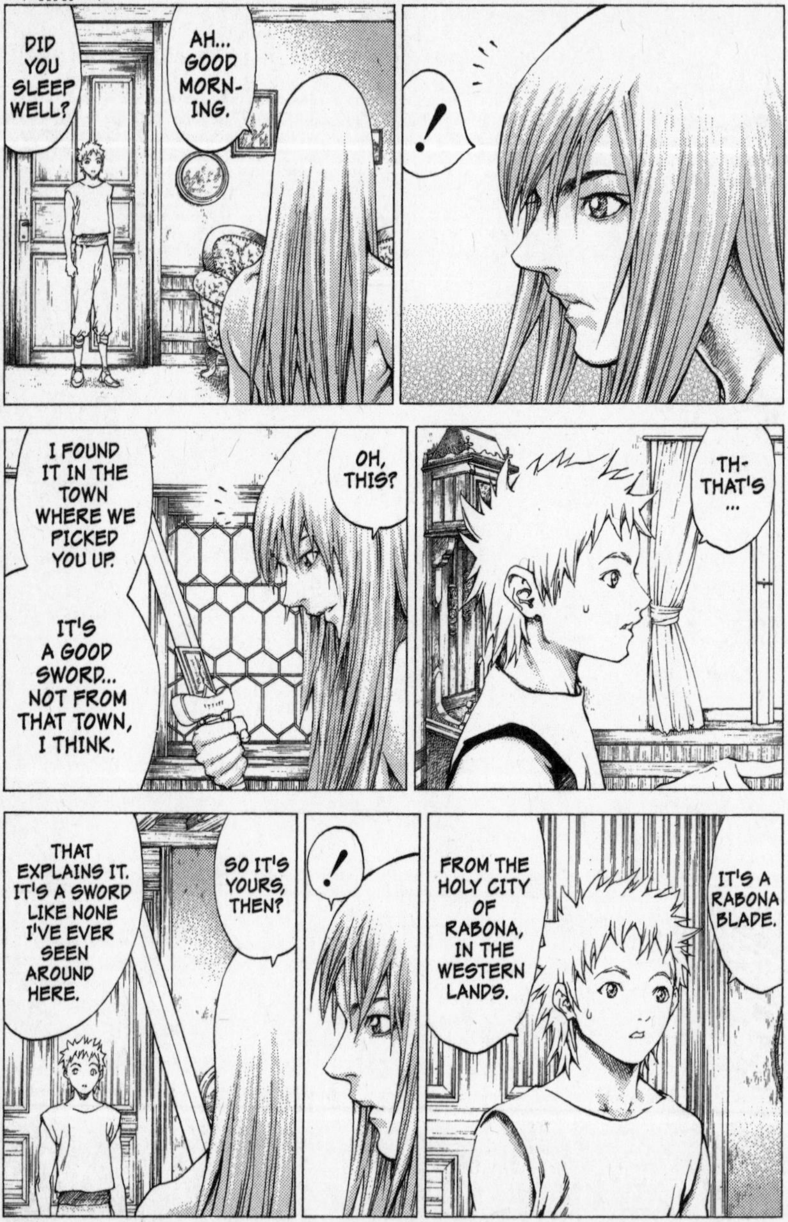
!
AH... GOOD MORN-ING.
DID YOU SLEEP WELL?
TH-THAT'S...
OH, THIS?
I FOUND IT IN THE TOWN WHERE WE PICKED YOU UP.
IT'S A GOOD SWORD... NOT FROM THAT TOWN, I THINK.
IT'S A RABONA BLADE.
FROM THE HOLY CITY OF RABONA, IN THE WESTERN LANDS.
!
SO IT'S YOURS, THEN?
THAT EXPLAINS IT. IT'S A SWORD LIKE NONE I'VE EVER SEEN AROUND HERE.

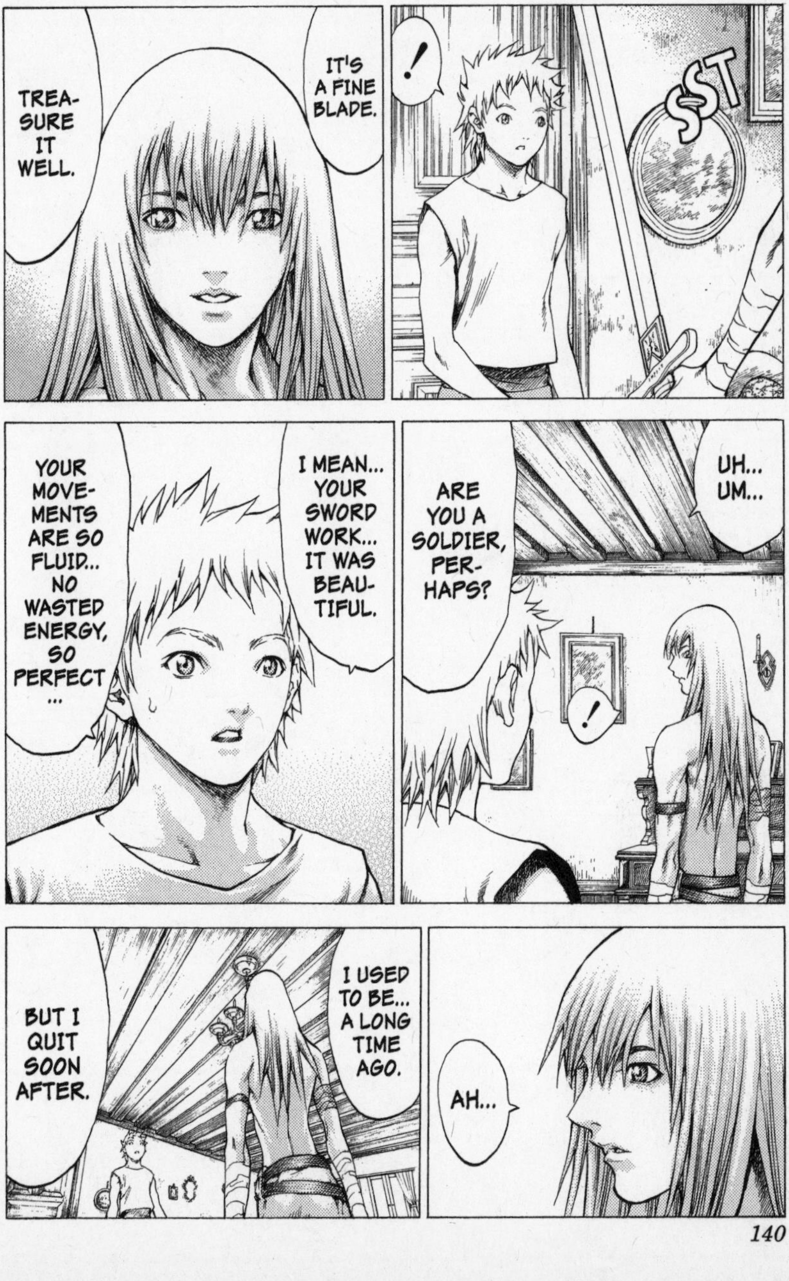
!
SST
IT'S A FINE BLADE.
TREA-SURE IT WELL.
UH... UM...
ARE YOU A SOLDIER, PER-HAPS?
!
I MEAN... YOUR SWORD WORK... IT WAS BEAU-TIFUL.
YOUR MOVE-MENTS ARE SO FLUID... NO WASTED ENERGY, SO PERFECT...
AH...
I USED TO BE... A LONG TIME AGO.
BUT I QUIT SOON AFTER.

READ THIS WAY

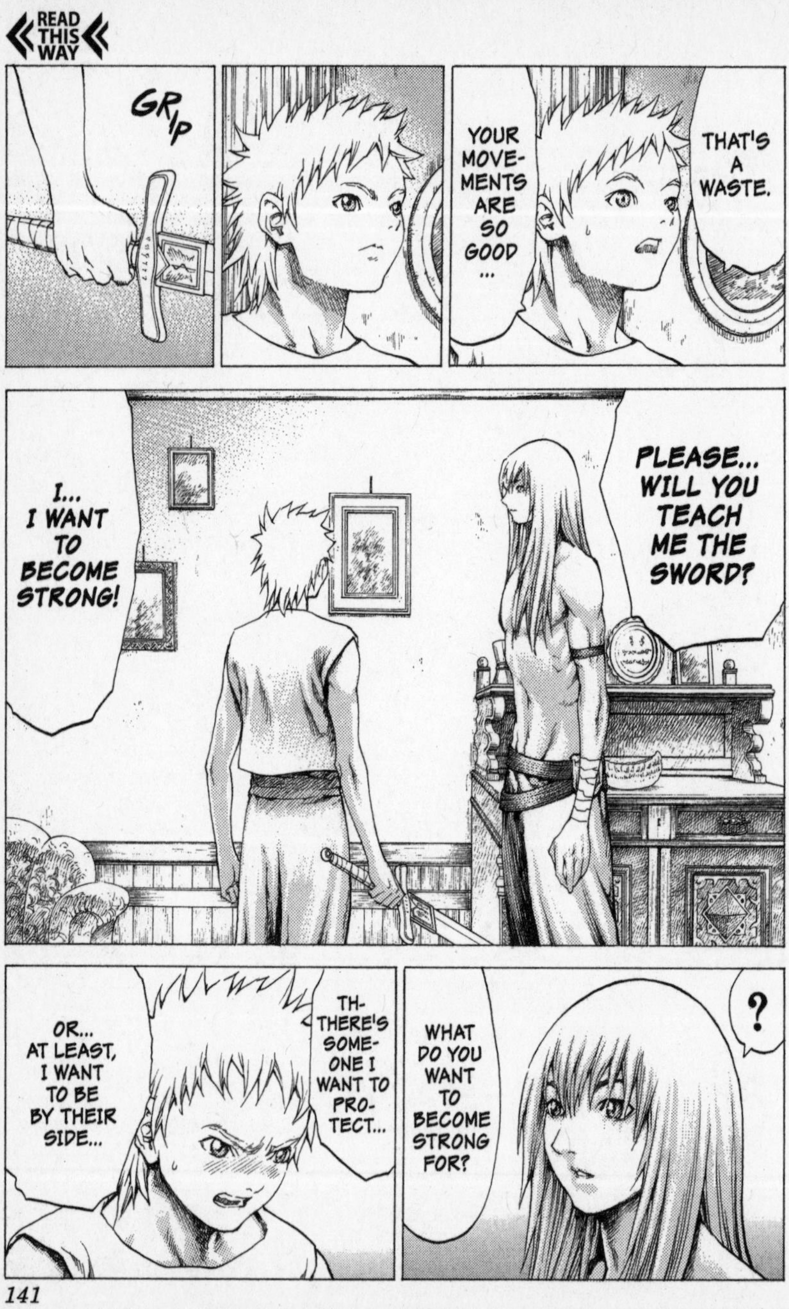
YOUR MOVEMENTS ARE SO GOOD ...
THAT'S A WASTE.
GRIP
PLEASE... WILL YOU TEACH ME THE SWORD?
I... I WANT TO BECOME STRONG!
?
WHAT DO YOU WANT TO BECOME STRONG FOR?
TH-THERE'S SOMEONE I WANT TO PROTECT...
OR... AT LEAST, I WANT TO BE BY THEIR SIDE...

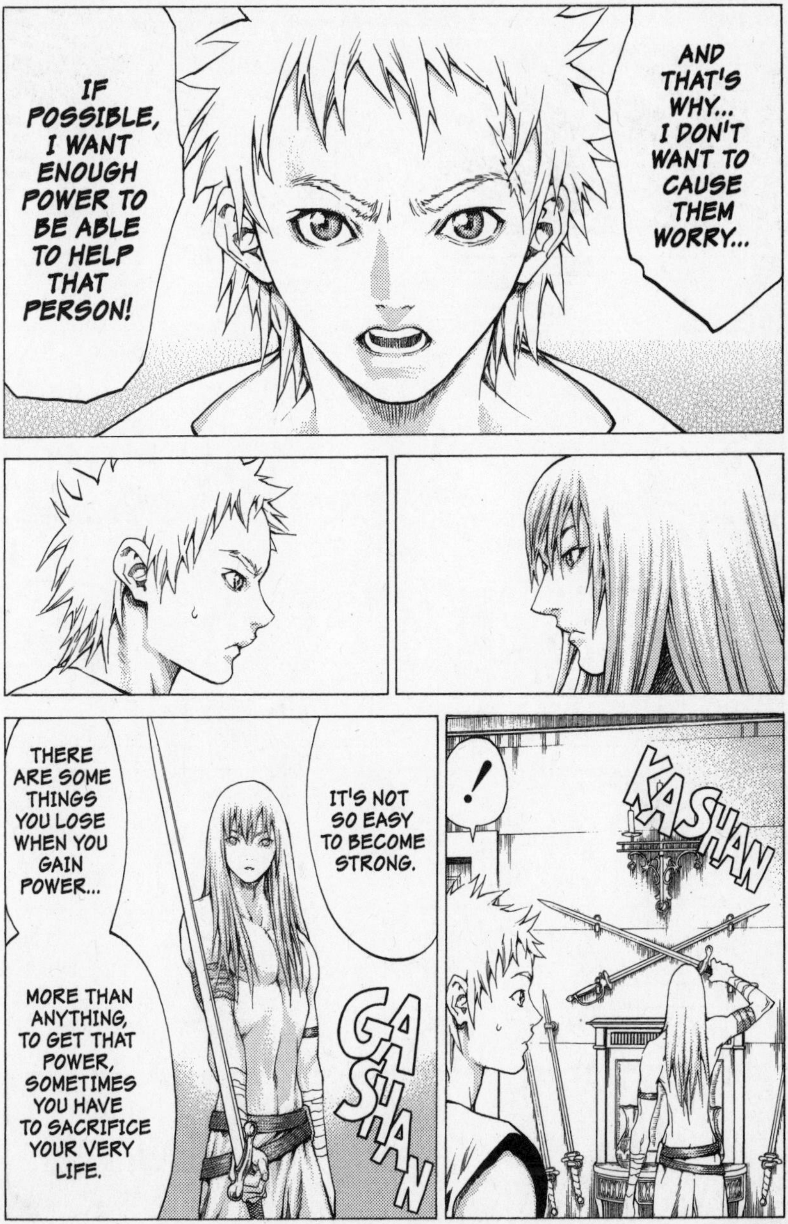
AND THAT'S WHY... I DON'T WANT TO CAUSE THEM WORRY...
IF POSSIBLE, I WANT ENOUGH POWER TO BE ABLE TO HELP THAT PERSON!
!
KASHAN
IT'S NOT SO EASY TO BECOME STRONG.
THERE ARE SOME THINGS YOU LOSE WHEN YOU GAIN POWER...
MORE THAN ANYTHING, TO GET THAT POWER, SOMETIMES YOU HAVE TO SACRIFICE YOUR VERY LIFE.
GASHAN

READ THIS WAY

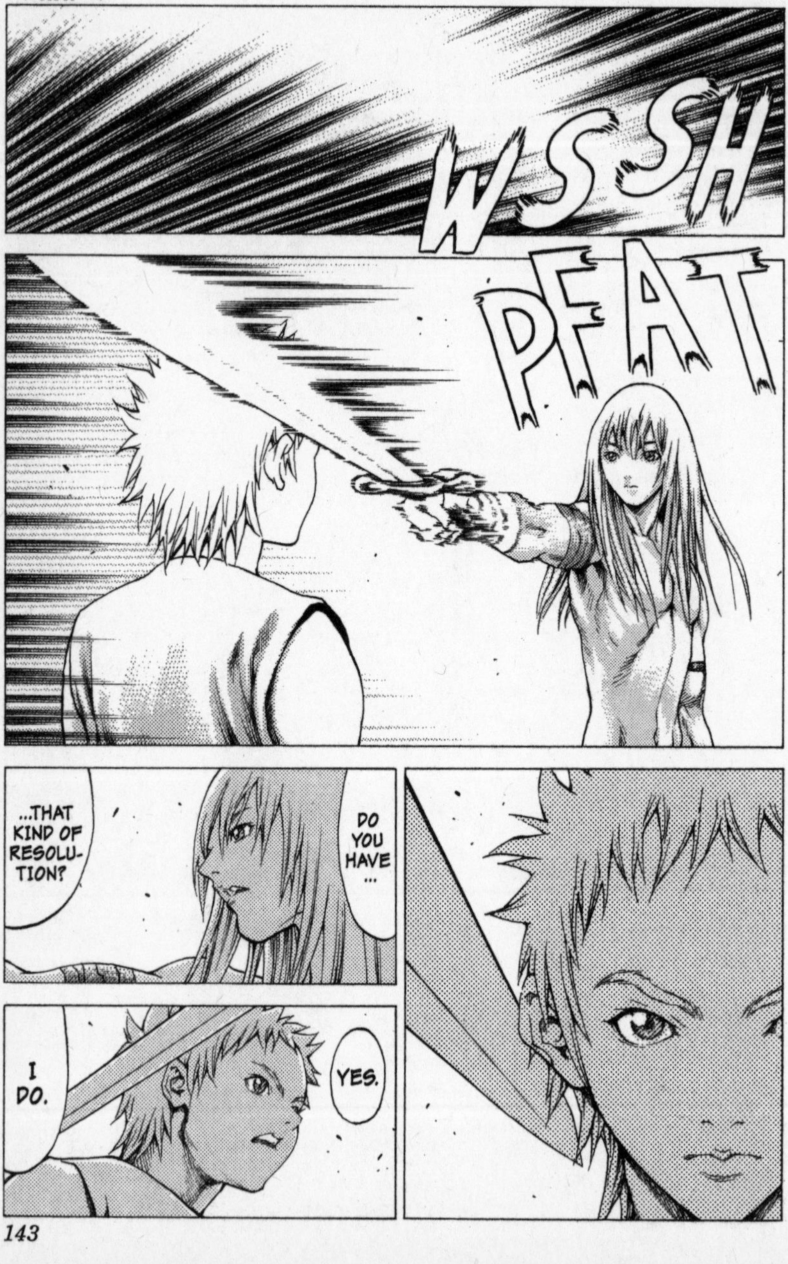
WSSH
PFAT
DO YOU HAVE ...
...THAT KIND OF RESOLUTION?
YES.
I DO.

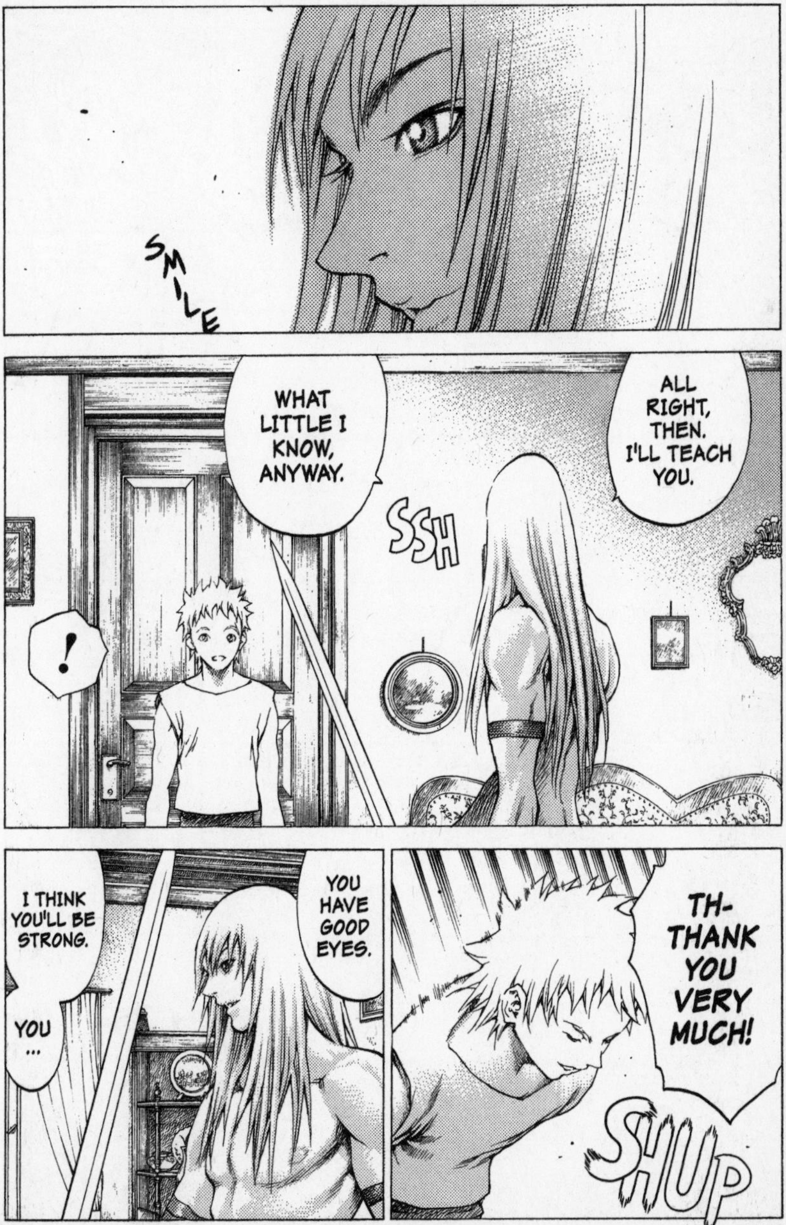
SMILE
ALL RIGHT, THEN. I'LL TEACH YOU.
WHAT LITTLE I KNOW, ANYWAY.
SSH
!
TH-THANK YOU VERY MUCH!
SHUP
YOU HAVE GOOD EYES.
I THINK YOU'LL BE STRONG.
YOU ...

READ THIS WAY

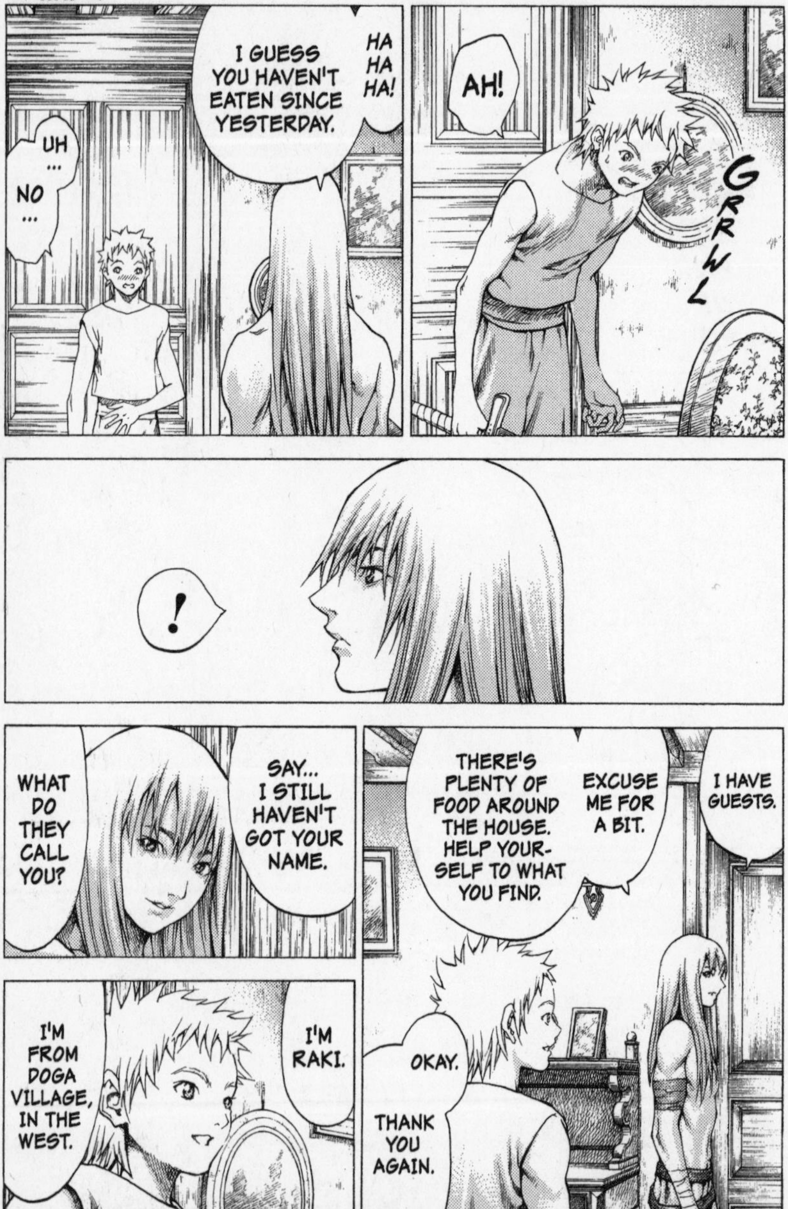
AH!
GRRWL
HA HA HA!
I GUESS YOU HAVEN'T EATEN SINCE YESTERDAY.
UH ... NO ...
!
I HAVE GUESTS.
EXCUSE ME FOR A BIT.
THERE'S PLENTY OF FOOD AROUND THE HOUSE. HELP YOURSELF TO WHAT YOU FIND.
OKAY.
THANK YOU AGAIN.
SAY... I STILL HAVEN'T GOT YOUR NAME.
WHAT DO THEY CALL YOU?
I'M RAKI.
I'M FROM DOGA VILLAGE, IN THE WEST.

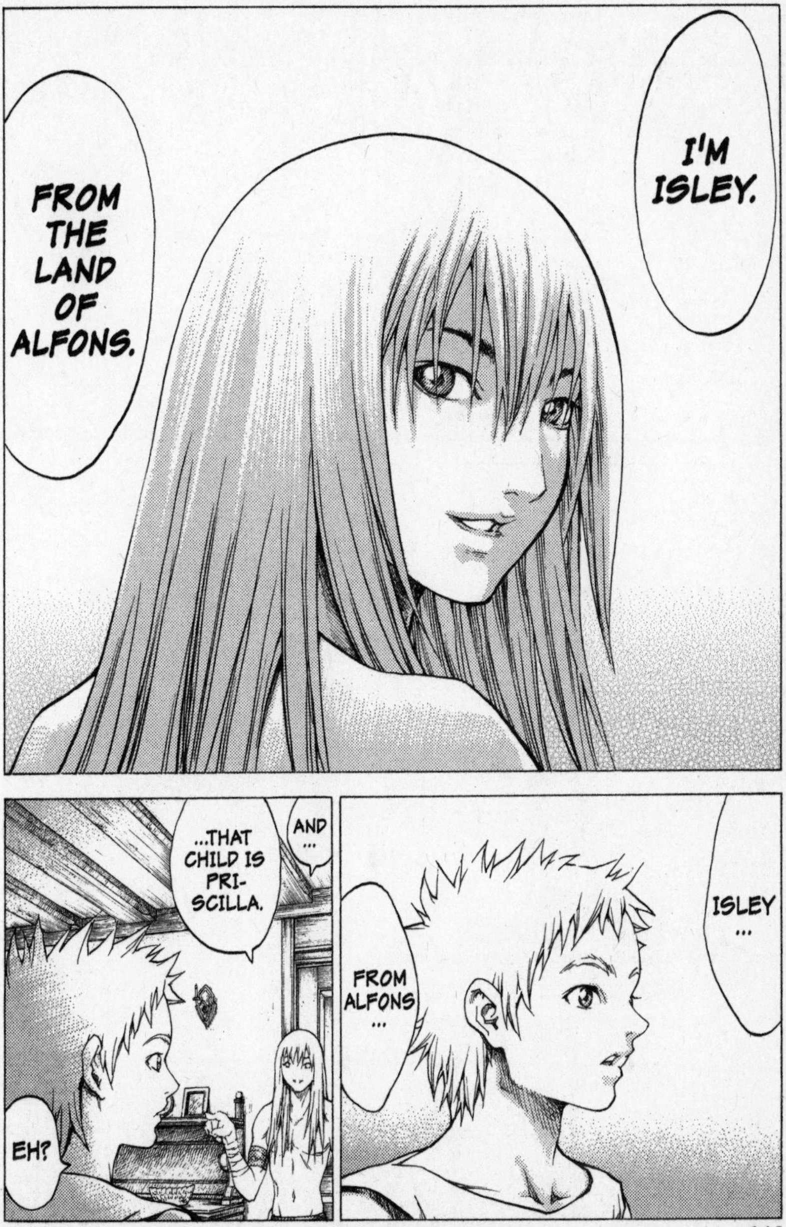
I'M ISLEY.
FROM THE LAND OF ALFONS.
ISLEY ...
FROM ALFONS ...
AND ...
...THAT CHILD IS PRI-SCILLA.
EH?

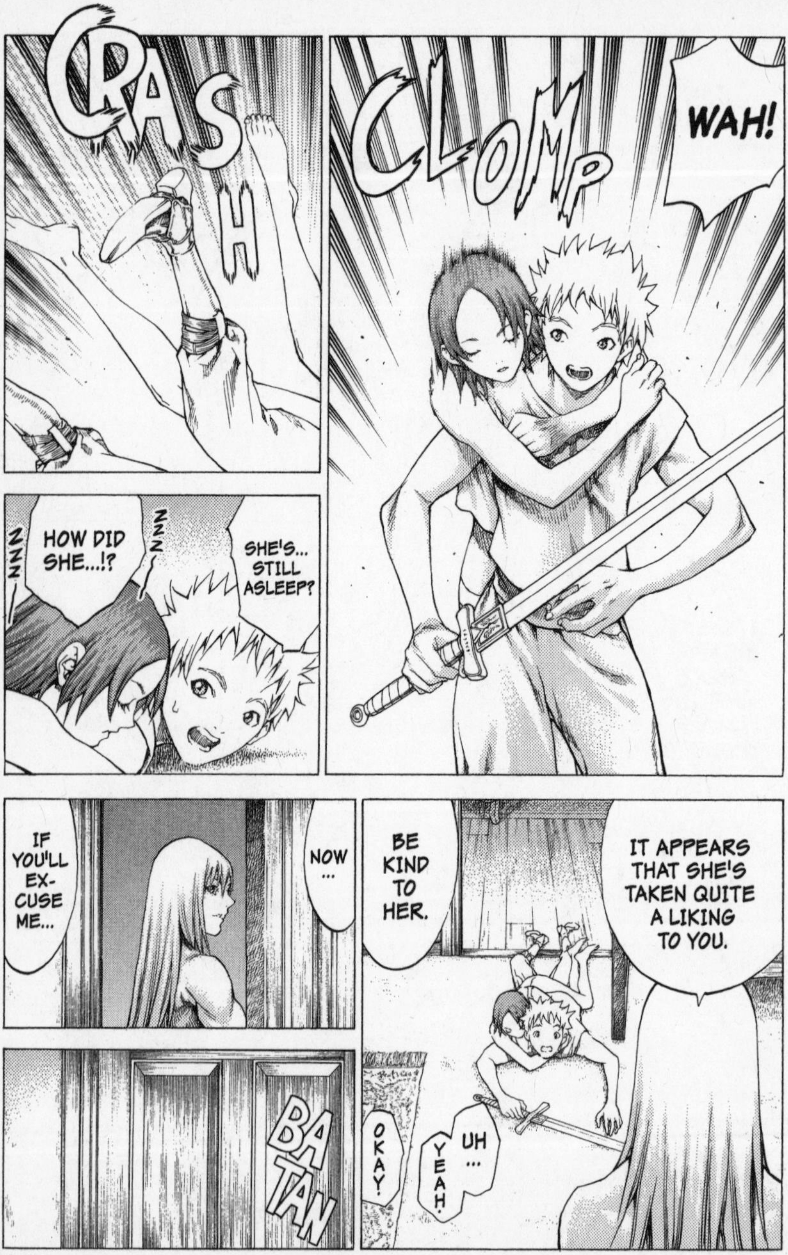
CLOMP
WAH!
CRASH
SHE'S... STILL ASLEEP?
ZZZ
HOW DID SHE...!?
ZZZ
IT APPEARS THAT SHE'S TAKEN QUITE A LIKING TO YOU.
BE KIND TO HER.
UH... YEAH.
OKAY!
NOW...
IF YOU'LL EX-CUSE ME...
BATAN

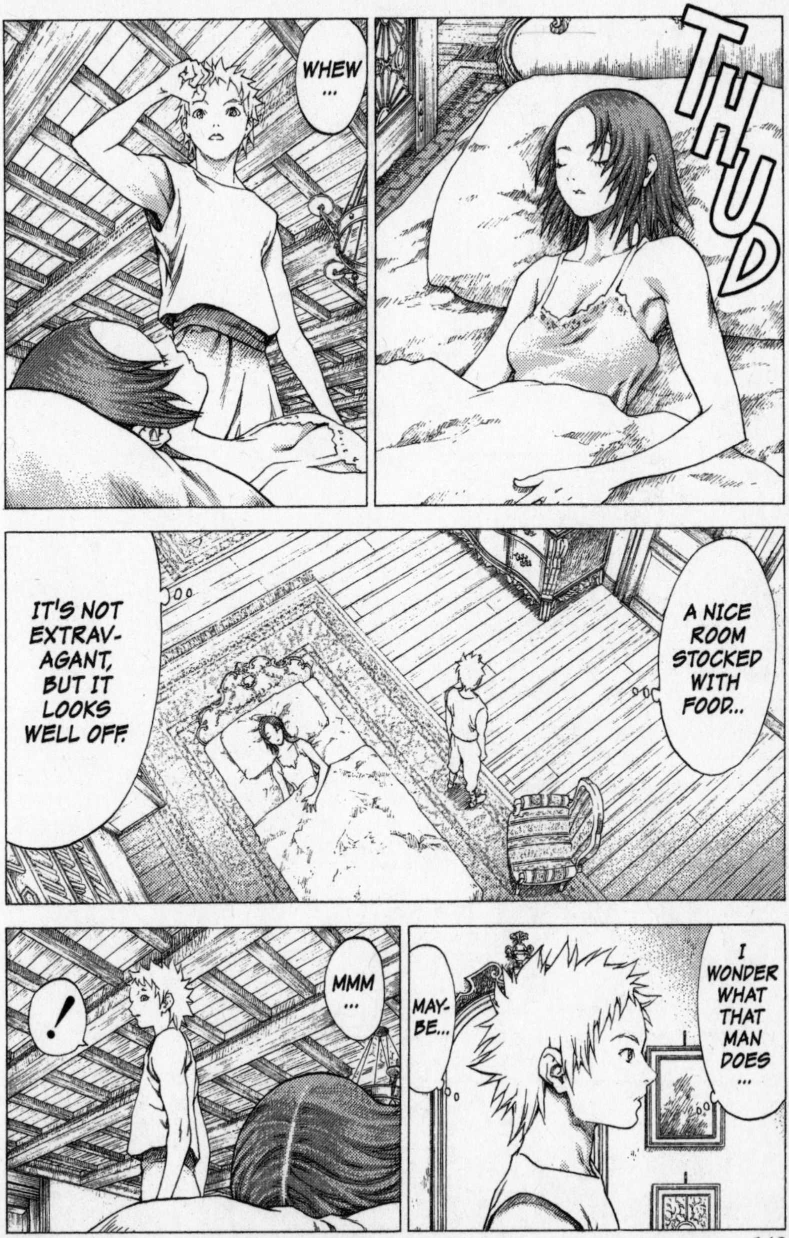
THUD
WHEW...
A NICE ROOM STOCKED WITH FOOD...
IT'S NOT EXTRAVAGANT, BUT IT LOOKS WELL OFF.
I WONDER WHAT THAT MAN DOES...
MAYBE...
MMM...
!

READ THIS WAY

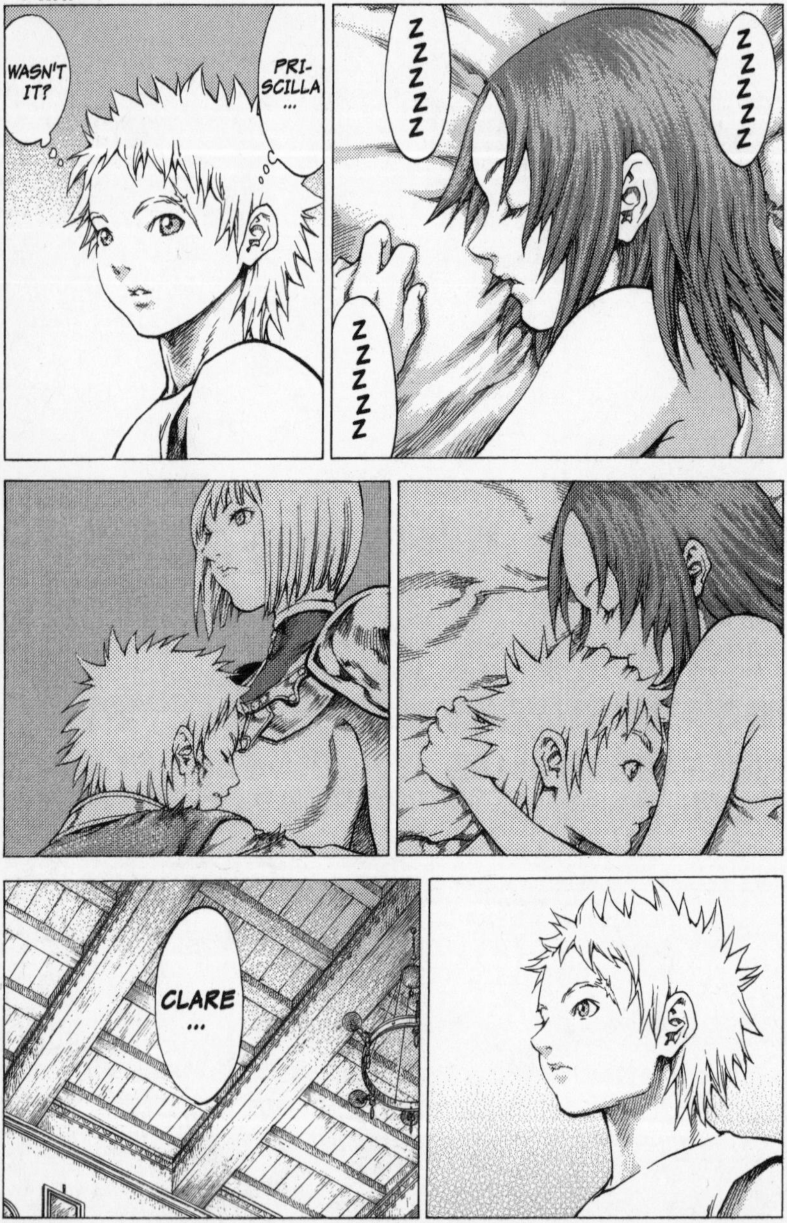
ZZZZZ
ZZZZZ
ZZZZZ
PRI-SCILLA...
WASN'T IT?
CLARE...

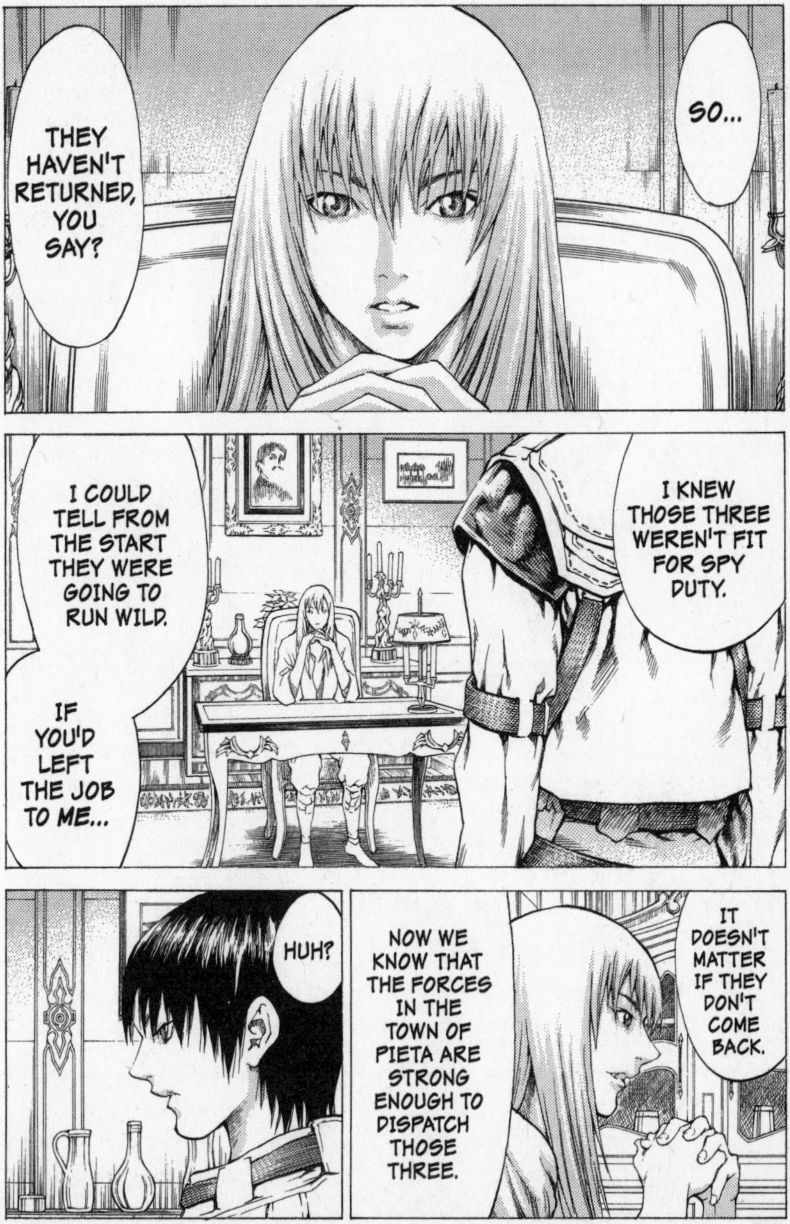
SO...
THEY HAVEN'T RETURNED, YOU SAY?
I KNEW THOSE THREE WEREN'T FIT FOR SPY DUTY.
I COULD TELL FROM THE START THEY WERE GOING TO RUN WILD.
IF YOU'D LEFT THE JOB TO ME...
IT DOESN'T MATTER IF THEY DON'T COME BACK.
NOW WE KNOW THAT THE FORCES IN THE TOWN OF PIETA ARE STRONG ENOUGH TO DISPATCH THOSE THREE.
HUH?

READ THIS WAY

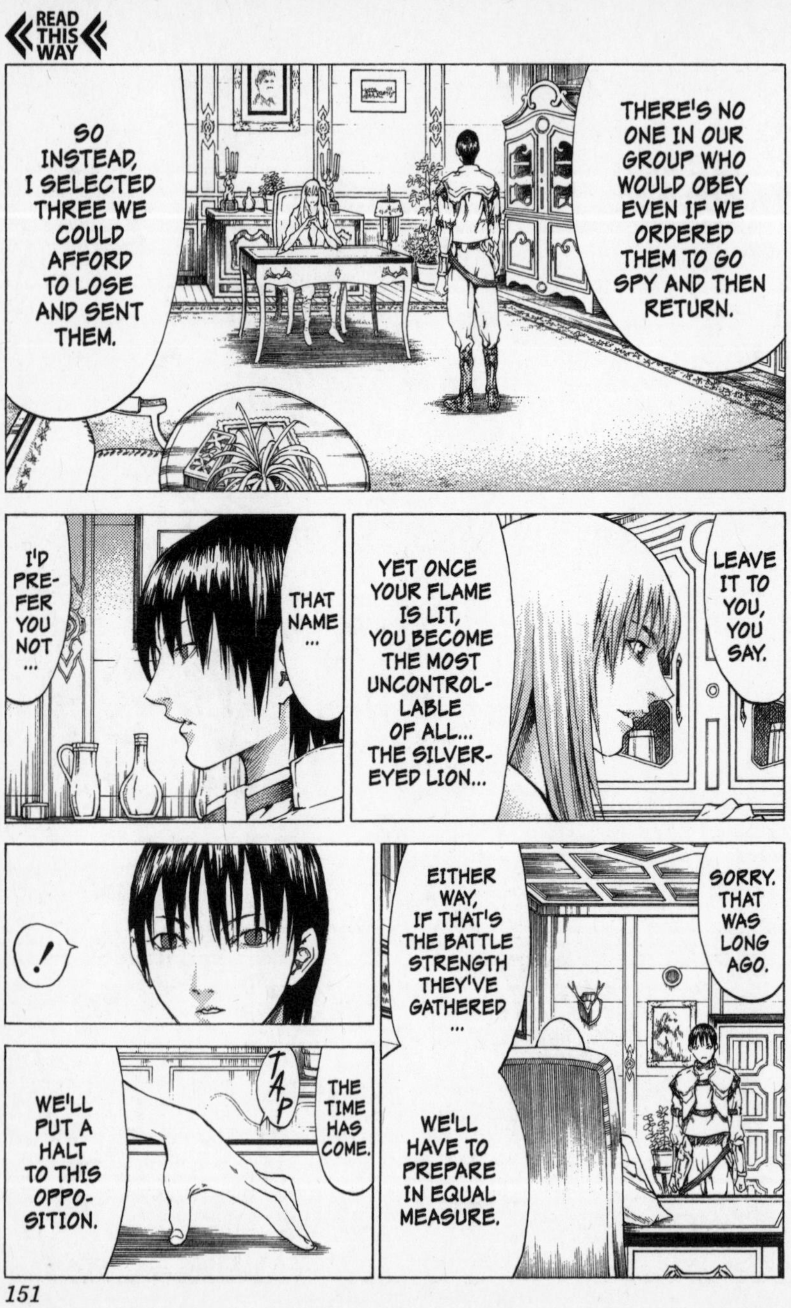
THERE'S NO ONE IN OUR GROUP WHO WOULD OBEY EVEN IF WE ORDERED THEM TO GO SPY AND THEN RETURN.
SO INSTEAD, I SELECTED THREE WE COULD AFFORD TO LOSE AND SENT THEM.
LEAVE IT TO YOU, YOU SAY.
YET ONCE YOUR FLAME IS LIT, YOU BECOME THE MOST UNCONTROL-LABLE OF ALL... THE SILVER-EYED LION...
THAT NAME...
I'D PRE-FER YOU NOT...
SORRY. THAT WAS LONG AGO.
EITHER WAY, IF THAT'S THE BATTLE STRENGTH THEY'VE GATHERED...
WE'LL HAVE TO PREPARE IN EQUAL MEASURE.
!
TAP
THE TIME HAS COME.
WE'LL PUT A HALT TO THIS OPPO-SITION.

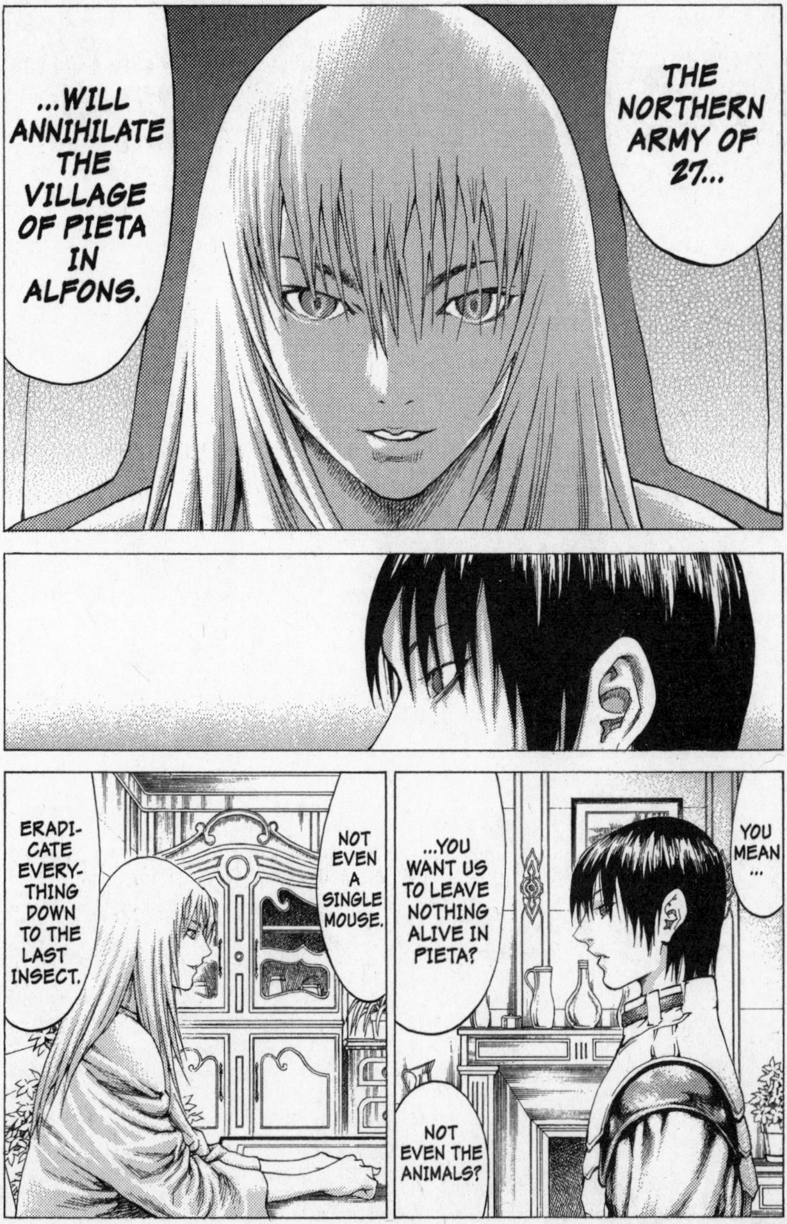
THE NORTHERN ARMY OF 27...
...WILL ANNIHILATE THE VILLAGE OF PIETA IN ALFONS.
YOU MEAN...
...YOU WANT US TO LEAVE NOTHING ALIVE IN PIETA?
NOT EVEN THE ANIMALS?
NOT EVEN A SINGLE MOUSE.
ERADI-CATE EVERY-THING DOWN TO THE LAST INSECT.

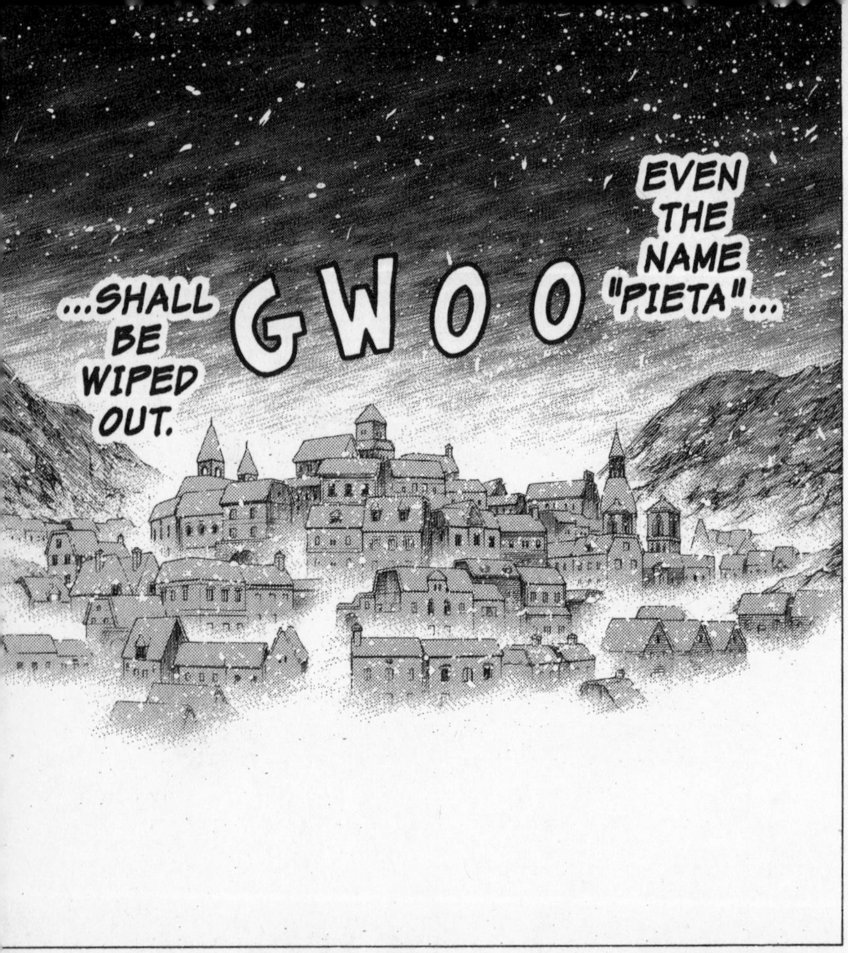
EVEN THE NAME "PIETA"...
GWOO
...SHALL BE WIPED OUT.

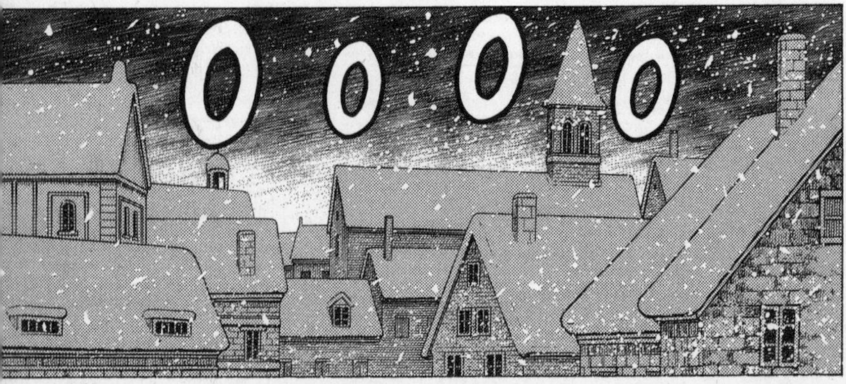
OOOO

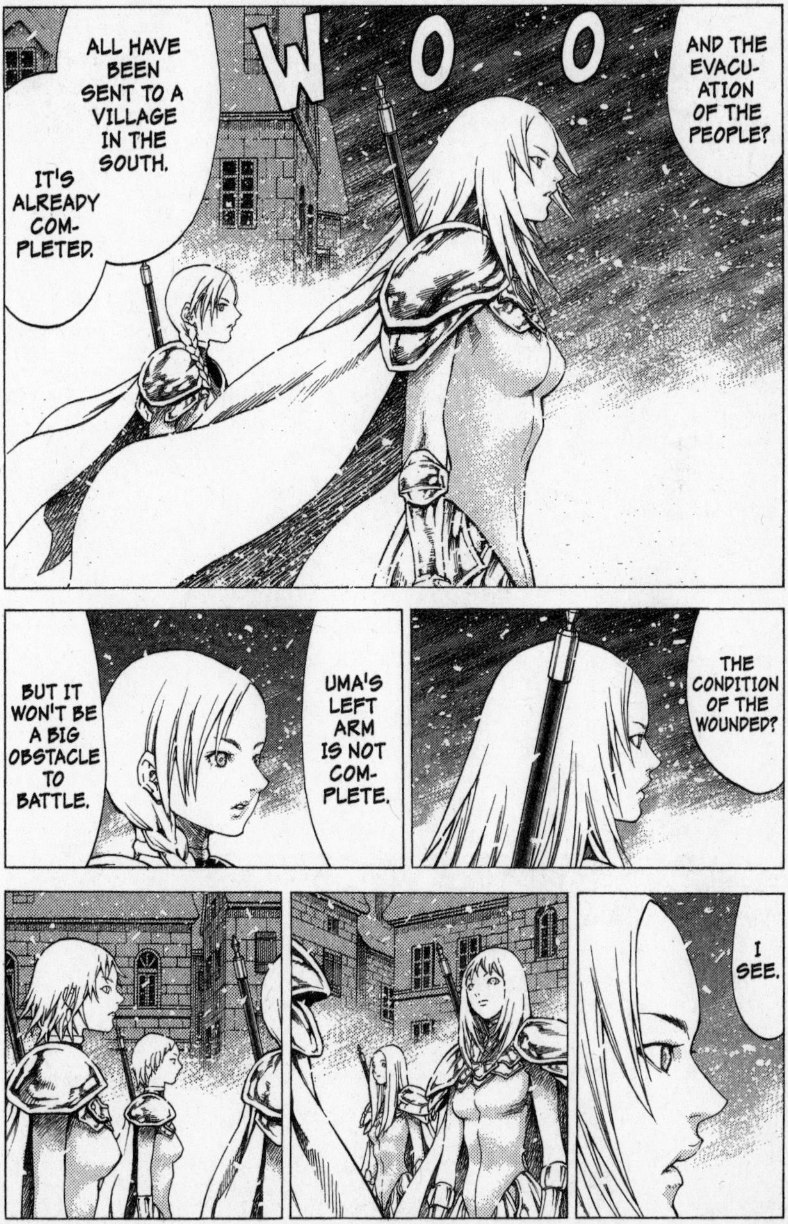
AND THE EVACUATION OF THE PEOPLE?
WOO
ALL HAVE BEEN SENT TO A VILLAGE IN THE SOUTH.
IT'S ALREADY COMPLETED.
THE CONDITION OF THE WOUNDED?
UMA'S LEFT ARM IS NOT COMPLETE.
BUT IT WON'T BE A BIG OBSTACLE TO BATTLE.
I SEE.

READ THIS WAY

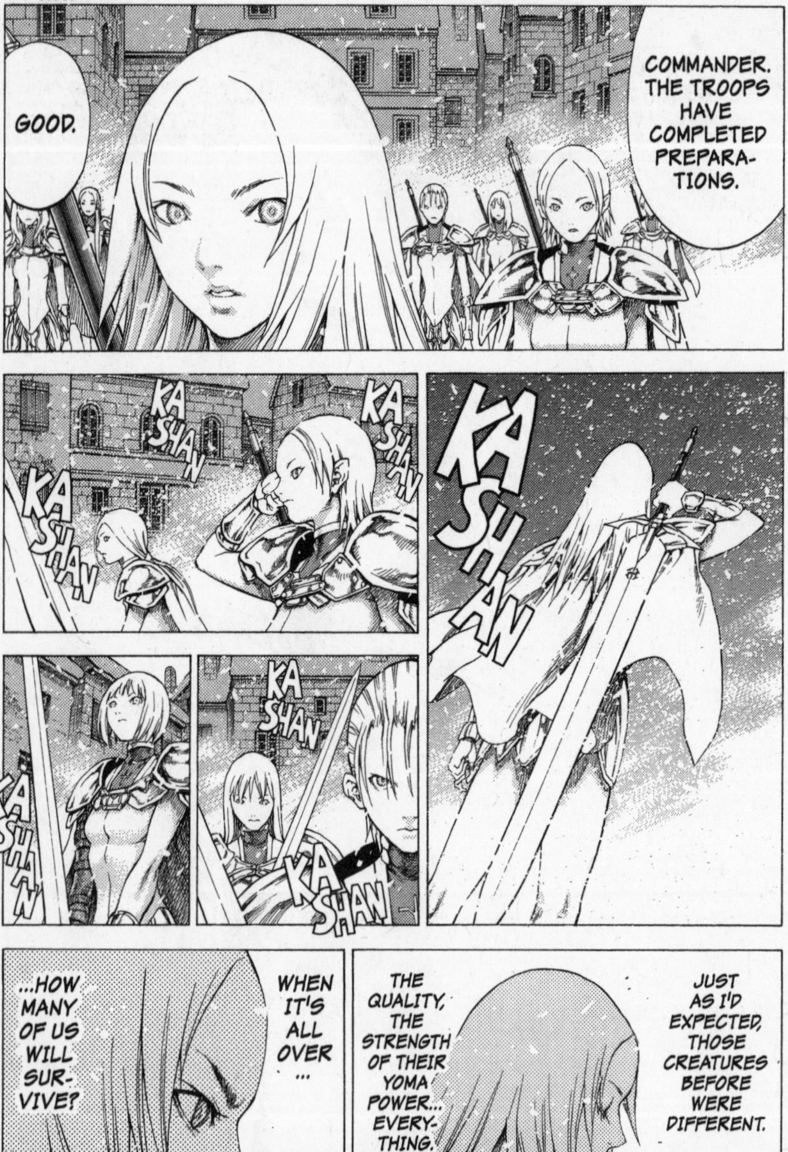
COMMANDER. THE TROOPS HAVE COMPLETED PREPARATIONS.
GOOD.
KA SHAN
KA SHAN
KA SHAN
KA SHAN
KA SHAN
KA SHAN
KA SHAN
JUST AS I'D EXPECTED, THOSE CREATURES BEFORE WERE DIFFERENT.
THE QUALITY, THE STRENGTH OF THEIR YOMA POWER... EVERYTHING.
WHEN IT'S ALL OVER...
...HOW MANY OF US WILL SURVIVE?

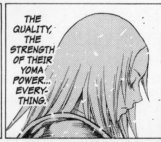

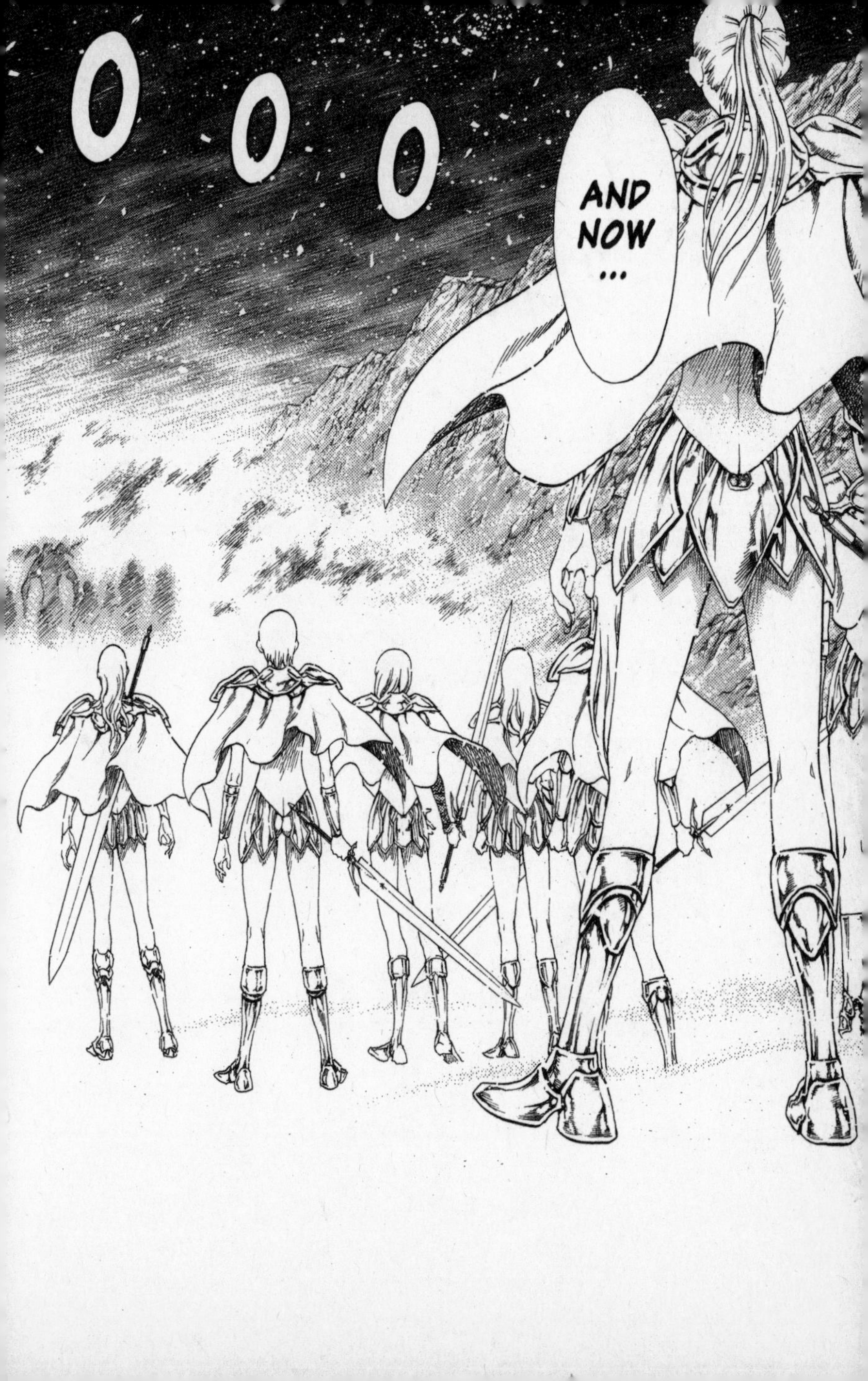
AND NOW ...
OOO

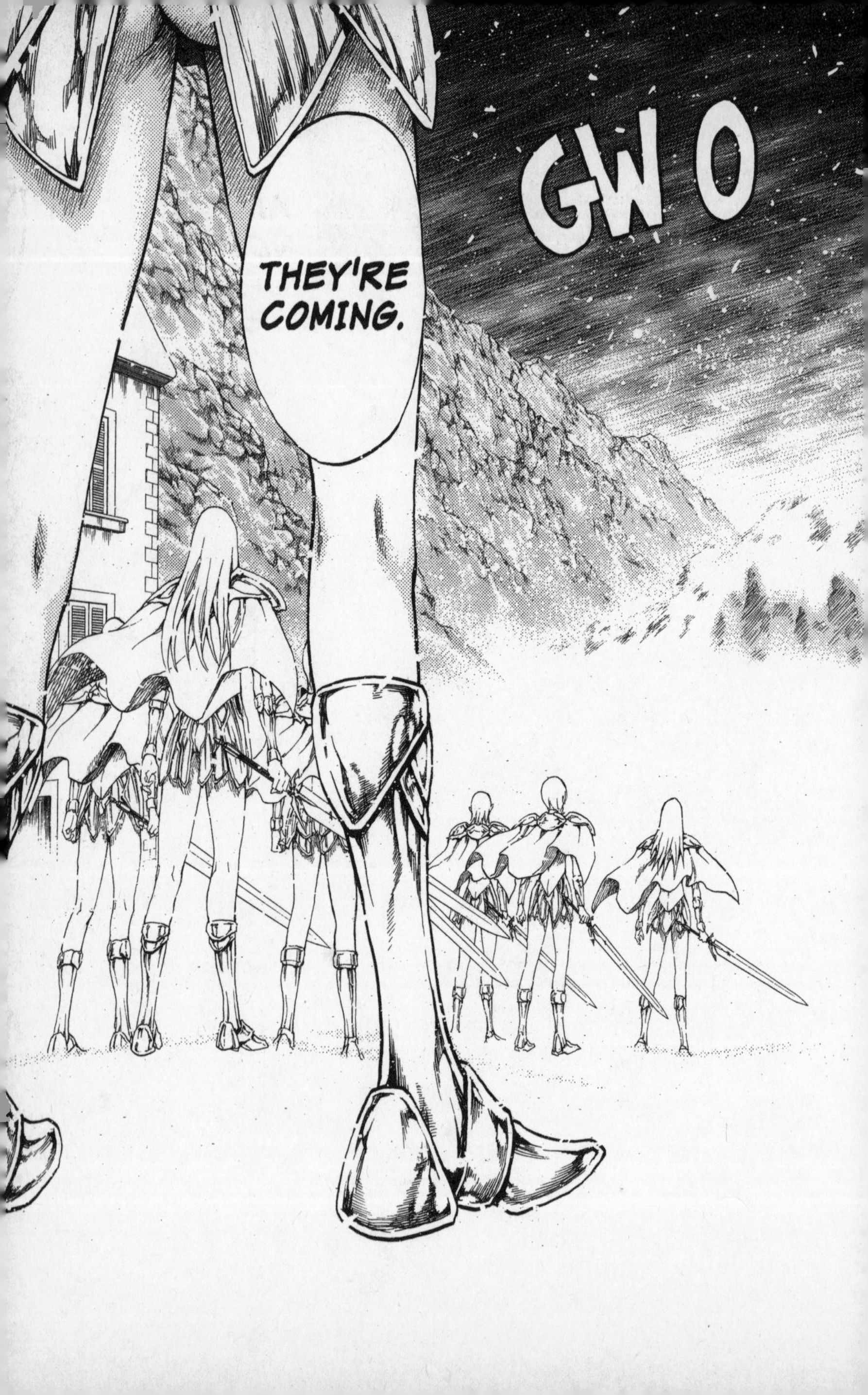
GW O
THEY'RE COMING.

SCENE 57: THE ASSAULT ON PIETA, PART 1

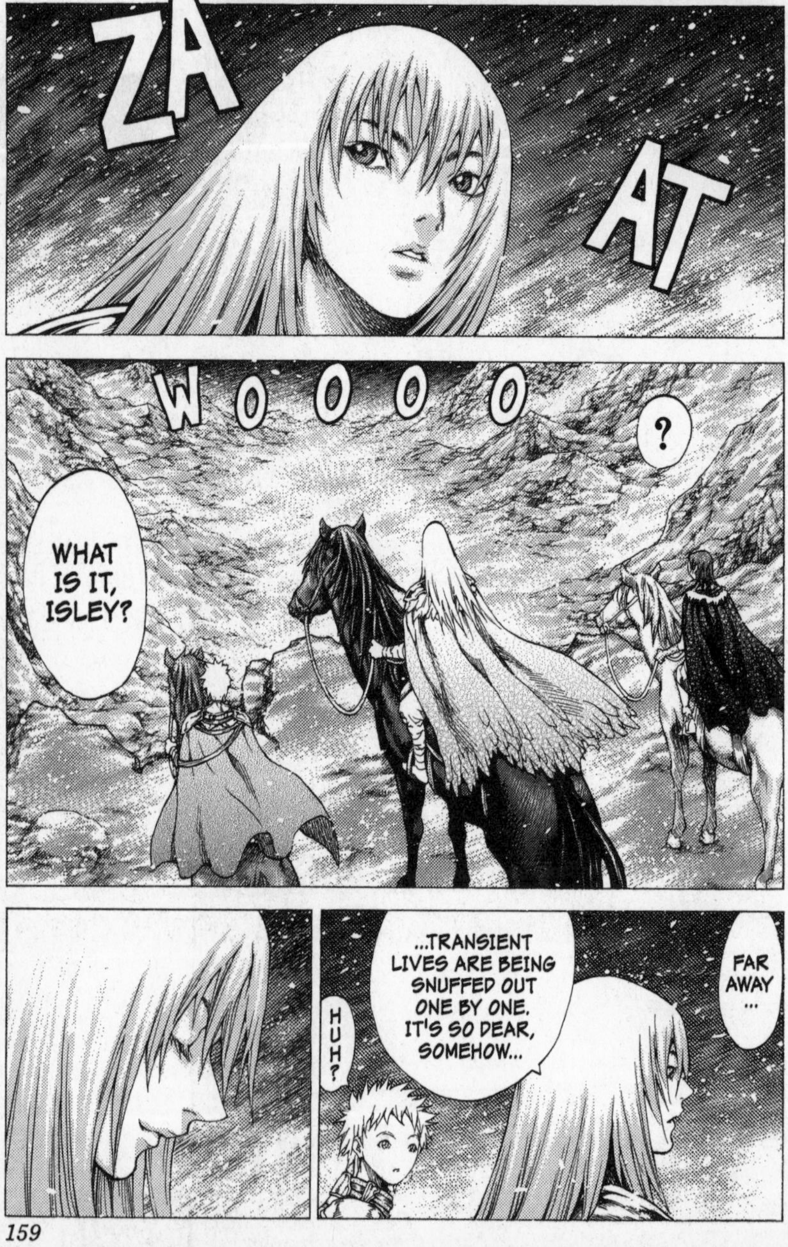
ZA
AT
WOOOO
?
WHAT IS IT, ISLEY?
FAR AWAY...
...TRANSIENT LIVES ARE BEING SNUFFED OUT ONE BY ONE. IT'S SO DEAR, SOMEHOW...
HUH?

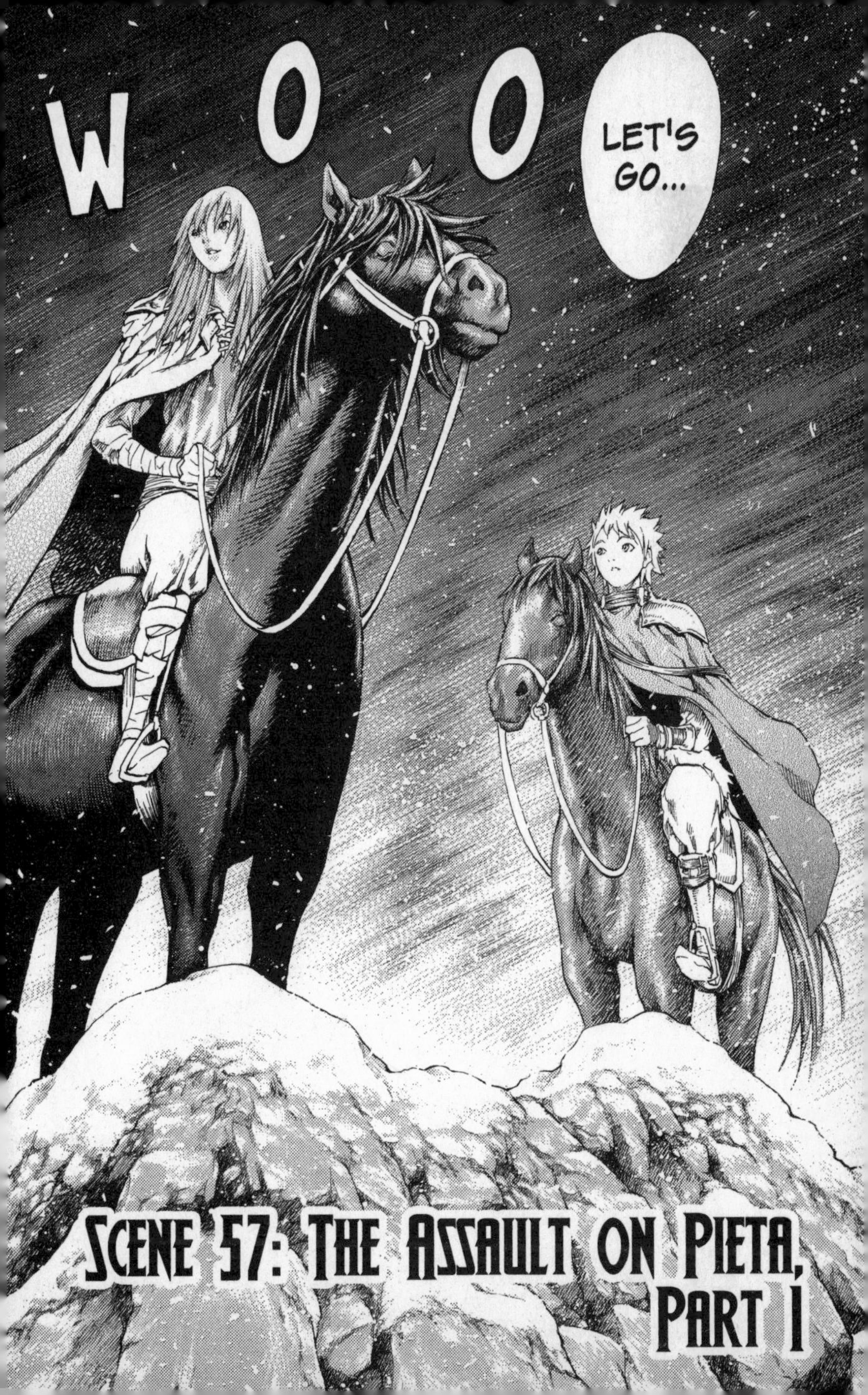
WOOO
LET'S GO...
SCENE 57: THE ASSAULT ON PIETA, PART 1

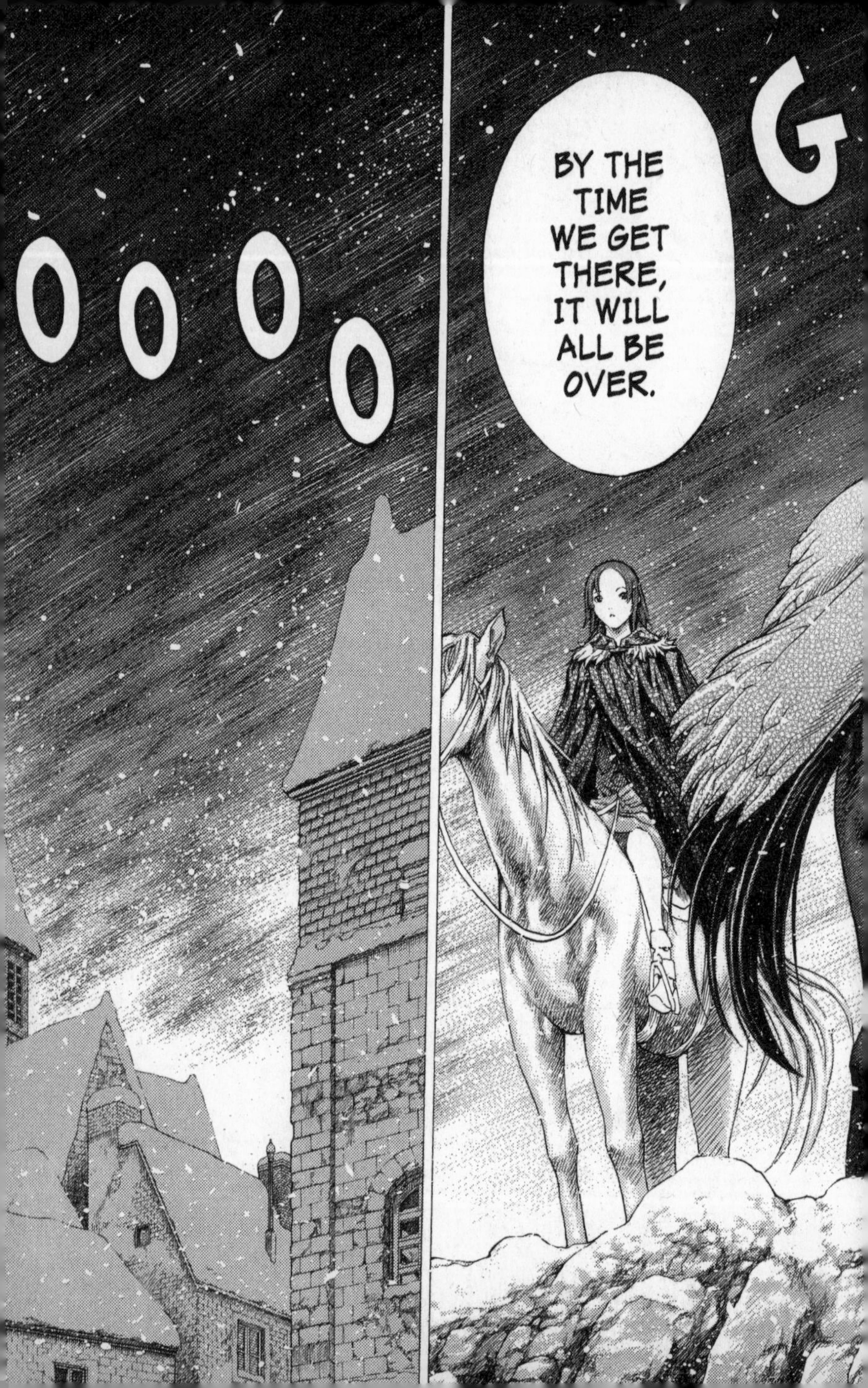
G
BY THE TIME WE GET THERE, IT WILL ALL BE OVER.
OOOO

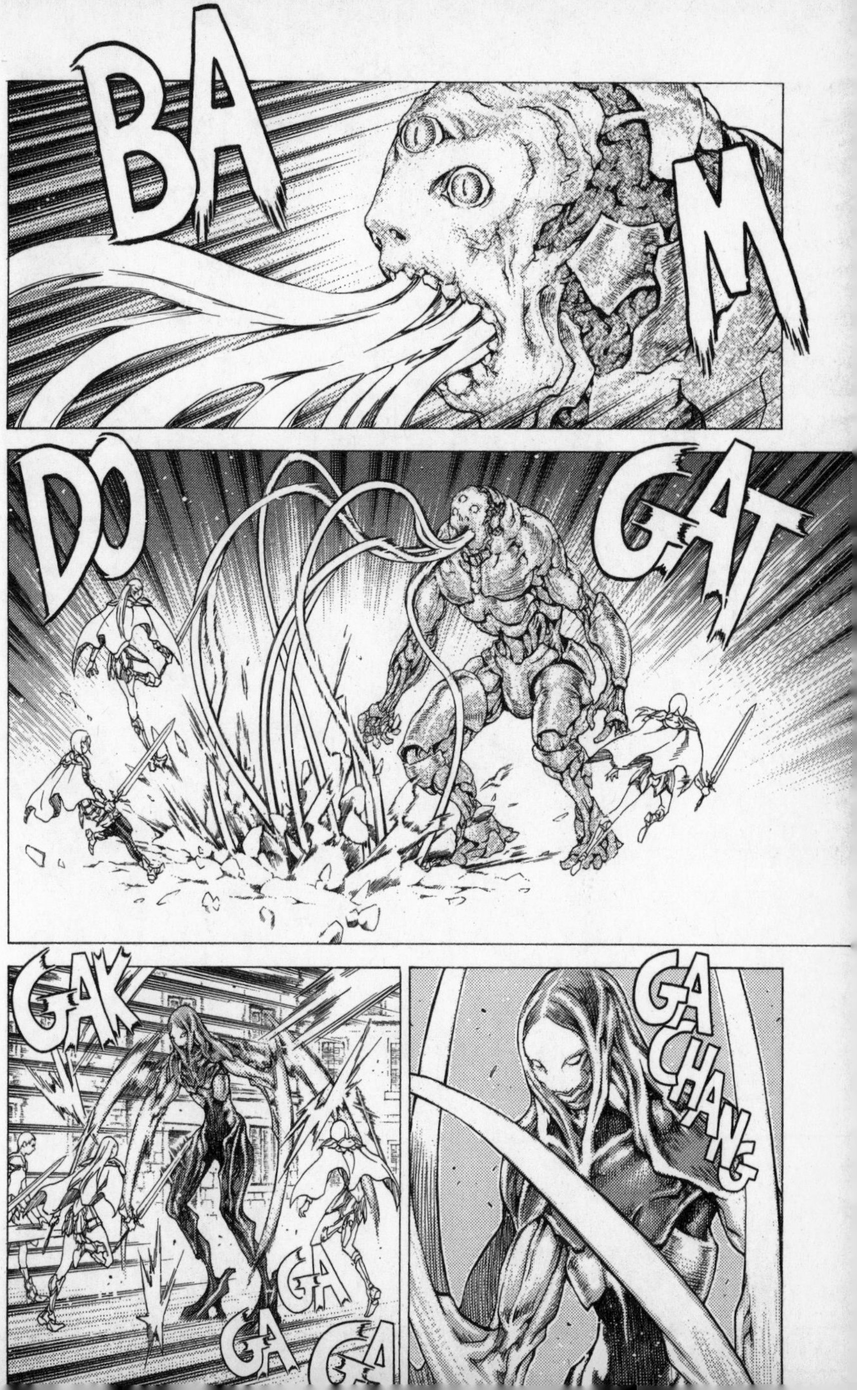
BAM
DO GAT
GA CHANG
GAK
GA GA
GA GA

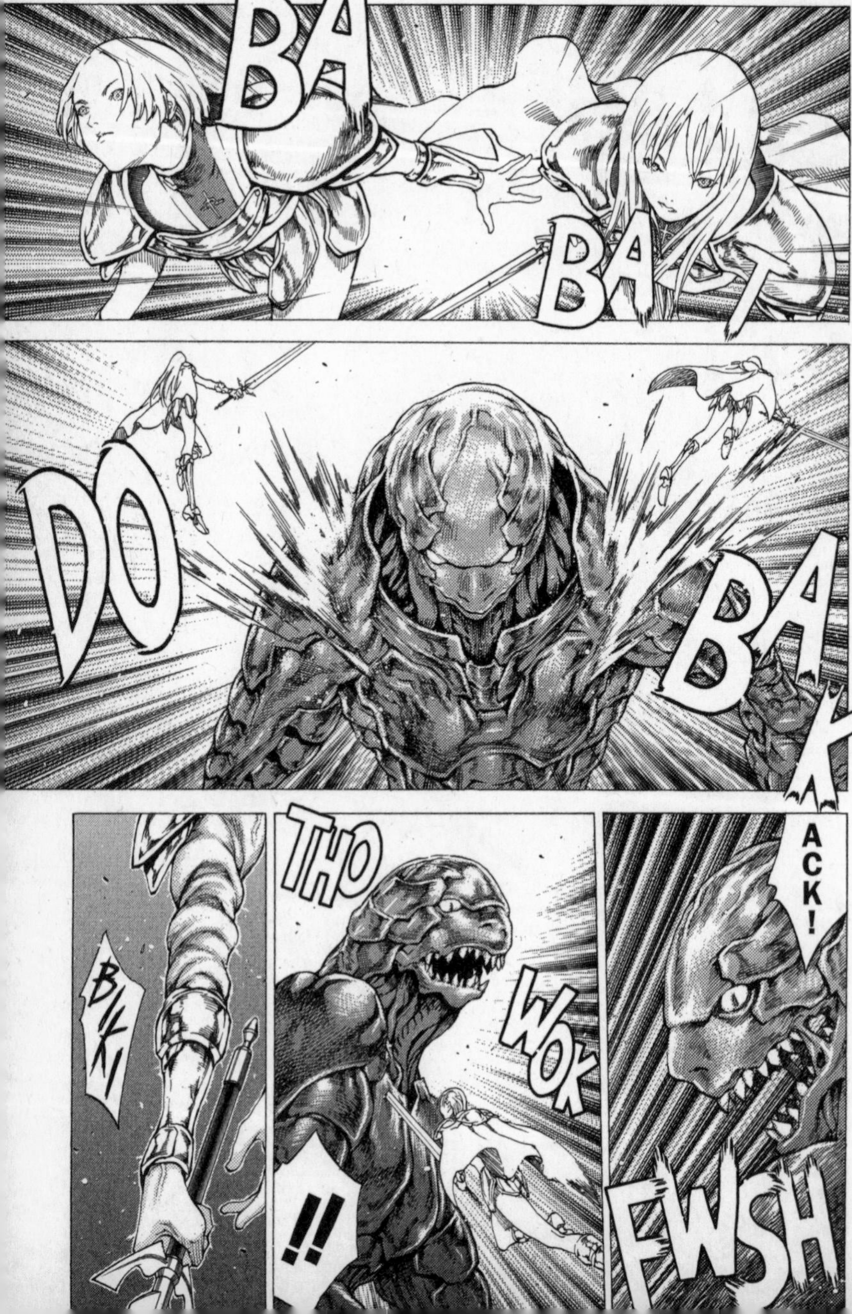
BA
BAT
BAK
DO
ACK!
FWSH
THO
WOK
!!
BIKI

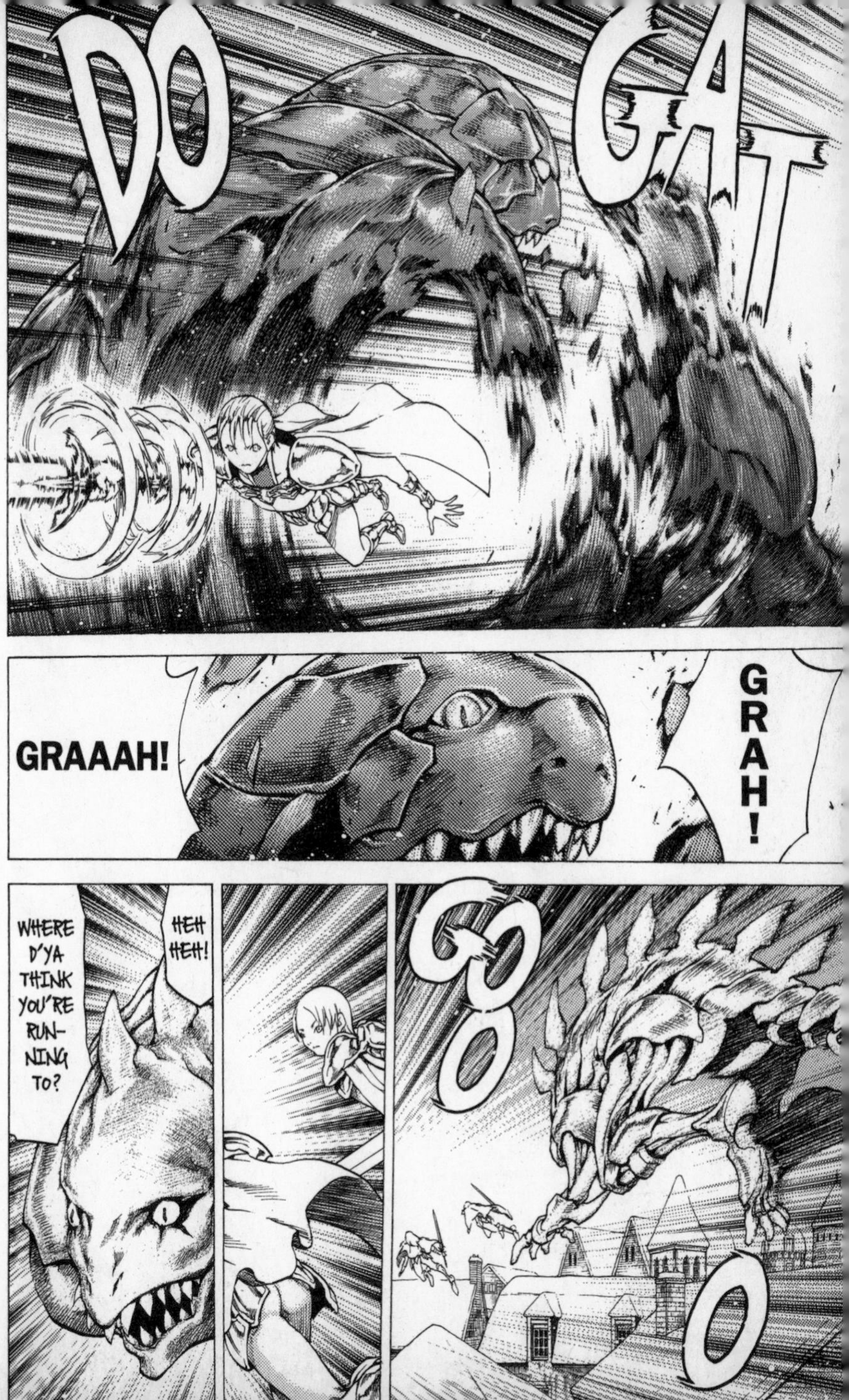
DO GAT
GRAH!
GRAAAH!
GOOO
HEH HEH!
WHERE D'YA THINK YOU'RE RUN-NING TO?

READ THIS WAY

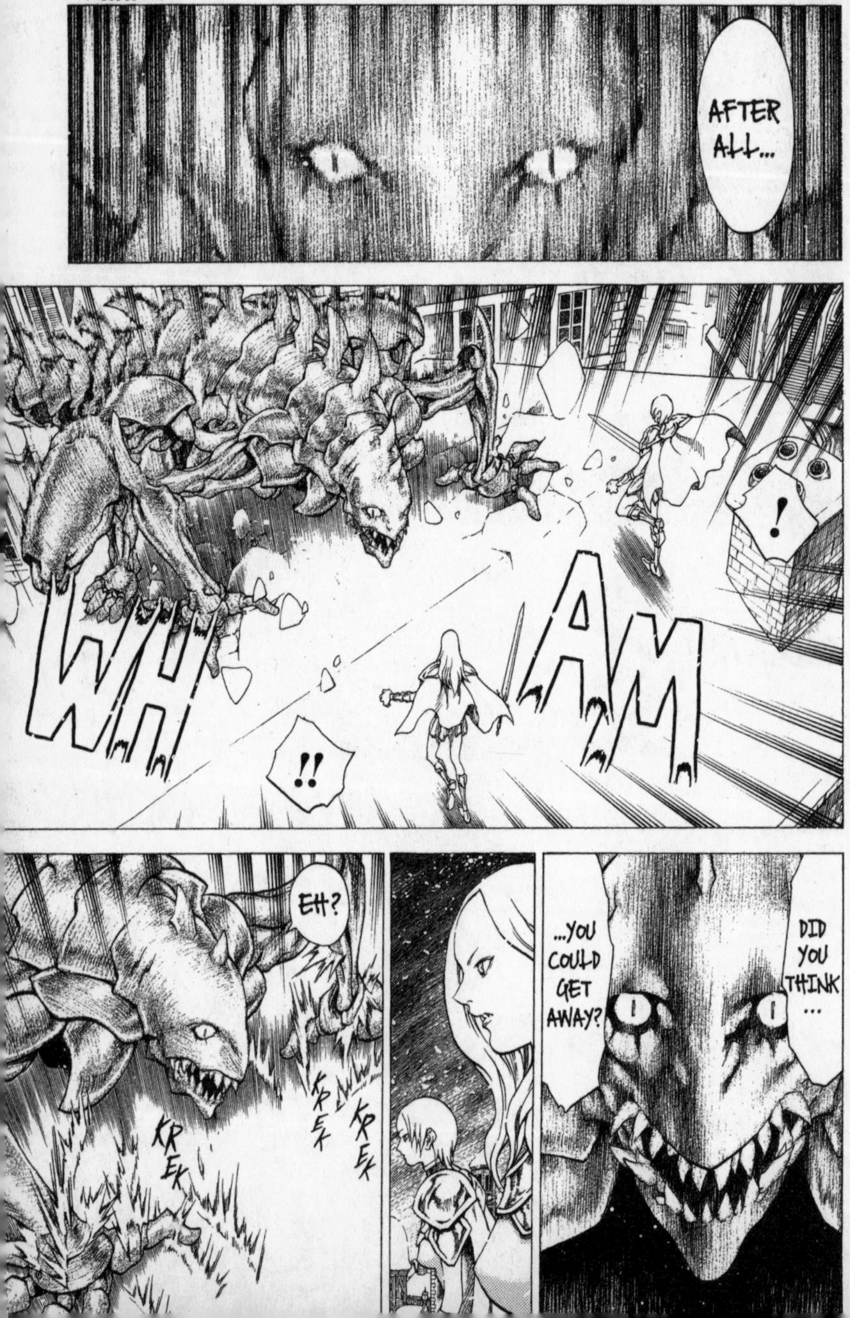
AFTER ALL...
!
WHAM
!!
DID YOU THINK...
...YOU COULD GET AWAY?
EH?
KREK
KREK
KREK

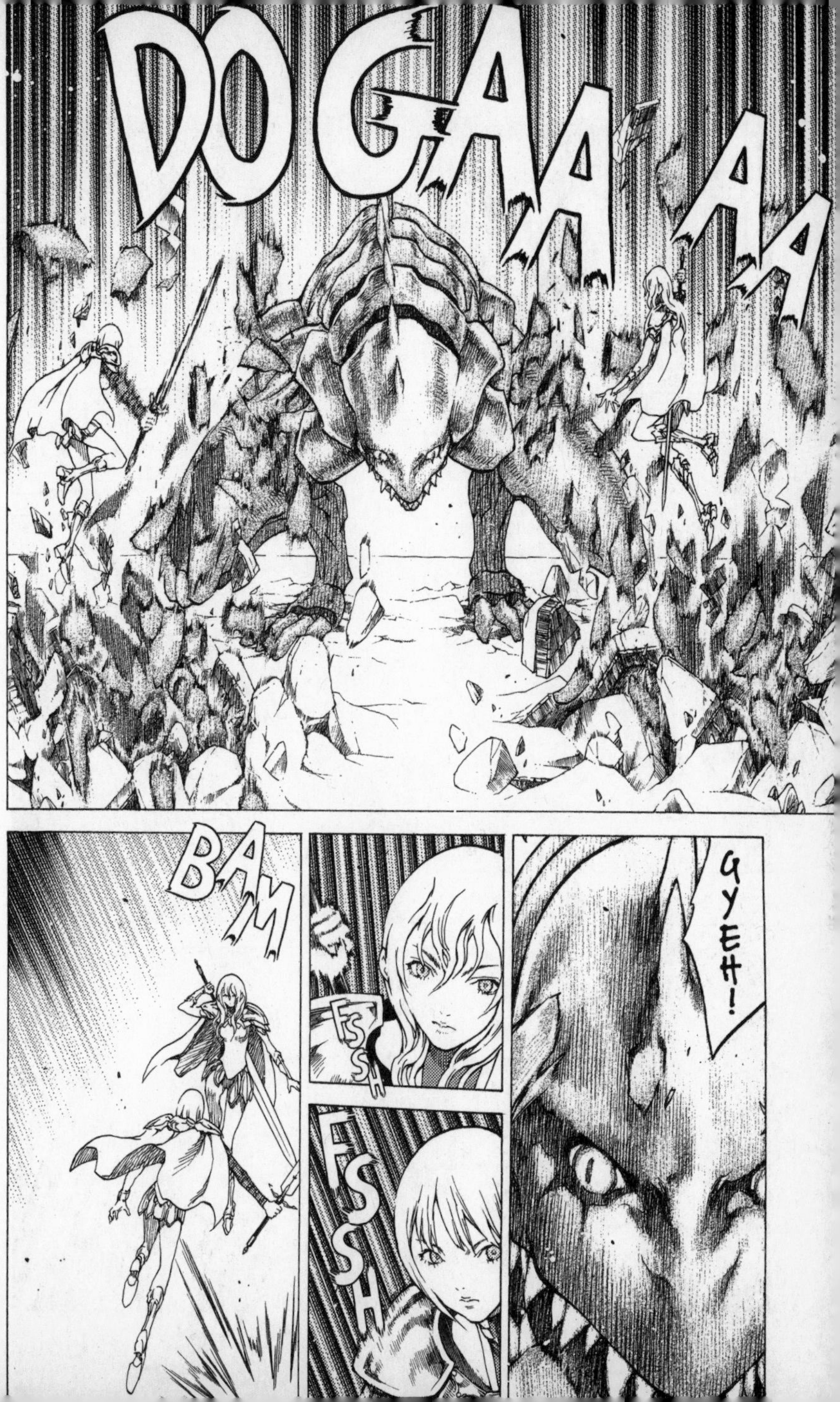
DOGAA AA
GYEH!
FSSH
FSSH
BAM

READ THIS WAY

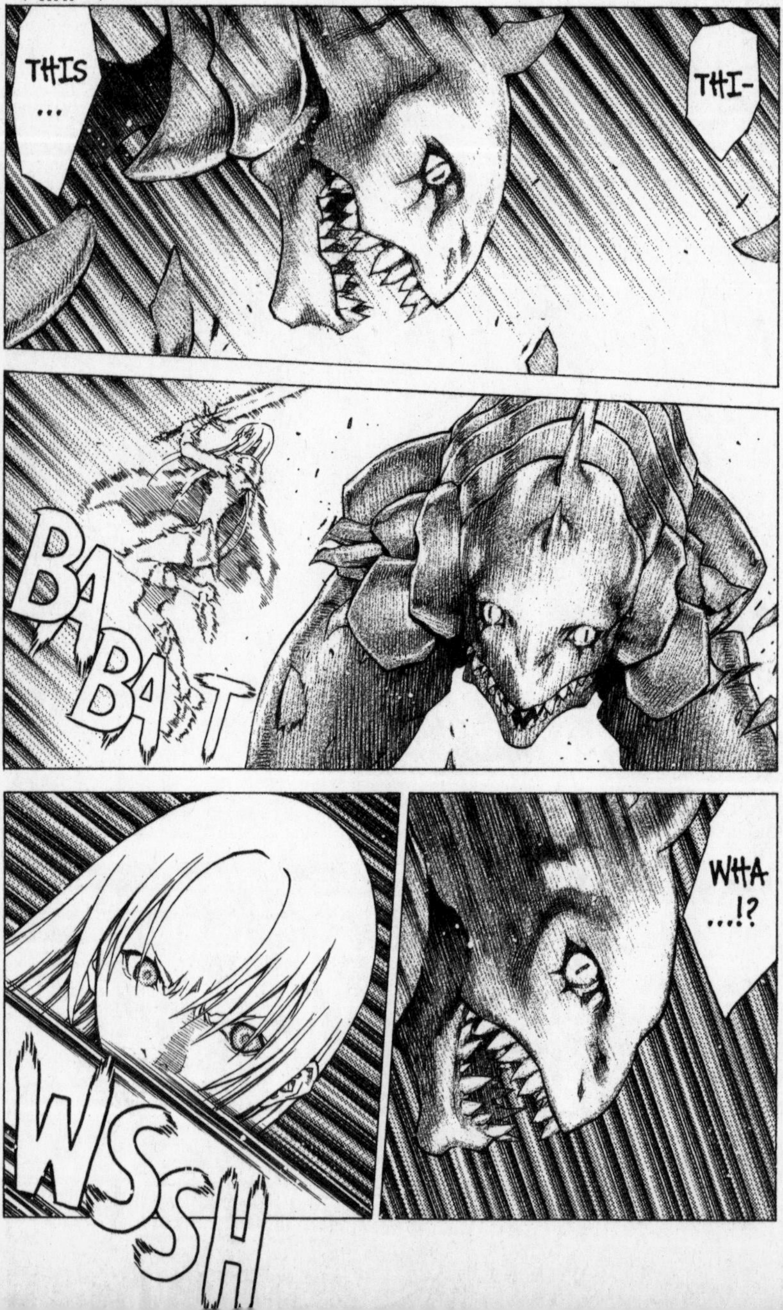
THI-
THIS ...
BA BA BAT
WHA ...!?
WSSH

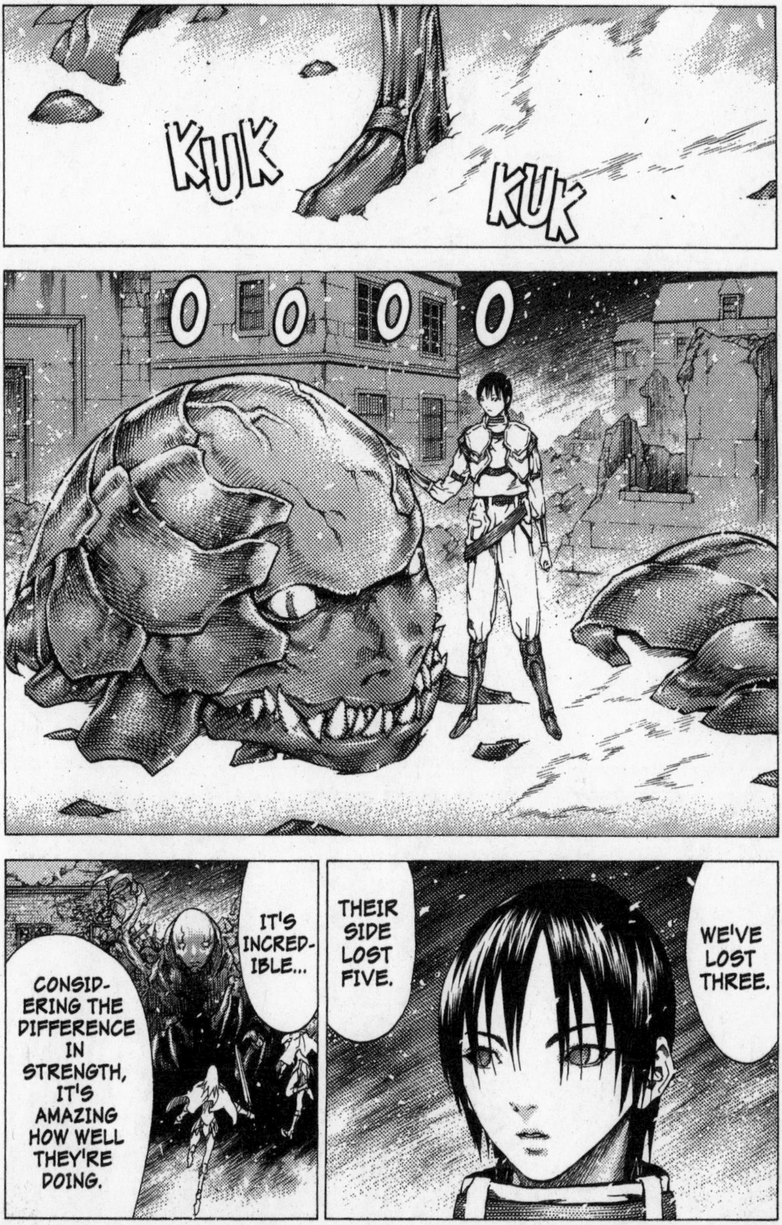
KUK
KUK
OOOO
WE'VE LOST THREE.
THEIR SIDE LOST FIVE.
IT'S INCREDIBLE...
CONSIDERING THE DIFFERENCE IN STRENGTH, IT'S AMAZING HOW WELL THEY'RE DOING.

READ THIS WAY

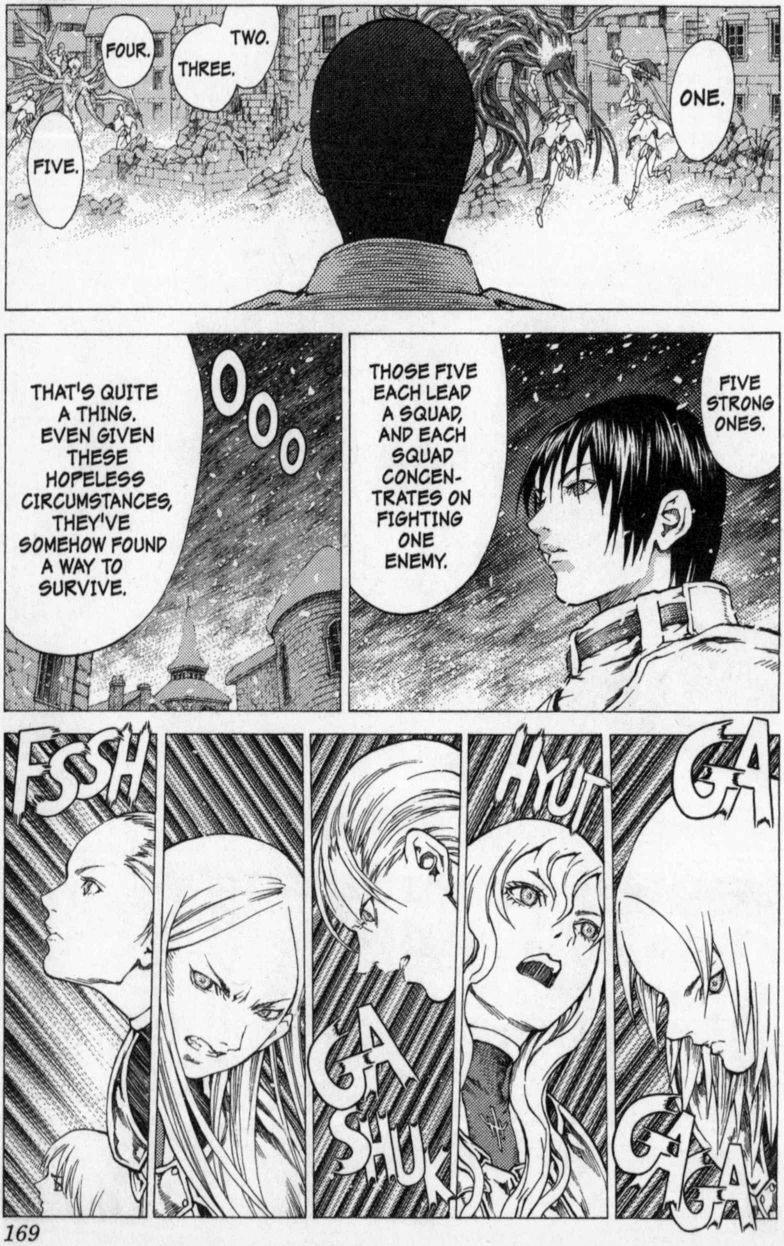
ONE.
TWO.
THREE.
FOUR.
FIVE.
FIVE STRONG ONES.
THOSE FIVE EACH LEAD A SQUAD, AND EACH SQUAD CONCEN-TRATES ON FIGHTING ONE ENEMY.
OOO
THAT'S QUITE A THING. EVEN GIVEN THESE HOPELESS CIRCUMSTANCES, THEY'VE SOMEHOW FOUND A WAY TO SURVIVE.
GA
GAGA!
HYUT
GA
SHUK
FSSH

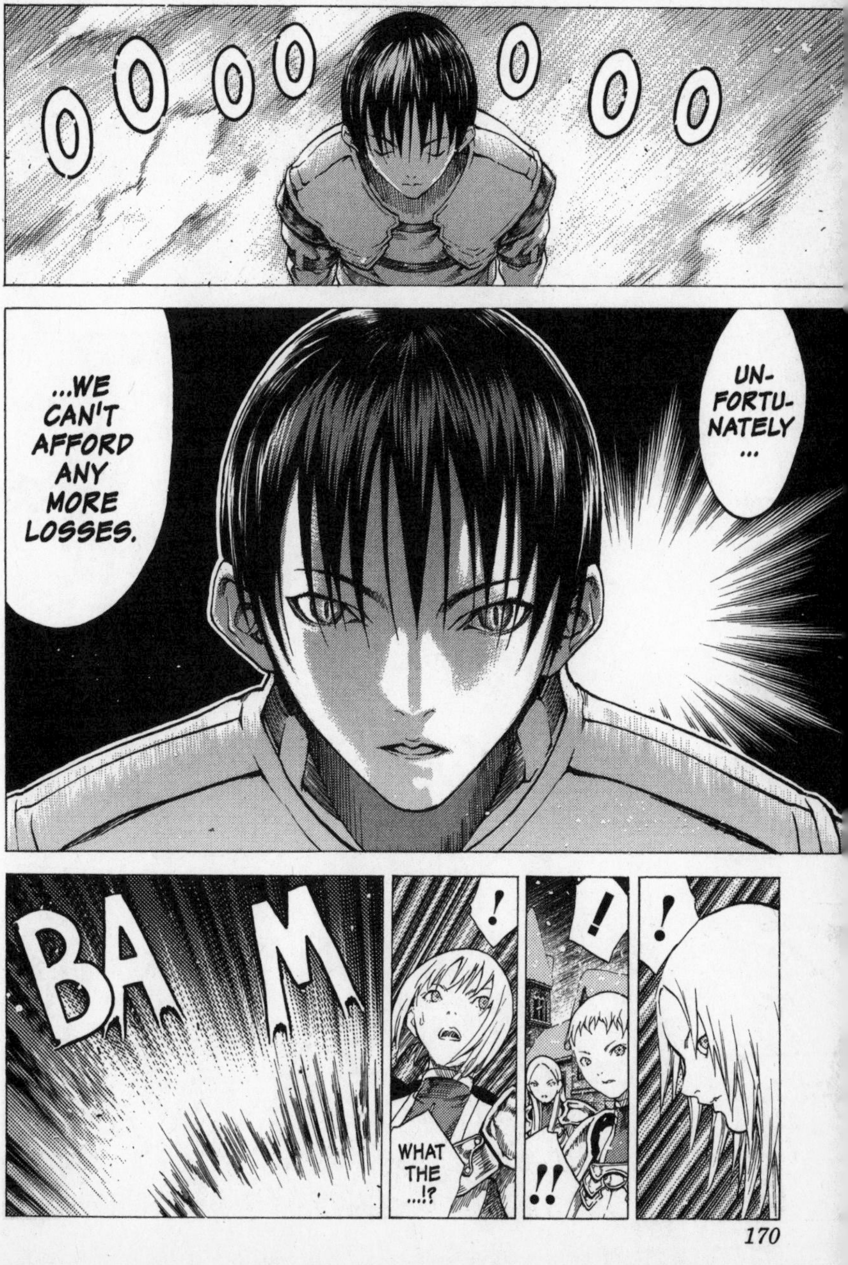

OOOO OOO
UN-FORTUNATELY...
...WE CAN'T AFFORD ANY MORE LOSSES.
!
!
!!
!
WHAT THE ...!?
BAM

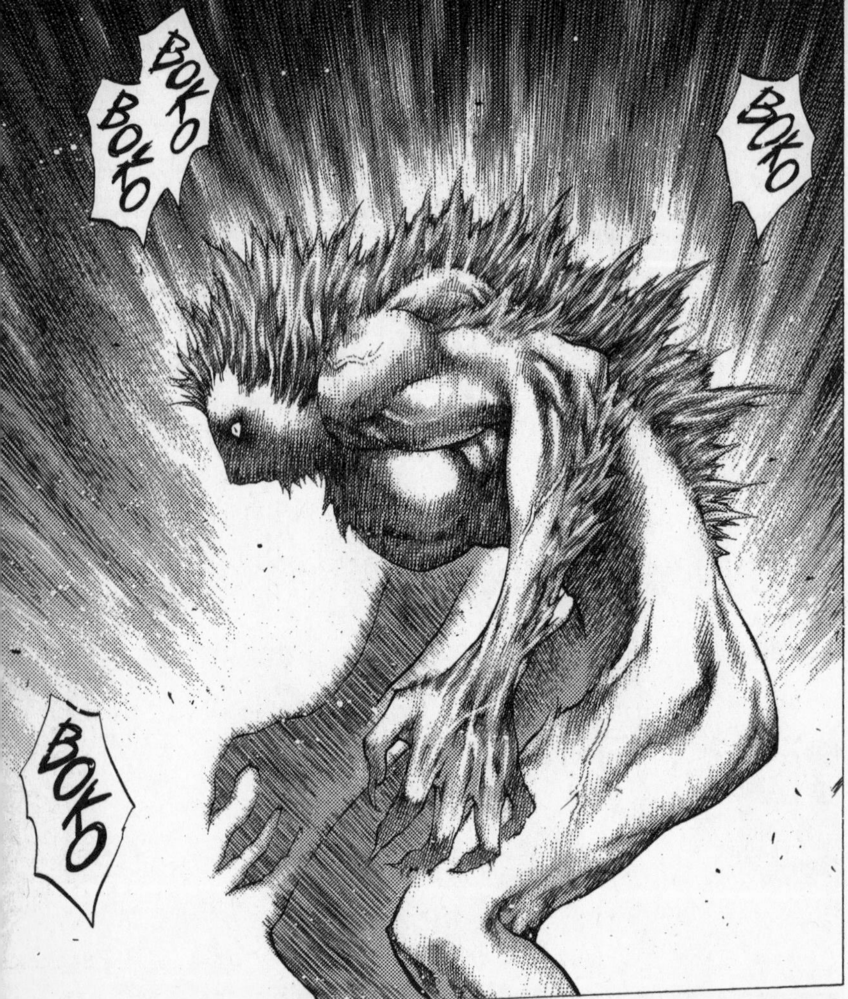
BOKO
BOKO BOKO
BOKO

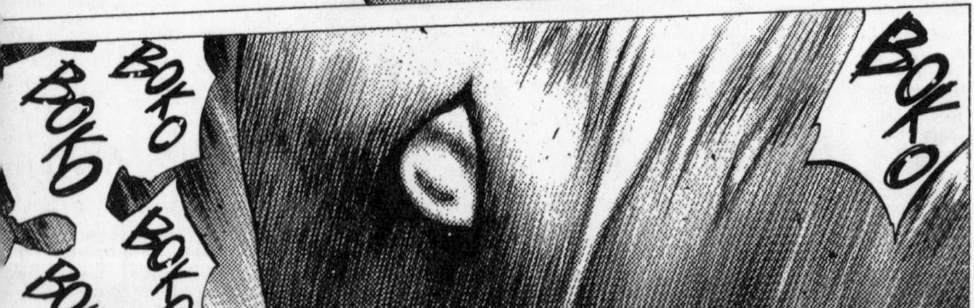
BOKO!
BOKO BOKO
BOKO BOKO

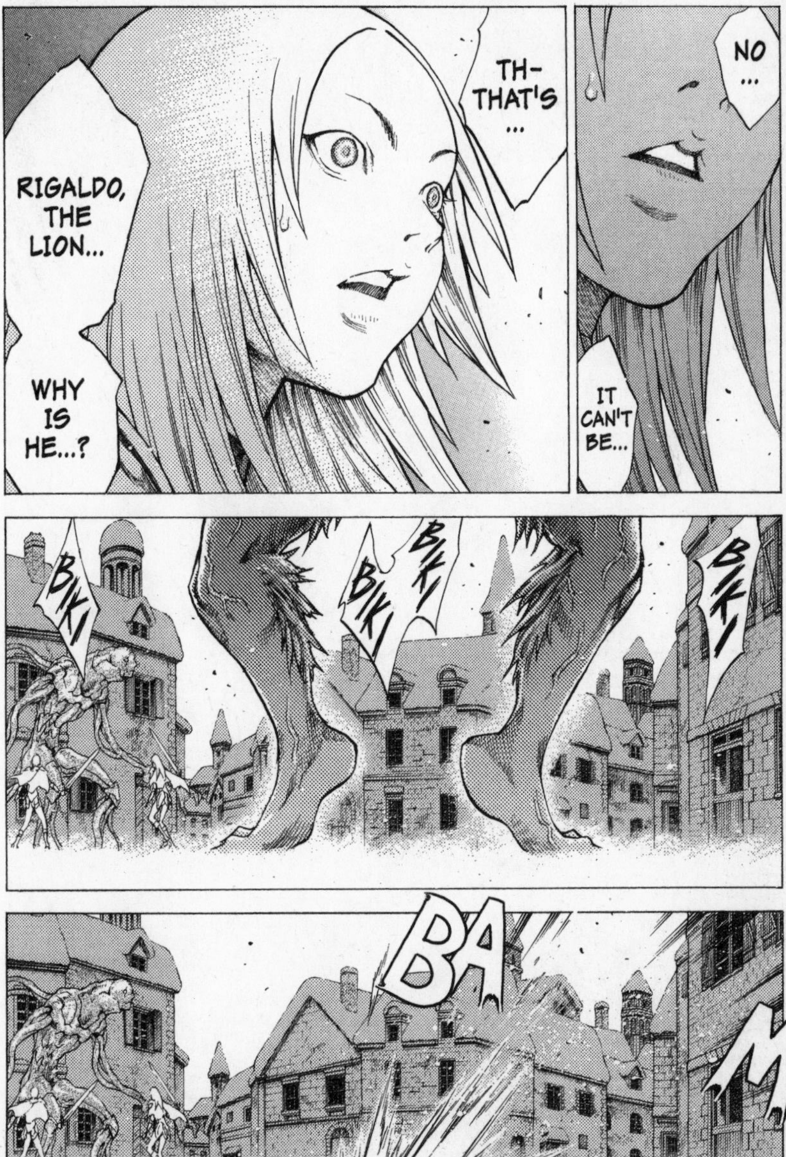
NO ...
IT CAN'T BE...
TH- THAT'S ...
RIGALDO, THE LION...
WHY IS HE...?
BIKI
BIKI
BIKI
BIKI
BAM

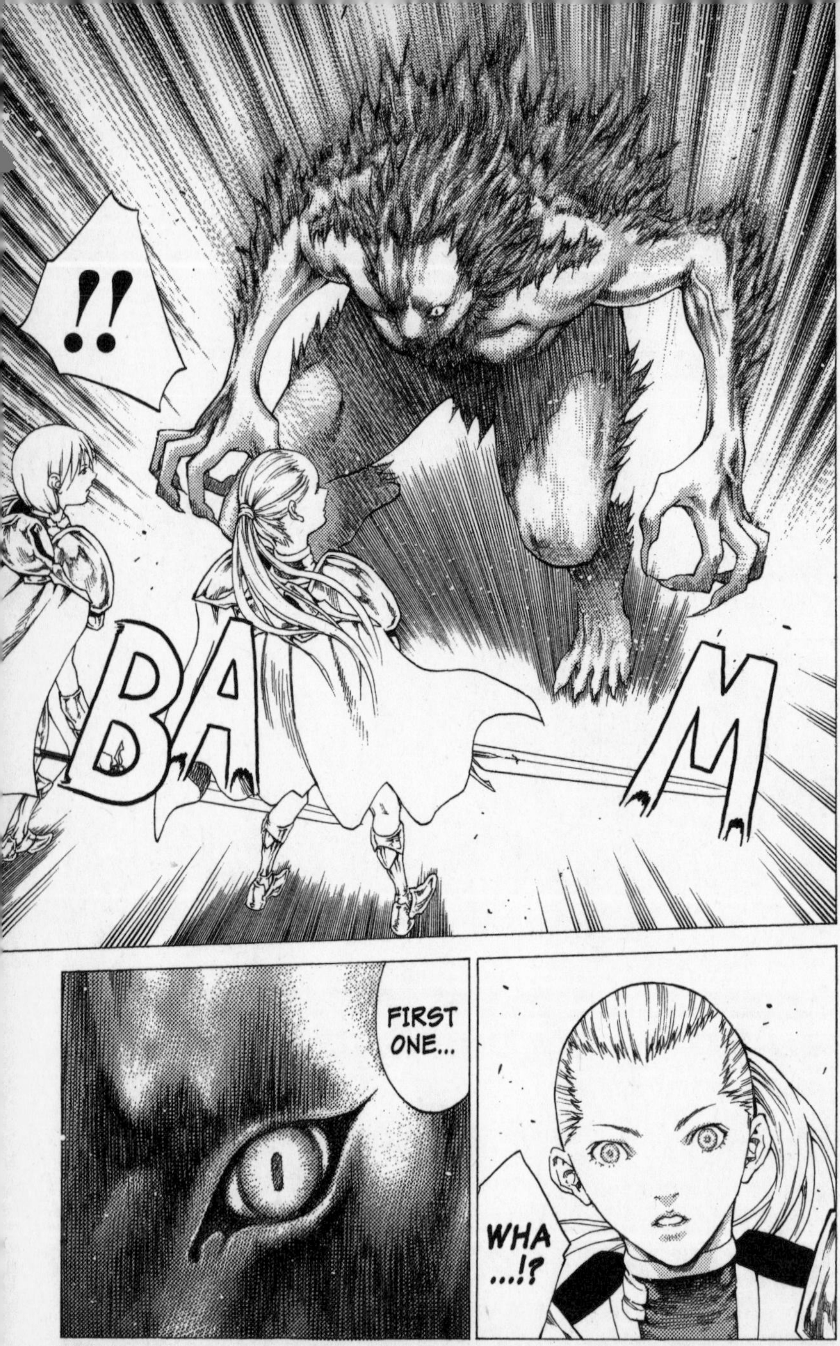
!!
BAM
WHA ...!?
FIRST ONE...

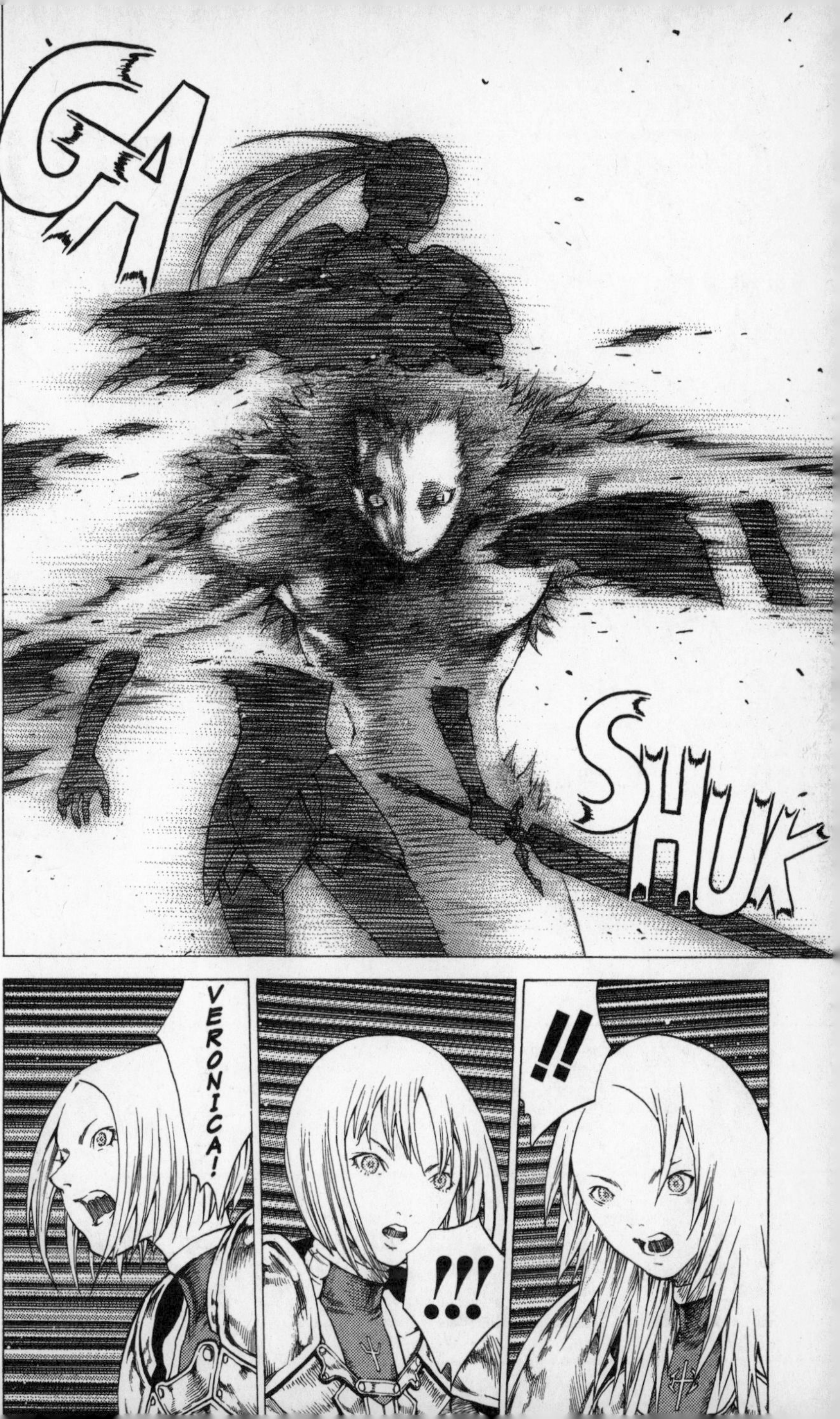
GA
SHUK
!!
!!!
VERONICA!

READ THIS WAY

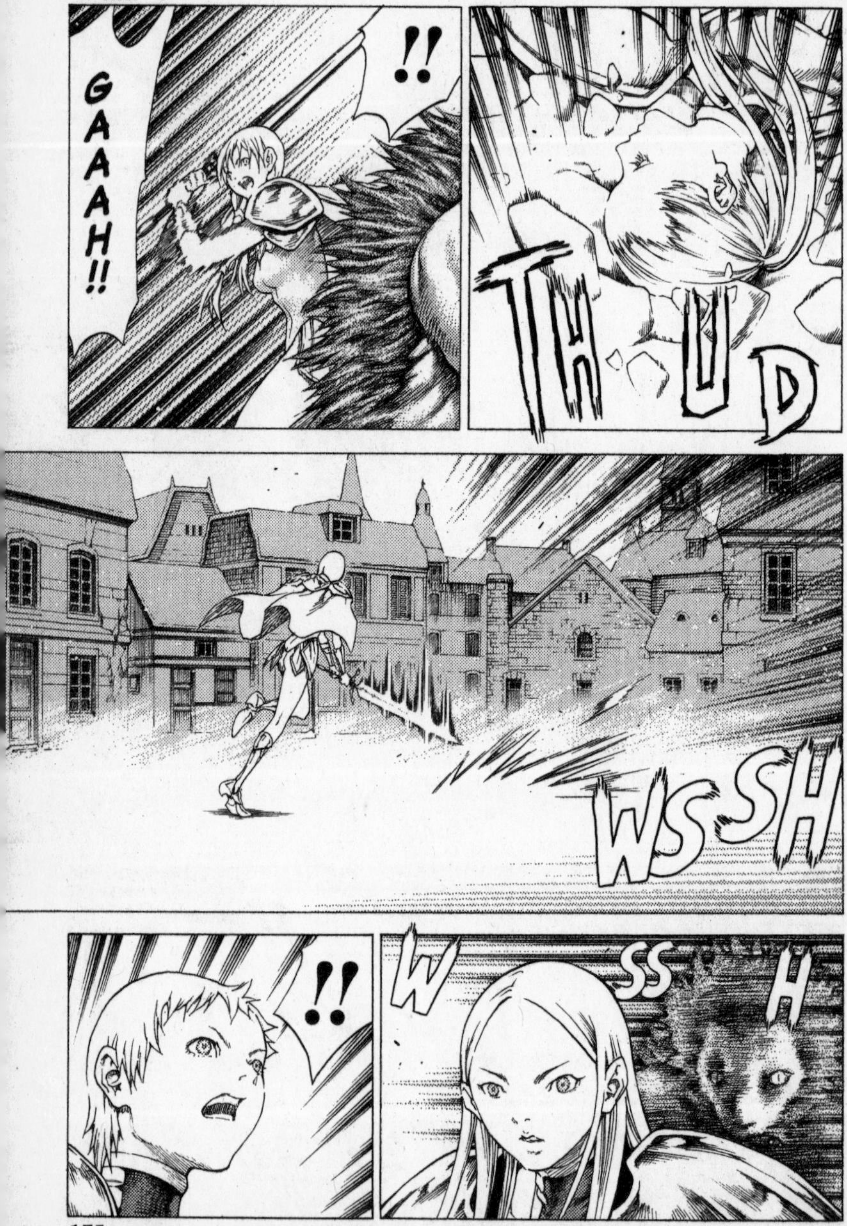
THUD
!!
GAAAAH!!
WSSH
WSSH
!!

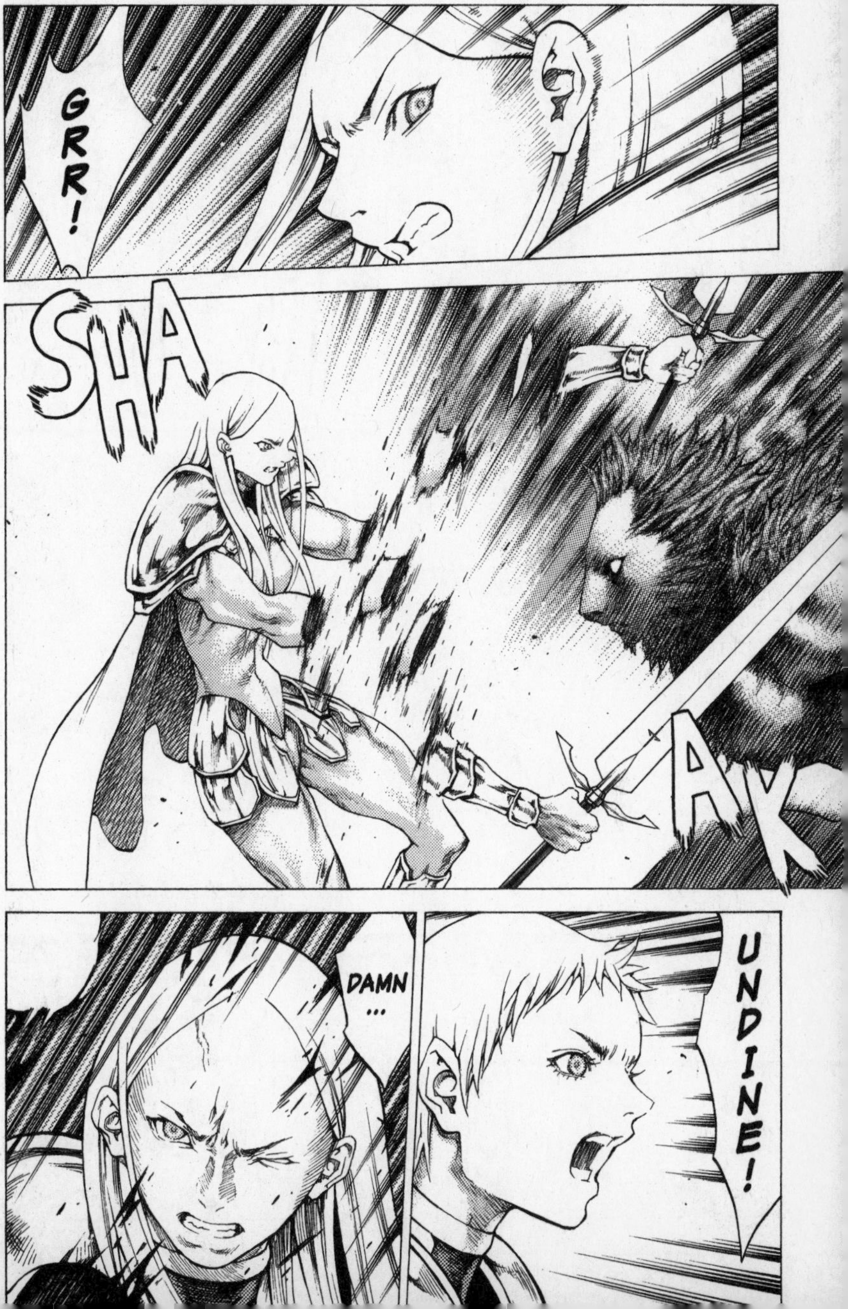
GRR!
SHA
AK
UNDINE!
DAMN ...

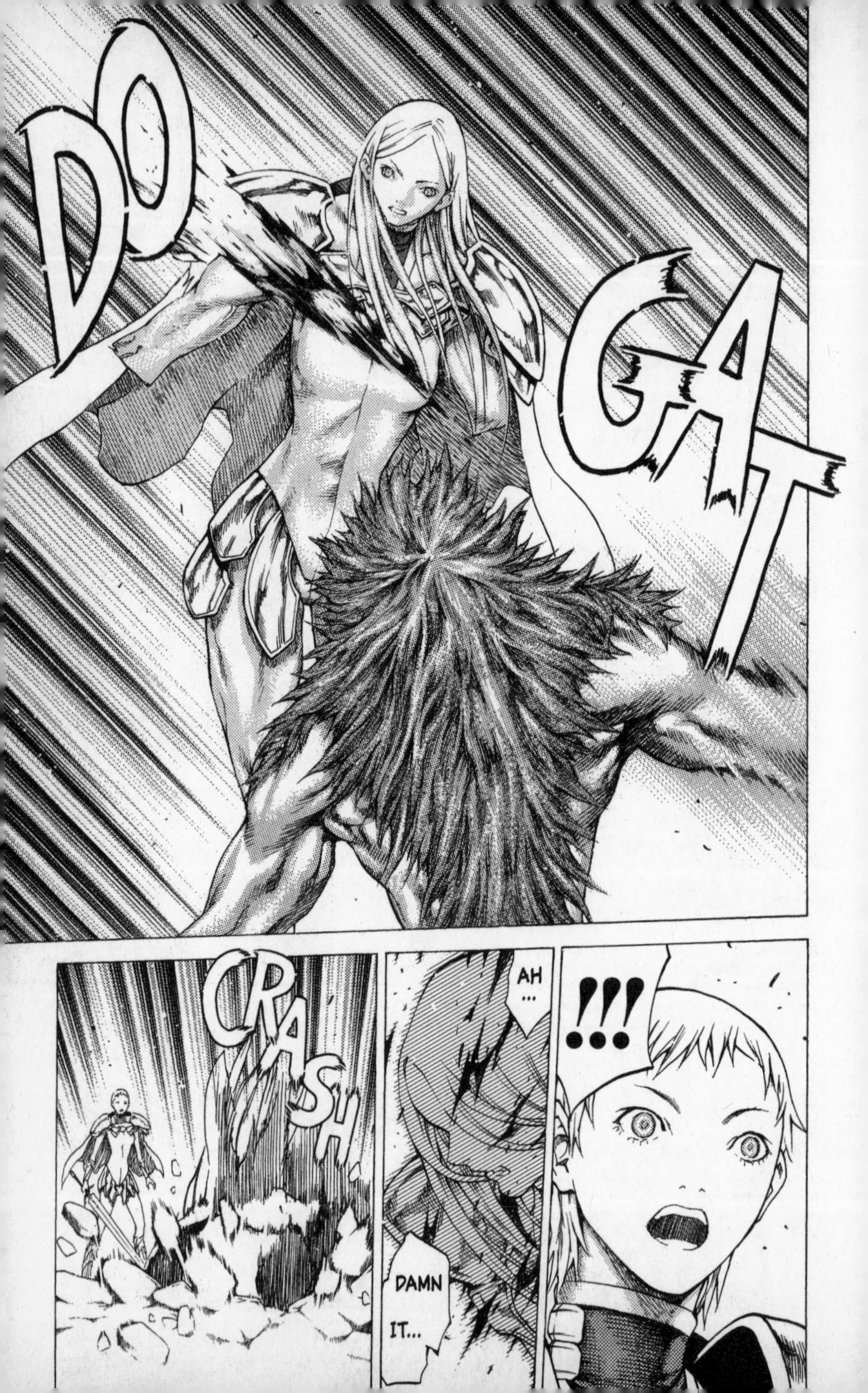
DO
GAT
!!!
AH...
DAMN IT...
CRASH

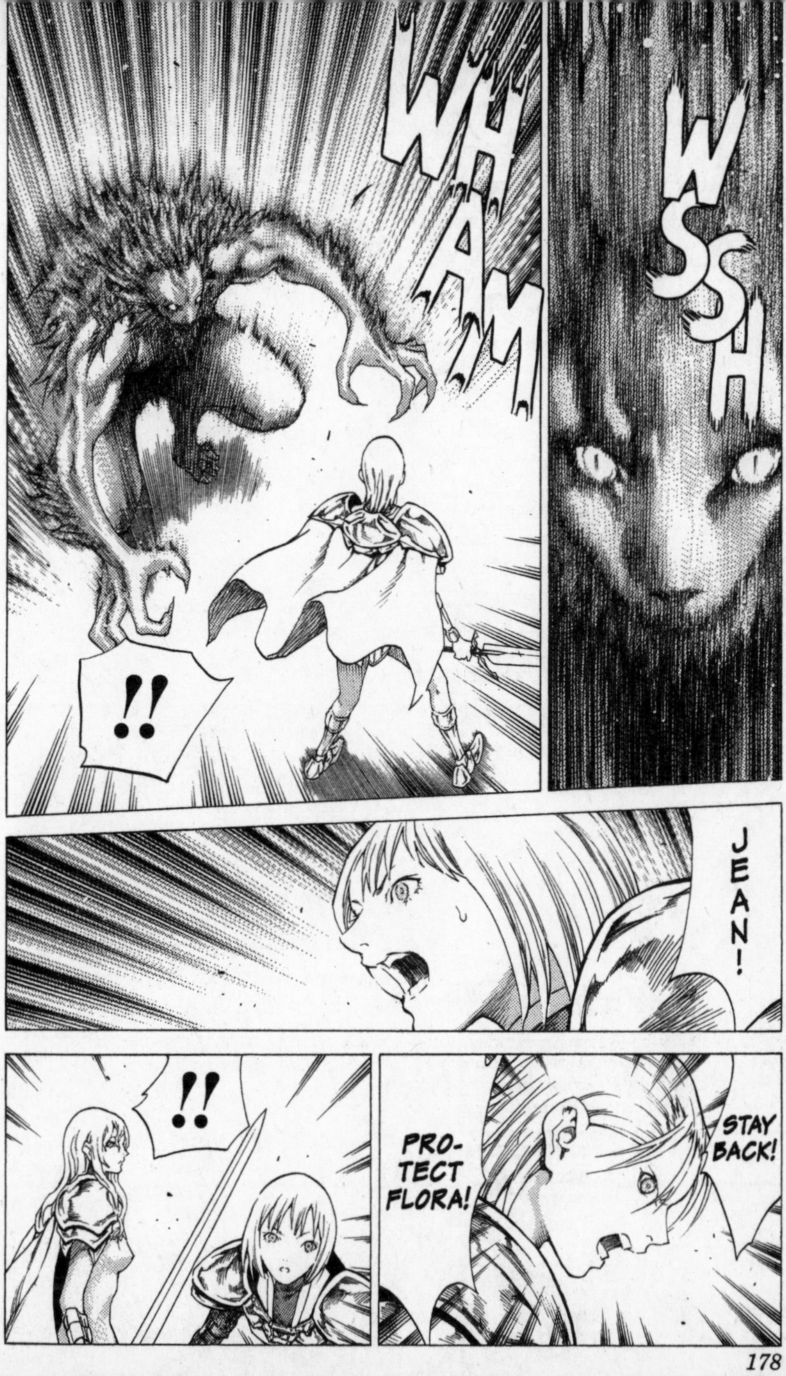
WSSH
WHAM
!!
JEAN!
STAY BACK!
PROTECT FLORA!
!!

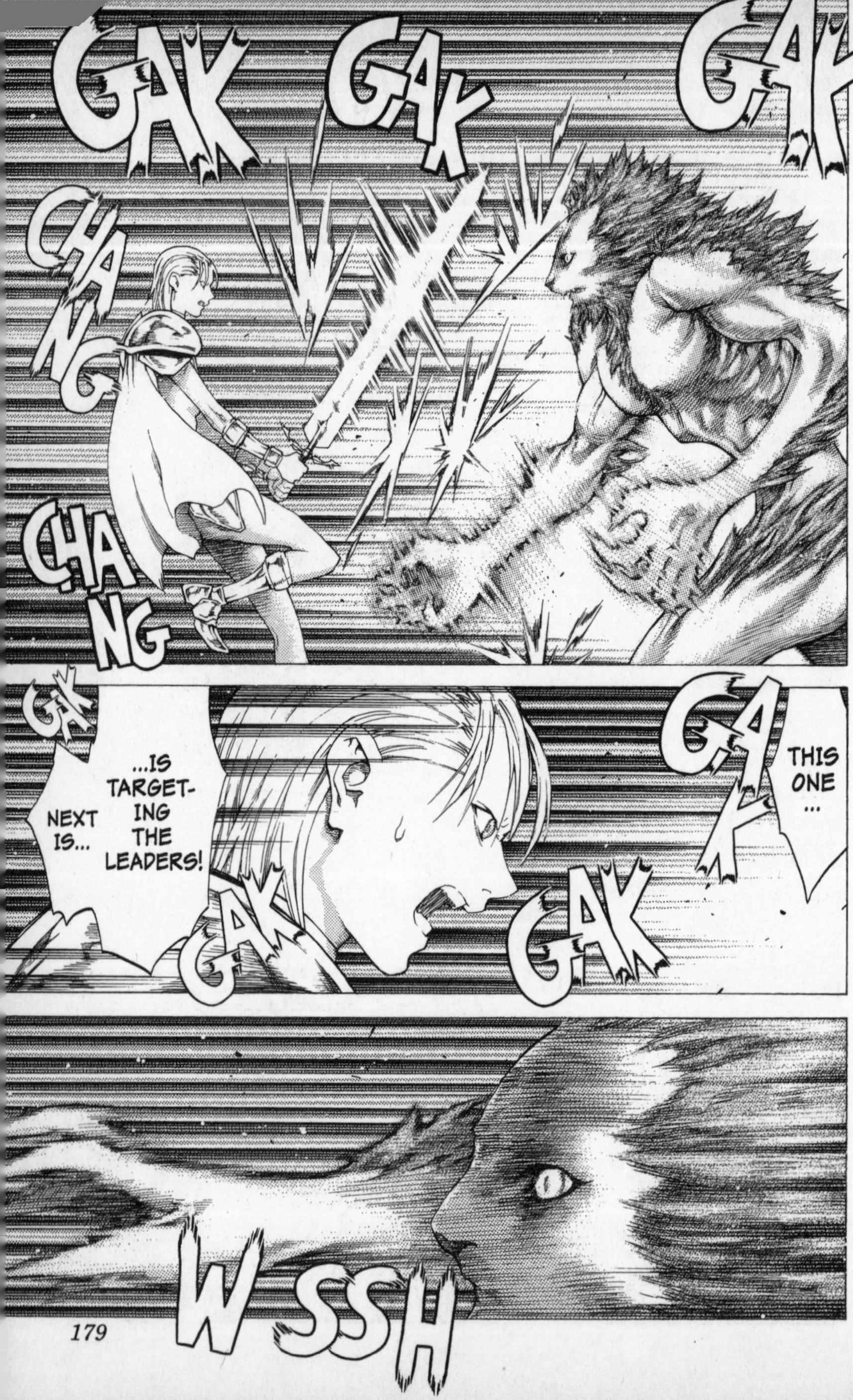
GAK
GAK
GAK
CHANG
CHANG
GAK
THIS ONE ...
GAK
...IS TARGETING THE LEADERS!
GAK
NEXT IS...
GAK
WSSH

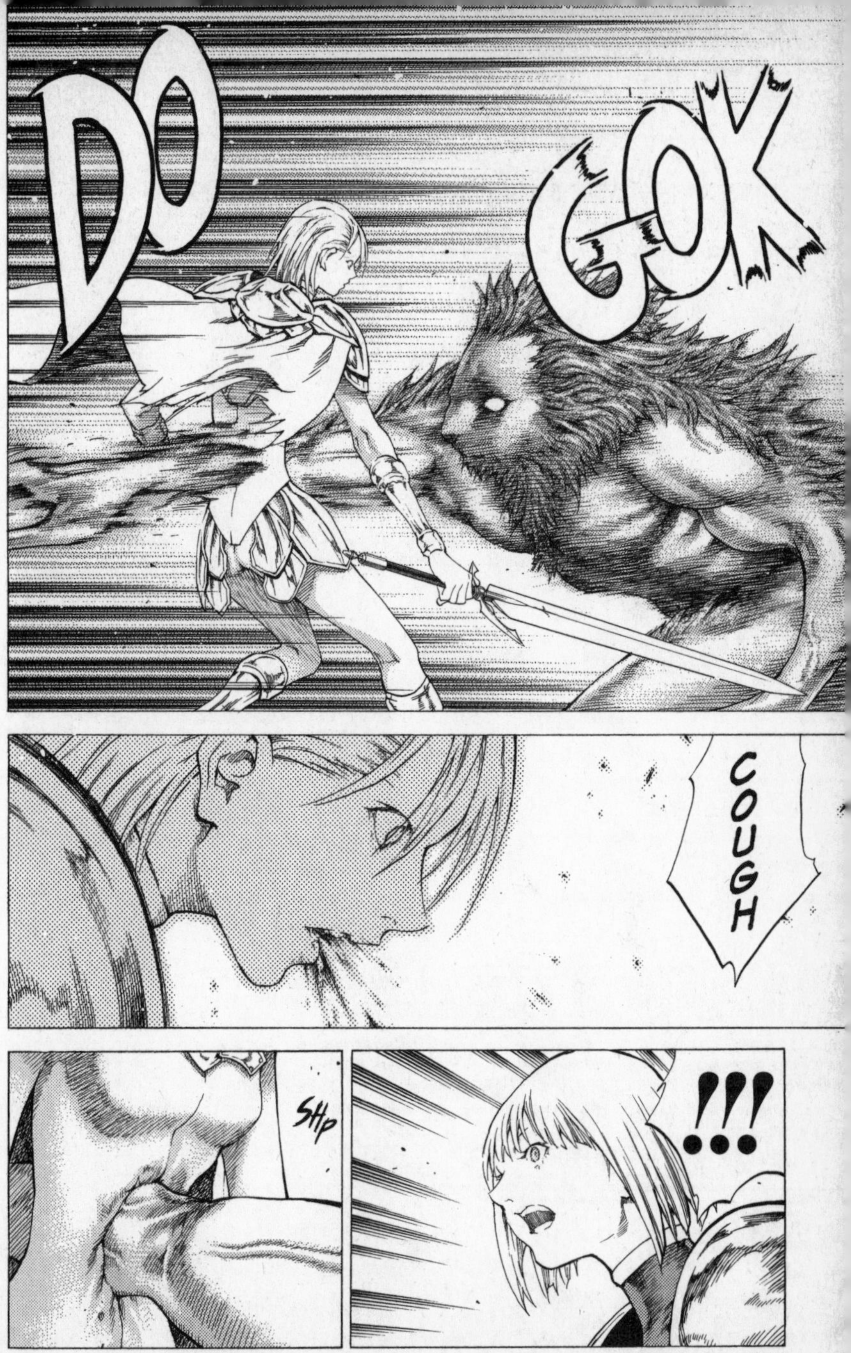
DO
GOK
COUGH
!!!
SHp

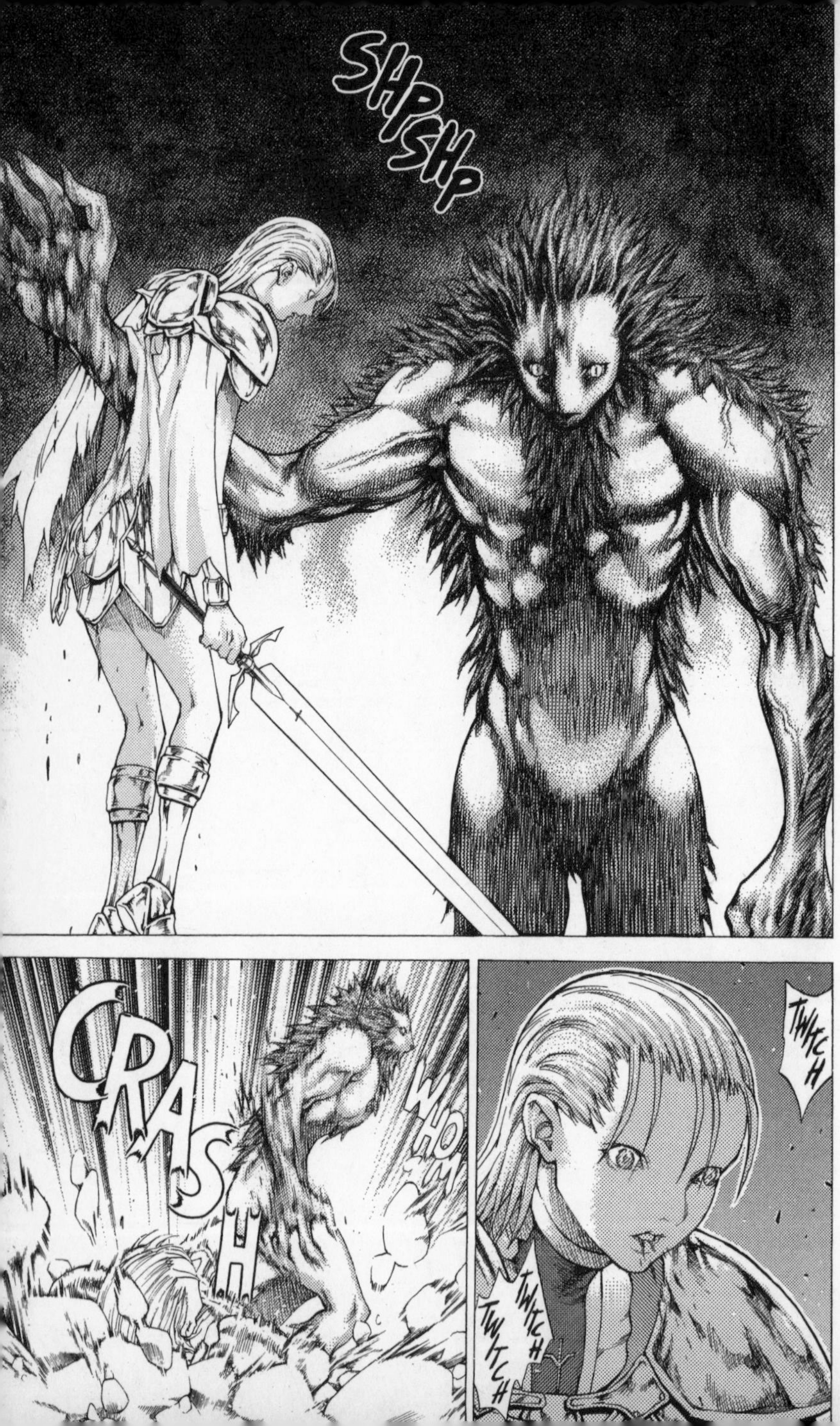
SHPSHP
TWITCH
TWITCH
TWITCH
CRASH
WHOM

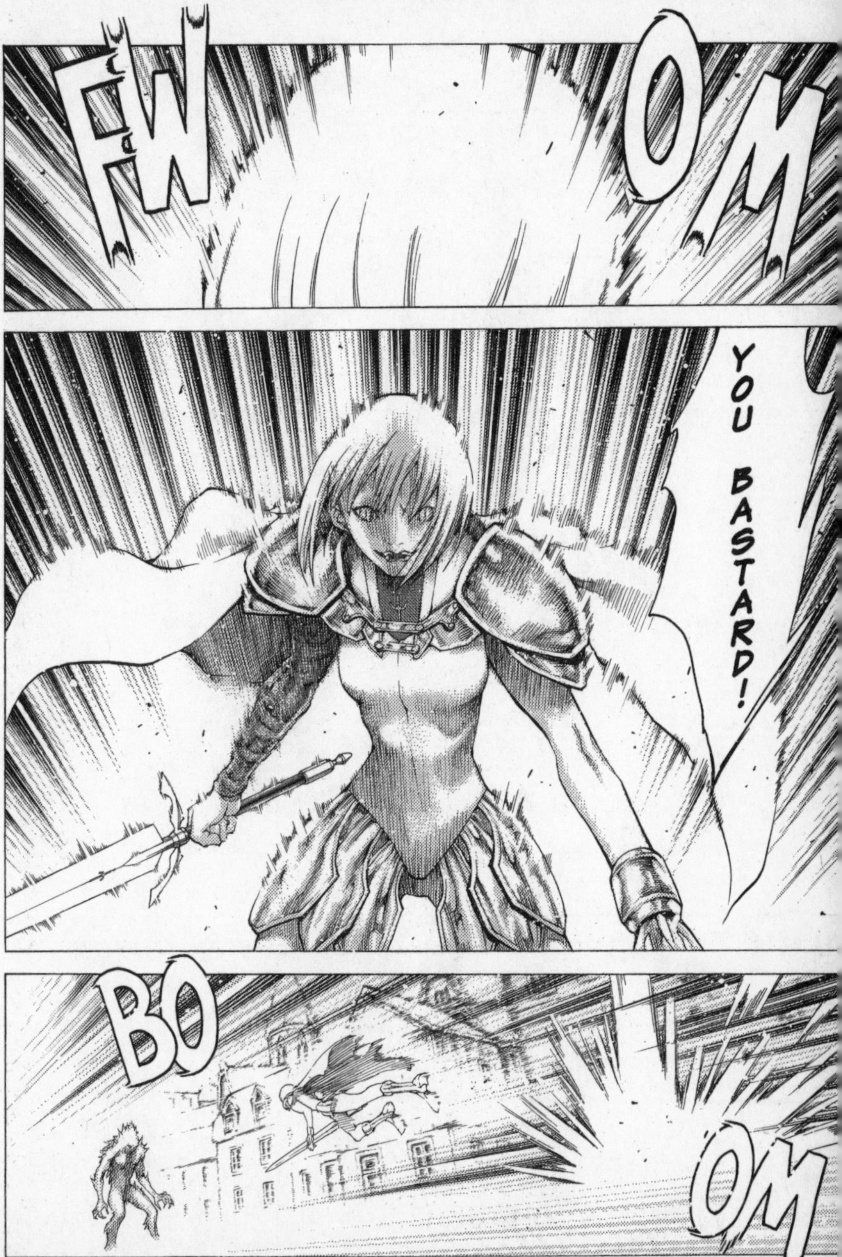
FWOOM
YOU BASTARD!
BOOM

READ THIS WAY

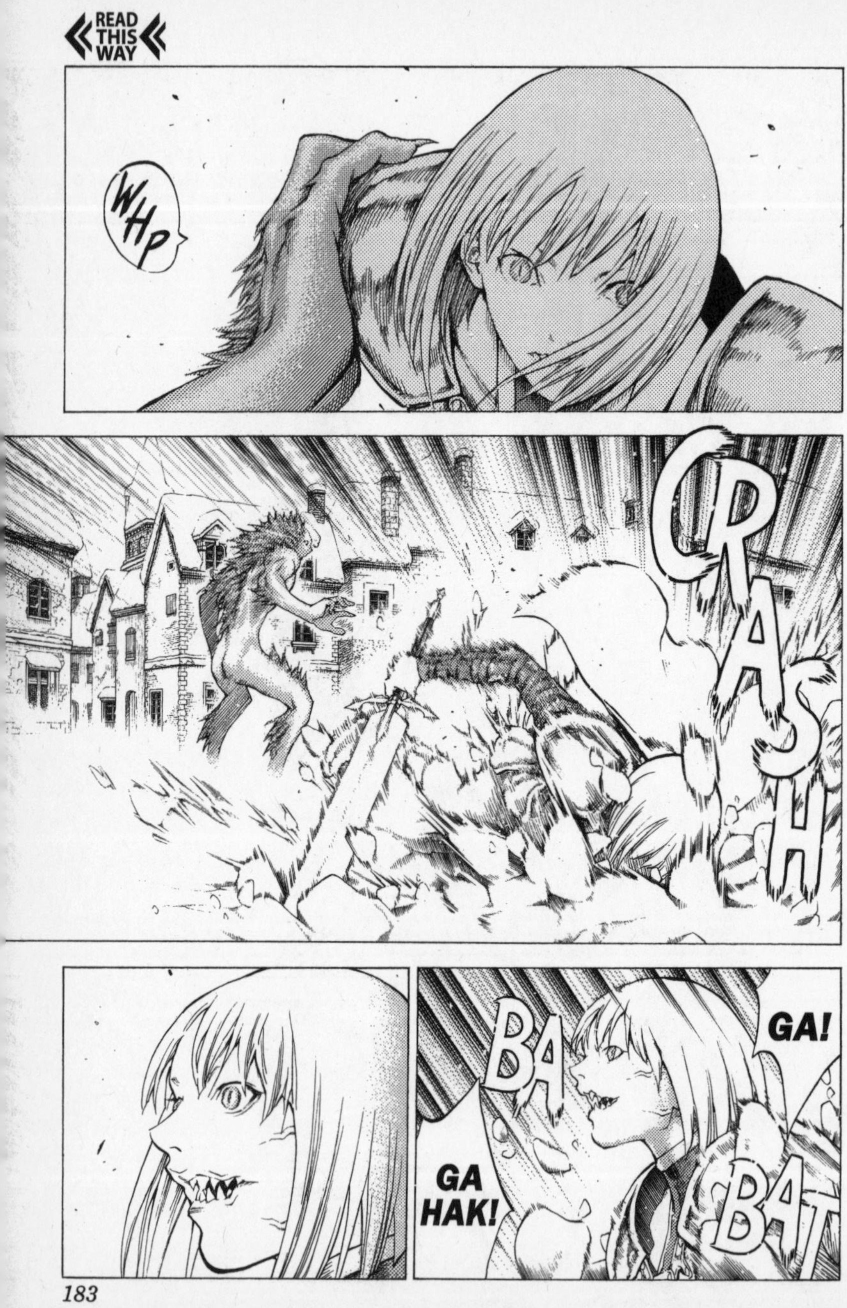
WHP
CRASH
GA!
BA
BAT
GA HAK!

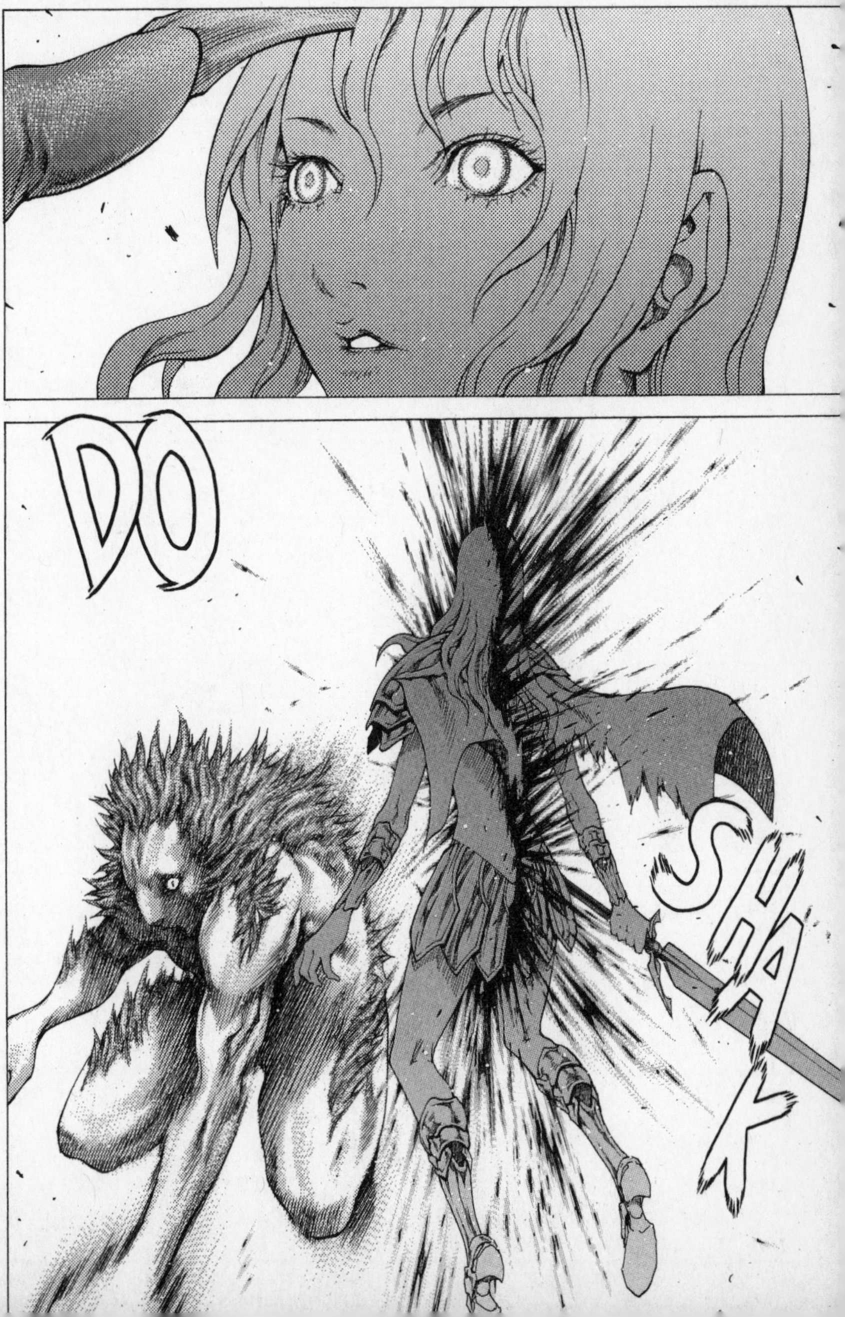
DO
SHAK

READ THIS WAY

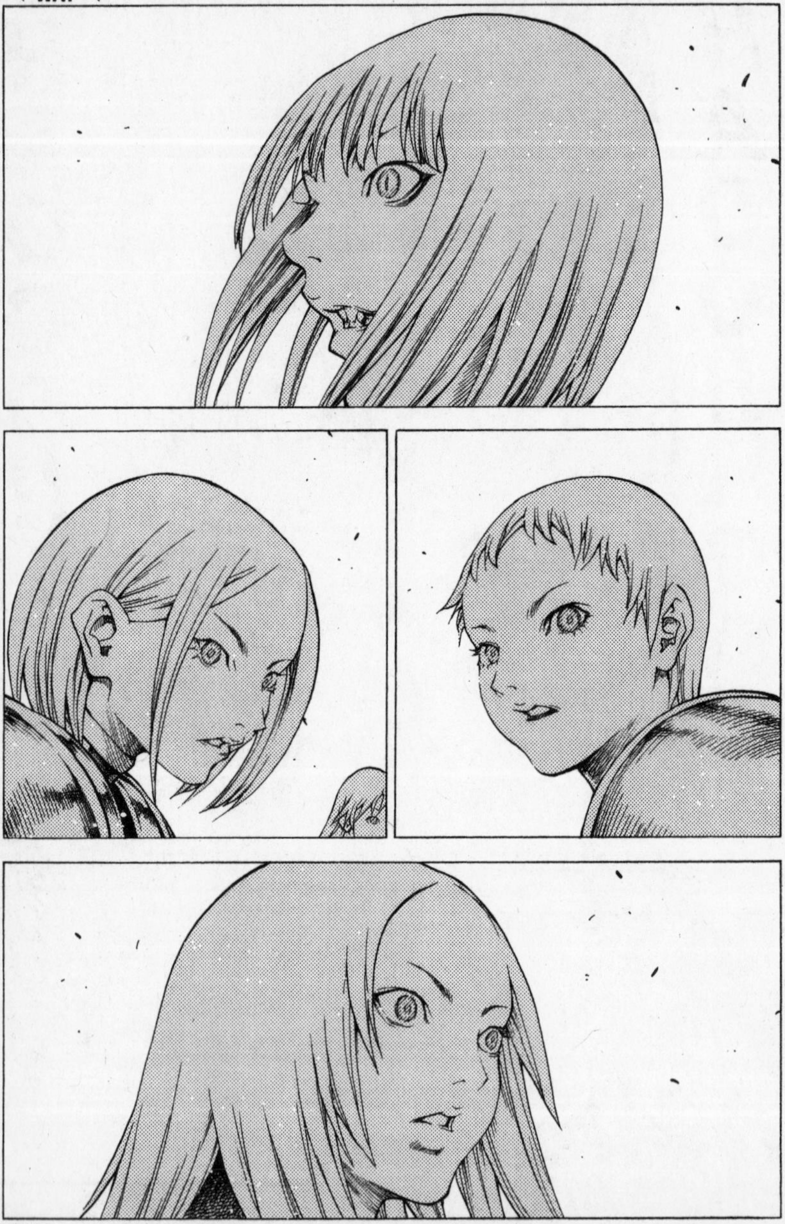

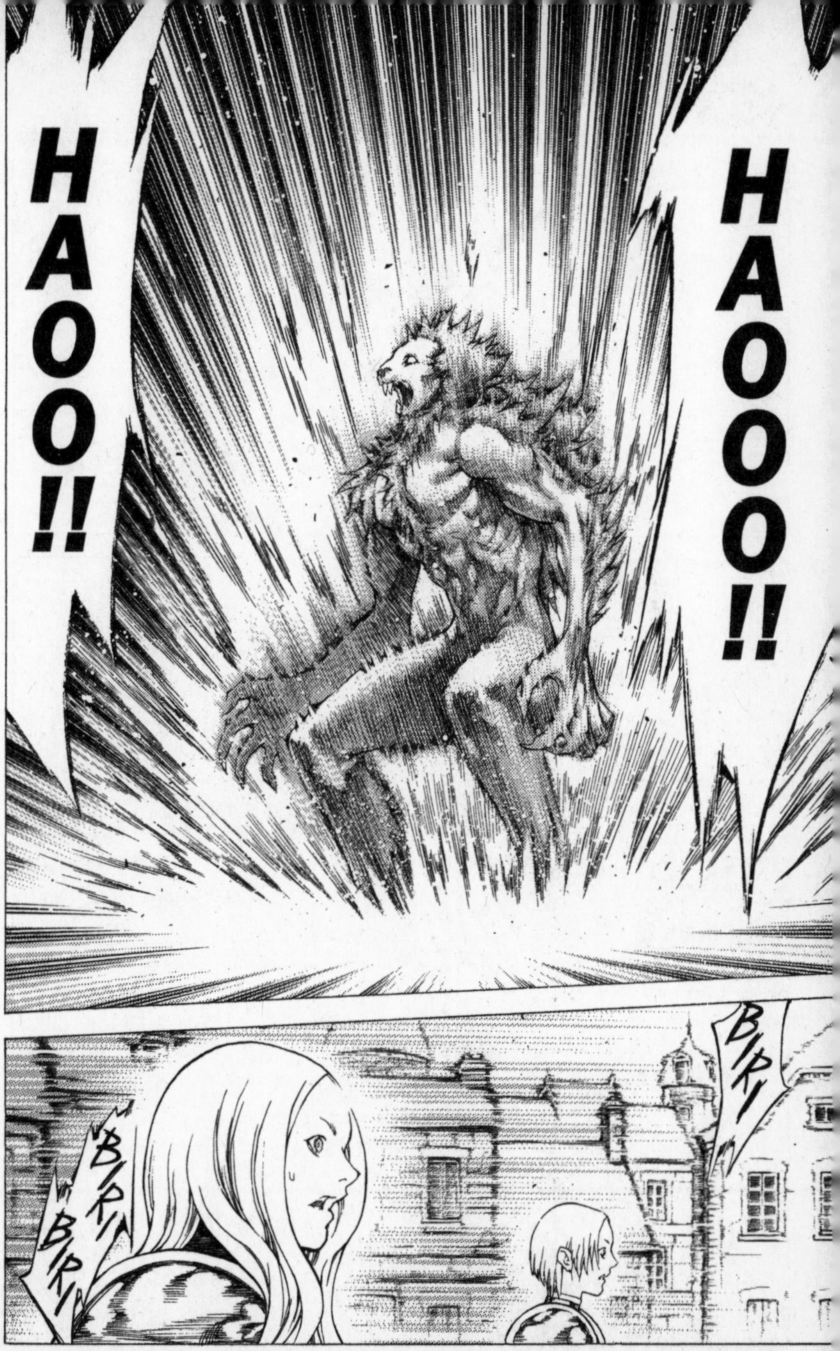
HAOOO!!
HAOO!!
BIRI
BIRI
BIRI

READ THIS WAY

GA ...
BIRI
BIRI
GASHAK
GLARE
!
BAM
!
!!

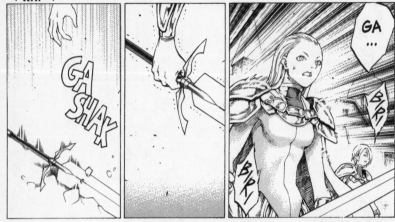

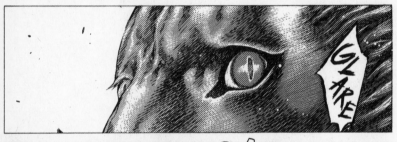

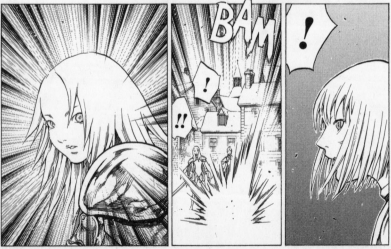

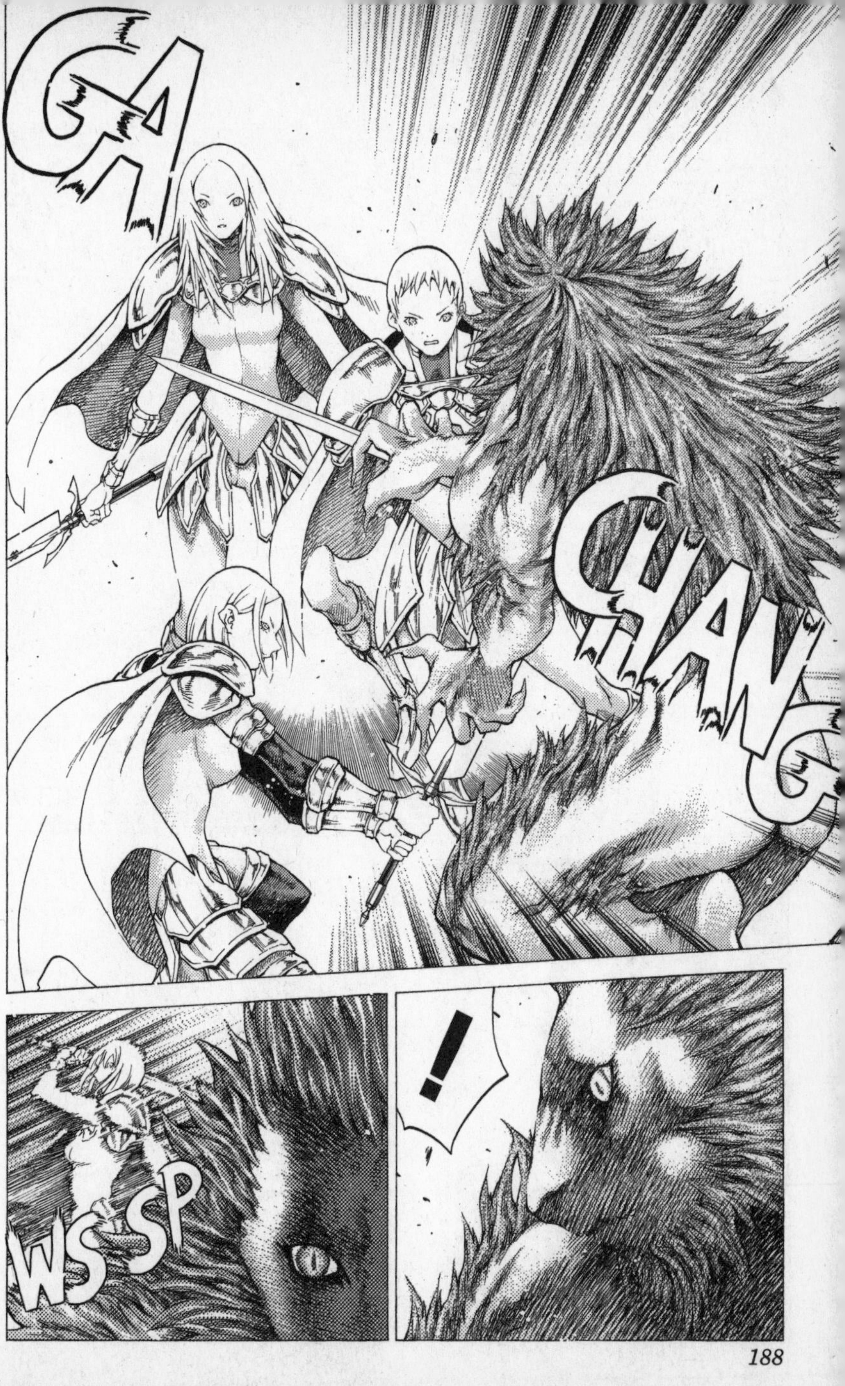
GA
CHANG
!
WSSP

READ THIS WAY

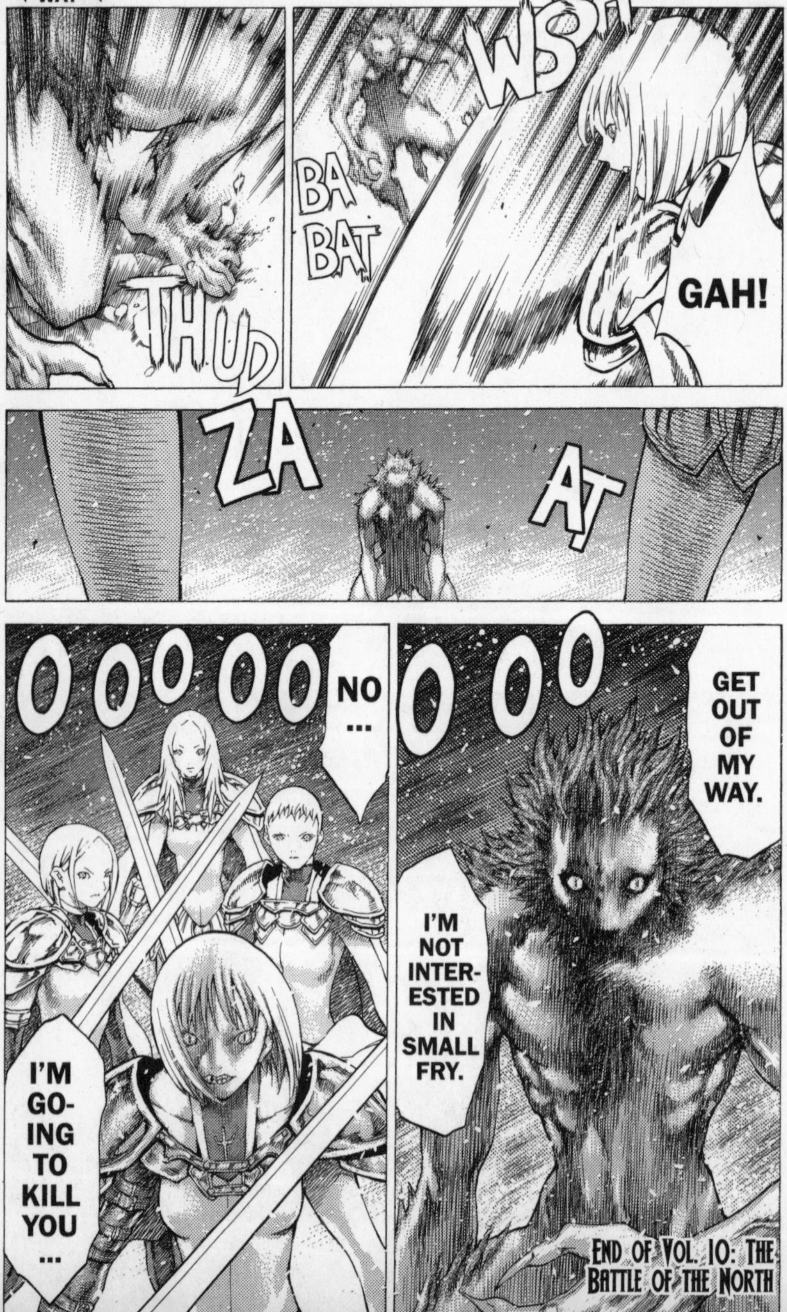
WSSH
BA BAT
GAH!
THUD
ZA
AT
OOO
GET OUT OF MY WAY.
I'M NOT INTER-ESTED IN SMALL FRY.
OOOOO
NO ...
I'M GO-ING TO KILL YOU ...
END OF VOL. 10: THE BATTLE OF THE NORTH

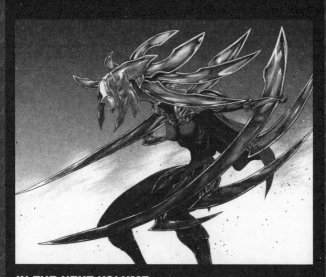

IN THE NEXT VOLUME

As the battle in Pieta with the Awakened Ones rages on, Clare
and the rest of the Claymores are pushed to their limits.
Surrounded and sustaining appalling losses, they prepare
themselves to make their final stand. Meanwhile Isley, the King
of the North, begins his assault on the forces of the South, and
the shadowy Organization, observing from afar, decides to
deploy its ultimate weapons.

Available in March 2008